W9-CXA-218

B, C.

PURITAN LONDON

Also by Tai Liu:

Discord in Zion: The Puritan Divines and the Puritan Revolution, 1640–1660.
Vol. 61 of International Archives of the History of Ideas.

(Editor-in-Chief) *New Studies in Chinese Cultural History* (in Chinese). 13
vols.

PURITAN LONDON

A Study of Religion and Society in the City Parishes

TAI LIU

Newark: University of Delaware Press
London and Toronto: Associated University Presses

© 1986 by Associated University Presses, Inc.

Associated University Presses
440 Forsgate Drive
Cranbury, NJ 08512

Associated University Presses
25 Sicilian Avenue
London WC1A 2QH, England

Associated University Presses
2133 Royal Windsor Drive
Unit 1
Mississauga, Ontario
Canada L5J 1K5

The paper used in this publication meets the
requirements of the American National Standard for
Permanence of Paper for Printed Library Materials Z39.48-1984.

Library of Congress Cataloging-in-Publication Data

Liu, Tai, 1930–
    Puritan London.

    Bibliography: p.
    Includes index.
    1. Parishes—England—London—History—17th
century.   2. London (England)—Church history.
3. Sociology, Christian—England—London—History—
17th century.   4. Puritans—England—London—History—
17th century.   I. Title.
BR764.L58   1986   274.21'06   85-40534
ISBN 0-87413-283-5 (alk. paper)

Printed in the United States of America

Contents

To
Lintung

Preface

Contemporary writers and modern historians alike have emphasized the crucial role played by the City of London in the course of the Puritan Revolution. At the outbreak of the Revolution, London was the main center of religious and political radicalism and opposition against both the Church and the Crown. In the middle of the Civil War, it became the stage of a fierce struggle between the Presbyterians and the Independents. At the end of the revolutionary era, the City was a major force in favor of the restoration of the monarchy. Although the importance of London on the national scene has been studied by many historians and from various perspectives, little attention has been given to what happened within the City during the twenty years of the revolutionary period. This study is intended to look at Puritan London from within, with special attention given to the various parochial communities of the City.

A series of questions may be raised, though few of them can be easily and definitely answered. To what extent, for instance, was Puritanism an influential force among the inhabitants of the City at the outbreak of the Revolution? Or, to put the question more specifically, in what areas or parochial communities of the City did Puritanism manifest itself strongly and unmistakably in the early years of the revolutionary era? And who were the Puritan civic leaders who came to power in either the civic or the parochial institutions of the City after 1641–42? Furthermore, was there a correlation between the religious and the socioeconomic configurations among the inhabitants of the City? In other words, was Puritanism a prevalent force among the substantial merchants and tradesmen or rather among the meaner sort of people and the poor? Questions may also be raised with regard to the Puritan experiment in the City during the revolutionary period. Were the Puritan forms of worship and discipline, whether Presbyterian or Independent, a success? In what City parishes was the Presbyterian church government firmly and successfully maintained and in what parishes did it fail to establish itself? In what City parishes did religious Independency prevail? Was there a difference in social composition between the parishes that were strongly Presbyterian and those that were Independent? And to what extent did the tradition of the parochial churches and Anglican clergymen survive in Puritan London? Finally, questions are also in order with regard to the social impact of the triumph of Puritanism in the City during the revolutionary era. With the bishop now gone and the ecclesiastical courts abolished, how was a minister chosen and how was he paid? What was the nature of the new relationship between the Puritan minister and the parochial community? Was this new relationship more rational and less customary than what had prevailed between the Anglican clergy and the parochial communities? How far was the Puritan discipline actually carried out in a parochial community? And did the Puritan experiment in the City bring about any radical change in the traditional governmental structure of the various City parishes?

It is with these questions in mind that this study of Puritan London has been pursued. Naturally, the decision to rely upon a systematic examination of the parochial records in the Guildhall Library and the Lambeth Palace Library and to focus upon the parochial communities of the City has resulted in a framework that presents both opportunities and limitations. Consequently, some of the questions raised above are fully explored, while others are only partially examined. Chapter 1 describes the social conditions of the City parishes on the eve and during the years of the Revolution, with special attention given to the presence of civic leaders in the various parochial communities. Since the Presbyterian church government was officially established in the City during the revolutionary period, chapter 2 gives a general survey of the Presbyterians in Puritan London, not only to show the successes and failures of Presbyterianism in the City but also to demonstrate the wide range of the sociopolitical spectrum among the Presbyterian civic leaders. In chapters 3 and 4, the Independents and the Anglicans in Puritan London are discussed. These two chapters are based mainly upon the information concerning the Independent ministers and Anglican clergymen in the City parishes. Chapter 5 deals with the new relationship, economic as well as ministerial, between the minister and the parish, while chapter 6 examines the continuity as well as change in the governmental structure of the City parish as a civic institution. In the concluding chapter the analyses in the preceding chapters are summarized and tentative interpretations are offered with regard to some of the questions raised above.

Acknowledgments

Throughout the years of my research on this work, I have received generous assistance from the librarians and staff members of the following libraries: The City of London Guildhall Library, the Corporation of London Records Office, the Lambeth Palace Library, the British Library, the Public Record Office, Dr. Williams's Library, the Folger Shakespeare Library, William Andrews Clark Memorial Library, U.C.L.A., and the Morris Library, University of Delaware. To all of them I wish to express my sincere thanks. I also wish to thank the American Council of Learned Societies for a research grant in the summer of 1976, William Andrews Clark Memorial Library for a Mellon Fellowship in the summer of 1977, and the University of Delaware for a research grant in the summer of 1984. The Dean's Office of the College of Arts and Science, University of Delaware, kindly gave me a grant for the typing of the manuscript. Mrs. Marie Perrone generously spent her time in helping me to prepare the typescript of this work.

I am indebted to my colleagues at the University of Delaware for their unfailing encouragement, especially Professors David F. Allmendinger, Jr., Daniel F. Callahan, Lawrence G. J. Duggan, Jack D. Ellis, Willard Allen Fletcher, George F. Frick, Reed G. Geiger, Ronald L. Lewis, Stephen Lukashevich, and Raymond Wolters. Special thanks are due to Professors Fletcher and Wolters, who kindly read the manuscript at the various stages of my writing and gave me many valuable suggestions for improvement. I have also imposed the reading of the manuscript upon Professor Leo F. Solt of Indiana University and Dr. Geoffrey F. Nuttall of King's College, University of London. I owe them more than I can ever express in words. During the last phase of the preparation I benefited greatly from the assistance of the editors of the Associated University Presses. The obliging efficiency and the gracious thoughtfulness of Miss Katharine Turok, the managing editor, blissfully facilitated the process, and the experienced eye and dexterous hand of Mrs. Mathilde E. Finch and Miss Beth Gianfagna, the copy editors, detected and corrected many inconsistencies and errors in the manuscript. I am deeply indebted to them and the high standard of their professionalism. Needless to say, the faults and mistakes remaining in this work, whether in research, in presentation, or in interpretation, are all mine.

Finally, I have to express my gratitude to my wife, Lintung, and my children, Lily, John, and Jeffrey, for their understanding and support of my own intellectual pursuits. I have disrupted their home life and their social life on far more occasions than I had any right to expect.

Abbreviations

Baillie	Robert Baillie, *Letters and Journals,* 3 vols., ed. David Laing (Edinburgh, 1841–42).
Beaven	A. B. Beaven, *The Aldermen of the City of London,* 2 vols. (London, 1908–13).
Biographical Dictionary	*The Biographical Dictionary of English Radicals in the Seventeenth Century,* 3 vols., eds. Richard Greaves and Robert Zaller (Brighton, Sussex, England, 1982–84).
BL Add. MS.	British Library, Additional Manuscript
C. J.	Great Britain, House of Commons, *Journals*
CLRO J. Co. Co.	Corporation of London Records Office, Journal of the Common Council
C. R.	G. A. Matthews, *Calamy Revised* (Oxford, 1934).
C. S. P. D.	*Calendar of State Papers, Domestic Series*
Dale	T. C. Dale, ed., *The Inhabitants of London in 1638* (London, 1931).
Firth and Rait	C. H. Firth and R. S. Rait, eds., *Acts and Ordinances of the Interregnum,* 3 vols. (London, 1911).
GLMS	Guildhall Library Manuscript
Green	Mary A. E. Green, ed., *Calendar of the Proceedings of the Committee for Advance of Money,* 3 vols. (London, 1888).
Harvey	W. J. Harvey, ed., *List of the Principal Inhabitants of the City of London 1640* (London, 1969).
Hill	Christopher Hill, *Economic Problems of the Church from Archbishop Whitgift to the Long Parliament* (Oxford, 1956).
Hist. MSS. Comm.	The Royal Commission on Historical Manuscripts
Jordan	W. K. Jordan, *The Charities of London, 1480–1660* (London, 1960).

L. J.	Great Britain, House of Lords, *Journals*
LPLMS CM	Lambeth Palace Library Manuscript, Carte Miscellanee
Newcourt	R. Newcourt, ed., *Repertorium Ecclesiasticum Parochiae Londinense,* 2 vols. (London, 1708–10).
Nuttall	Geoffrey F. Nuttall, *Visible Saints: The Congregational Way, 1640–1660* (Oxford, 1957).
Pearl	Valerie Pearl, *London and the Outbreak of the Puritan Revolution* (Oxford, 1961).
PRO SP	Public Record Office, State Papers
Ruthworth	John Ruthworth, *Historical Collections.* 8 vols. (London, 1659–1722).
Seaver	Paul S. Seaver, *The Puritan Lectureships: The Politics of Religious Dissent, 1560–1662* (Stanford, 1970).
Shaw	William A. Shaw, *A History of the English Church during the Civil Wars and under the Commonwealth 1640–1660,* 2 vols. (London, 1900).
Surman	Charles E. Surman, ed., "The Records of the Provincial Assembly of London, 1647–1660," 2 vols. (typescript in Dr. Williams's Library)
Tolmie	Murray Tolmie, *The Triumph of the Saints: The Separate Churches of London, 1616–1649* (Cambridge, 1977).
Woodhead	J. R. Woodhead, *The Rulers of London 1660–1689* (London, 1965).
W. R.	G. A. Matthews, *Walker Revised* (Oxford, 1948).

List of Parishes
within the Jurisdiction of the City

1. PARISHES WITHIN THE WALL

1 Allhallows Barking
2 Allhallows Bread Street
3 Allhallows the Great
4 Allhallows Honey Lane
5 Allhallows the Less
6 Allhallows Lombard Street
7 Allhallows London Wall
8 Allhallows Staining
9 Christ Church
10 Holy Trinity the Less
11 St. Alban Wood Street
12 St. Alphage
13 St. Andrew Hubbard
14 St. Andrew Undershaft
15 St. Andrew by the Wardrobe
16 St. Anne and St. Agnes Aldersgate
17 St. Anne Blackfriars
18 St. Antholin
19 St. Augustine
20 St. Bartholomew by the Exchange
21 St. Benet Fink
22 St. Benet Gracechurch
23 St. Benet Paul's Wharf
24 St. Benet Sherehog
25 St. Botolph Billingsgate

26 St. Christopher le Stocks
27 St. Clement Eastcheap
28 St. Dionis Backchurch
29 St. Dunstan in the East
30 St. Edmund Lombard Street
31 St. Ethelburga
32 St. Faith under St Paul's
33 St. Gabriel Fenchurch
34 St. George Botolph Lane
35 St. Gregory by St. Paul's
36 St. Helen
37 St. James Duke's Place
38 St. James Garlickhithe
39 St. John the Baptist
40 St. John the Evangelist
41 St. John Zachary
42 St. Katherine Coleman
43 St. Katharine Cree
44 St. Lawrence Jewry
45 St. Lawrence Pountney
46 St. Leonard Eastcheap
47 St. Leonard Foster Lane
48 St. Magnus the Martyr
49 St. Margaret Lothbury
50 St. Margaret Moses
51 St. Margaret New Fish Street
52 St. Margaret Pattens
53 St. Martin Ironmonger Lane
54 St. Martin Ludgate
55 St. Martin Orgar
56 St. Martin Outwich
57 St. Martin Vintry
58 St. Mary Abchurch
59 St. Mary Aldermanbury
60 St. Mary Aldermary
61 St. Mary Bothaw
62 St. Mary le Bow
63 St. Mary Colechurch
64 St. Mary at Hill
65 St. Mary Magdalen Milk Street
66 St. Mary Magdalen Old Fish
    Street
67 St. Mary Mounthaw
68 St. Mary Somerset

69 St. Mary Staining
70 St. Mary Woolchurch
71 St. Mary Woolnoth
72 St. Matthew Friday Street
73 St. Michael Bassishaw
74 St. Michael Cornhill
75 St. Michael Crooked Lane
76 St. Michael Queenhithe
77 St. Michael le Querne
78 St. Michael Paternoster Royal
79 St. Michael Wood Street
80 St. Mildred Bread Street
81 St. Mildred Poultry
82 St. Nicholas Acons
83 St. Nicholas Cole Abbey
84 St. Nicholas Olave
85 St. Olave Hart Street
86 St. Olave Old Jewry
87 St. Olave Silver Street
88 St. Pancras Soper Lane
89 St. Peter Westcheap
90 St. Peter Cornhill
91 St. Peter Paul's Wharf
92 St. Peter le Poor
93 St. Stephen Coleman Street
94 St. Stephen Walbrook
95 St. Swithin
96 St. Thomas the Apostle
97 St. Vedast

2. PARISHES OUTSIDE THE WALL

98 St. Andrew Holborn (part of)
99 St. Bartholomew the Great
100 St. Bartholomew the Less
101 St. Botolph without Aldersgate
102 St. Botolph without Aldgate
      (part of)
103 St. Botolph without Bishops-
      gate
104 St. Bride
105 Bridewell Precinct (extra paro-
      chial)

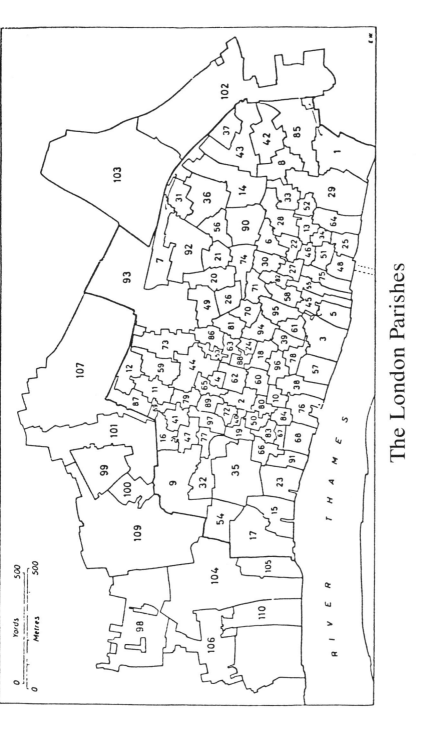

The London Parishes

1

Social Conditions in the City Parishes

IN any study of religion and society in Puritan London, a reconstruction of the social conditions in the various parishes of the City on the eve and during the years of the Puritan Revolution, however sketchy and incomplete, is requisite as a basic historical framework for analysis and interpretation. Admittedly, historical data for such a study are scarce, for there was no comprehensive and official census in the City before almost the end of the seventeenth century, when, in 1695, an assessment of London inhabitants under the Act of 6 & 7 Wm. & M., c. 6 produced, perhaps for the first time in London history, a full range of demographic data about the population of the City.[1] Fortunately, there are extant now in both the Guildhall Library and the Lambeth Palace Library a large number of parochial and ecclesiastical documents, from which a great amount of valuable information can be gathered about the general social conditions in the various parishes of the City during the early part of the seventeenth century.[2]

Within her jurisdiction in the early seventeenth century, the City of London consisted of one hundred and ten parishes, with ninety-seven of them located inside the Wall of the City and another thirteen outside it.[3] For the sake of convenience in this analysis, it may be appropriate to divide the City parishes, in accordance with the known number of their tithable houses, into four groups: (1) parishes with no more than fifty tithable houses, (2) parishes with about sixty to a hundred tithable houses, (3) parishes with about one hundred to two hundred tithable houses, and (4) parishes with more than two hundred tithable houses. If the number one hundred is used as the dividing line between the large and small parishes, fifty-five of the City parishes were small. Furthermore, only two of these fifty-five small parishes were outside the Wall; the other fifty-three were located within the Wall close to the center of the City. And of these fifty-five small parishes, the number of

tithable houses in nineteen, all within the Wall, was often well below fifty.
Clearly, early seventeenth-century London had a large number of small
parochial communities.

                                             I

From the ecclesiastical point of view, these nineteen smallest parishes
constituted a special group in the City in the early seventeenth century.
Owing to their small number of tithable houses, these parishes, as ecclesiastical benefices, had an extremely low value of tithes. In fact, few of them
paid tithes worth more than £50 a year. In the parish of St. Mary Staining, the
annual value of tithes was estimated at only £21.12s.4d.; in St. Mary
Mounthaw, at £26. 10s. 8d.[4] In eleven other parishes of this group, the annual
value of tithes was estimated at between £30 and £50. Only six of these
nineteen parishes paid slightly over £50 in tithes, if, indeed, tithes were all
collected.[5] Even in terms of the augmented tithes proposed by the London
clergy in 1638, only in five of these nineteen parishes was the value of tithes
to be raised to £100 or more.[6]

These nineteen parishes were undoubtedly among the poor ecclesiastical
benefices in early seventeenth-century London. It is important to point out,
however, that with the exception of three, namely, St. Mary Mounthaw, St.
Mary Staining, and St. Margaret Pattens, none of the other sixteen parishes
in this group was really an impoverished parochial community in the City in
the early seventeenth century. On the contrary, as we shall see, in most of
these sixteen smallest parishes there was a concentration of substantial
merchants and well-to-do tradesmen, who were often prominent and influential civic leaders in Puritan London. However, owing to the fact that these
parishes were small in size and population, modern historians sometimes
wrongly conclude that they were the impoverished and decayed parochial
communities in early seventeenth-century London.

The inhabitants in the parish of St. Mary Mounthaw were, indeed, generally poor. In 1638 the parish itself stated that its inhabitants were "few &
poore," the truth of which statement can be corroborated by the assessment
figures returned by the minister of the parish. In November 1642 the parish
contributed only £13 to Parliament—in all probability the smallest amount
among all the contributions from the City parishes. During the revolutionary
period, only one of its inhabitants appears to have acted in civic and ecclesiastical affairs in the City, but he was a rather obscure, minor figure.[7] The
social composition of the parish of St. Mary Staining was not much better.
Both the Haberdashers' Hall and the Scriveners' Hall were located either in
part or entirely in this parish. Yet most of its inhabitants were poor. In fact,
the parish complained in 1638 that the "two halls in it [are] as large as the
rest" and that it "stands in a place out of trade & very poore." And some

years later, in a petition to the City government, the parish again described itself both as "one of the least in the Citty for number of inhabitants and circuit of ground" and as "one of the poorest for the quality of the inhabitants, having many poor to maintaine and very little maintenance of orphans."[8] Similarly, the parish of St. Margaret Pattens stated in 1638 that sixteen of its fifty-nine houses were in alleys and the poor inhabitants were "chargeable to the parish."[9] And few of the inhabitants of these two parishes became prominent civic leaders during the revolutionary period.[10]

In his study of charities in the City of London during the sixteenth and seventeenth centuries, W. K. Jordan included among the impoverished and decayed parishes in the City four of the remaining sixteen smallest parochial communities in this group: St. John the Evangelist, St. Benet Gracechurch, St. George Botolph Lane, and Allhallows Honey Lane.[11] A closer examination of their social composition, however, points to a different conclusion. In actuality, it appears that these four parishes rank relatively high among the London parishes in our period both in terms of the wealth of their inhabitants and in terms of the status of their civic leaders.

Of these four parishes, St. Benet Gracechurch clearly had a concentration of wealthy inhabitants. In 1640 at least six of its parishioners were included in the list of the able inhabitants of Bridge Ward Within. More important, among its civic leaders were some of the most influential men in Puritan London.[12] Similarly, Allhallows Honey Lane was still a relatively substantial parochial community in the early seventeenth century, though its civic leaders appear to have been fewer in number and less prominent in status than those of St. Benet Gracechurch. Yet, among its inhabitants were two masters of the Clothworkers' Company, and both were also relatively prominent civic figures in the revolutionary period.[13] It is true that St. John the Evangelist was the smallest parish in the City and the parish itself stated in 1638 that it "consists but of 24 howses and the trade there is decayed." But there can be no doubt that its inhabitants comprised a group of well-to-do tradesmen and that the parish was not totally lacking in relatively well-known civic leaders.[14] The social composition of St. George Botolph Lane appears to have been more diversified; yet, again, it was far from being an impoverished parish. Among its parishioners were a number of Dutch merchants, all of whom appear to have been very rich indeed. In 1640 at least seven of its householders were included among the able inhabitants of Billingsgate Ward, though its civic leaders during the revolutionary era were relatively minor figures.[15]

As for the remaining twelve of this group of the smallest parishes in early seventeenth-century London, there was in almost all cases a rather high proportion of substantial and well-to-do inhabitants. In view of the social and political status of their civic leaders during the revolutionary period, some of these twelve parishes were, indeed, among the most important and influential parochial communities in Puritan London. Among the civic leaders of St.

Stephen Walbrook during the Puritan era, for example, were one Lord Mayor of the City of London, four Aldermen, and a number of other active figures. In November 1642 twenty-eight of its parishioners contributed £953 to the Parliament—a very respectable amount from such a small parish.[16] Equally prominent were the civic leaders of St. Mary Magdalen Milk Street, who played a crucial role either during the years of the revolution or on the eve of the Restoration.[17] The civic leaders of St. Mary Colechurch during the Puritan era included both prominent Aldermen and active Common Councilmen. Four of its parishioners became masters of the Apothecaries' Company in the early seventeenth century.[18] The parish of St. Martin Outwich appears to have had a rather mixed social composition, but in the words of its rector in 1638, "the parishioners are (for ye most part) wealthy men and doe inhabit faire and comodious howses, both for dwelling & for trading." In 1640 at least nine of its parishioners were included among the principal inhabitants either of Broad Street Ward or of the neighboring Bishopsgate Ward. In any case, among its civic leaders during the revolutionary period were no fewer than five Aldermen of the City.[19] The parishioners of St. Pancras Soper Lane were all well-to-do and substantial in wealth, especially those in Cheapside and Soper Lane, though the parish maintained in 1638 that it had "much decayed in few years" and that it was "very poore and in debt." In November 1642 twenty-eight of its parishioners contributed £568 to the Parliament, in addition to thirty-eight men and arms raised and maintained by its parishioners. Among its civic leaders during the revolutionary era were three Aldermen of the City and a number of other relatively noted minor figures.[20] Similarly, in the parish of St. Nicholas Acons, there were a prominent Common Councilman and two Aldermen of the City in the early part of the revolutionary period, and two other men of its parishioners were to become masters of the Salters' Company and Aldermen of the City after the Restoration.[21]

In comparison, the remaining six parishes of this group were inferior either in their general social composition or in the social status of their civic leaders. However, it must be once again emphasized that none of the six was actually a poor or impoverished parochial community in the early seventeenth century. Among these six, the parish of St. Margaret Moses was the least prominent in its social composition. Its parishioners were mostly small tradesmen, and it had no eminent civic leaders during the Puritan era.[22] The parish of St. Mary Bothaw, too, consisted mostly of small tradesmen; yet in 1640 eight of its parishioners were included among the principal inhabitants of Walbrook Ward and the Alderman of the Ward also had his residence in this parish.[23] In 1638 the parish of St. Martin Ironmonger Lane maintained that it was "in a narrow lane and small trade," but, in fact, it was neither lacking in wealth among its parishioners nor obscure in its civic leadership. In 1642, for instance, one of its parishioners, Lady Rumney, "(a vertuous and most charitable ancient Matron in this our Israel) did voluntarily and freely send into the treasury at Guildhall 2000l. not in way of loans, but as a free gift."[24] In the parishes of St. Benet Sherehog, St. Clement Eastcheap, and St. Matthew Friday Street, there were in each case a number of well-to-do tradesmen and relatively well-known civic leaders, though these men were neither great merchants nor leading City Fathers of London during the revolutionary period.[25]

II

A second group of the small parochial communities in early seventeenth-century London includes thirty-six of the City parishes, with thirty-four within the Wall, each of which had a larger number of inhabitants, ranging from about sixty to about one hundred tithable houses. In comparison with the nineteen smallest London parishes surveyed above, it is clear that in some of these parishes there was already an increasing number of the meaner sort of people and the poor. It is to be noted, however, that of the thirty-four parishes within the Wall, the inhabitants in twenty-four were still generally substantial merchants and well-to-do tradesmen. There was, therefore, a high degree of social coherence in these parochial communities. Furthermore, even in the few parishes among them in which there was a slightly higher proportion of the poor, the wealthy and the well-to-do either constituted the majority of the inhabitants or were adequate in number for the maintenance of parochial stability during the revolutionary era. For the other ten parishes of this second group, there was clearly an overwhelming number of the poor people and, perhaps more important, a very low proportion of substantial inhabitants. Consequently, we find these ten parishes all lacking, to a greater or lesser degree, in social coherence or parochial stability, especially with regard to religious and ecclesiastical affairs. Geographically, it is noteworthy that among these ten parishes, five were located on the north bank of the River and the other five were adjacent to it.

Six of the twenty-four substantial parochial communities of this second group were also very small in size, with the known number of tithable houses in each still well below seventy. It is again in these small parishes, all near the center of the City, that one finds a concentration of both wealth and prominent civic leadership. The parish of Allhallows Bread Street can be cited as an example. Although the parish itself maintained in 1638 that it "consists but 64 houses; many of ye househoulders [are] of meane condicōn and not owners," Jordan correctly considered it as one of the richest parishes in the City in the early seventeenth century. In the light of the parish register, in which the occupations of the parishioners are given, the inhabitants of this parish were mostly merchant tailors, drapers, grocers, ironmongers, salters, and haberdashers. In November 1642 the parish contributed £847 to the Parliament—a respectable amount from a parish of its size. Perhaps the prominence of this parish in its social composition can be seen more clearly from an analysis of its civic leadership during the revolutionary period. Among its civic leaders of this period were three Aldermen of the City, another three important Common Councilmen, two masters of the Merchant Taylors' Company, a master of the Salters' Company, four commissioners of the London Militia Committee in 1647, a colonel in the London militia, and the Lieutenant of the Tower of London in 1648.[26]

St. Olave Old Jewry, for another example, was also a small but extremely prominent parochial community in early seventeenth-century London. In 1638 sixty-two houses were assessed by the parish clergyman, though the parish itself stated that it "consists of 59 titheable howses, most of them small and poore, [and it] standeth in a place much out of trade." In fact, neither the assessment figures nor the statement of the parish reveals the true picture of this parochial community. In any case, among its civic leaders during the revolutionary era were, at one time or another, six Lord Mayors of the City of London. Indeed, even the lesser civic leaders of the parish were prominent men in the City. Not surprisingly, Jordan considered it also one of the richest parishes in seventeenth-century London.[27]

The other four small parishes of this second group were likewise substantial in wealth and prominent in civic leadership. In 1638 the parish of Allhallows Lombard Street maintained that it was "small consistinge of 66 houses & meane trades and 27 households of poore [are] relieved by ye p^ish." Yet, in November 1642 fifty-seven of its parishioners contributed £763 to the Parliament.[28] The parish of St. Antholin Budge Row stated in 1638 that it "consists of 55 ffamilies whereof many of them poore," but in 1640 at least seven of its parishioners were included among the principal inhabitants of Cordwainer Street Ward. In fact, all its parishioners appear to have been substantial merchants and tradesmen.[29] Nine of the parishioners of the parish of St. Christopher were listed among the principal inhabitants of Broad Street Ward and Cornhill Ward in 1640, and in November 1642 twenty-eight of its parishioners contributed £583 to the Parliament.[30] In 1638 the parish of St. Leonard Eastcheap, too, maintained that it was small, "consistinge of meane trades." Yet, of its inhabitants in 1638, one was to be chosen Lord Mayor of the City in 1645–46, two were to be elected Aldermen in 1649 and 1650, and another was to become the Chamberlain of the City of London in the latter part of the revolutionary period.[31]

Of the other eighteen substantial parochial communities of this second group, wealthy merchants and well-to-do tradesmen clearly constituted a solid majority of the inhabitants in at least twelve. Only in six does there appear to have been a higher proportion of the meaner sort of people and the poor. Among these six parishes St. Mildred Poultry and St. Bartholomew by the Exchange were located, perhaps rather surprisingly, quite close to the center of the City. In the case of St. Mildred Poultry, it is understandable that with the Poultry Compter in it, the area surrounding the prison was unlikely to be a place suitable either for trade or for residence for the rich and the well-to-do. There was in all probability a concentration of the poor in that area. However, the parish was anything but an impoverished community, for James Howell spoke of the "divers fair houses" in this parish. In any case, parochial stability appears to have been maintained by a group of substantial inhabitants during the revolutionary era.[32] The parish of St. Bartholomew by the Exchange also appears to have had a higher proportion of poor people in it, but there can be little doubt that it was one of the bustling marketplaces in the City in the early seventeenth century. Although there were no great merchants among its parishioners of our period, the majority of its inhabitants were substantial and well-to-do tradesmen. In November 1642 twenty-seven of them contributed £397 to the Parliament. More important, a number of its civic leaders during the years of the revolution played active roles both in religion and in politics in the City.[33] The other four parishes were located relatively farther from the center of the City, especially St. Gabriel Fenchurch toward the east end of the City and St. Helen at the northeast corner. St. Andrew Hubbard maintained in 1638 that "it is a poore parish standinge out of trade" and that there were "but 80 houses in the parish whereof 23 receive Almes."[34] Similarly, the parish of St. Margaret Lothbury stated that it was "litle & in small trade" and that "ye p[ishioners] for ye most p[te] [are] handicraftsmen." Besides, there were in it "30 familyes relieved wth Almes."[35] Nonetheless, none of the four was a decaying or impoverished parochial community. While the inhabitants of St. Andrew Hubbard were generally substantial tradesmen, there was in each of the other three parishes a cluster of very rich men, though the rich were more often than not royalists during the revolutionary period.[36]

The remaining twelve of the substantial parochial communities of this second group were all located in the center of the City. Among these twelve St. Mary Aldermanbury was undoubtedly one of the most important parishes in Puritan London. Neighboring the Guildhall, it was a prestigious area both for trade and for residence. And there was clearly a concentration of wealthy merchants and prominent civic leaders in this parish during the revolutionary period. In November 1642 sixty-four of its inhabitants contributed £924 to the Parliament—one of the largest contributions among the London parishes. Not surprisingly, the parish produced a large number of influential civic leaders in Puritan London, of whom at least five were elected Aldermen of the City. Indeed, in 1640, when the Earl of Warwick came to London, he requested a pew in the church of this parish. Perhaps the reputation of this parish can also be seen from the ministers it chose. At the beginning of the Puritan era, its ministry was supplied by Edmund Calamy, one of the most influential Puritan divines in Puritan London. Upon his ejection in 1662, he was succeeded by John Tillotson, the future Archbishop of Canterbury.[37]

To the south of St. Mary Aldermanbury were another five of these twelve substantial parishes. Although the parish of St. Augustine complained in 1638 of "the great decay of tradinge," at least eight of its parishioners were included among the principal inhabitants of Bread Street Ward in 1640.[38] Similarly, five of the parishioners of St. Mary le Bow were listed among the able inhabitants of Cheap Ward and Cordwainer Ward. And in November 1642 forty-nine of its parishioners contributed £530. 13s. 4d. to the Parliament.[39] Jordan considered St. Mary Aldermary as one of the City parishes in which there was a concentration of great merchants, though in 1640 only two of its parishioners were listed among the principal inhabitants of Cordwainer Ward. However, the parish records reveal that the inhabitants of the parish were generally substantial tradesmen: merchant tailors, skinners, drapers, and the like. In November 1642 the parish contributed £581 to the Parliament.[40] The parish of St. Peter Westcheap maintained in 1638 that it "consists of 60 houses & more then third of them [are] poore," but eighty-nine houses and shops were actually assessed. And it appears that the inhabitants of the parish—especially those along Cheapside and on both sides of Wood Street—were generally substantial tradesmen. In November 1642 the parish also contributed £510 to the Parliament.[41] Similarly, the parish of St. Michael le Querne also stated in 1638 that it was "small and they [are] Tenants to other men." Yet, during the years of the revolution, four of its inhabitants were chosen masters, respectively, of the Vintners' Company, the Mercers' Company, the Skinners' Company and the Ironmongers' Company.[42]

Three other parishes of the twelve were located near Lombard Street, another prosperous trade area on the east side of the center of the City. The parish of St. Mary Woolchurch, for example, near the west end of Lombard Street and with the Stocks Market in it, must have been a parochial community of substantial tradesmen. In November 1642 the parish contributed £550 to the Parliament. Although it appears to have no great merchants or prominent City Fathers during the revolutionary period, its civic leaders included three Aldermen, one colonel, and a lieutenant colonel in the London militia.[43] To the east of St. Mary Woolchurch was the parish of St. Mary Woolnoth, an apparently very wealthy parochial community with a number of goldsmiths among its parishioners. In 1640 at least twelve of the parishioners of St. Mary Woolnoth were included among the principal inhabitants of Langborne Ward. Of its civic leaders of the revolutionary period, one was chosen Lord Mayor of the City in 1653–54.[44] On the east side of St. Mary Woolnoth was the parish of St. Edmund the King. Although the parish itself maintained in 1638 that it was "small and divers places of it [are] out of trade," seven of its parishioners were also listed among the principal inhabitants of Langborne Ward. In fact, among its parishioners of 1638 were two senior Aldermen of the City.[45]

Of the remaining three of the twelve, St. Swithin had no assessments of the individual tithable houses in 1638, but it was said to have ninety-five houses in it. According to James Howell, St. Swithin Lane "is replenished (on both sides) with fair builded houses." Although it does not seem to have had great merchants, its parishioners were generally substantial tradesmen. In November 1642 forty-nine of its parishioners contributed £468 to the Parliament.[46] The other two were a little farther from the center of the City, but each was located in an area of trade. St. Peter le Poor, along Broad Street in the northern part of the City, was said to have eighty-four houses, though no assessments of its tithable houses were returned in 1638. It, too, appears to have been a substantial parochial community; in 1642 twenty-three of its parishioners were named as wealthy inhabitants who had either refused to contribute to the Parliament at all or declined to contribute adequately. Fourteen of these twenty-three parishioners of St. Peter le Poor had been included among the principal inhabitants of Broad Street Ward in 1640. It is to be noted, however, that few of its parishioners became known civic leaders of London during the revolutionary era.[47] The parish of St. Magnus was located at the north end of London Bridge. Rather unique among the parishes on the north bank of the River, St. Magnus was a prosperous marketplace for well-to-do tradesmen. Although it had neither great merchants nor prominent City Fathers during the period of the revolution, it produced a fairly large number of minor but active civic leaders in Puritan London.[48]

As has been indicated above, ten parishes of this second group, all located near the north bank of the River, had either an overwhelmingly large number of poor or a very low proportion of substantial inhabitants. Among the five located directly upon the bank of the River, St. Peter Paul's Wharf was clearly the poorest in wealth and the least prominent in social composition. In fact, it was in all probability the most impoverished parochial community in early seventeenth-century London. In 1638 the parish itself stated that "most of the p[ish] [are] handicraftsmen," which, in this case, appears to be borne out by the parish register. The occupations of its parishioners are identified mostly as dyers, brewers, tailors, firkinmen, embroiderers, vintners, victualers, and watermen. No notable civic leaders in the City during the revolutionary period appear to have come from this parish, with the exception of one or two minor figures, who, in any case, do not appear to have exercised strong influence in the affairs of the parish.[49]

Farther down the River closer to London Bridge were another three of these five parishes. Because the northern boundaries of these parishes reached into the centers of trade, they were not totally lacking in wealthy inhabitants. Among the civic leaders of Allhallows the Less, for instance, were a captain in the London militia, an Alderman's deputy, a number of Common Councilmen, and a future Lord Mayor of London.[50] The parish of St. Martin Orgar had at least three Aldermen of the City, while the parish of St. Lawrence Pountney had six masters of the London livery companies, two of the Ironmongers' Company, and one each of the Grocers' Company, the Salters' Company, the Saddlers' Company, and the Clothworkers' Company. And two of these men were also elected Aldermen of the City.[51] However, there were a large number of poor people in each of these parishes. The parish of Allhallows the Less, for instance, maintained in 1638 that it "consists for the most parte of poore handicraftsmen & impotent people to whom is yearely paid for Relieve 50l."[52]

The parish of St. Botolph Billingsgate, which was located on the east side of London Bridge, also had a group of substantial and well-to-do tradesmen. In 1640 at least eight of its parishioners were included among the principal inhabitants of Billingsgate Ward; and among the eight, one was to become master of the Clothworkers' Company in 1641, one was chosen master of the Vintners' Company in 1649, and two others were leading members respectively of the Grocers' Company and the Fishmongers' Company. Yet the statement of the parish in 1638 would suggest otherwise and provides a vivid picture of its social composition: "The parish consists of 27 houses in the Streetside of mean trade especially of the decayed trade of Salts. . . . The rest of the parish is upon wharfes inhabited by victualers, watermen & ye like."[53]

Of the other five poorer parishes of this second group, three were located next to one another near Queenhithe. Of these the parish of St. Nicholas Olave was the smallest in size and the least prominent in social composition. The parish stated in 1638 that it was "small & [there are] many poore in it," and Jordan correctly included it among the impoverished parochial communities in early seventeenth-century London. None of its parishioners appears to have become a known civic figure in the City during the revolutionary era.[54] On the east side of St. Nicholas Olave was the parish of Holy Trinity the Less, which also maintained in 1638 that its parishioners were mostly handicraftsmen. Although Jordan suggested that it was still a preferred area of residence for substantial and old-fashioned vintners, only one of its parishioners was actually identified as a vintner in 1638. However, on its vestry in 1647–48 was the master of the Vintners' Company for that year.[55]

To the north of these two parishes was that of St. Mildred Bread Street. Although the parish also stated in 1638 that it was "generally poore, trade decayinge," among its parishioners were a past master of the Bowyers' Company and a future master of the Wax-chandlers' Company. Both men were also relatively active civic leaders in the City during the revolutionary era.[56] Farther to the east was the parish of St. Michael Paternoster Royal, yet another impoverished parochial community in early seventeenth-century London. In 1638 the parish stated that "there are but 86 howses & two halls in the parish of wch 30 are small tenements and the people meane, many of them receivinge pentions. The rest for the most part [are] sleepinge houses."[57] In comparison, St. Margaret New Fish Street, the last one of these five parishes, appears to have been of a more substantial social composition. Located along New Fish Street near London Bridge, it was one of the marketplaces in the eastern side of the City. Although there were no great merchants in this parish and many poor people in it, it had an adequate number of substantial and well-to-do tradesmen. It is no surprise, therefore,

that among these five parishes, only St. Margaret New Fish Street maintained its parochial stability in an orderly and sustained fashion during the
years of the revolution.[58]

The two extramural parishes of this second group were not regular or
ordinary parochial institutions in the early seventeenth century: Bridewell
chapel belonged to the Bridewell Hospital; St. Bartholomew the Less, while
an impropriation in the hands of the Lord Mayor and the Corporation of the
City of London, belonged to St. Bartholomew's Hospital. Nor were they
important parochial communities in either wealth or civic leadership. In
November 1640 fourteen inhabitants of St. Bartholomew the Less contributed only £38 to the Parliament. A few inhabitants of Bridewell also contributed, but none of them more than £10. In any case these were insignificant
parochial communities in early seventeenth-century London. No inhabitants
of these two parochial communities appear to have played any role in the
City, either in religion or in politics during the revolutionary era.[59]

III

The contemporary assessment records and estimations indicate that there
were thirty-two London parishes within the Wall and one outside it each with
about one hundred to two hundred tithable houses. These thirty-three parishes constitute a third group in our study. Generally speaking, in almost
every one of these larger parishes of early seventeenth-century London, the
poor and the meaner sort of people made up a much higher proportion
among the inhabitants and, in some of them, an overwhelming majority. Yet,
in at least sixteen of the thirty-two parishes within the Wall, the number of
substantial merchants and well-to-do tradesmen was still proportionately
large, so that they were able to provide a broad basis for social coherence and
parochial stability during the revolutionary period. Indeed, in terms of the
social and political status of their civic leaders, six parishes of this third
group were among the most prominent and influential parochial communities
in Puritan London.

The other sixteen parishes within the Wall of this third group may be
considered impoverished or decaying parishes in the City in the early seventeenth century. They were all poor in their general social composition and
insignificant in their civic leadership. It is interesting to observe that again,
geographically, four of these parishes were located on the north bank of the
River and another four close to it, all to the west of London Bridge. Among
the remaining eight of the sixteen, four were located at the northwestern
corner of the City and the other four near the northern section of the Wall.
Obviously, all these sixteen parishes were neither prosperous places of trade
nor areas of residence preferred by the rich and the well-to-do in the City.

Of the six richest parishes of this group, St. Lawrence Old Jewry and St.

Michael Bassishaw were located respectively to the south and the north of the Guildhall in the ancient and prestigious part of the City. Jordan included both of these two parishes among the wealthy London parochial communities in the early seventeenth century. In November 1642, for instance, fifty-four of the parishioners of St. Lawrence Old Jewry contributed £1,184 to the Parliament—the third largest contribution among all the parishes of the City. Among its civic leaders during the Puritan era were two senior Aldermen of the City, three masters of the Haberdashers' Company, two masters of the Salters' Company, two master of the Innholders' Company, and a master of the Grocers' Company. It should be added that Lady Elizabeth Camden, widow of Baptist Hicks, Viscount Camden, was a leading parishioner of this parish, and she alone contributed £200 in 1642.[60] Similarly, St. Michael Bassishaw was a very wealthy parochial community, though the parish itself maintained in 1638 that "the number of houses in ye parish [is] 190 whereof 60 receive almes & 40 [are] so meane that they are not assessed to the poore." In fact, in 1638 Richard Fenn, Lord Mayor of the City, was an inhabitant of this parish, and among its civic leaders during the revolutionary period were two masters of the Drapers' Company, a master of the Merchant Taylors' Company, a master of the Mercers' Company, and a master of the Barber-Surgeons' Company. And three of these men were to be elected Aldermen and one was to be chosen Lord Mayor of London.[61] A little distance to the southwest of these two parishes was the parish of St. Vedast Foster Lane, which covered a large part of Westcheap, one of the prosperous areas of trade in the City in the early seventeenth century. Among its parishioners were a large number of goldsmiths, though the parish complained in 1638 that "tradinge much decayed espetially amongst Gouldsmithes whose shops are now shut vp or possessed by pettie trades & ye unruly markett checks their entercourse with customs." Nonetheless, during the revolutionary period, at least six of its inhabitants were elected Aldermen of the City: four goldsmiths, a merchant tailor, and a fishmonger. And in 1638 Richard Gurney, Alderman of Dowgate Ward and a future Lord Mayor of London, was also an inhabitant of this parish.[62]

The other three of the six richest parishes of this group were located in the eastern side of the City. The parish of St. Dionis Backchurch, for example, consisted of a large number of substantial merchants and tradesmen. In 1640 at least six of its parishioners were included among the principal inhabitants in the City, and in November 1642 the parish contributed £960 to the Parliament. During the period of the revolution, four of its parishioners became masters, respectively, of the Apothecaries' Company, the Merchant Taylors' Company, the Clothworkers' Company, and the Cordwainers' Company, and five were elected Aldermen of the City. In addition, in the mid-1650s, two older Aldermen also appear to have been associated with this parish church, if they were not actually inhabitants in this parish.[63] To the north of St. Dionis Backchurch was the parish of St. Andrew Undershaft. As Jordan has pointed out, John Stow, who "described the virtues of this parish with loving pride, would suggest that this was a bustling and highly prosperous urban region." Among its inhabitants of 1638 were two senior Aldermen of the City, and in November 1642 twenty-six of its parishioners contributed £875 to the Parliament. Two of the chief contributors were to be elected Lord Mayors of the City in 1644–45 and 1655–56, respectively, while another one was a great merchant and financial supporter of the Parliament.[64] The parish of St. Olave Hart Street was near the Customs House in eastern London; understandably, among its inhabitants in 1638 were two great Customs Farmers. Although few of its parishioners appear to have been actively involved in either religion or politics in the City during the early part of the revolution, one was elected Alderman in 1651 and another was to be chosen Lord Mayor of London in 1670. And all these men were royalists in Puritan London.[65]

In another ten parishes of this group, the social composition was evidently inferior. Unlike the six described above, none of these ten parishes appear to have had many extremely rich merchants in our period. This is not to say, however, that they were poor or impoverished parochial communities in the City. Furthermore, their civic leaders during the revolutionary period, though mostly well-to-do tradesmen, played important roles both in religion and in politics in Puritan London.

Five of these ten parishes were located in the eastern side of the City, and of the five, the parish of St. Michael Cornhill was probably the most important, at least in terms of the activities of its civic leaders during the revolutionary period. In 1638 only one of its parishioners was a great merchant and senior Alderman in the City, and in November 1640 forty-one of its parishioners contributed £371 to the Parliament, with no single contribution above £20. Yet at least ten of its parishioners were included among the principal inhabitants of Cornhill Ward in 1640, and during the period of the revolution its civic leaders included two Aldermen, two deputies, two colonels in the London militia, and a number of active Common Councilmen.[66]

Next on its eastern side was the parish of St. Peter Cornhill, which had at least five of its parishioners included among the principal inhabitants of Cornhill Ward in 1640. Among its civic leaders were one Alderman, a major in the London militia, two masters of the Armourer-Brasiers' Company, and a master of the Saddlers' Company. It also had a number of active Common Councilmen.[67] The parish of St. Benet Fink, on the northern side of St. Michael Cornhill, maintained in 1638 that "the number of houses in the p[ish] is 108 in which the almes people are included." Yet in 1640 at least twelve of its parishioners were listed in the various categories of the principal inhabitants of Broad Street Ward. During the revolutionary period one of its parishioners became the master of the Clothworkers' Company, another fined both for the mastership of the Merchant Taylors' Company and the office of Alderman, and some others were active Common Councilmen in the City.[68]

Farther to the east was the parish of Allhallows Staining, which maintained

in 1638 that it "hath few p^sons of worth in it & consists most of handicraftsmen and poor people." It appears that the parish did indeed have an
overwhelming number of poor people. However, it seems clear that there was
also in this parish a cluster of very rich merchants. Among its inhabitants in
1638, for example, was a wealthy merchant and customs farmer, and two
others were to be elected Aldermen of the City. In fact, one was to be chosen
the Lord Mayor of London in 1651–52.[69] The parish of St. Mary at Hill, the
last of the five in the eastern side of the City, was actually located on the bank
of the River to the east of the Bridge. The parish also maintained in 1638 that
it was a small parish with the greater part of it in lanes and alleys inhabited by
poor people, while the rest of the parishioners were engaged in "the decayed
salte trade." The truth is that it had a fairly large number of well-to-do
tradesmen, and among its civic leaders during the revolutionary period were
a well-known physician, a master of the Salters' Company, and one of the
most active colonels in the London militia.[70]

Of the five parishes in the western part of the City, two were located near
Aldersgate. The parish of St. Anne and St. Agnes Aldersgate stated in 1638
that its parishioners were generally "poore and handicraftsmen" and that "a
great parte of the parish is in the liberties of St. Martin le Graund." However,
among its civic leaders during the Puritan era were a past master of the
Barber-surgeons' Company, a master of the Clock-makers' Company, and a
master of the Innholders' Company. Besides, some of them were active
Common Councilmen in the City.[71] On the east side of St. Anne and St.
Agnes was the parish of St. John Zachary, which also claimed in 1638 that it
"consists of many poor Artificers." Yet, in addition to a leading Alderman in
Puritan London, the parish also produced a number of important Common
Councilmen.[72] To the south of these two parishes was St. Faith, which
appears to have been much richer in its social composition. During the
revolutionary period, however, few of its parishioners became prominent
civic leaders of London.[73] The parish of St. James Garlickhithe was on the
north bank of the River but, unlike other parishes along the north bank of
Thames, it was not an impoverished community. A fair number of tradesmen
appear to have been able to maintain the parish affairs in an orderly fashion,
and among its civic leaders were a colonel and a captain of the London
militia.[74] Finally, St. John the Baptist, which was located farther to the north
and closer to the center of the City, also had a better social composition and a
number of relatively noted civic leaders during the revolutionary period.[75]

As was pointed out earlier, sixteen parishes of this third group were poor in
their general social composition and insignificant in their civic leadership. Of
the four parishes on the north bank of the River, the parish of St. Benet Paul's
Wharf asserted in 1638 that it was "a small p^ish where are divers great houses
[which] containe more than halfe of it." One of the great houses was, of
course, Baynard Castle, which was the residence of the Earl of Pembroke and
Montgomery in 1640. Among its ordinary parishioners, however, there were
neither rich merchants nor prominent civic leaders. It should be noted,

however, that the parochial stability of this parish appears to have been relatively well maintained during the revolutionary era.[76] Farther down the River were the parishes of St. Michael Queenhithe and St. Mary Somerset, both of which appear to have had an overwhelming number of poor and a very low proportion of well-to-do inhabitants. Surprisingly, in November 1642 the former contributed £214 to the Parliament, and its churchwardens' accounts recorded two more collections for the maintenance of soldiers. Yet, again no prominent civic leader in Puritan London seems to have come from either of these two parishes.[77] The parish of St. Michael Crooked Lane was located next to the Bridge on its west side. Its civic leaders, few in number and all minor tradesmen, also failed to maintain a social and religious coherence during the revolutionary period.[78]

Of the four parishes near the River, the parishes of St. Mary Magdalen Old Fish Street and St. Nicholas Cole Abbey were located next to each other in the west side of the City. Both were insignificant parochial communities in early seventeenth-century London. During the revolutionary period the number of substantial tradesmen and civic leaders in both parishes was simply too small to provide a firm basis for parochial unity.[79] The other two parishes were St. Thomas the Apostle and St. Mary Abchurch, both of which were, in a sense, rather important parochial communities in Puritan London. As we shall see in this study, while the latter was one of the havens for religious Independency in the City during the years of the Civil War, the former became a center of religious radicalism and the Fifth Monarchy movement under the Commonwealth and the early Protectorate. The parish of St. Thomas the Apostle itself stated in 1638 that "most p^{te} of the houses are small & inhabited by handicraftsmen & poore." During the revolutionary period, its known civic leaders clearly had no influence in the parish.[80] The parish of St. Mary Abchurch appears to have had a fair number of small tradesmen, and in November 1642 thirty-eight of its parishioners contributed £399 to the Parliament. Yet few of its civic leaders became really noted figures in Puritan London.[81]

Of the four parishes at the northwestern corner of the City, St. Olave Silver Street was included by Jordan among the five richest parishes in early seventeenth-century London, though he added that only one merchant lived in this "otherwise quite humble parish." The parish stated in 1638 that it was "in a place out of trade. Of 111 houses there are not above fowr p^{sons} of quality. There are 55 poore families & 17 almshouses." It is true that there were still a few rich men in this parish, but the bulk of its inhabitants were very poor.[82] Similarly, the parish of St. Alphage stated in 1638 that it was "the poorest within the Walls. The parishioners [are] generally of meane quality & poor handicraftsmen, there being noe parishioners of quality." During the Puritan era, it produced a few relatively noted civic leaders in the City, but their number was small.[83] To the south of these two parishes was St. Alban Wood Street, which also had a large number of poor people, though a group of well-to-do tradesmen appears to have maintained its parochial stability during the revolutionary era. Its civic leaders during the revolutionary era included a master of the Apothecaries' Company and two Aldermen of the City.[84] Farther to the south was the parish of St. Michael Wood Street. According to the statement of the parish in 1638, "the parishioners for the most part are handicraftsmen and have little trade in respecte of the Compter in the parish." Here, too, the parochial stability of the parish was well maintained by a group of well-to-do tradesmen, though besides John Bastwick, one of the famous Laudian martyrs, none of the parishioners became noted figures in Puritan London.[85]

The other four parishes along the northern section of the Wall were all poor and insignificant parochial communities in the City in the early seventeenth century. Although the assessments of the parish of Allhallows London Wall included a house of a nobleman and another house of a former Alderman of the City, there was no sign of other wealthy men in this parish. Indeed, the leading vestrymen of the parish during the revolutionary era included a weaver, a currier, a pewterer, a fletcher, an innholder, and two yeomen.[86] The parish of St. Ethelburga appears to have been better in its social composition, but again, its leading parishioners during the Puritan era were innholders and other minor tradesmen.[87] The parish of St. Katherine Coleman claimed in 1638 that it was "one of the poorest within ye walls [with] many allies & noe trade in it" and that all houses in it were "sleeping houses" and the parishioners were "mechaniques."[88] And similarly the parish of St. James Duke's Place stated in 1638 that it was "poore & consists of mechaniques" and that its houses "are sleeping houses & have noe shops."[89]

The remaining extramural parish of this third group, St. Bartholomew the Great, was located to the northwest of the City and had its own peculiar parochial status. An Augustinian Priory before the Henrician Reformation, it was made a parish and a rectory after the dissolution of the monastery. The inhabitants of the parish, however, still enjoyed the traditional privilege of the priory and paid no tithes. Jordan included it among the five richest parishes of the City in late sixteenth-century and early seventeenth-century London, and we find that among the contributors for the poor of the parish in 1645 were the Earl of Bolingbroke, the Earl of Westmorland, the Countess of Middlesex, and Lady Hastings. Major-General Philip Skippon was also among its inhabitants in 1645. It is to be noted, however, that no wealthy London merchants or well-to-do tradesmen of the City can be detected from a poor rate assessment list of one hundred and ten householders for the year 1652. In November 1642 only eleven of its inhabitants contributed to the Parliament. In any case, with the exception of Skippon, none of its parishioners during the Puritan era became noted civic figures in London.[90]

IV

In addition to the three groups of eighty-eight parishes described in the previous sections of this chapter, a fourth group comprises another twenty-one parishes, each of which had more than two hundred tithable houses in the early seventeenth century. Of these twenty-one parishes, twelve were located within the Wall and the other nine outside the Wall but within the jurisdiction of the City. They were the largest parochial communities in and about the City. Geographically speaking, even the twelve largest parishes within the Wall were all farther away from the center of the City: one in the north, three in the east end (with two actually on the bank of the River), six in the west end (also with two on the bank of the River), and the remaining two on the north bank of the River and at a little distance to the west of the Bridge. Socially speaking, in almost all of these parishes, the number of poor was overwhelming. However, in some of these twelve parishes, there were a large number of wealthy merchants or well-to-do tradesmen as well. Consequently, they were among the most important parochial communities in early seventeenth-century London.

Among the twelve parishes within the Wall, St. Stephen Coleman Street was, indeed, one of the most influential parishes in the City. Valerie Pearl appropriately considered it "the Faubourg St. Antoine of London" during the English Revolution. Unfortunately, in 1638 the vicar of the parish, John Goodwin, who was one of the most radical Puritan ministers in the City, did not return assessments of the tithable houses of the parish, so that we have no information with regard to the general picture of its social composition. It is known, however, that two hundred and seventy-eight houses were assessed in the parish for Poll Tax in 1641 and there were also about a hundred tenements in it. It was thought to have about four hundred families in 1642. What is clear is that there was in it a large concentration of very rich merchants and substantial trademen. In November 1642 ninety-three of its parishioners contributed £1,310. 19s. to the Parliament—the second largest contribution among all the parishes of the City. It is no surprise, therefore, that this parish produced a large number of prominent civic leaders during the revolutionary era: the first parliamentarian Lord Mayor of the City, four Aldermen, a colonel in the London Militia, a master of the Mint under the Commonwealth, and a host of Common Councilmen. Furthermore, it was a center of radical agitation in religion as well as in politics throughout the revolutionary period.[91]

Equally prominent in wealth and in civic leadership was the parish of St. Dunstan in the East. Although it was actually located on the bank of the River, it was a very rich parochial community. In November 1642 fifty-eight of its parishioners contributed £1,407 to the Parliament—the largest of all the contributions from the City parishes. During the twenty years of the revolutionary period, one of its parishioners was to be elected Lord Mayor of the City, another six were to be chosen Aldermen, and a total of eight men were to become masters of the London livery companies: two masters of the Skinners' Company and a master each, respectively, of the Clothworkers' Company, the Grocers' Company, the Haberdashers' Company, the Salters' Company, the Apothecaries' Company, and the Cutlers' Company.[92] To the east of St. Dunstan in the East was the parish of Allhallows Barking. In comparison, the parish of Allhallows Barking had a much higher proportion of poor people, but it also had a group of royalists in the early years of the revolutionary era. One was a captain of the Honourable Artillery Company in 1641, master of the Clothworkers' Company in 1642, and later a colonel in the Royal Army; two other men were officers of the Customs House.[93] Farther to the north near Aldgate was the parish of St. Katherine Cree. No assessments were returned from this parish in 1638, but it appears to have been one of the largest parochial communities in early seventeenth-century London. In 1641 the vestry minutes recorded about four hundred and fifty names of people who had subscribed to the Protestation and, in the churchwardens' accounts for 1655–56, about three hundred names of its parishioners were listed for the assessment of tithes. Although its general social composition is not known, it is obvious that this parish was not an impoverished community. During the revolutionary period its civic leaders included a deputy, an Alderman, and a Lord Mayor of the City. Besides, there were a colonel and possibly three captains in the London militia. Three of its parishioners also became masters respectively of the Fishmongers' Company, the Haberdashers' Company, and the Skinners' Company.[94]

Of the six parishes of this group in the west end of the City, St. Gregory by St. Paul's appears to have had a large group of rich tradesmen. There was a concentration of merchant tailors among the inhabitants of this parish, and many of them became wardens of the Company during the revolutionary period. And one of its parishioners was elected Alderman of the City in 1652 and master of the Barber-surgeons' Company in the following year. Furthermore, its civic leaders were unmistakably Puritans and parliamentarians; indeed, one of them was selected as a member of Barebone's Parliament in 1653. In the latter part of our period, however, this parish became a well-known center of the Anglican clergymen in London.[95] To the west of St. Gregory by St. Paul's was the parish of St. Martin Ludgate, which appears to have had a much larger proportion of poor people and few extremely rich merchants. Yet it did have a large number of substantial tradesmen, who were able to provide a firm basis for social coherence and parochial stability during the revolutionary era. Among its civic leaders in our period were two Aldermen, one of whom was elected Master of the Haberdashers' Company, and a number of active Common Councilmen. Besides, one of its parishioners was the president of St. Bartholomew's Hospital and another was a captain of the London militia.[96] To the north of these two parishes were St. Leonard Foster Lane and Christ Church, both of which appear to have been much poorer in their general social composition. Jordan included the parish of St. Leonard Foster Lane among the impoverished parochial communities in early seventeenth-century London, though the number of well-to-do tradesmen in this parish was adequate for the maintenance of its parochial stability during the revolutionary period. It had no prominent civic leaders.[97]

Christ Church was a very large parochial community. No individual assessments of its tithable houses were returned in 1638, but we learn from other estimations that the number of communicants in this parish was about 6,500 and its total value of rents was given at £5,500. The parish itself maintained that "the most p^te of ye p^ishioners [are] poore & ye rest are charged with 7. or 800 poore people to ye yearely value of 300l. & in time of visitation much more." Its known civic leaders, though numerous and active, were rather minor figures in the City.[98]

The parishes of St. Anne Blackfriars and St. Andrew by the Wardrobe were both located on the bank of the River in the west end of the City, and they were clearly decaying parochial communities. In 1638 the parish of St. Anne Blackfriars had no individual assessments of its tithable houses, but in 1695 three hundred and seventy-three houses were assessed in this parish. A modern historian has observed that "the levelling-down of the social composition of the parish can be seen in the parish registers, which as the century goes on reveal fewer and fewer gentry and titled persons, and more and more lodgers, foundlings, itinerants and foreigners." The process of decline was already evident in the Puritan era, for although it had long been recognized as a strongly Puritan parish in the City, it produced few noted civic leaders during the revolutionary period.[99] The parish of St. Andrew by the Wardrobe claimed in 1638 that it was "small and out of tradinge" and that it was "inhabited for ye most parte wth carmen, watermen & other handicraftsmen." It further added that the two brewhouses in the parish, which had "relieved ye poore much," had declined. In any case, its known civic leaders during the Puritan era were mostly minor and obscure figures.[100] Farther to the east on the bank of the River were the parishes of St. Martin in the Vintry and Allhallows the Great. Both parishes had an overwhelmingly large number of poor people. In 1638 the parish of St. Martin in the Vintry stated that it had "much decayed in trade & tradesmen" and "the houses are meane." During the revolutionary period, no noted civic leader of the City appears to have come from this parish.[101] Allhallows the Great did not have noted civic leaders, either, during the Puritan era, though its parochial stability was relatively well maintained by a group of small tradesmen. Perhaps because of its diversified social composition, it became one of the most important centers of religious radicalism in the City. Its pulpit was to be monopolized by Fifth Monarchy preachers in the early 1650s.[102]

Of the nine extramural parishes of this group, four were located to the west of the City, two to the north, another two to the east, and one on the south bank of the River near London Bridge. Among the four to the west of the City, the parish of St. Dunstan in the West appears to have been a very substantial parochial community. Located along Fleet Street, it had a large number of well-to-do tradesmen, though it appears to have few extremely rich merchants. And it was undoubtedly one of the radical parishes in Puritan London. Indeed, in 1641, in a highly irregular and contested election, the old civic leaders of the parish were replaced by new men. During the period of revolution, this parish produced a large number of active and often radical Common Councilmen in the City.[103] To the east of St. Dunstan was the parish of St. Bride, which was a huge parochial community. No individual assessments were returned in 1638, but it was said that the parish spent "to the value of eight hundred pounds per ann. to the maintenance of our miserable poor which are betwixt seven and eight hundred families with nursing of poor children and Orphans left upon our charge." In 1652, in an assessment for the poor, it was again stated that the parish had five hundred and ten families able to pay the poor rate, eight hundred and seventy poor families, one hundred and sixty families receiving poor relief, and eleven hundred and sixty poor children. Yet it appears that the parish was not totally lacking in well-to-do tradesmen, for the parochial affairs of St. Bride were well managed by a group of thirty to forty parishioners throughout the revolutionary period. It also had a number of active civic leaders.[104] To the north of St. Bride was the parish of St. Sepulchre, another huge parochial community. According to Pearl, it was one of the poorest outparishes, crowded with craftsmen and laborers. It appears, however, that its parochial affairs were also well maintained by a group of well-to-do tradesmen.[105] Farther to the northwest was the parish of St. Andrew Holborn, which was partly within the jurisdiction of the City and partly in the county of Middlesex. Although the City section appears to have been a wealthy community, few men of this parish seem to have been active in London affairs during the Puritan era.[106]

The two northern outparishes were St. Botolph without Aldersgate and St. Giles without Cripplegate, both of which were huge parochial communities. Although its inhabitants of 1638 included both noblemen and gentry families, the parish of St. Botolph must have had an overwhelmingly large number of poor people. More important, however, there was also a large cluster of well-to-do tradesmen in this parish, who were able to provide a firm basis for parochial coherence and stability. Some of its civic leaders during the revolutionary period were relatively noted figures in the City.[107] The general social composition of the parish of St. Giles without Cripplegate appears to have been much poorer. In 1638 the parish clergyman listed one hundred and nineteen entries for the assessment of tithes, of which only four were actually for individual houses, three for brewhouses, two each for an inn and a tavern, and one for a warehouse. All the rest were for tenements. The number of poor people in the parish must have been overwhelming. Yet its parochial life appears to have been well maintained during the revolutionary era. In fact, as we shall see in this study, this huge and impoverished parochial community kept the most comprehensive and well-managed poor relief system among all the City parishes. Its parochial leaders must have been men able to govern such a community, and indeed, some of them became relatively noted civic leaders as well in Puritan London.[108]

The parish of St. Botolph without Bishopsgate, located to the northeast of the City, also had a large number of tenements. Again, like the parish of St. Giles without Cripplegate, a group of well-to-do tradesmen in this parish were able to maintain its parochial stability. It also had a consistent and well-managed poor relief system. Its civic leaders, though mostly minor figures in the City, were numerous and active.[109] The parish of St. Botolph without Aldgate was located outside the Wall on the east side of the City. In 1638 the parish itself maintained that "there are 1100 houses beinge halfe ye pish that receive almes." If there is any truth to this statement, it must have been a huge and extremely impoverished parochial community. During the revolutionary period, however, it did produce a number of relatively active civic leaders, though they were neither great merchants nor prominent City Fathers.[110] The parish of St. Olave Southwark, on the south bank of the River, had only a small portion of it within the jurisdiction of the City, with the greater part of it in the County of Middlesex. Yet it was one of the parishes in which radical and violent iconoclastic actions took place at the very beginning of the revolutionary era. Although not an important parochial community in the City, some of its civic leaders were at times deeply involved in both religion and politics in Puritan London.[111]

V

In light of the preceding survey of the social conditions of the various parishes in early seventeenth-century London, it becomes clear that the parochial communities and their social composition in the different parts of the City were indeed very complex and diversified. To the outside world, the City of London represented one political entity; and it has also been treated as such in modern studies of the English Revolution. Yet, in a closer look at London itself, these complexities and diversities would soon reveal themselves. This is particularly true when attention is focused on the events in the parochial communities in the City during the period of the Revolution. It is from this perspective of looking at Puritan London from within that a reconstruction of the social conditions in the various parishes of the City becomes necessary as a basic historical framework for analysis and interpretation of religion and society in Puritan London.

While no simple generalizations can be attempted with regard to the social configurations in the City as a whole, the following observations may be made as to the basic features that have more or less clearly revealed themselves in this survey. First, as noted earlier, with the exception of a small number of specific cases, the small London parishes were by no means impoverished or decayed parochial communities in the City, though they might have been poor ecclesiastical benefices for the ministers of these parish churches. If we look at the small London parishes from the social, rather than the ecclesiastical, perspective, they were unmistakably wealthy communities. There was in almost every one of them a cluster of substantial and well-to-do merchants and tradesmen. More important, these small London parishes possessed a relatively high degree of social coherence and parochial stability. Furthermore, in view of the social and political status of their civic leaders during the revolutionary period, these small parishes constituted a group of highly important parochial communities in the City.

Second, geographically speaking, almost all the wealthier parochial communities were located close to the center of the City: an area extending from Cheapside in the west to Cornhill and Lombard Street in the east, from the Guildhall and Coleman Street in the north to Old Fish Street and Eastcheap in the south. Obviously, the London citizens still preferred the center of the old City both for purpose of trade and for residence. The migration of the urban rich from the inner city to the suburbs, which has become a common feature of modern cities, had not fully, if at all, begun in early seventeenth-century London. In any case, for our period, the closer to the center of the City a parish was located, the more substantial its social composition appears to have been. To be sure, there are some exceptions to this general pattern, such as St. Dunstan in the West and some parishes at the east side of the City. Yet all such parishes were rather unique in their geographical location. St. Dunstan in the West, which was located along Fleet Street, then a thoroughfare from the City to Westminster, was a prosperous area for well-to-do tradesmen. The few parishes in the east end, in which there was a concentration of rich inhabitants, were located near the Customs House and thus became convenient places of residence for customs officials and overseas merchants.

Third, this survey has revealed two regions in the City where truly impoverished parochial communities existed in early seventeenth-century London: the north bank of the River especially to the west of London Bridge, and the area along the northern section of the Wall. The parishes on the north bank of the River or close to it all had large numbers of poor people and relatively fewer substantial merchants and tradesmen. Exceptions were some of the parishes near the north end of London Bridge, where apparently was still a prosperous marketplace for well-to-do tradesmen. Generally speaking, the parishes on the north bank of the River to the west of London Bridge were all impoverished parochial communities. So also were the parishes along the northern section of the Wall, especially those at the northwestern corner of the City. Obviously, these were regions far away from trade centers and marketplaces in early seventeenth-century London.

Fourth, I must emphasize that the society of early seventeenth-century London, even during the revolutionary period, was basically still one of social status. It is true that the larger a parish was in size, the greater was the number of the poor in it. As a result, the social composition in a large parish became much more diversified and its social coherence was more precarious. It is important to note, however, that even in some of the largest parishes, the presence of an adequate number of well-to-do tradesmen could and did provide a firm basis for the maintenance of parochial stability. As noted in the previous survey, this was often the case in some of the extramural parishes in which the number of the poor and the meaner sort of people was overwhelming.

Finally, a noteworthy feature in the general social composition of early seventeenth-century London is the absence of a stark spatial segregation between the rich and the poor among its inhabitants. In no area of the City was there an exclusive concentration of either the poor or the rich.[112] While, on the one hand, we find the poor living in alleys and lanes of the substantial parochial communities, there were, on the other, well-to-do tradesmen and occasionally rich merchants in the impoverished parishes of the City. As just observed above, the presence of well-to-do tradesmen in a poor or large parish was an important factor in the maintenance of parochial stability. More important, due to this mixed distribution of rich and poor in the City, the lower classes of the London inhabitants did not constitute a distinct sociopolitical entity in any large area. Perhaps also thanks to this mixed social composition in the parochial communities, life in Puritan London remained one of social status and deference in spite of the fact that it was an age of political and religious radicalism.

In the ensuing chapters we shall look more closely at the London parochial communities during the revolutionary era.

NOTES

1. See D. V. Glass, ed., *London Inhabitants within the Walls 1695* (London, 1966), especially Introduction, pp. ix–xxxviii.

2. For the ecclesiastical records in the Lambeth Palace Library, in addition to T. C. Dale, ed., *Inhabitants of London in 1638* (London, 1931), see LPLMSS CM VIII/4, ff. 1–2, 4–5; CM VIII/18, ff. 1–3; CM VIII/23, ff. 1–5; CM VIII/25; CM VIII/37, ff. [1]–[4]; CM VIII/43, ff. 1–4; CM VIII/45, ff. A1–A2; CM IX/25, ff. 1–4; CM IX/50; CM IX/58; CM IX/82. For the parochial records of the City parishes, see Guildhall Library, *Vestry Minutes of Parishes within the City of London: A Handlist* (London, 1964) and *Churchwardens Accounts of Parishes within the City of London: A Handlist* (London, 1969).

3. See map and list of the London parishes. Strictly speaking, the City of London had within her jurisdiction one hundred and eight parochial communities and two extraparochial precincts (Bridewell and Whitefriars), and four of her extramural parishes, especially St. Andrew Holborn and St. Olave Southwark, lay partly in the boundaries of the City and partly in the County of Middlesex. Furthermore, it appears that for ecclesiastical purposes, Whitefriars Precinct was within the parish of St. Dunstan in the West. See LPLMS CM VIII/37, f. [4].

4. Dale, pp. 117, 120. Cf. also Newcourt, 1: 452, 457. For more statistical information about the social conditions of the London parishes and the value of their tithes as given in 1635–38, see Appendix A.

5. Allhallows Honey Lane (£42.1s.), St. Benet Sherehog (£31. 5s.8d.), St. Clement Eastcheap (£40), St. John the Evangelist (£44.10s.), St. Margaret Pattens (£44.17s.8d.), St. Martin Ironmonger Lane (£40.3s.), St. Mary Bothaw (£41.10s.4d.), St. Mary Colechurch (£44), St. Matthew Friday Street (£49.14s.), St. Pancras Soper Lane (£36. 17s. 4d.), and St. Stephen Walbrook

(£39.10s.). Dale, pp. 13, 41, 46, 78, 104, 111, 113, 125, 136, 173, 181. Cf. also Newcourt, 1: 251, 303, 326, 373, 407, 411, 439 [447], 449, 474, 538. St. Benet Gracechurch (£57. 18s. 6d.), St. George Botolph Lane (£58. 5s.), St. Margaret Moses (£62. 6s. 8d.), St. Martin Outwich (£57. 17s. 2d.), St. Mary Magdalen Milk Street (£74. 8s. 3d.), and St. Nicholas Acons (£68. 18s.). Dale, pp. 40, 64, 100, 131, 137, 160. Cf. also Newcourt, 1: 300, 352, 403, 419, 470, 504.

6. Strictly speaking, only in two of the nineteen parishes, namely, St. Mary Magdalen Milk Street and St. Stephen Walbrook, were the values of tithes raised clearly to £100 or more in the proposals by the London clergy in 1638. Two lists of such increased value of tithes desired and proposed by the London clergy are extant among the documents now at the Lambeth Palace Library. See LPLMS CM VIII/4, ff. 4–5; LPLMS CM IX/82.

7. See Dale, p. 116; LPLMS CM VIII/37, f. [3]; Green, 1: 9; BL Add. MS. 15671, f. 233b.

8. LPLMS CM VIII/37, f. [3]; Dale, p. 120; GLMS 1541/2, f. 1; PRO SP 16/492, f. 90.

9. LPLMS CM VIII/37, f. [2]; Dale, p. 104; GLMS 4571/1, ff. 22, 28.

10. See GLMS 1542/2, ff. 39, 44, 46; GLMS 4571/1, ff. 22, 28. The scope of this chapter does not permit identification of the civic and parochial leaders of the City parishes. However, many of them will be identified in the following chapters.

11. Jordan, p. 41n.

12. Dale, p. 40; Harvey, p. 4; GLMS 1568/1, ff. 676, 698, 719, 725; GLMS 4214/1, ff. 12–46, *passim*.

13. Dale, p. 13; Harvey, pp. 11–12; PRO SP 19/78, f. 91D; GLMS 5026/1, no folio number, see churchwardens' account for 1642.

14. Dale, p. 78; Harvey, p. 3; Green, 1: p. 15.

15. Dale, p. 64; Harvey, p. 2; GLMS 952/1, ff. 14–22, *passim*.

16. Dale, p. 181; Harvey, p. 18; PRO SP 16/492, f. 75; GLMS 594/2, 1648–60, *passim*, esp. f. 46.

17. Dale, p. 137; Harvey, pp. 13–14; LPLMS CM VIII/37, f. [3]; GLMS 2597/1, ff. 53–124, *passim*.

18. Dale, pp. 112–13; GLMS 64/1, ff. 86–166, *passim*. In 1640 at least seven of its parishioners were included among "the most able p'sons of worth" of Cheap Ward. See Harvey, pp. 11–12.

19. Dale, p. 131, LPLMS CM IX/75; GLMS 11394/1, 1640–60, *passim;* Harvey, pp. 3, 4–5; PRO SP 19/78, f. 91B.

20. Dale, p. 173; LPLMS CM VIII/37, f. [4]; GLMS 5019/1, f. 84; PRO SP 19/78, f. 91C.

21. Dale, p. 160; LPLMS CM VIII/37; f. [3]; GLMS 4060/1, ff. 57–140, *passim;* Harvey, p. 16; PRO SP 16/492, f. 82.

22. Dale, p. 99; PRO SP 19/78, f. 91; W. Bruce Bannerman, ed., *The Registers of St. Mildred, Bread Street, and of St. Margaret Moses, Friday Street, London* (London, 1912), pp. 18–23. Nine wealthier inhabitants of the parish were included only in the second or third sort of the able citizens of Bread Street Ward. See Harvey, p. 3.

23. Dale, p. 111; Harvey, p. 18; PRO SP 19/78, ff. 11, 91. The parish contributed £371 in 1642.

24. Dale, p. 125; LPLMS CM VIII/37, f. [3]; John Vicars, *God in the Movnt. Or, Englands Parliamentarie-Chronicle* (London, 1644), p. 128.

25. For these three parishes, see, respectively, the following:

(a) Dale, p. 41; LPLMS CM VIII/37, f. [1]; PRO SP 16/492, f. 95.

(b) Dale, p. 46; LPLMS CM VIII/37, f. [1]; PRO SP 16/492, ff. 66–66b; PRO SP 19/78, f. 91B; GLMS 978/1, f. 7 and 1642–62, *passim*.

(c) Dale, p. 136; PRO SP 16/492, f. 89; PRO SP 19/78, f. 91D; GLMS 3579, ff. 61–121, *passim*.

26. Dale, p. 9; LPLMS CM VIII/37, f. [1]; W. Bruce Bannerman, ed., *The Registers of All Hallows, Bread Street, and of St. John the Evangelist, Friday Street, London* (London, 1913), pp. 22–31; Jordan, p. 52; PRO SP 19/78, f. 91B.

27. Dale, p. 171; LPLMS CM VIII/37, ff. [3]–[4]; Jordan p. 35; GLMS 4415, ff. 100b–204, *passim*.

28. Dale, p. 16; LPLMS CM VIII/37, f. [1]; PRO SP 16/492, f. 79; PRO SP 19/78, ff. 2B, 91B;

GLMS 4049/1, f. 19b (eighteen assessments in Langbourne Ward, twelve assessments in Bridge Ward Within, and thirty-seven assessments in Billingsgate Ward in 1635); ibid., ff. 21–31.

29. Dale, pp. 32–33; LPLMS CM VIII/37, f. [1]; Harvey, pp. 12–13; PRO SP 16/492, ff. 84–84b; PRO SP 19/78, f. 91C; GLMS 1045/1, 1648–62, *passim.*

30. Dale, p. 45 (£150 for the shops and cellars rated collectively); PRO SP 16/492, f. 86; PRO SP 19/78, f. 91D; LPLMS CM VIII/37, f. [1]; E. Freshfield, ed., *Minutes of the Vestry Meetings and Other Records of the Parish of St. Christopher le Stocks* (London, 1886), pp. 33–46; Harvey, pp. 4–5, 13.

31. Dale, pp. 88–89; LPLMS CM VIII/37, f. [2].

32. Dale, pp. 158–59; PRO SP 19/78, f. 91C; GLMS 62/1, ff. 1–53b, especially f. 10; James Howell, *Londinopolis* (London, 1657), p. 111.

33. Dale, pp. 36–37; LPLMS CM VIII/37, f. [1]; PRO SP 16/492, f. 94; PRO SP 19/78, ff. 91C–91D; E. Freshfield, ed., *The Vestry Minute Books of the Parish of St. Bartholomew Exchange in the City of London, 1587–1676* (London, 1890), pt. 1, pp. 133–46; pt. 2, pp. 1–78.

34. Dale, p. 22; LPLMS CM VIII/37, f. [1]; PRO SP 16/492, ff. 81–81b; PRO SP 19/78, f. 91D; GLMS 1278/1, 1638–60, *passim.*

35. Dale pp. 97–98; LPLMS CM VIII/37, f. [2]; GLMS 4352/1, 1639–60, *passim,* especially ff. 148b–49, 175b.

36. For the other two parishes of these four, namely, St. Gabriel Fenchurch and St. Helen, see, respectively, the following:

(a) Dale, p. 62; Harvey, p. 15. In November 1642 the parish contributed £638.10s. to the Parliament. PRO SP 19/78, f. 91. It appears, however, that no prominent Puritan civic leader came from this parish during our period with the exception of Stephen White. See BL Add. MS 15669, f. 69.

(b) Dale, pp. 69–70; Harvey, p. 3; GLMS 6836, ff. 305b–309b, 310, and *passim;* GLMS 6844/1, ff. 1–20, *passim.* It appears that Abraham Cullen and John Lawrence took their residence here in this parish in the early 1650s.

37. LPLMS CM IX/80; PRO SP 19/78, ff. 91B, 102; Green, 1: 9; GLMS 3570/2, 1639–62, *passim,* especially ff. 43, 43b, 98b.

38. Dale, pp. 34–35; LPLMS CM VIII/37, f. [1]; GLMS 635/1, 1640–60, *passim.* In 1642 the parish contributed £365 to the Parliament. PRO SP 19/78, f. 91; Harvey, p. 3.

39. Dale, pp. 109–10; PRO SP 16/492, ff. 88–88b; PRO SP 19/78, f. 91B; Harvey, pp. 11–12, 13.

40. Dale, p. 107; Jordan, p. 35; LPLMS CM VIII/37, f. [2]; PRO SP 19/78, f. 91; GLMS 4863/1, ff. 15b–35b, *passim;* Harvey, p. 13.

41. Dale, pp. 174–75; LPLMS CM VIII/37, f. [4]; PRO SP 16/492, ff. 72–72b; PRO SP 19/78, f. 91D; GLMS 642/1, 1638–53, *passim.*

42. Dale, p. 152; PRO SP 16/492, f. 97; PRO SP 19/78, f. 91B; GLMS 2895/2, 1638–60, *passim.*

43. Dale, p. 121; GLMS 1013/1, ff. 168b–244b, *passim;* GLMS 1012/1, 1648–61, *passim;* PRO SP 19/78, f. 91.

44. Dale, p. 123; LPLMS CM VIII/37, f. [3]; GLMS 1002/1B, 1639–41; Harvey, p. 15; PRO SP 19/78, f. 2b.

45. Dale, pp. 53–54; Harvey, p. 15; LPLMS CM VIII/37, f. [2].

46. LPLMS CM VIII/4, f. [5]; LPLMS CM IX/41; LPLMS CM IX/80; PRO SP 16/492, f. 73; PRO SP 19/78, f. 91. See also GLMS 560/1, 1647–60, *passim;* Howell, *Londinopolis,* p. 83 [93].

47. LPLMS CM VIII/4, f. 5; LPLMS CM IX/41; LPLMS CM IX/80; PRO SP 16/492, f. 102; Harvey, pp. 4–5.

48. Dale, pp. 94–96; GLMS 1179/1, 1639–60, *passim.* In November 1642 thirty-four inhabitants of the parish contributed £262 to the Parliament, with only a few contributions above £10. See PRO SP 16/492, f. 85; PRO SP 19/78, f. 91C.

49. Dale, p. 179; LPLMS CM VIII/37, f. [4]; Willoughby A. Littledale, ed., *The Registers of St. Benet and St. Peter Paul's Wharf* (London, 1909), pp. 165–75.

50. Dale, pp. 14–15; LPLMS CM VIII/37, f. [4]; GLMS 824/1, 1644–60, *passim.*

51. For these two parishes, see, respectively, the following:

(a) Dale, pp. 129–30; LPLMS CM VIII/37, f. [3]; GLMS 959/1, 1638–60, *passim*. In November 1642 the parish contributed only £123 to the Parliament. PRO SP 19/78, f. 91C.

(b) Dale, pp. 86–87; GLMS 3908/1, 1638–60, *passim*. In 1642 the parish contributed only £262 to the Parliament. PRO SP 19/78, f. 91.

52. LPLMS CM VIII/37, f. [4].

53. Dale, p. 42; LPLMS CM VIII/37, f. [1]; GLMS 943/1, 1638–50, *passim*. Unlike the parish of St. Peter Paul's Wharf, St. Botolph Billingsgate produced a larger number of civic leaders during the Puritan era, though they were mostly minor figures in the City.

54. Dale, p. 165; LPLMS CM VIII/37, f. [3]. In November 1642 the parish contributed £123 to the Parliament. PRO SP 19/78, f. 91B.

55. Dale, pp. 184–85; LPLMS CM VIII/37, f. [4]; Jordan, p. 40; PRO SP 16/492, f. 70; GLMS 4835/1, 1638–60, *passim*. In 1638 the parson of the parish stated that "the parish is not a place of trading, few shopkeepers in it, most of the inhabitants make no shew outward but use their employments inward." See Dale, p. 184.

56. Dale, pp. 156–57; LPLMS CM VIII/37, f. [3]; PRO SP 16/492, f. 87; GLMS 3470/1A, 1648–60, *passim*.

57. Dale, p. 154; LPLMS CM VIII/37, f. [3].

58. Dale, pp. 101–3. In 1638 the parish maintained that it "consists but of 50 houses whereof many are in lanes inhabited by chargeable poor." LPLMS CM VIII/37, f. [2]. See also GLMS 1175/1, 1639–60, *passim*.

59. Dale, pp. 199–200, 202; PRO SP 16/492, f. 99; PRO SP 19/78, ff. 2B, 8.

60. Dale, pp. 84–85; Jordan, p. 52; PRO SP 16/492, f. 71; PRO SP 19/78, f. 91C; GLMS 2590/1, 1640–60, *passim;* GLMS 2593/2, 1640–60, *passim*.

61. Dale, pp. 141–43; Jordan, pp. 38, 52; PRO SP 16/492, f. 96; GLMS 2601/1, 1638–60, *passim*.

62. Dale, pp. 60–61; Jordan, p. 51; LPLMS CM VIII/37, f. [2].

63. Dale, pp. 47–48; Harvey, pp. 3, 15–16; GLMS 4216/1, 1647–60, *passim;* GLMS 4215/1, 1639–60, *passim;* PRO SP 19/78, f. 91; Green, 1: 9.

64. Dale, pp. 24–26; Jordan, pp. 36, 52; PRO SP 16/492, f. 82; PRO SP 19/78, f. 91.

65. Dale, pp. 166–67; Jordan, p. 38; Alfred Povah, *The Annals of the Parishes of St. Olave Hart Street and Allhallows Staining* (London, 1894), p. 240.

66. Dale, pp. 144–45; PRO SP 16/492, ff. 69–69b; PRO SP 19/78, f. 91C; GLMS 4072/1, 1639–60, *passim;* Harvey, p. 13.

67. Dale, pp. 176–78; PRO SP 19/78, ff. 1, 2B; Green, 1: 2; GLMS 4165/1, 1645–60, *passim;* Harvey, p. 13.

68. Dale, pp. 38–39; LPLMS CM VIII/37, f. [4]; GLMS 1303/1, 1638–60, *passim;* Harvey, pp. 4–5. In 1642 twenty-seven of its inhabitants contributed £390 to the Parliament. GLMS 1303/1, churchwardens' account, 1641–42.

69. Dale, pp. 17–18; LPLMS CM VIII/37, f. [4]; GLMS 4956/3, 1645–60, *passim;* Povah, *Annals of the Parishes of St. Olave Hart Street and Allhallows Staining*, pp. 321–22, 349. In 1642 the parish contributed £370.10s. to the Parliament. PSO SP 19/78, f. 2B; Green, 1: 9.

70. Dale, pp. 114–15; Jordan, p. 52; LPLMS CM VIII/37, f. [3]; GLMS 1240/1, 1640–60, *passim;* PRO SP 19/78, f. 91B.

71. Dale, pp. 30–31; LPLMS CM VIII/37, f. [1]; PRO SP 19/78, f. 91C; GLMS 587/1, 1638–60, *passim*.

72. Dale, pp. 79–80; LPLMS CM VIII/37, f. [2]; PRO SP 19/78, f. 91C; GLMS 590/1, 1639–60, *passim*.

73. Dale, pp. 57–58. The parishioners complained in 1638 that "their trade much decayed by shutting up of dores into St. Paules Church." LPLMS CM VIII/37, f. [2].

74. Dale, pp. 74–75; GLMS 4813/1, 1640–60, *passim;* GLMS 4810/2, 1638–60, *passim;* PRO SP 19/78, f. 2B; Green, 1: 9.

75. Dale, pp. 76–77; GLMS 577/1, 1638–60, *passim;* GLMS 1543, 1638–60, *passim*.

76. LPLMS CM VIII/4, f. 5; LPLMS CM IX/41; LPLMS CM IX/80; LPLMS CM VIII/37, f. [1]; PRO SP 19/78, f. 2B; LPLMS Comm. XIIa/20, f. 6; GLMS 878/1, 1638–60, *passim;* GLMS 877/1, 1638–60, *passim.*

77. For these two parishes, see, respectively, the following:

(a) Dale, pp. 150–51; PRO SP 19/78, f. 91; GLMS 4825/1, 1638–60, *passim,* especially f. 61b. Cf. also LPLMS CM VIII/37, f. [3]: "ye parish consistinge most of laboringe people."

(b) Dale, pp. 118–19; PRO SP 19/78, f. 91; GLMS 5714/1, 1638–60, *passim;* BL Add. MS 15671, f. 60.

78. Dale, pp. 147–49; PRO SP 19/78, f. 91; GLMS 1188/1, 1640–60, *passim.*

79. For these two parishes, see, respectively, the following:

(a) Dale, p. 138–39; LPLMS CM VIII/37, f. [3]; GLMS 1341/1, 1648–60, *passim.*

(b) Dale, pp. 161–62; LPLMS CM VIII/37, f. [3].

80. Dale, pp. 182–83; LPLMS CM VIII/37, f. [4]; GLMS 662/1, 1639–60, *passim.*

81. Dale, pp. 105–6, LPLMS CM VIII/37, f. [2]; PRO SP 19/78, f. 2B; Green, 1: 9; GLMS 3891/1, 1638–60, *passim.*

82. Dale, pp. 169–70; LPLMS CM VIII/37, f. [4]; Jordan, p. 35; PRO SP 16/492, ff. 98–98b; PRO SP 19/78, f. 91C; GLMS 1257/1, 1638–60, *passim.*

83. LPLMS CM VIII/4, f. 5; LPLMS CM IX/41; LPLMS CM IX/80; LPLMS CM VIII/37, f. [1]; GLMS 1431/2, 1638–60, *passim.*

84. Dale, pp. 1–2; GLMS 7673/1, 1638–60, *passim.*

85. LPLMS CM VIII/4, f. 5; LPLMS CM IX/41; LPLMS CM IX/80; LPLMS CM VIII/37, f. [3]; GLMS 524/1, 1637–60, *passim.* Strangely, Bastick's name was never given in the church-wardens' accounts either as a churchwarden or as an auditor.

86. Dale, pp. 19–21; LPLMS CM VIII/37, f. [1]; GLMS 5090/2, 1639–60, *passim;* PRO SP 19/78, f. 91B.

87. Dale, pp. 55–56; PRO SP 19/78, f. 2B; GLMS 4241/1, 1639–60, *passim.*

88. Dale, pp. 81–83; LPLMS CM VIII/37, f. [2]; PRO SP 16/492, ff. 91–91b; PRO SP 19/78, f. 91D.

89. Dale, pp. 71–73; LPLMS CM VIII/37, f. [2].

90. Dale, p. 198; Jordan, pp. 34–35; PRO SP 19/78, f. 2B; Green, 1: 9; GLMS 3989/1, collections for the poor, 1645; GLMS 4047/1, poor rate list, 1652.

91. David A. Kirby, "The Radicals of St. Stephen's Coleman Street," *The Guildhall Miscellany* 3, no. 2 (April 1970): 98–119; PRO SP 16/492, ff. 76–76b; PRO SP 19/78, ff. 2B, 91D; Jordan, p. 52; Pearl, p. 183; GLMS 4458/1, 1639–60, *passim.*

92. Dale, pp. 49–51; PRO SP 16/492, f. 83; PRO SP 19/78, f. 91B; GLMS 4887, 1639–51, *passim;* GLMS 7882/1, 1639–60, *passim.*

93. Dale, pp. 3–7; Joseph Maskell, *Collections in Illustration of the Parochial History and Antiquities of the Ancient Parish of Allhallows Barking in the City of London* (London, 1864), pp. 149–51. In 1642 the parish contributed only £385 to the Parliament. PRO SP 19/78, f. 2B; Green, 1: 9.

94. GLMS 1196/1, f. 19; GLMS 1198/1, no folio number, churchwardens' account, 1655–56. For the civic leaders of this parish during the Puritan era, see GLMS 1196/1, 1639–60, *passim.*

95. Dale, pp. 65–67; PRO SP 16/492, f. 77; GRO SP 19/78, f. 2B; GLMS 1336/1, 1643–60, *passim.*

96. Dale, pp. 126–28; GLMS 1311/1, especially ff. 137b, 139b; GLMS 1313/1.

97. Dale, pp. 126–28; PRO SP 19/78, f. 91; GLMS 1311/1, 1640–60, *passim;* Dale, pp. 90–92; Jordan, p. 41.

98. Dale, p. 44; LPLMS CM VIII/4, f. 4; LPLMS CM IX/58; LPLMS CM VIII/37, f. [4]; GLMS 9163. In 1652–53, Alderman John Ireton and William Steel, Recorder of the City, appeared to be inhabitants of this parish.

99. LPLMS CM VIII/4, f. 4; LPLMS CM IX/80; Brian Burch, "The Parish of St. Anne's Blackfriars, London, to 1665," *The Guildhall Miscellany* 3, no. 1 (October 1969): 14; Glass, *London Inhabitants . . . 1695,* p. xxiv.

100. Dale, pp. 27–29; LPLMS CM VIII/37, f. [1]; PRO SP 16/492, ff. 92–92b; PRO SP 19/78, f. 2B; GLMS 2088/1, churchwardens' accounts, 29 November 1642 and 19 January 1642/3.

101. Dale, pp. 132–35; LPLMS CM VIII/37, f. [3]; PRO SP 19/78, f. 91D; BL Add. MS 15671, f. 53. In 1642 only £108 was contributed to the Parliament from this parish.

102. Dale, pp. 10–12; GLMS 819/1, 1639–60, *passim.* In 1642 sixty-two of its inhabitants contributed £233. 5s. 6d. to the Parliament. PRO SP 16/492, ff. 93–93b. See also chap. 3 below.

103. Dale, pp. 230–34; GLMS 3016/1, 1638–60, *passim;* GLMS 3018/1, 1638–60, *passim.* See also chap. 6 below.

104. Dale, p. 201; GLMS 6554/1, 1646–60, *passim,* esp. f. 120b.

105. Pearl, p. 40; GLMS 3146/1, especially ff. 10b, 12, 100b; GLMS 3149/1, especially ff. 2, 4–5, 6–7.

106. Dale, pp. 187–91; LPL MS CM VIII/37, f. 4; PRO SP 19/78, ff. 60d, 60f.

107. Dale, pp. 203–8; GLMS 1453/1, 1643–60, *passim;* GLMS 1455/1, 1638–60, *passim;* GLMS 1453/2, 1651–60, *passim.*

108. Dale, pp. 236–38; GLMS 6048/1, ff. 1–4b; GLMS 6047/1, 1648–60, *passim.* In 1642 the parish contributed £452 to the Parliament. PRO SP 19/78, f. 2B.

109. Dale, pp. 225–28; LPLMS CM VIII/37, f. [4]; GLMS 4526/1, 1638–60, *passim;* GLMS 4524/1, 1636–60, *passim.* In 1642 the parish contributed £452 to the Parliament. PRO SP 19/78, f. 2B.

110. Dale, pp. 210–23; GLMS 9234/8, 1640–60, *passim;* GLMS 9235/2, 1638–60, *passim;* LPLMS CM VIII/37, f. [4].

111. Dale, p. 240, Hist. MSS Comm., *Fourth Report,* Appendix, pp. 7, 74; *L. J.,* 4: 270.

112. I owe this idea to my colleague Professor David F. Allmendinger, Jr. And my colleague Professor George Basalla called to my attention K. H. Schaeffer and Elliot Sclar, *Access for All. Transportation and Urban Growth* (Harmondsworth, Middlesex, England, 1975), in which chap. 2: "The Walking City" also emphasizes this characteristic of the old city before the developments of modern transportation.

2

The Presbyterians in Puritan London

When Clement Walker published his pamphlet *The Mysterie of the Two Ivnto's* in 1647, he apparently believed that the two cliques in the Long Parliament, that is, the Independent and Presbyterian leaders—the "grandees," as he called them, "for that is now Parliament language"—each had a power base on its side. According to Walker's opinion, the Independent faction "groundeth [its] strength upon the Army," whereas for the Presbyterians, "the City is their chief foundation with which they keepe a strict correspondencie and daily communication of Councells."[1] It seems that in the eyes of contemporaries like Walker, at least in 1647, the Army had become an instrument of the Independents in their struggle for political power and religious toleration, while the City of London was the main "pillar" of the political façade of the Presbyterians in their confrontation with the Independents and the Army. "Upon this consideration," Walker continued, the Presbyterians "have lately put the Parliament Purse into the Cities Pocket" and "settled and inlarged the City Militia."[2] In short, the City of London had become Presbyterian in its religious persuasion and in its political alliance.

Some traditional historians of English Presbyterianism appear to have adopted a similar view. To these historians the City of London during the English Revolution was, indeed, a Presbyterian London. The following quotation from an old standard history of the English Presbyterians by A. H. Drysdale may be cited as a revealing testimony to this traditional interpretation:

> To speak of Presbyterian London, is to use no exaggerated language. Strange as it may sound to modern ears, it describes exactly what London became under the Long Parliament. From the meeting of the Westminster Assembly in July, 1643, and the public adoption by Parliament of the Solemn League and Covenant in September of that same year, London

grew intensely Presbyterian in its sympathies, although Presbyterian worship and order did not fully come into operation over the City and suburbs
till August 1646. . . . Traditionally Puritan in temper, London struggled for
and welcomed the new religious Establishment. Presbyterian Puritanism
may have subsisted longer in Lancashire; but in London it achieved its
earliest triumph and its highest renown.[3]

Of course, neither Walker nor Drysdale is entirely right in his respective
characterization of the City of London. Modern historians have demonstrated that the picture was far more complex. In fact, the very labels
Presbyterians and *Independents* have been called into question.[4] In any case,
it is to be noted that the Presbyterian movement in the City during the
revolutionary period was far from being a complete success. Not only was the
City as the main pillar of the Presbyterian faction in the Long Parliament
soon to collapse but the Presbyterian worship and order, as we shall see in
this chapter, never did "come fully into operation over the City and suburbs"
after August 1646, when the Presbyterian church government was finally and
officially established under parliamentary ordinances. Yet, on the other hand,
neither Walker nor Drysdale is entirely wrong, either. During the years of the
Civil War, there was, indeed, a strong Presbyterian faction gradually taking
shape in the City, and the London Presbyterian leaders, both lay and clerical,
were prepared, at least for some dangerous months in 1647, to confront the
Independent Army with the City militia in what has been called London's
counterrevolution.[5] Furthermore, the Presbyterian church government and
discipline had been officially established by the Parliament, first and foremost, for the City of London, and the London Provincial Assembly, however
incomplete, did come into existence from 1646 to 1660.[6] In this chapter, we
shall have a closer look at the successes and failures of the Presbyterians in
Puritan London.

Before we examine the establishment of the Presbyterian church government among the various London parishes, it may be appropriate to make
some preliminary observations. First, it should be pointed out that with the
calling of the Long Parliament, the outbreak of the Civil War, and especially
the convening of the Westminster Assembly of Divines, there began a constant and tremendous influx of Puritan ministers into the City of London—a
phenomenon that probably had never happened before and was never to
happen again in London history.[7] During the years of the Civil War, London
had become truly the center stage of Puritanism and Puritan politics in the
nation. To be sure, there was a great variety of opinion among the Puritan
divines on almost every important point of ecclesiastical polity—church
government, ordination, elderships, discipline, and so on.[8] And it is true that
not even the English Presbyterian divines had ever wished to have the rigid
Scottish Presbyterian system introduced into England. However, as most of
them were opposed, on the one hand, to episcopacy and the arbitrary powers
of the bishops and, on the other, to Independency and the disruptive con-

sequences of gathered churches, a modified form of Presbyterianism was the only choice left them. It is not strange, therefore, that most of the Puritan divines did become Presbyterians and supported the new Presbyterian church government. More significant, since many of them replaced the old Anglican incumbents as ministers of the City parishes, they were able to persuade and finally to win over a large number of the civic leaders of London for the Presbyterian system, which, designed to protect the traditional parochial structure and social order but shorn of any means of exercising coercive power, would, ideologically and practically, appeal to these men, too. To say this, I should hasten to add, is not to deny that many of the London civic fathers during the Puritan era were genuine religious Presbyterians.[9]

Second, a few words may be said as to the Presbyterian system itself. Theoretically, the complete Presbyterian church government consisted of four different levels of institutions: the National Assembly or Synod, the Provincial Assemblies, the Classical Presbyteries, and the parochial elderships. The National Assembly would be the highest court of this new church government in regard to doctrinal resolutions, ecclesiastical policies, and disciplinary measures. In actuality, such a national synod never came into being in England during the Puritan era, and, we may reasonably believe, it was probably never intended by the Parliament to be constituted. Jealous of their own privileges and resentful of clerical authority of whatever kind, the members of the Parliament had no intention of elevating the Presbyterian ministers to a national institution and thus enhancing their power. In response to the petitions of London Presbyterians, the House of Commons went no further than the creation of an independent parliamentary commission.[10] Under the National Assembly were the Provincial Assemblies, each of which would cover a county or, in the case of the London Provincial Assembly, the Cities of London and Westminster, the surrounding Liberties, Southwark, and the adjoining parishes south of the Thames. The membership of a provincial assembly was composed of ministers and lay ruling elders delegated from each of the classes within the bounds of the province. Similarly, under the Provincial Assembly were the Classical Presbyteries, each of which comprised delegates, ministerial and lay, from all of the constituent parishes of the classis. At the bottom were the individual parish elderships, each of which included a minister and a number of lay ruling elders elected by the parishioners. The lay ruling elders constituted probably the most important feature in the new Presbyterian church government and discipline. With their assistance, the minister of the parish was to maintain the doctrinal orthodoxy and the spiritual edification of the parishioners and their families.

On the surface it might appear that England had adopted the Scottish Presbyterian system, albeit without a national assembly. In fact, this was far from being the case. Neither the Provincial Assemblies nor the Classical Presbyteries were given any coercive superior jurisdiction, in spite of the fact that during the years of 1645 and 1646, the London Presbyterian leaders did, in a series of concerted campaigns, petition for a stronger Presbyterian system. "But in London," as a contemporary pamphleteer wrote, "it goes but slowly forward; for the *Provincial Assembly* there, have *petitioned* both *Houses* for *removing of Obstruction in their church discipline,* yet receive they no *answer* . . . so that the Presbyterian Government, as it is yet settled, is but (as the *Scots* have told them) *a dead Forme without Life, or Power.*" It is also for these reasons that Robert Baillie, the Scottish clerical commissioner in London, dubbed the English Presbyterian church government "a lame Erastian" Presbyterianism.[11]

Nevertheless, it was this Presbyterian church government that was lawfully established in the City of London and adopted and maintained by the London citizens in a large number of the City parishes. However "lame" in its authority and however incomplete in its organization, the London Provincial Assembly comprised not only the majority of the Puritan ministers in the City but also many of the prominent civic leaders in the various parishes. In what parishes of the City was the Presbyterian church government established? In what parishes did it fail to establish itself? Is there any correlation between the economic and social conditions of a City parish and the success or failure of Presbyterianism during the Puritan era? These are some of the questions I shall attempt to answer in the ensuing survey of the Presbyterians in Puritan London.

According to the parliamentary ordinance, the London Provincial Assembly consisted, within its jurisdiction, of twelve classes and one hundred and thirty-six parishes.[12] As was noted earlier, it covered a much larger area than the City of London itself. Partly because the City of Westminster, Southwark, and the surrounding Liberties lie outside the scope of this study and partly because three of the four classes beyond the boundary of the City were never formed, the present examination of the successes and failures of Presbyterianism in Puritan London will be concerned with the City parishes themselves.

It should be pointed out that as an ecclesiastical institution, the Presbyterian church government was a new and, one may even say, a rather artificial creation, that had no historical roots in the City parishes, in spite of the fact that Presbyterianism apparently evoked an unmistakably strong and wide following not only among the Puritan parish ministers in the City but also among the civic leaders of various London parishes as well. Unlike the old episcopacy, the London Provincial Assembly, for instance, had no traditional and customary relationship or ecclesiastical and institutional ties with a parish ministry or vestry. There was, therefore, a conspicuous absence from the London parish records of this period of any direct references to the jurisdiction or the existence of the London Provincial Assembly. Only rarely do we find a parish voluntarily consulting the classical presbytery on certain particular issues.[13] Even the election of the ruling elders, which was perhaps the most essential feature of the Presbyterian system on the parochial level, was seldom officially acknowledged in the vestry minutes of the City parishes. In fact, among the extant parish records of our period, only ten parishes recorded the names of the ruling elders elected in 1646. And only one later election was ever recorded again in future years.[14] It is to be emphasized, however, that while the lack of direct references to the new church government in contemporary parish records is arresting to a modern researcher, it is also rather deceptive as evidence for interpreting the strength of Presbyterianism in Puritan London.

In a collation of the City parochial records with those of the London Provincial Assembly and the Fourth London Classis, the only official records of the Presbyterian experiment in London that have come down to posterity, we shall find that in at least sixty-four of the City parishes, the new Presbyterian church government appeared to have been established. To be sure, the nature of the Presbyterian church order in these sixty-odd London parishes varied greatly. In some, it was fully organized and continued to function effectively throughout the revolutionary period; in others, it was only partially constituted and increasingly declined afterward. Of course, in a fairly large number of the City parishes, it was not adopted at all or, as in the unformed classes, its function was confined to the parochial elderships. For the sake of convenience in this survey, I shall follow the classical divisions of the Province of London and have a closer look at the Presbyterian parishes, with special attention given to both the Presbyterian divines and the Presbyterian civic leaders in the various parishes of the City. Such a survey may reveal, at least indirectly, the geographical distribution and social composition of the Presbyterians in Puritan London.

The success of Presbyterianism in a London parish depended on a combination of favorable conditions, economic and social as well as religious. Economically, the parish needed to be a substantial community able to maintain a minister by tithes and contributions.[15] Socially, it had to have a group of civic leaders who were able to provide a broad basis of social coherence and stability within the parochial community. Religiously, and most important, the success of the Presbyterian experiment in a London parish required the presence and support of active and influential Presbyterian leadership, either clerical or civic, or, ideally, both. A few examples from each of the constituted London classes may be cited as illustrations of this fundamental nature of London Presbyterianism.

The First Classis of the London Provincial Assembly included fifteen City parishes, of which nine appear to have adopted the Presbyterian church government. In three of these parishes, the favorable conditions outlined above clearly existed and, understandably, the Presbyterian church government was firmly established in all three of them. The parish of Allhallows Bread Street may be given as a revealing example. Although not one of the large parishes in seventeenth-century London, it was undoubtedly a substantial parochial community with a concentration of wealthy merchants, and it had long been preeminent in the history of London Puritanism.[16] There was therefore the favorable coalescence of clerical and civic Presbyterian leadership, which provided a firm foundation for the success of Presbyterianism in the parish. With adequate tithes and a lectureship, Lazarus Seaman, who had been lecturer and curate of the parish from 1638, became its rector in 1643 and remained in the cure until his ejection in 1662.[17] One of the influential and politically minded Puritan divines in the revolutionary period, Seaman was chosen a member of the Westminster Assembly, elected president of Sion College, London, in 1651–53, and appointed Vice-Chancellor of Cambridge University in 1653–54. Although Seaman appears to have supported the Commonwealth and the Protectorate in future years, he was undoubtedly a Presbyterian in his views of ecclesiastical polity and, indeed, has been considered by Robert Baillie as one of the English divines who would support the Scottish position. In any case, Seaman actively participated in the proceedings of the London Provincial Assembly, being the only founding member who also attended its very last session in 1660.[18]

Perhaps more important, there was in this parish a group of eminent civic leaders such as William Kendall, Morris Gething, Tempest Milner, John Mellish, and John Box. In addition, Francis West and Richard Turner were probably also inhabitants of the parish in the early years of the revolutionary period.[19] During the years of the Civil War, all the civic leaders of the parish played an important role in the City in both political and religious events. In 1642 Kendall and Gething were appointed assessors for subscriptions and contributions to the Parliament, and Gething and Box, probably churchwardens in that year, collected £847 from their own parish. And in the following two years, Gething and Milner, along with Richard Turner and William Hawkins of St. Andrews Undershaft, jointly lent £42,929. 12s. 8d. to the Parliament themselves.[20] Kendal, Gething, and Milner were all prominent Common Councilmen and sat on various important committees of the Court of the Common Council—the committee concerning malignant, scandalous, and seditious ministers, the committee to draw a counter-petition against the peace movement in the City, the committee on borrowed arms, the committee to enlist auxiliaries for the City militia, the committee for the reforms of the City market, and the committee for the maintenance of the Puritan ministers in the City parishes. More significant, all three appear to have been involved in the Presbyterian movement in the City and were appointed to the Militia Committee in 1647 when the Presbyterian faction in the City government attempted to control the London militia in a possible military confrontation with the Army.[21] In 1645–46, four lesser men of the parish— Thomas Sadler, John Norwood, Thomas Came [or Carne], and Captain John Lanne—signed the Presbyterian petitions for a stronger church government. And Box, too, was clearly a staunch Presbyterian and signed the City's engagement for a personal treaty with the King in 1648.[22] Although its more prominent civic leaders, who had invested heavily in the revolutionary cause, had to compromise their religious convictions and support the Commonwealth, the parish was undoubtedly one of the strongly Presbyterian parishes in Puritan London.

Similarly, in the neighboring parish of St. Augustine Watling Street, the Puritan minister during the years of the Civil War was Francis Roberts, who was a confidant of Robert Baillie and acted frequently as an intermediary between the City ministers and the Scottish commissioners in London. It was probably Roberts who, in response to and under the pressure of Baillie, instigated and organized the Presbyterian agitation in the City in favor of a stronger Presbyterian church government. In future years Roberts was succeeded as minister of St. Augustine by Simeon Ashe, another influential Presbyterian divine—"a burning and shining light," as Edmund Calamy would say in 1662, and "one whom many Ministers and other good Christians called Father, insomuch that it was a common proverb in the City, Father Ash."[23] On the civic side, the leading parishioners of the parish were Presbyterian in their religious persuasion and prominent in their social status. In fact, the civic leaders of St. Augustine and those of Allhallows Bread Street were closely associated. In 1640 Morris Gething and Tempest Milner of Allhallows served as sureties for the churchwardens of St. Augustine, while Richard Turner and Francis West, who were Common Councilmen and leading parishioners of St. Augustine, had been and probably still were inhabitants in the parish of Allhallows Bread Street.[24] Turner continued to be one of the Common Councilmen from this parish until 1648, and the other Common Councilmen from 1641 onward were successively John Orlibear and Henry Ashurst, who were also Presbyterians.[25] Turner was an assessor for parliamentary contributions and assessments in 1642 and, as Common Councilman, sat on the committee concerning scandalous ministers in the City. Again, what was even more significant, Turner, a colonel himself in the London militia, was appointed to the Presbyterian Militia Committee in 1647.[26] Orlibear appears to have had a closer relationship with the Scots, for in 1646 the Scottish commissioners in London wrote to their army officers in Ulster for the restitution of goods seized from an agent of Orlibear, who, as the Scottish commissioners stated, was "our very good friend . . . he being a person well-effected and forward in the cause."[27] Among the three leading civic figures of the parish, Henry Ashurst was probably a more moderate man in Puritan politics during the years of the Civil War. He was, however, to become a leading Nonconformist in London after the Restoration. Richard Baxter's "most intire friend," to whom Baxter dedicated his *Directions for weake distempered Christians* in 1669 and for whose funeral Baxter preached, Ashurst was to become an Alderman of the City in 1668, master of the Merchant Taylors' Company in 1670, and treasurer of the Trust for the Propagation of the Gospel to the Indians, of which Robert Boyle was president. And Ashurst was a ruling elder of the parish and an overseer of the will of Simeon Ashe.[28] Among the lesser men of the parish, there were, too, a number of known Presbyterians, at least five of whom signed the Presbyterian petitions in 1645–46. Two of these men deserve some explanation. William Barton was probably Colonel William Barton, in whose house Christopher Love preached in 1650 and who was implicated in Love's plot; and Thomas Gellibrand was a captain in the London militia who was purged in 1648 because, in the words of a contemporary pamphleteer, he was "of too much honesty to serve any base designe."[29]

The parish of St. Martin Ludgate may be cited as one more example. Although a much larger parish with a greater number of poor people, it was one of the substantial parochial communities in the City, with a concentration of well-to-do merchants in it. As we shall see later in this study, the parochial governmental structure of the parish was more effectively reorganized during the revolutionary period.[30] During the years of the Civil War, its minister was Stanley Gower, and its civic leaders included Thomas Arnold, William Hobson, William Jeston, and Matthew Fox. Gower, who had been rector of Brampton Bryan, Herefordshire, had had close ties with the famous Puritan family of Sir Robert and Lady Brilliana Harley; and like Harley, Gower became a Presbyterian.[31] Among the civic leaders, Arnold was probably the most important. An assessor for parliamentary contributions in 1642 and a prominent Common Councilman, Arnold was appointed to the committee to draw a counterpetition against the peace movement in the City, the committee for the fortification of London, and the committee for the consideration of the church government. In 1647 Arnold was also appointed to the Presbyterian Militia Committee.[32] Similarly, Hobson was a member of the committees concerning the malignant ministers in the City, for the drafting of a counterpetition and for the consideration of the church government.[33] And Hobson and Jeston must have been known Presbyterians, for, according to Thomas Edwards, both of them were among the candidates for the Common Council in 1645, who were openly opposed by the sectarians in the City. In addition, there were also a number of Presbyterians among the lesser civic figures of the parish: Hugh Radcliffe, Edward Toking, Captain Walter Lee, and so on.[34] With such ministerial and civic leaders for Presbyterianism, it is understandable that St. Martin Ludgate was one of the few London parishes in which the Presbyterian church government was officially adopted by the vestry. At a vestry meeting on 19 June 1646, as the vestry minutes clearly recorded, "it was unanimouslie consented unto that the Ordinance of Parliament touching the Presbyterian Govnment should goe forward and be put in execucon."[35]

In six other parishes of the First London Classis, the Presbyterian church government was also established, but it appears that the success of Presbyterianism in these parishes was due more to the dedication and efforts of their Puritan ministers than to the influence of their civic leaders. In fact, in all these six parishes, the known civic leaders during the Puritan era were fewer in number and far less prominent in social status. In this respect the parish of St. Anne Blackfriars may be cited as a good example. Sociologically speaking, the parish, as noted in the preceding chapter, was a rapidly declining parochial community in seventeenth-century London, with an increasingly larger and larger number of the poor and fewer and fewer substantial householders. During the years of the Civil War, no prominent civic figure appeared in this parish except for Richard Browne, who, though appointed as a lay trier in 1645 as of Blackfriars, was in all probability not a regular inhabitant of the parish.[36] Yet, it is to be noted that the parish of St. Anne Blackfriars had long been privileged with the ministry of William Gouge, perhaps the most renowned and respected Puritan divine in the City of London. For more than thirty years the preaching of Gouge, first as lecturer and then as minister, had made Blackfriars one of the main centers of Puritanism in prerevolutionary London. "How great was the influence of hearers," as William Jenkyn afterward recalled in his sermon at Gouge's funeral, "which in former times not only from all parts of this famous City, but of many parts of England, frequented the lectures at Black-Fryars. . . . When the godly Christians of those times came to London, they thought not their business done unless they had been at Black-Fryars lectures." One of the feoffees for Puritan lectureships and purchased impropriations in the 1630s and an eminent member in the Westminster Assembly, Gouge was a venerable figure among the Presbyterian ministers in London. The esteem he commanded among his London brethren was expressed unmistakably by the fact that he was chosen the moderator for the very first London Provincial Assembly in 1647.[37] In general, the First London Classis appeared to be one of the better constituted classical presbyteries in Puritan London, though for various reasons, as we shall see, the Presbyterian church government was either languidly formed or was never adopted at all in six of its constituent parishes.[38]

In comparison, the Third London Classis appears to have been a weaker organization. Out of the twelve parishes with which it was composed, the Presbyterian system was well established only in five, though in three others it was adopted at the beginning but soon afterward ceased to function.[39] Yet the five Presbyterian parishes of this classis deserve further examination in order to reveal the circumstances surrounding the Presbyterian experiment in Puritan London. The case of St. Mary Woolchurch, for instance, offers a good example of the role played by civic Presbyterian leaders in maintaining the Presbyterian system in a City parish during the Puritan era. During the years of the Civil War, the new Puritan civic leaders of the parish were Colonel Thomas Gower, Michael Herring, and Lieutenant Colonel Robert Thompson, all of whom were undoubtedly Presbyterians in their religious belief and political association. In fact, Gower was to become a predominant figure in the parish—both as a vestryman and as a new feoffee for the parish lands. A colonel in the London militia as well as a Common Councilman,

Gower sat on the committees for borrowed arms and for the consideration of the church government. In 1647 he was also appointed to the Presbyterian Militia Committee.[40] Herring was appointed as assessor for parliamentary contributions and assessments in 1642 and, also a Common Councilman, sat on the committee concerning malignant ministers in the same year. In 1645 he was appointed a lay trier of the Third Classis.[41] And both Gower and Herring were ruling elders of the parish and, as such, were chosen as delegates to the London Provincial Assembly.[42] Thompson, too, was undoubtedly a Presbyterian, for in 1648, after the triumphant march of the Army upon London and the collapse of the Presbyterian faction in the City government, he was one of the officers purged from the London militia, though, as a contemporary pamphleteer maintained, he had been "a valiant and faithful commander."[43] The importance of the civic Presbyterian leaders for the establishment of the Presbyterian church government in the parish of St. Mary Woolchurch can be seen from the fact that the two ministers of the parish during the Puritan era, Thomas Wheatley and Richard Ball, do not appear to have been involved in the Presbyterian experiment in the City. Wheatley, who was the parish minister from 1646 to 1650, was apparently a Presbyterian but, rather strangely, never officially became a member of the London Provincial Assembly; whereas Ball, who became the minister of the parish in 1652, was probably an Anglican at heart and never participated in the proceedings of the Assembly in the eight remaining years of its existence.[44]

On the other hand, the parish of St. Stephen Walbrook may be cited as a revealing example of the ambiguous and shifting positions the civic leaders had to take in religion and politics in Puritan London. It was also one of the London parishes in which the Presbyterian church government existed under a group of influential political Independents. There can be no doubt that the parish of St. Stephen Walbrook was one of the strongly Puritan parishes in the City and its civic leaders played crucial roles in municipal and national events throughout the revolutionary period. In 1641 the parish threatened to petition against the old incumbent, Dr. Thomas Howell, and finally forced him to resign, and in the following year, as noted before, a group of twenty-eight of its inhabitants contributed £953 to the Parliament.[45] Although a small parish, it was one of the substantial parochial communities in seventeenth-century London, with a concentration of wealthy merchants.[46] More significant, during the revolutionary period, the parish produced a number of prominent and influential civic leaders: John Warner (Sheriff, 1639–40; Alderman, 1640–48; Lord Mayor, 1647–48), Samuel Warner (Alderman, 1643–45), Samuel Mico (Alderman, 1653–56), William Underwood (Alderman, 1651–58) and William Thompson (Alderman, 1653–61). In addition, three other parishioners of the parish, namely, Charles Lloyd, Arthur Juxon, and John Sadler, were also Common Councilmen in the City. Juxon was master of the Salters' Company in 1648; Sadler was chosen Town Clerk of the City in 1649;

and Lloyd was also chosen Alderman in 1651.[47] It is to be noted, however, that some of the civic leaders of the parish were to become leading political Independents in the City. John Warner was elected the Lord Mayor of London upon the triumphant occupation of the City by the Army.[48] Underwood, a colonel in the London militia, had apparently abandoned the cause during the crucial hours in the confrontation between the City and the Army. "In the Blew Regiment," as a contemporary pamphleteer observed, "shakerag *Vnderwood* may serve their turn well enough; he basely hid his head when he should have been at the head of his Regiment."[49] When he died in 1658 it was George Cokayne, a leading Independent divine in the City, who preached his funeral sermon.[50] And we may assume that Sadler, chosen as he was as Town Clerk in 1649, must have also been a political Independent. Nevertheless, John Warner had been appointed a lay trier for the Third Classis in 1645, and in 1647, both before and after his election as Lord Mayor, he attended the London Provincial Assembly as a delegate from the Third Classis. As such, he must have been a ruling elder of the parish as well.[51] And Underwood, too, was a ruling elder and he continued to participate in the proceedings of the London Provincial Assembly as late as 1652.[52] In the light of these shifty positions of Warner and Underwood in Puritan politics, modern students of the Puritan era should, indeed, be wary of the danger in using the factional labels too rigidly. While a moderate Presbyterian could become a political Independent under the logic of the necessity of immediate events, a political Independent could well remain a Presbyterian in religious or parochial affairs or, at least, continue to support a Presbyterian ministry.[53] This can be seen clearly from the career of Thomas Watson, minister of the parish from 1647 to 1662 and a staunch Presbyterian divine in the City. In spite of the political changes in the City and the changing positions of the parish civic leaders, Watson was able to maintain his ministry in the parish and continue to have undiminished support of his parishioners. Although the value of tithes in the parish amounted to less than £50 a year, Watson had an annual salary of £120 when he came to the cure in 1647 and his salary was increased to £150 from 1658 to 1662.[54]

There was a more favorable coalescence of ministerial and civic Presbyterian leadership in the other three parishes of the Third London Classis: St. Mary Woolnoth, St. Nicholas Acons, and St. Swithin.[55] Without examining in detail the Presbyterian civic leaders in these parishes, a few observations should be made as to the wide scope of the Presbyterian appeal among the civic figures in Puritan London. In the parish of St. Mary Woolnoth, for instance, the minister, Ralph Robinson, was one of the staunch Presbyterian divines in the City who participated actively and consistently in the proceedings of both the Third Classis and the London Provincial Assembly, serving on several occasions as scribe and moderator of both bodies. Or, as Simeon Ashe said in 1655 in his funeral sermon for Robinson: "In his judgment, affection and practice, he was a thorow, well-ground Presbyterian" and "he was conscientiously constant to his Covenant; neither hopes nor fears, caused him to warp, or to decline either to the right hand or to the left."[56] Among his parishioners and supporters was no less a civic figure than Sir Thomas Vyner, who was Alderman in 1646–65, Sheriff in 1648–49, Lord Mayor in 1653–54 and a famous financier for the Commonwealth, the Protectorate, and the restored Monarchy.[57] It is perhaps rather strange for a modern student of Puritan London to include Vyner among the civic Presbyterians; yet it was to Vyner that in 1655 Ashe dedicated his sermon for Robinson's funeral, and when Lady Honor Vyner died in the following year, her funeral sermon was preached by William Spurstowe, another eminent Presbyterian divine in the City, who also dedicated the sermon to Sir Thomas Vyner.[58] In the parish of St. Nicholas Acons, the civic leaders included William Ashwell, John Babington, Nicholas Skinner, and Henry Gray. Ashwell, a known ruling elder of the parish, was Deputy in 1642 and Alderman in 1643–44.[59] Babington, who was Common Councilman from 1639 to 1648, was in all probability also a Presbyterian.[60] During the Commonwealth and the Protectorate the Common Councilmen in the parish were Skinner and Gray, who were brothers-in-law and perhaps also related to Babington. In the future, both Skinner and Gray became Aldermen of London and masters of the Salters' Company.[61] During the Puritan era, the ministers of the parish, Francis Peck and John Meriton, were unmistakably Presbyterian divines.[62] The Presbyterian experiment in Puritan London was not just the creation of zealous men, who were undoubtedly important both in the Presbyterian movement in the City and in the actual formulation of the London Provincial Assembly; it also enjoyed the support of men ranging from a great financier like Thomas Vyner to moderate London merchants like William Ashwell, Nicholas Skinner, and Henry Gray.

As has been noted earlier in this chapter, the Fourth London Classis has left its register-book to posterity, which is now the only source to provide us with a complete picture of the proceedings and activities of a London classical presbytery during the revolutionary period. From its records we know that the Fourth Classis was first convened in November 1646 and continued to function until the end of 1659. In appearance and in the nominal sense, it seemed to be a well-constituted ecclesiastical institution under the new Presbyterian system in London. In actuality, a closer scrutiny of the classical register-book and the parochial records of the individual parishes of the classis would reveal that out of the fourteen parishes that constituted the Fourth London Classis, four appear never to have adopted the Presbyterian system.[63] In another three parishes the Presbyterian church elderships, which had been formed in 1646 at the initial stage of the classical presbytery, were soon to become at least partially inoperative, with Independent divines as their parish ministers; whereas in still another two, Anglican influences prevailed either on the part of the parish minister or among the parishioners in general.[64] As a result we may conclude that the Presbyterian church order was more or less firmly established and maintained in only five parishes of the Fourth Classis.[65] Yet, to look at the same evidence from a different perspective, the records of the Fourth Classis also reveal to us that civic Presbyterian leaders were, indeed, just as important as Presbyterian clergymen for whatever success Presbyterianism could achieve in Puritan London.

The Fourth Classis comprised a group of eleven parishes at the northern end of London Bridge, with three additional parishes farther to the north. With one or two exceptions, these were parishes of well-to-do tradesmen. Although few of them could boast of a large number of great merchants among their inhabitants, some of these parishes produced active and influential Presbyterian civic leaders in Puritan London—such as James Bunce of St. Benet Gracechurch, John Bellamy of St. Michael Cornhill, Edward Hooker of St. Mary at Hill, John Gase of St. Andrew Hubbard, Edward Bellamy of St. Magnus, Richard Hill and Thomas Manwaring of St. Dionis Backchurch, Tobias Lisle and John and Nehemiah Wallingham of St. Leonard Eastcheap, and so forth. James Bunce might be what modern historians would call a political Presbyterian,[66] but all the other civic leaders mentioned above were unmistakably Presbyterians in their religious belief no less than in their political associations. In fact, in most of these parishes, it was the civic Presbyterian leaders who were instrumental in the adoption and maintenance of the Presbyterian system as well as in the continuation of the Fourth Classis. The parish of St. Michael Cornhill, for example, was actually without a settled minister in 1646, when the Presbyterian system was to be established in the City. Yet, in a vestry meeting on 28 June, after having read and endorsed the protestation of the London ministers in regard to the imperfections of the Presbyterian church government under parliamentary ordinances, the civic leaders resolved to follow the ministers' advice "to put the Presbyteriall government into execution." On 31 July it was further decided that elders were to be elected among the parishioners in the middle of August, and on 16 August the election duly took place with six elders chosen: Francis Mosse, William Rowell, James Martin, John Bellamy, William Webb, and John Turlington.[67]

Among the six chosen ruling elders of the parish of St. Michael Cornhill, John Bellamy deserves some special attention. In 1616, while still a young apprentice, Bellamy, who had "a most pious, quiet and tender conscience" and desired "to know more of the mind and will of God," joined the separatist church of Henry Jacob in Southwark, and he remained with the Southwark congregation until the middle of the 1620s. In the meantime he had become a successful bookseller and one of the first publishers in London of the works of such eminent Separatists and Independents as John Robinson, Henry Ainsworth, William Bradford, John Winthrop, Edward Winslow, and John Cotton.[68] Bellamy's association with the radical sectarians appeared to have continued until the early years of the revolutionary era; for, as the writer of *Mercurius Aulicus* maintained in 1642, his shop "at the three golden Lyons neare the old Exchange" had become "the *Medley* and *Brownists Nest* wither all the Brethren flutter."[69] It was probably with the rising tide of radical sectarianism in these years that Bellamy became more conservative in his religious stance and eventually embraced Presbyterianism.[70] In any case, throughout the years of the Civil War, he was one of the most active new civic leaders in religion as well as in politics in Puritan London. Elected Common Councilman in a disputed election in 1641–42, he was appointed an assessor for parliamentary contributions and subscriptions in 1642 and, in the Common Council, sat on committees between 1642 and 1646 over a wide range of important matters: for the fortification of the City, for the suppression of scandalous pamphlets and books, and for the maintenance of the ministers of the London parishes. Also a colonel in the London militia, he was appointed to the Presbyterian Militia Committee in 1647.[71] In the parochial life of St. Michael Cornhill, Bellamy also appears to have been a dedicated leader.[72]

Similarly, Edward Hooker of the parish of St. Mary at Hill was an important figure of the Presbyterian faction in the City. A captain in the London militia in 1642, he became lieutenant colonel in 1643 and colonel in 1644. Also a Common Councilman, Hooker sat on a number of important committees—concerning the expulsion of the royalist Common Councilman Robert Alden, for the malignant ministers in the City, for the consideration of church government, for borrowed arms, and for the suppression of scandalous pamphlets and books. In 1647 Hooker was also appointed to the Presbyterian Milita Committee.[73] Perhaps more militant than Bellamy in the dangerous confrontation between the City and the Army, Hooker was soon to be purged from the London militia. He was described by a contemporary pamphleteer as "a valiant prudent godly and faithful Captain" and as "a man that stood up with the first and acted with the best, for the safety of King, Parliament, Kingdom, and City."[74] And Hooker was the leading vestryman in the parishes of both St. George Botolph Lane and St. Mary at Hill.[75]

I have given special attention to Bellamy and Hooker because they were good examples of ordinary London tradesmen who played highly important roles in Puritan politics in the City during the years of the Civil War. The establishment of the Presbyterian church government in these parochial communities depended also upon the participation and support of other civic leaders. In the parish of St. Michael Cornhill, Francis Mosse, James Martin, and William Rowell were all Common Councilmen in the Civil War period. William Webb was probably not Colonel William Webb, though this might well be the same man. In any case, Webb was chosen Common Councilman in Cornhill Ward in 1648 but "not sworn," and he was again listed as Common Councilman in the following year. And John Turlington, a noted spectacle maker, was elected Common Councilman in 1658.[76] Similarly, the fellow ruling elders of Hooker in the parish of St. Mary at Hill were also relatively important civic leaders in the City. Thomas Lenthall was Common Councilman from 1643 to 1651. He had been appointed an assessor for parliamentary subscriptions in 1642 and sat on the committees for church government in 1644 and for borrowed arms in 1645. Dr. Edward Alston, a noted physician, was elected fellow of the College of Physicians in 1631 and became its president from 1655 to 1666. William Harris, a minor figure, was a wealthy cheesemonger and served as a commissioner for Billingsgate Ward in 1648.[77] John Gace, one of the ruling elders of the parish of St. Andrew Hubbard, was another important civic leader in Puritan London. He was appointed an assessor for parliamentary subscriptions in 1642 and a lay trier for the Fourth Classis in 1645; and, also a Common Councilman, he sat on the committees for the City's remonstrance about church government and for the maintenance of ministers in the City. In 1647 he too was appointed to the Presbyterian Militia Committee.[78] The presence of Presbyterian civic leaders in the parish of St. Peter Cornhill was perhaps even more necessary, for the old civic leader of the parish was Thomas Lusher, a Royalist and Anglican, who had been replaced as Common Councilman by John Bellamy in 1641. And Lusher and a group of his friends apparently remained to have some influence in the parish. Among the six ruling elders of the parish, Philip Meade was an assessor in 1642; William Peace and Francis Cooling were Common Councilmen; Miles Robinson was master of the Company of Armourers-Brasiers in 1635 and William Bromwich, master of the Company in 1652; and Lewis Bicker, who was to be warden of the Grocers' Company in 1660, was one of the leading vestrymen during the revolutionary period.[79] What is more significant is that civic Presbyterian leaders such as Thomas Manwaring and Richard Best of St. Dionis Backchurch and John and Nehemiah Wallington of St. Leonard Eastcheap, continued to participate in the proceedings of the Fourth Classis in spite of the fact that the minister of the former had been converted to the Anglican church polity and the ministry of the latter had fallen into the hands of a radical Independent.[80]

The Fifth London Classis occupies a unique place in the Presbyterian movement in Puritan London because there gathered among its constituent parishes a large number of eminent and, in some cases, the most militant Presbyterian ministers during the years of the Civil War. Among the ministers of this classis were William Jenkyn and Thomas Edwards at Christ Church, Richard Heyrick and Christopher Love at St. Anne and St. Agnes Aldersgate, Roger Drake at St. Peter Westcheap, James Nalton at St. Leonard Foster Lane, Simeon Ashe at St. Bride, John Conant and Thomas Jaggard at St. Botolph Aldersgate, Anthony Tuckney and Matthew Poole at St. Michael le Querne, Nicholas Proffett at St. Vedast Foster Lane, and William Barton at St. John Zachary. Some brief accounts of the activities of these men will not only elucidate the success of the Presbyterian experiment in these parishes but also shed much light on the militant aspect of London Presbyterianism during the revolutionary period.

Born to devout Puritan parents, William Jenkyn was destined to play an important role in Puritan politics. Coming to London in 1641, he was chosen minister in the parish of Christ Church and, a few months later, appointed to a lectureship as well in the parish of St. Anne Blackfriars. During the period of the Civil War, in the words of Edmund Calamy, the Nonconformist biographer, "he continu'd to fill up this double Station with great Diligence and Acceptance." A strong advocate of the Presbyterian discipline, Jenkyn was one of the Presbyterian remonstrants in London who signed the ministerial petition for a more authoritarian Presbyterian system in 1645, the *Testimony* of the London ministers in 1647, and their *Vindication* and *A serious and faithful Representation* in 1649. In fact, he must have long turned the pulpit into a political forum, for he had been summoned early in October 1647 before the House of Commons to answer charges against him. Perhaps his staunch, pro-Scottish position can be seen more clearly from the writings of John Price, who called him "that pertinatious," "that imperious," and "that Metropolitan-like Mr. Jenkyn." According to Price, he was one of the London Presbyterian divines who, after the triumph of the Army and the Independents, declined to acknowledge the legitimacy of the Parliament, "for the word of Parliament is now dissolved in some of their mouthes." In one of his sermons, he said, "O that the people of God would rather feare an Army of lusts within them, than an Army of Rebels without them. God shall disband them, and you shall see them melt and pine, and moulder away, and come to nothing." In another, preached probably on the eve of the second Scottish invasion, he openly prayed for Scotland and said that "Wee thank thee for any hopes thou hast given us to make them further instrument for the advance of truth amongst us. Lord, Blow up those Sparks into a Flame." As a result, Jenkyn was suspended from his ministry in 1650. He retired temporarily into Essex and returned to London in the following year only to become involved in Love's plot.[81] Under Jenkyn's ministry, Christ Church must have become a stronghold of Presbyterianism in the City, so much so that it was chosen by the London Presbyterian brethren sometime in 1644–45 as the place for a weekly lecture for Thomas Edwards, the most outspoken opponent of Independency and an acrimonious Presbyterian propagandist. "It was here," as Pearl has put it, "that Edwards over the next two years rehearsed the substance of *Gangraena,* that most virulent, unrestrained, irrational attack on the Independents."[82]

Christopher Love, the only true martyr for the Presbyterian cause during the revolutionary period, was undoubtedly a man of bold and indomitable spirit. On the eve of the Revolution, while still a young Welsh Puritan preacher, Love already became notorious for refusing to receive episcopal ordination and to subscribe to the new canons of Archbishop Laud. In 1639 he came to London on the invitation of John Warner, Sheriff of the City, to serve as chaplain to the Warner family. With the outbreak of the Civil War, Love was appointed chaplain to the regiment of Colonel John Venn, and when Venn was made governor of Windsor Castle, he followed Venn there as chaplain to the garrison. While at Windsor Castle, Love in early 1645 preached an inflammatory sermon at Uxbridge against peace negotiations between the King and the Parliament. Shortly afterward he was chosen minister and lecturer in the parish of St. Anne and St. Agnes Aldersgate. In spite of his earlier associations with Warner and Venn, both eminent political Independents in the City, Love joined the London Presbyterian brethren's campaign for a stronger Presbyterian church government. Also one of the Presbyterian remonstrants in London, Love probably drafted part of their *Vindication.* In fact, during the years 1646–49, he was engaged in an open and pugnacious pamphlet war against the sectarians both in the Army and in the City, with a thinly veiled attack upon the Independents in the House of Commons as well. In 1646 he told General Thomas Fairfax that the dangerous sectarian doctrines "would not only blemish, but disturbe your Army; and though God hath cloathed them with strength to conquer men, yet if such doctrines should spread among them, errours will conquer them in the end." In the following year, probably shortly after the Army's triumphant march upon London, Love published a pamphlet entitled *Works of Darkness Brought to Light. Or A true Representation to the Whole Kingdome of the Dangerous Designes driven on by the Sectaries in the Army,* in which he reflected upon the Independents in the House of Commons, the sectarians in the City and the Army. "When the Sectaries, in and about London, Petition," he wrote in one place, " 'tis only to their own House of Commons, they never take notice of the Lords House at all; witness that factious Petition from *Lambes* Congregation, and another Petition from the Sectaries of London, delivered to the House of Commons, by that Turn-coate *Samuel Warner, Tichbourn* and others, in opposition to the Renouned Remonstrance of the City." And the teachings of the Army chaplains, he wrote in another place, "have so corrupted their hearers and disciples from the simplicity of the Gospel that the whole Army now contends for Toleration by the sword in the Field." Still undaunted by the victory of the sectarians, Love ended his pamphlet with the following doggerel:

> Ye Presbyterian starrs, in Christs right hand
> Though Armies pul you down, yet shall you stand.
> Out live you shal, these troubles, do what can
> *Hobson,* or *Hughson, Del,* or *Quarterman.*

And it is no surprise that Love ended his own life as a central figure in a plot that bears his name, in 1649–51 against the Commonwealth and for the return of the future Charles II.[83]

Among the other ministers of the Fifth Classis, Simeon Ashe, James Nalton, and Roger Drake were also strong advocates of Presbyterianism in Puritan London. Ashe, as has been noted earlier in this chapter, was a highly esteemed figure among his London Presbyterian brethren. "A *Nonconform-*

ist of the Old Stamp," he had long been an ejected Puritan minister because of his opposition to the Laudian ceremonies and the Book of Sports. On the eve of the Revolution, Ashe came to London, and it appears that even at this early date he, along with William Rathband, had been concerned about the possible dangers of Independency. In the middle of May 1642 he preached before "the Commanders of the Military Forces of the Renowned Citie of London" a sermon entitled "Good Covrage Discovered, and Encovraged," and on the outbreak of the Civil War, he was appointed chaplain to the Earl of Manchester, a Lord General of the parliamentary army. At the battle of Edgehill, according to a contemporary report, Ashe was one of the chaplains who "rode up and down the army through the thickest dangers, and in much personal hazard, mostly faithfully and courageously exhorting and encouraging the soldiers to fight valiantly and not to fly." And in his capacity as the Lord General's chaplain, Ashe wrote in defense of Manchester's military conduct and became involved in the conflict between Manchester and Cromwell. More important for our subject, he also became a leading spirit in the Presbyterian movement in the City. In 1645 he was one of the signatories in the ministerial petition for a stronger Presbyterian church government. Early in 1646 he preached, along with Edmund Calamy, before the Lord Mayor, Aldermen, and the Common Council in a public fast for a renewal of the Solemn League and Covenant by oath and subscription. And in July 1647, during the dangerous confrontation between the City and the Army, he again preached at Guildhall for new recruitments for the London militia. The prominent place occupied by Ashe among the London Presbyterian brethren was recognized by the Army, for after the latter's occupation of the City, he was invited by Robert Tichborne to meet the Army's Council of Officers at Whitehall for a conference about "liberty in worship." To be sure, Ashe declined the invitation unless, he declared, "the Councell of the Army would come to a debate, whether they had sinned or no." In later years Ashe continued to oppose the Commonwealth and the Protectorate, and "fell under the Obloquy of the *Cromwellians*." In 1660 he had "a considerable Hand in bringing in King *Charles* II."[84]

Nalton and Drake were perhaps less influential among the London Presbyterian ministers but hardly less committed to the Presbyterian cause. Nalton was said to be "a good Linguist, a zealous excellent Preacher, commonly called the *Weeping Prophet*, because his Seriousness oft expressed itself by Tears." He served as assessor of the London Provincial Assembly in 1649 and its moderator in 1650. Also one of the London ministerial remonstrants, he was implicated in Love's plot and temporarily fled to Holland in 1651.[85] In comparison with the other London Presbyterian divines, Drake had an unusual career. Educated at Leiden University, Drake was an able and distinguished physician and a believer in the Harveian doctrine. In 1645, a year before he resolved to enter the ministry, Drake became deeply engaged in the Presbyterian agitation in the City, and signed both of the citizens' petitions for a strong Presbyterian system in late 1645 and early 1646. His name headed the list of sixty signatories of the first petition, which had probably been drafted by him. Scribe of the London Provincial Assembly in 1649 and its moderator in 1653, Drake, too, was implicated in Love's plot and imprisoned in the Tower.[86] And it may be added that Richard Heyrick, who was to become the leading exponent of Presbyterianism in Lancashire, might have retained his connections with London and was probably the only non-London minister implicated in Love's plot in 1651. And Thomas Jaggard, who had probably more direct complicity in the plot and was among the first accomplices apprehended for treason, was chosen minister first at St. Peter Westcheap in 1646 and then at St. Botolph Aldersgate in 1647.[87]

The other five Presbyterian divines associated with the Fifth London Classis during the years of the Civil War were comparatively moderate men in Puritan politics; yet they all supported the position of their London Presbyterian brethren. Four of them were recognized learned divines in seventeenth-century England. Anthony Tuchney was afterward master of Emmanuel College and St. John's College at Cambridge, Vice-Chancellor of the University, and the Regius Professor of Divinity, while John Conant, was master of Exeter College, Vice-Chancellor and the Regius Professor of Divinity at the University of Oxford.[88] Matthew Poole was "a Celebrated Critick and Casuist" in biblical studies, whereas William Barton was a noted hymnologist and published verse translations of the Psalms. And Poole, who was an active participant in the proceedings of the London Provincial Assembly, wrote in defense of ordained ministry and against lay preaching in 1658 "by the Appointment of the Provincial Assembly at London."[89] Not much is known about Nicholas Proffett and his involvement in Puritan politics in the City. A member of the Westminster Assembly, Proffett was twice invited to preach before the Parliament and he later signed all the three testimonial and vindicative declarations of the London Presbyterian ministers from 1647 to 1649.[90]

The preceding account of the Presbyterian divines of the Fifth London Classis may serve as a revealing example of the immense clerical influence in the City of London during the years of the Civil War. It is, indeed, an arresting phenomenon to a modern researcher that such a group of eminent and indomitable Presbyterian clergymen gathered together among such a small group of neighboring parishes in London. The impact of their preaching in the pulpits and their persuasion by personal association with their parishioners cannot be overestimated. It may not be too wrong to say that the strength of Presbyterianism in the Fifth Classis lay primarily in its clerical leadership. Perhaps it is because of this that, as we shall see later in this chapter, the Presbyterian system in this classis declined more conspicuously during the later years of the Puritan era, when some of these Presbyterian divines either left their cures for better preferments or became implicated in political intrigues. This is not to deny, of course, that there were active and in some cases equally militant Presbyterian civic leaders among the parishes of the Fifth Classis, whose participation and support were essential for the success of the Presbyterian experiment in the earlier years of the Puritan era. Now we may turn our attention to the civic side of the Fifth London Classis and have a closer look at some of the leading Presbyterian laymen.

The Fifth London Classis consisted of eleven parishes and Bridewell Precinct. Clearly due to the clerical leadership, the Presbyterian church government was established in nine of these parochial or extraparochial communities,[91] which was, comparatively speaking, a greater success than most of the other London classes, at least in the early part of the revolutionary period. It is also to be noted that with the exceptions of St. Vedast Foster Lane and St. Michael le Querne, none of the other parishes appear to have had a large concentration of great merchants and substantial tradesmen. Bridewell Precinct was not a regular parochial community, nor was it socially or politically important in seventeenth-century London. And St. Mary Staining and St. Olave Silver Street were among the truly impoverished parishes in the City.[92] It is no surprise, therefore, that the parishes of St. Vedast Foster Lane and St. Michael le Querne provided some of the prominent civic Presbyterian leaders in this classis. St. Vedast Foster Lane, which was located at the western end of Cheapside, was probably one of the main centers of goldsmiths in the City. During the revolutionary period, five of its inhabitants were elected Aldermen, four being members of the Goldsmiths' Company.[93] More pertinent to our subject was the presence of three important Presbyterian civic leaders in the parish: Richard Glyde, Francis Ashe, and John Perrin. All three were Common Councilmen during the years of the Civil War, and Glyde, who was more actively involved in Puritan politics, sat on a number of important committees in the Common Council over matters ranging from resolving the disputes between the militia committee and the subcommittee in 1643 to borrowed arms and reforms of common markets in the City in 1645. In 1647 both Ashe and Perrin were members of the committee for the nomination of the Presbyterian militia committee and Glyde was nominated to it. Also one of the treasurers for the £32,000 to be raised for the fortifications of the City in 1647, Glyde was undoubtedly one of the most staunch and militant Presbyterian Common Councilmen in the City. In fact, he was one of the lay Presbyterians whose candidacy for the Common Council was openly opposed by the sectarians in the election of 1645. And Glyde was a delegate to the very first session of the London Provincial Assembly.[94] The parish of St. Michael le Querne, which was also located at the western end of Cheapside, had a large number of substantial tradesmen. Of the two known Presbyterian civic leaders, John Gellibrand, who was appointed an additional assessor for parliamentary subscriptions and assessments in 1642 and elected Common Councilman from 1643 to 1647, was probably more actively engaged in the Presbyterian movement in the City. As ruling elder of the parish, he was frequently delegated as a representative to the London Provincial Assembly. The other was Edward Honeywood, who was appointed a lay trier for the Fifth Classis in 1645 and, later as ruling elder, also a delegate to the Assembly. Though perhaps less important as a political figure during the years of the Civil War, Honeywood was to become master of the Ironmongers' Company in 1652 and in 1664 he was elected Alderman of the City.[95]

The Presbyterian civic leaders from some of the other parishes were generally less substantial in wealth and less prominent in social status, though they were hardly less active in Puritan politics. In the parish of St. Peter Westcheap, for instance, the elected ruling elders of the parish were Richard Floyd, John Dod, Richard Overton, [James?] Harbert, and, later in 1652, Maximilian Bard. Floyd and Overton had been engaged in the Presbyterian agitation in the City and signed the citizen's petitions for a strong Presbyterian government in 1645–46. Among these men, however, only Bard was to become a relatively important political figure in the City. Master of the Girdlers' Company in 1652 and 1663, Bard was to be elected Alderman and Sheriff in 1651, appointed a commissioner of the London Militia Committee in 1660, and chosen Common Councilman in 1660–62.[96] Similarly, in the parish of Christ Church, the known Presbyterian civic leaders were William Hart, William Greenhill, and Peter Mills. Hart was appointed a lay trier for the Fifth Classis in 1645, but otherwise he was a rather obscure figure, though he might well be the Hart whose candidacy for the Common Council in 1645 was opposed by the sectarians in the City. Greenhill and Mills, on the other hand, were noted radical men in London in the early days of the revolutionary period. As we shall see in another chapter of this study, Greenhill was accused by the old incumbent as "the Arch-incendiary of Christ Church Parish," whereas Mills was a notorious iconoclast both in the parish church and at St. Paul's. During the years of the Civil War, both men were elected Common Councilmen and sometimes they sat on important committees. Yet, their election to the Common Council was probably due more to their radical position than to their social status.[97] It should be added, however, that the ministry of William Jenkyn unmistakably had its concrete result, for, according to a modern historian, a number of the parishioners of Christ Church, including John Vicars, the Presbyterian pamphleteer, and Captain Nicholas Widmerpole, who was to be purged from the London militia in 1648, had also been engaged in the Presbyterian agitation in the City and signed the petitions for a strong Presbyterian church government in 1645–46.[98] The Presbyterian civic leaders in the parish of St. Anne and St. Agnes Aldersgate were also minor tradesmen. John Sherman, who was appointed a lay trier in 1645, was upper-bailiff of the Weavers' Company, while Josiah Hammes, a known ruling elder of the parish, was an ordinary haberdasher. Both Sherman and Hammes were, however, Common Councilmen during the years of the Civil War. It should also be added that the leading men of the vestry during the 1640s, when Christopher Love was minister, included Henry Blackley and John Nicasius. Although not political figures in the City, Blackley was master of the Barber-Surgeons' Company in 1637, and Nicasius was master of the Clock-makers' Company in 1653 and 1655.[99]

Next we shall examine the parishes of St. Botolph Aldersgate and St. Bride, both of which were outside the Wall and among the largest parochial communities in seventeenth-century London. The social composition of these large parishes, as noted in the previous chapter, was of a much greater diversity, and, as was the case of St. Bride, there was an overwhelming number of poor. Yet it is to be noted that the parochial governance could well be maintained by a group of substantial or well-to-do tradesmen. Furthermore, it was often these same men who provided the civic leadership for the Presbyterian church government. In the parish of St. Botolph Aldersgate, for instance, the most prominent and perhaps most respected civic leader during the years of the Civil War was John Johnson. Common Councilman and later also Deputy of Aldersgate Ward Without during the years of 1638–47, Johnson was appointed an assessor for parliamentary subscriptions and assessments in 1642 and a lay trier for the Fifth Classis in 1645. When the London Provincial Assembly was convened in 1647, he was a delegate to the very first session of the Assembly. In light of this, Johnson was at least a moderate Presbyterian and a supporter of the Presbyterian system in the parish.[100] Although other Presbyterian civic leaders of the parish cannot be identified with certainty, it is possible to arrive at some tentative identifications from other evidence. During the years of 1648–52, five civic leaders of the parish were elected Common Councilmen but "not sworn," which was in all probability because of their subscription to the City's engagement for a personal treaty with Charles I. Among these men were Miles Fletcher and John Allen. Fletcher, who had been elected to the Common Council from 1644 to 1647, was one of the leading publishers in early seventeenth-century London. Master of the Stationers' Company in 1652 and 1662, he was elected Alderman in 1661.[101] Similarly, Allen was to become master of the Painter-Stainers' Company in 1654, Deputy of Aldersgate Ward Without in 1648–57 and Alderman of London in 1658–59.[102] Another two of these Presbyterian civic leaders were William Yardley and John Whitturne. Though not politically important, the former was master of the Founders' Company in 1655, while the latter became master of the Innholders' Company in 1660. It is also to be noted that the leading vestrymen of the parish during the Puritan era included Ralph Hutchinson, Lawrence Blomley, and James Glassbrooke. Hutchinson was Common Councilman in 1641–43, 1647, and 1652–57; Blomley was Common Councilman and later Deputy in 1654–64; and Glassbrooke, who was elected Alderman and Sheriff in 1651, was the benefactor of the poor of several London parishes in 1656.[103]

The parish of St. Bride presents another fascinating case for the study of the Presbyterians in Puritan London, for the ruling elders of the parish, twelve in number, were officially elected by the vestry, and, in light of the parish records, the governance of the parish affairs was unmistakably in the hands of these men throughout the revolutionary period. To be sure, the governance of such a parish as St. Bride, which was immense in size and complex in social composition, was not easy. In 1645, for instance, when the election of a minister was conducted in a general meeting of the parishioners, Thomas Coleman was chosen shortly after he had created a storm among the Scottish and English Presbyterian ministers with a sermon in favor of Erastianism. In the following year, in the midst of the heated campaign for a strong Presbyterian church government in the City, Hugh Peters, the "Soliciter General for the Sectaries," desired and was allowed to preach in the parish church.[104] With the reorganization of the vestry and the election of the ruling elders in 1646, however, the Presbyterian civic leaders were able to consolidate their governance of the parish. It is to be noted that although all the twelve ruling elders appeared to be minor tradesmen, they were relatively important and active civic leaders in the Puritan era. Ten of the ruling elders were elected Common Councilmen at one time or another during the revolutionary period.[105] Two were also officers in the London militia.[106] Perhaps the strength of Presbyterianism among the civic leaders of the parish can be seen from the fact that two of the ruling elders had been actively engaged in the Presbyterian agitation in the City and signed the petitions in 1645–46, and another two were known to have subscribed to the City's engagement for a personal treaty with Charles I in 1648.[107] In actuality, the number of men involved in the latter event was undoubtedly greater, for after the election of the Common Councilmen in 1648, the vestry minutes clearly stated that "All or most of the other Officers for Brides parish were not chosen nor confirmed there [i.e., in the Wardmote], although chosen by the parish, having subscribed to the Engagement in the year 1648 concerninge the Treaty to be att London."[108] In 1652, while the Presbyterian church government was collapsing in most parishes of the classis, the eldership of St. Bride was reported still "complete."[109]

Among the constituted classical presbyteries in Puritan London, the Sixth Classis was probably the strongest, because in none of the other London classes does there appear to have existed a more favorable coalescence of clerical and civic leadership. Like the Fifth Classis, just examined in the previous section of this chapter, there was, too, a group of eminent and influential Presbyterian divines in this classis; yet the social compositions of the various constituting parishes of the latter were far superior both in terms of the wealth and in light of the social status of their inhabitants. As to the ministerial leadership of the Sixth Classis, there were Edmund Calamy and Matthew Newcomen at St. Mary Aldermanbury; Thomas Case and Thomas Manton at St. Mary Magdalen Milk Street; Anthony Burgess and later Christopher Love at St. Lawrence Old Jewry; Arthur Jackson at St. Michael Wood Street; Peter Witham at St. Alban Wood Street; Thomas Burdall and

John Wells at St. Olave Old Jewry; John Arrowsmith and John Wallis at St. Martin Ironmonger Lane; and Thomas Horton at St. Mary Colechurch. A closer look at some of these men will be in order.

In any study of Puritan London, Edmund Calamy would deserve the foremost attention. An anti-Arminian and an opponent of the Laudian innovations during the prerevolutionary decades, Calamy had suffered deprivation in 1626 from his lectureship at Bury St. Edmunds (Suffolk) under Bishop Matthew Wren of Norwich. For a few years after his deprivation, he lived in Essex under the "wings" of "the Noble Earl of Warwick," who presented him to the rectory of Rochford. Coming to London in 1639 on the eve of the Revolution, Calamy succeeded Dr. John Stoughton as curate of St. Mary Aldermanbury, and his former patron "did not lose, but followed him to London," requesting a pew in his parish church. With the outbreak of the Puritan Revolution, Calamy rose rapidly to eminence both in the City and on the national scene. One of the Smectymnuans, he opposed Bishop Joseph Hall's claim of *jure divino* episcopacy and testified to the same effect before the parliamentary committee on religion. Also a member of the Westminster Assembly of Divines, he preached frequently before the Houses of Parliament and the City authorities during the years of the Civil War, first for further reformation of the Church of England and then for the establishment of the Presbyterian church government. More pertinent to our subject in this study is the fact that Calamy commanded unparalleled prestige and exercised an irrefutable influence in the City of London during the revolutionary era. As his grandson would later say:

> No Minister in the City was more follow'd; nor hath there ever been a Week-day lecture so frequented as his; which was attended not only by his own Parish, but by other Eminent Citizens, and many Persons of the Greatest Quality, and constantly for 20 years together; for there seldom were so few as 60 coaches.

Indeed, it was often in Calamy's house in Aldermanbury that strategy and actions of the London Puritan brethren were planned, and "he generally had the Chair among the City ministers." During the Presbyterian agitation in the City in 1645–47, Calamy was undoubtedly one of the leading ministers involved. On 14 January 1646 Calamy preached before the Lord Mayor, Aldermen, and the Common Council for the renewal of the Solemn League and Covenant, and in July of the following year he again preached at Guildhall for recruitments of the London militia. Even after the occupation of the City by the triumphant Army, Calamy openly denounced the latter in a sermon for the morning exercise at St. Michael Cornhill, so much so that a temporary pamphleteer chided: "When we come to hear you, we expected to be instructed in Divinity, and not to be corrupted in Civility; if we had a desire to learn the language of *Billingsgate,* we should not have gone to Michael Cornhill in London, especially when Mr. Calamy was the Teacher."

In fact, Calamy's prestige among the City ministers was such that the Army in triumph had to solicit his understanding and cooperation.[110]

Among the other Presbyterian ministers of the Sixth Classis, Case, Witham, Burgess, and Jackson were also involved more or less militantly in the political struggle in the City during these years. Case had preached frequently before the Parliament and it was Case who initiated the famous morning exercises in the City of London. In early 1648 Case too openly preached against the Independents both in the Army and in the Parliament. "Lord," he said in one sermon, "they have fallen fearfully, let them not fall finally; let not them that were appointed for our salvation, prove our perdition; them that were intended for physick, prove poysonous: if they will not doe us good, let them not do us hurt." In another sermon preached at Christ Church he made "almost every particular of his sermon to reflect dishonour, reproach and contempt upon the Parliament." In future years Case defiantly refused to take the Engagement for the new Commonwealth and was implicated in the plot of Christopher Love. On the eve of the Restoration, to quote from Thomas Jacomb's funeral sermon in 1682, "as none (in his Sphere) did more cordially endeavour to promote it, before it was accomplished; so none more cordially rejoice in it, when it was accomplish'd."[111] Witham was more acrimonious in his attack upon the Independents in 1648. He called the Parliament a "sinful Parliament" and the Army "the Beast spoken of by the Prophet Daniel." Indeed, Witham was to be deprived of his ministry because of such unbecoming words in his prayers.[112] Jackson was an old Puritan minister in the City and the prominent place he occupied among his London brethren can be seen from the fact that he was to be chosen by the London Provincial Assembly in 1660 to present the Bible to Charles II at the head of the City ministers during the king's triumphal progress through the City. And Jackson was also implicated in Love's plot in 1651.[113] Even Anthony Burgess, otherwise a moderate and nonpolemical man, preached at Guildhall in 1647 for the recruitments of the London militia and he was succeeded by Christopher Love in the ministry of St. Lawrence Old Jewry in 1649–50.[114] Finally, I may add that among the Presbyterian ministers of the Sixth Classis during the years of the Civil War, there was no lack of men of academic achievement. Arrowsmith was to become master successively of St. John's College and Trinity College at Cambridge University, Vice-Chancellor of the University in 1647, and the Regius Professor of Divinity in 1657. Arrowsmith was succeeded in the ministry of St. Martin Ironmonger Lane, for a brief period in 1649, by John Wallis, the renowned mathematician and future Savilian Professor of Geometry at Oxford. And Horton was President of Queen's College at Cambridge University, Vice-Chancellor of the University in 1650, and Gresham Professor of Divinity in London.[115]

Similarly, the civic leaders in most of the twelve constituting parishes of the Sixth Classis were equally important in Puritan London. Like its minister, Edmund Calamy, the parish of St. Mary Aldermanbury deserves special attention. Having long leased the rectory and advowson from the Crown, the parish had always chosed Puritan divines for its ministry during the decades before the Revolution: Robert Harris, Thomas Taylor, John Stoughton, and Edmund Calamy. There can be little doubt, therefore, that it was a strongly Puritan parish. During the Civil War period the civic leaders of St. Mary Aldermanbury included Symon Edmonds, Gabriel Newman, George Witham, James James, John Holland, William Methwold, Humphrey Onby, Bartholomew Edwards, and Walter Boothby. Five of these men (Edmonds, Newman, Witham, James, and Boothby) were chosen as Common Councilmen; three (Edmonds, Witham, and Boothby), elected Aldermen; and another three (Onby, Edwards, and Boothby), appointed assessors for parliamentary subscriptions and assessments in the City. And the family connections among some of these men were also worthy of notice: Edmonds was the father-in-law of Christopher Pack; Witham, the father-in-law of Walter Boothby; and Edmonds and Boothby were probably related, too.[116] Among these men Boothby appeared to have been more actively involved in Puritan politics in the City during the years of the Civil War. Appointed a member of the subcommittee for parliamentary subscriptions in Cripplegate Ward in 1642, Boothby was apparently in charge of the purchase of arms in 1643. As Common Councilman from 1643 to 1648, Boothby sat on the committees for the consideration of church government in 1645 and for the maintenance of the ministers in the City in 1646. In 1647 he was also appointed to the Presbyterian Militia Committee during the struggle for the control of the City forces. A faithful supporter of Calamy in all parish affairs, Boothby was ruling elder and delegate to the London Provincial Assembly.[117] Although the religious convictions of the other parish leaders can only be conjectured, there is little doubt that Calamy's ministry received irrefutable and undiminishing support from these civic leaders. In fact, lay ruling elders of the parish were chosen as early as January 1645, almost a year and half ahead of the establishment of the Presbyterian church government in the City under parliamentary ordinances. And the Presbyterian church order was firmly maintained in the parish.[118]

The civic leadership in the parish of St. Olave Old Jewry was even more impressive, if we look at it from a broader perspective and not merely in terms of the strength of civic Presbyterianism in Puritan London. At the beginning of the revolutionary era, the leading parishioners of St. Olave were Alderman Edmund Wright, Alderman Richard Gurney, Moses Tryon, and Oliver Neve. Wright was Lord Mayor in 1640–41; Gurney was Lord Mayor in 1641–42 but was replaced by Isaac Pennington in the middle of his term; Neve was Common Councilman in 1639–41; and Tryon was listed the leading man among the wealthiest inhabitants of Coleman Street Ward in 1640. All four were Royalists.[119] In addition, I should add, John Wollaston was given Gurney's house during his term as Lord Mayor in 1643–44, and Thomas Foot, Lord Mayor in 1649–50, was also living in this parish in 1646–48 and again in the mid-1650s.[120] With the rise of the Puritan faction in the City in 1642, the governance of the parish affairs fell into the hands of new men, among whom were William Vaugham, George Almery, John Mascall, and John Frederick. All four were officially chosen ruling elders of the parish on 19 July 1646. Vaugham and Mascall were also chosen Common Councilmen during the years of the Civil War. While the former was appointed an assessor for parliamentary subscriptions in 1642, the latter was to become a member of the London militia committee in 1659–60. The political career of Frederick was a far more impressive one. He became master of the Barber-Surgeons' Company in 1654 and 1658, Alderman in 1653–83, Sheriff in 1655–56 and Lord Mayor in 1661–62.[121]

Similarly, the parish of St. Lawrence Old Jewry had Alderman John Cordell and Alderman George Clarke as its leading civic leaders at the beginning of the Revolution. Both Cordell and Clarke were to become opponents of the parliamentary cause.[122] The new leaders of the parish during the Civil War period were William Addams, William Bisbey, George Hadley, and William Medlicott. Although none of these men became really prominent civic figures in Puritan London, both Bisbey and Addams were appointed assessors in 1642 for parliamentary subscriptions in the City. Addams was Deputy in 1642, and Bisbey was to become master of the Salters' Company in 1646. And Addams and Hadley were Common Councilmen of the Presbyterian faction during the years of the Civil War and later fined for the office of sheriff.[123] What made the parish of St. Lawrence really stand out among the City parishes during the Puritan era is the fact that with perhaps the richest endowments for lectureships in seventeenth-century London, it was able to attract prominent divines for its ministry. The parish stipend for the lecturer was raised from £10 per annun in 1570 to £100 in 1643. By the 1650s, the lecture money for the minister was again raised to £140 a year. In 1639 an endowment of £1,142 was established, with the largest portion of the income for the payment of £40 per annum to a lecturer, and in 1643 Lady Camden left £600 for the parish with the income of £30 a year also for a lectureship.[124] It is no surprise, therefore, that the ministers of the parish during the Puritan era included Anthony Burgess, Peter Witham, Christopher Love, Richard Vines, and Edward Reynolds. With the presence of such eminent Presbyterian ministers, we may safely assume that the Presbyterian church order was reasonably well maintained.[125]

Special attention should also be given to the civic leaders of two small parishes in the Sixth Classis: St. Mary Magdalen Milk Street and St. Mary Colechurch. In spite of the fact that the number of inhabitants was relatively small in these two parishes, each had a concentration of substantial tradesmen who were able to provide effective civic leadership for and maintain social stability in the parish. During the years of the Civil War, the leading parishioners in the parish of St. Mary Magdalen Milk Street were Richard Aldworth, Robert Story, Francis Waterhouse, Anthony Webster, George

Cornish, and Lawrence Brinley. Aldworth was elected sheriff in 1641; Story, Waterhouse, and Webster were successively Common Councilmen during the Civil War period; and Brinely was appointed an assessor in 1642 and a lay trier in 1645. These men were also among the feoffees named by Lady Camden in 1643 when she bequeathed £600 for a lectureship in this parish. From the parish records we learn that the parishioners of St. Mary Magdalen Milk Street faithfully subscribed the Protestation in 1641, took the Solemn League and Covenant in 1643, and officially elected George Cornish, Anthony Webster, Lawrence Brinley, and Francis Waterhouse as their ruling elders on 19 July 1646 "to join with the ministers in settling the presbyteriall government." Only in the middle of the 1650s, when Case was deprived of his ministry in the parish and when Alderman John Robinson, the future Lord Mayor in 1662–63, was the leading parishioner, the Presbyterian church order, as we shall see in another chapter, suffered a temporary decline.[126] The civic leaders of the parish of St. Mary Colechurch during the Civil War period included John Towse, Randall Manwaring, William Pitchford, Edmund Sleigh, and Thomas Jackson. Towse, who was Alderman from 1640 to 1645 and died in the latter year, did not appear to have played any important role in parish affairs, which were well managed by the other men. Pitchford, Sleigh, and Jackson were successively Common Councilmen during the years of the Civil War, and Manwaring and Jackson were prominent officers of the London militia. While Manwaring, who was a known radical from the very beginning of the Revolution, was probably to become a political Independent in the City, Jackson was a staunch Presbyterian and became implicated in Love's plot in 1651. It may also be worth noticing that, during the revolutionary era, three of the parishioners of this parish became masters of the Apothecaries' Company: William Shambrooke in 1644–45, John Lawrence in 1647–48, and John Lorymer in 1654–55.[127]

In general, the civic leaders of the other parishes of the Sixth Classis were relatively fewer in number. Still, some of them require further explanation in order to present a full picture of the strength of civic Presbyterian leadership in the Sixth London Classis. Philip Christian of St. Mildred in the Poultry and William Haynes of St. Alphage London Wall were both Common Councilmen during the years of the Civil War and in all probability of the Presbyterian faction in the City. Robert Manwaring of St. Giles Cripplegate, a colonel in the London militia, was appointed a lay trier in 1645 and a member of the Presbyterian militia committee in 1647; whereas Robert Winch, a ruling elder of St. Martin Ironmonger Lane, was to be elected Alderman in 1658 and master of the Drapers' Company in 1663–64. And the last but by no means the least among the civic leaders of the Sixth Classis who must be included in this study was no other than John Bastwick, a ruling elder of the parish of St. Michael Wood Street, who had been one of the three famous Laudian martyrs in London before the Revolution and who, unlike his fellow martyrs

Henry Burton, the Separatist minister, and William Prynne, the Erastian lawyer, had become a staunch Presbyterian.[128]

Of the constituted London classical presbyteries during the revolutionary era, the Seventh Classis was institutionally an anomaly; for, on the one hand, it had some of the most militant Presbyterian leaders, lay as well as clerical, in Puritan London, while, on the other, there was lacking a broad social basis for the success of the Presbyterian experiment. The Seventh Classis was composed of nine parishes, among which only two, namely, St. Bartholomew by the Exchange and St. Christopher le Stocks, can be identified as truly Presbyterian. The minister of St. Christophers le Stocks was James Cranford, who, as Anthony Wood correctly observed, was "a zealous Presbyterian." It was Cranford who, as a licenser for books of divinity, approved of and wrote a prefatory epistle for Thomas Edwards's notorious work, *Gangraena,* in which, he said, the reader "mayest discerne the mischief of Ecclesiasticall Anarchy, the monstrousnesse of the much affected Toleration, and be warned to be wise to sobriety, and fear and suspect the pretended New lights." Of course, Cranford was himself an able polemicist, but what is more important is the fact that he acted as an agent for the Scottish commissioners in the City and became deeply involved in Puritan politics during the Presbyterian agitation in London in 1645–46. In early June 1645, goaded by Robert Baillie, he spread rumors at the Royal Exchange in a plot to defame and politically to destroy the Independent leaders of the Parliament, and on 1 February 1646, when the agitation in the City for a strong Presbyterian church government reached its highest point, he again attacked toleration in a sermon, *Haereseo-Machia; or the mischiefe which Heresies doe,* which he preached before the Lord Mayor of London.[129] Equally involved in Puritan politics and perhaps even more defiant of the triumphant Independents in the Parliament and in the Army was Thomas Cawton, minister of St. Bartholomew by the Exchange. According to a contemporary pamphleteer, in a morning lecture on 17 February 1648 Cawton "did most uncivilly and maliciously inveigh against the Army" and called it "that generation of Vipers." Two years later, on 25 February 1649, less than a month after the death of Charles I, he openly prayed for the royal family and Charles II during a sermon he preached before the Lord Mayor and the Aldermen of the City at Mercers' Chapel. In 1650–51 Cawton was also implicated in the plot of Christopher Love and escaped to Holland.[130]

It was also from these two parishes that the most active and influential civic Presbyterian leaders of the Seventh Classis appeared during the years of the Civil War. In the parish of St. Bartholomew by the Exchange there was a solid group of staunch civic Presbyterians such as Samuel Harsnett, John Jones, Richard Venner, and Stephen White. Harsnett was elected common councilman in 1641–42 in a disputed election in which Alderman Henry Garway refused to put his name "to hands" in the wardmote—a clear indication that Harsnett had already been known as a radical in the City. He was appointed an assessor for parliamentary subscriptions in 1642, and as sergeant major and later as colonel in the City's forces, he was added to the London Militia Committee in 1643 and appointed a commissioner of the London Court Martial in 1644 and 1646. Harsnett was also appointed a lay trier in 1645.[131] More deeply involved in the Presybterian agitation in the City were Jones and Venner, both of whom were captains in the London militia and assessors for parliamentary subscriptions in 1642. It was Jones whom Cranford sought out in 1645 in the attempt to defame the Independent leaders in the Parliament, in which Venner, too, was involved. And Jones also signed the citizens' petition for a strong Presbyterian church government in 1645. As Common Councilmen, both Jones and Venner sat on the committee for the suppression of scandalous and unlawful pamphlets and books, and the latter sat on the committee for the maintenance of ministers in the City as well. A minor literary pamphleteer himself, Jones published in 1646 *Plain English: or the Sectaries Anatomized, Wherein this City of London and their Remonstrance is Vindicated*. More important, in 1647 both Jones and Venner were nominated to the Presbyterian militia committee when the City was for a while preparing itself to confront the Army with force. In fact, the activities of Jones in 1647 were such that he was voted guilty of "high misdemeanour" and committed to the sergeant-at-arms.[132] The career of White lay in the future, though he was also an assessor in 1642 for parliamentary subscriptions. Fined for the office of Alderman in 1654, White was chosen master for the Grocers' Company in 1659 and Common Councilman in 1659–60. Although knighted by Charles II in July 1660, White was to be secluded from the Court of Assistants of his company.[133]

The parish of St. Christopher le Stocks was both religiously and politically more divided. At the beginning of the Revolution, the parish had a number of known Royalists such as Sir William Middleton, Sir Peter Rickaut, Edmund Underwood, Thomas Culling, and William King.[134] During the years of the Civil War, however, the governance of the parish affairs was clearly in the hands of a group of Presbyterian civic leaders, among whom were William Williamson, John Roberts, John Hinde, and, above all, Joseph Vaugham. Roberts was Common Councilman from 1639 to 1647 and probably of the Presbyterian faction in the City. In 1643 he sat on the committee to quicken the assessments for the fortification of the City, and two years later he was on the committee to enlist auxiliaries for the City militia.[135] Hinde, a captain in the London militia, was purged in 1648; in the words of a contemporary pamphleteer, he was "a man that hath done the very eminent service at the beginning of these troubles, as a Commissary of Horse, and *gratis* too," and a man who "truly fears God, and walks close with him."[136] Williamson, a ruling elder of the parish, was appointed an assessor for parliamentary subscriptions in 1642 and a layer trier in 1645. Although he did not appear to have held civic offices in Puritan London, Williamson was warden of the

Painter-Stainers' Company in 1646 and master of the Company in 1651.[137] Far more important was Vaugham, who was appointed an assessor for parliamentary subscriptions in 1642 when he was not really a prominent parishioner of St. Christopher le Stocks. He was chosen churchwarden in 1643–44. However, he must have been a known staunch Presbyterian, for he was one of the candidates for the Common Council whom the London sectarians openly opposed in 1645. As captain and later colonel in the London militia, Vaugham was to become deeply and dangerously involved in Puritan politics. He sat on the committee for the nomination of the London Militia Committee in 1647 and in the following year he was found "guilty of High Treason" and purged from the City militia. He was, in the words of a contemporary pamphleteer, guilty "of City High Treason, that is for retaining so much courage and prudence as to defend the City." Two years later, Vaugham was involved in the plot of Christopher Love.[138]

To a lesser degree, the parish of St. Michael Bassishaw may also be considered Presbyterian in its religious life, though at the beginning of the Revolution, the leader parishioner of St. Michael Bassishaw was Deputy Robert Alden, who was soon to be expelled from the Common Council, while in the latter part of the Puritan era, the parish, as we shall see, returned to the Anglican stance.[139] During the years of the Civil War, however, the parish did have a number of Presbyterian civic leaders such as George Dunne, Walter Pell, Edwin Browne, and Christopher Pack. All four were assessors for parliamentary subscriptions in 1642. Dunne, Pell, and Browne were all Common Councilmen during the Civil War period and clearly of the Presbyterian faction in the City. While Dunne sat on the committee for the maintenance of the ministers in the City in 1646, both Pell and Browne sat on the committee for the nomination of the London militia committee in 1647 and Browne was himself nominated.[140] It is indeed difficult to think of a future Lord Mayor in 1653–54 during the first year of the Protectorate, and of a Lord in the Cromwellian Upper House as a Presbyterian; yet it is important to point out that Pack, while Common Councilman during the Civil War period, sat on such committees as for the consideration of the church government in 1644, for the suppression of scandalous pamphlets and books in 1646 and for the nomination of the London militia committee in 1647. In fact, Pack was nominated to the Presbyterian militia committee himself. As a lay trier appointed in 1645 and probably also a ruling elder, Pack was twice delegated to the London Provincial Assembly in 1648 and 1649.[141]

To be sure, there were Presbyterian civic leaders in the other parishes of the Seventh Classis such as James Story of St. Benet Fink, Robert Launt and George Poyner of St. Peter le Poor, and John Everett of St. Botolph Bishopsgate.[142] Yet in none of these parishes did the civic Presbyterians appear to have been large enough in number to provide a broad foundation for the Presbyterian church government and discipline. Perhaps the anomalous nature of the Presbyterian church government in Puritan London can be seen from the parishes of St. Margaret Lothbury and St. Stephen Coleman Street, in both of which the Presbyterian system was officially established. In the parish of St. Margaret Lothbury, for instance, six ruling elders were officially elected in 1646: Miles Corbet, Anthony Bedingfield, Ralph Hugh, Edward Chad, Thomas Essington, and Robert Lowther. Admittedly, Corbet and Bedingfield were elected because they were members of the Parliament; yet, if Bedingfield can be identified as a Presbyterian, Corbet, the future regicide, was certainly an Independent. In fact, neither Bedingfield nor Corbet was involved in parish affairs. Thomas Essington was possibly the son of William Essington, a prisoner-of-war of General Edward Massey at Gloucester, who had been "a malignant who frequented the enemy's quarters and refused to lend anything to Parliament." Lowther played a more important role in City affairs in 1647. As Common Councilman, he sat on a total of five committees: about the decay of trade, for the nomination of the London militia committee, to draft an answer to the Army, to request the Army not to quarter within twenty-five miles of the City, and for removing the misunderstandings between the Parliament and the City. It appears, however, that Lowther was more concerned with his business than religion. In 1646 he had cheated in his assessment payment and said passionately that "the City was abused and cozened." As ruling elders, all these four men were strange choices, and none of them appeared to have acted as such in the Presbyterian church government. In fact, in 1652 it was reported that not one elder of this parish was acting.[143]

The parish of St. Stephen Coleman Street has received much attention from modern historians both for its religious Puritanism and for its political radicalism in the City before as well as during the Revolution. From 1624 to 1633, John Davenport served as its minister, and after Davenport emigrated first to Holland and then to the New World, he was succeeded by John Goodwin. At the beginning of the Revolution, the parish was unmistakably Puritan and parliamentarian. Indeed, as is well known, in January 1642 it was in Coleman Street that the Five Members of the Long Parliament sought refuge from the King. As we shall see in a future chapter of this study, however, Goodwin was deprived of his ministry in 1645 in the midst of the Presbyterian campaign in the City, and he was replaced by the Presbyterian divine William Taylor. And early in the following year, a "parish covenant" was adopted by the general vestry, with thirteen of the leading parishioners elected as "ruling elders" to assist Taylor with the administration of the Holy Communion. Taylor, whom Anthony Wood called "the Loyal Presbyterian," participated faithfully in the proceedings of the London Provincial Assembly and twice served as the scribe of the Seventh Classis, which, incidentally, also held its meetings at least twice in the parish church of St. Stephen Coleman Street.[144] In appearance, therefore, the Presbyterian church government and discipline seem to have been well established in this parish.

With a closer look at the religious conditions of the parish, however, the anomalous nature of the Presbyterian experiment at St. Stephen Coleman Street would soon reveal itself. Among the thirteen "ruling elders" chosen in early 1646, for example, were Alderman Isaac Pennington, Colonel Owen Rowe, James Russell, and Richard Ashurst, all of whom were Independents—unmistakably in politics and possibly in religion as well. As we shall see in another chapter in this study, many of the London Independents and sectarians, as civil leaders, never abandoned their civic responsibilities and, on the contrary, faithfully fulfilled their duties in their parochial communities. Yet it is doubtful that they would join the Presbyterian church government beyond the parochial level and there is, indeed, no sign that they ever did.[145] Furthermore, even some of the leading parishioners who were not of Goodwin's faction and whom we may reasonably describe as Presbyterians did not appear to have supported the Presbyterian church government as enthusiastically as could have been expected. During the conflict between Goodwin and the parish, which eventually led to the former's sequestration, the civic leaders who represented the interests of the parish were Samuel Avery, Thomas Fitzwilliams, Joseph Sibley, Edward Lucas, Andrew Kendrick, and Thomas Barnardiston.[146] Among these men, Avery not only was an important civic figure in Puritan London but, in the light of his activities during the years of the Civil War, he had all the marks of being a staunch Presbyterian as well. Common Councilman in 1644–45, master of the Merchant Taylors' Company in 1645–46, Sheriff in 1647–48, and Alderman in 1645–58, Avery sat on almost all the important committees concerning religion and the Presbyterian church government between 1644 and 1646. In 1647 he was a member of the committee for the nomination of the London militia committee and was himself nominated.[147] Barnardiston and Kendrick were clearly substantial merchants, and Sibley was a future Common Councilman in 1652–55, 1658–59, and 1668–80. Yet the two known ruling elders, who faithfully participated in the proceedings of the London Provincial Assembly, were Edward Lucas and Thomas Fitzwilliams, both of whom were lesser men in the parish of St. Stephen Coleman Street.[148] Finally, the anomaly of the Presbyterian church government in the parish cannot be fully comprehended without mentioning the fact that having long been noted for its disorder and nonconformity, St. Stephen Coleman Street was a breeding ground for gathered churches of sectarians. Even before the Revolution there had been the Baptist congregation in White's Alley, an Independent conventicle led first by John Canne and later by Samuel How; another Baptist meeting in Bell Alley under the leadership of Edward Barber and Thomas Lamb; and perhaps other sectarian groups. And, of course, John Goodwin's own gathered congregation must be added, which, after his ejection from the ministry in 1645, first met in another place but after 1649 held their services in the parish church itself.[149] Admittedly, the case of St. Stephen Coleman Street was a peculiar one; yet, like the parish of St. Margaret Lothbury, it further testifies to the fact that the success of the Presbyterian church government in London depended upon a favorable coalescence of clerical and civic leaders.

The Eighth Classis was the last constituted classical presbytery within the jurisdiction of the old City, though it contained three out-parishes—St. Leonard Shoreditch, Hackney, and St. Mary Stoke Newington, all of which lay to the northeast of London. Although two of the most prominent Puritan divines of our era, namely, William Spurstow and Thomas Manton, both came from these out-parishes, the parishes lie outside the main scope of this study. In any case, the lay Presbyterian leaders of the out-parishes played little if any part in Puritan politics in the City during the years of the Civil War.[150] The following analysis will be directed, therefore, mainly to the seven City parishes of this Classis. Among these seven parishes, St. Andrew Undershaft and St. Helen Bishopsgate were among the substantial parochial communities in early seventeenth-century London, and as such their ministries were relatively well settled during the Puritan era. Elidad Blackwell was minister at St. Andrew Undershaft from 1645 until his death in 1658; George Walker was lecturer at St. Helen from 1639 to 1647; and Arthur Barham was minister of St. Helen from 1647 until his ejection in 1662. All three were Presbyterians, and they participated in the proceedings of the London Provincial Assembly actively and consistently.[151] On the civic side, however, few of the prominent civic leaders of these two parishes appear to have joined the Presbyterian church with enthusiasm. For the parish of St. Andrew Undershaft the parochial records for our period have unfortunately been lost to us and there is no way to know the social composition of its vestry. In the light of the list of its parishioners who subscribed contributions to the Parliament in November 1642, there was indeed a group of very wealthy and influential civic leaders and merchants among the inhabitants of the parish, including Thomas Atkins, Abraham Chamberlain, Abraham Cullen, John Dethick, and William Hawkins. Atkins was Sheriff of London in 1637–38, Alderman in 1638–61, and Lord Mayor in 1644–45. Although during his term as Lord Mayor Atkins did little to head off the clerical and civic Presbyterian agitation in the City, he was to become a political Independent. And so too did Dethick, who was Alderman in 1649–60, Sheriff in 1649–50, and Lord Mayor in 1655–56. In fact, none of these men is known to have taken part in the London Provincial Assembly.[152] Rather ironically, the known ruling elder and delegate of St. Andrew Undershaft was Sir David Watkins, who had long been associated with the Independents in the City.[153] The parish of St. Helen, whose social composition was much the same, did not produce any staunch Presbyterian civic leaders in Puritan London, either.[154]

In the remaining five City parishes of the Eighth Classis, the ministry did not seem to have been well settled in the Puritan era, and few of the ministers who served the cures at various times of the revolutionary period were really eminent men.[155] More significant, in none of the five parishes was there an adequate number of committed Presbyterian civic leaders to provide a broad social foundation for the success of the Presbyterian church government. In the parish of St. Katherine Cree, the civic leaders during the early years of the Revolution included such important figures as John and William Bond, Richard Chiverton, William Thompson, John Owfield, and Richard Shute, none of whom is known as a Presbyterian. In fact, Thompson and Shute were leading Independents in the City.[156] Similarly, the civic leaders of the parish of St. Martin Outwich during the years of the Civil War were Richard Bateman, Rowland Wilson, Henry Hunt, John Beale, Richard Clutterbuck, and William Vincent. While Clutterbuck and Vincent were probably Presbyterians, Wilson was one of the most influential Independents in London and Bateman had been associated with the Royalist groups in the City in early 1642. And the names of Bateman and Wilson always appear as the leading signatories in the parish records.[157] In the parish of St. Ethelburga, Richard Hardmet and William Eveleigh were possible Presbyterians, but both were minor civic figures in London.[158] The parish of St. James Duke's Place had neither a settled ministry nor known civic Presbyterians.[159] Finally, the parish of St. Botolph Aldgate, located outside the Wall and one of the largest parochial communities in seventeenth-century London, was deeply divided both religiously and politically among its civic leaders.[160] Although the Presbyterian church government seemed to have been established in most of these parishes, it is very doubtful that it had ever functioned effectively. In the light of the preceding analyses, we may safely conclude that the Eighth Classis was probably the weakest among the constituted classical presbyteries in Puritan London.

Of the remaining five classes of the London Province, the Tenth Classis was formed, but since it was composed of the parishes in Southwark, Bermondsey, and Rotherhithe, it lies outside the scope of this study. It is worth noticing, however, that in spite of the fact that Southwark was generally a radical community in the early seventeenth century, the parishes to the south of the Thames had a number of both prominent Presbyterian divines and militant Presbyterian laymen. Among the ministers of the Tenth Classis were John Rawlinson of Lambeth, Jeremiah Whitaker and later William Whitaker of St. Mary Magdalen Bermondsey, and Thomas Gataker of Rotherhithe. All these men were highly esteemed divines and played important roles in the revolutionary period.[161] On the civic side, two of the officers of the Southwark militia, Lieutenant-Colonel Jeremiah Baines and Colonel Daniel Sowton, appear to have been staunch Presbyterians. In 1647 both men were involved in the riots in and about London to intimidate the Parliament, so much so that charges of high treason were later brought against them in the House of Commons. In the future, both men were to be implicated in the plot of Christopher Love in 1651.[162]

As to the four unformed London classes, three lay largely outside the Wall of the City. Their constituent parishes were not only farther removed from the center of the City but also much more diversified in their social make-up. The Ninth Classis covered a large area from the parishes in the east end of the City within the Wall to the eastern suburbs of Stepney and Wapping. These eastern suburbs were especially diverse in their social components and had been unusually radical in both religion and politics during the revolutionary era. Even among the seven City parishes within the Wall, there was in none of them an adequate number of Presbyterian civic leaders. In fact, in three of these parishes—Allhallows Barking, St. Olave Hart Street, and St. Gabriel Fenchurch—there had been a number of Royalists at the beginning of the Revolution, but few eminent Puritan leaders appeared during the Puritan era.[163] In another three, namely, Allhallows Staining, St. Katherine Coleman, and St. Margaret Pattens, the ministry was not firmly settled.[164] And the parish of St. Dunstan in the East, which was indeed one of the most important parochial communities in Puritan London, was both religiously and politically divided among its civic leaders. It was after all dominated by such influential Independents as John Fowke, Maurice Thompson, and Robert Russell during the revolutionary period.[165] The Eleventh Classis comprised the parishes in and about the City of Westminster, stretching from Drury Lane on the east to Knightbridge on the west, from St. Giles in the Fields on the north to Tothill Fields on the south. As the center of national government and politics, the City of Westminster was an arena of political forces far too complex and powerful to be contained by the classical structure.[166] The Twelfth Classis was composed of eight parishes outside the Wall to the west and northwest of the City. The core of this classis was obviously the Ward of Farringdon Without and especially the parish of St. Dunstan in the West. Although there were a large number of Presbyterian civic leaders in this part of the City and twelve ruling elders were actually elected in the parish of St. Dunstan in the West, the civic leaders were also deeply divided both in religion and in politics. Like St. Dunstan in the East, there were also strong Independent elements in the parish of St. Dunstan in the West. After all, it was here that Praise-God Barebone had both his business and his gathered church.[167]

The failure of the Second London Classis to form its classical government certainly calls for special attention, for geographically it lay in the very heart of the old City. Furthermore, among the fifteen parishes that made up the Second Classis was the parish of St. Antholin Budge Row, which had for almost a century served as the center of the Puritan movement in London. In 1559, at the very beginning of the reign of Queen Elizabeth I, the famous St. Antholin lectureship was founded. For generations to come the bells of the parish church would ring at five o'clock in the morning to summon the godly to morning prayer, psalm singing, and the lecture at six—all after the Genevan pattern as a contemporary diarist observed. Richly endowed and continuously Puritan, the parish of St. Antholin, unique even in the City of

London, had a lecture every weekday. In the early years of the Civil War, when the Scottish clerical commissioners came to London, it was in this parish church that they preached to the London citizens. The parish minister, Charles Offspring, a renowned Puritan divine, also supported the Presbyterian movement in the City and signed the London ministers' petition for a strong Presbyterian church government. In fact, throughout the Puritan era, the lecturers chosen for the Antholin lectures were all known Presbyterian ministers.[168] Yet, surprisingly, neither the personal influence of Offspring nor that of the parish of St. Antholin was able to serve as a nucleus for the formation of the Second London Classis.

A closer examination of the individual parishes of the Second Classis would reveal the true cause of its failure. Out of the fifteen parishes, nine were reported in October 1648 to be without a minister, which was primarily due to the poor economic conditions of these parishes and consequently the inadequate means to maintain a settled ministry.[169] At least five parishes of the Second Classis are included by Jordan as among the impoverished parochial communities in early seventeenth-century London. In fact, twelve of the fifteen parishes were located on the north bank of the River or close to it, and all of them were either decayed areas or with large numbers of poor people among their inhabitants.[170] And one of the remaining three parishes was the second smallest parish in the City.[171] As a result, in twelve of the fifteen parishes of the Second Classis, the ministry was never firmly settled throughout the revolutionary period. This lack of settled ministry in so many of the parishes of the Second Classis was undoubtedly a decisive factor for its failure to establish the Presbyterian classical government. Although, as we shall see in the following chapter, there were Independent groups in four of these parishes, it is to be noted that Presbyterianism did not fail to have its appeal among these poorer parochial communities. In addition to the parish of St. Antholin Budge Row, which was definitely Presbyterian in both its clerical and civic leadership, Presbyterians were also present in some other parishes of the Second Classis. The parish of Holy Trinity the Less, where Matthew Haviland was minister from 1644 to his ejection in 1662, was basically Presbyterian in its religious persuasion. So probably was the parish of St. John the Baptist, where Peter Witham became minister in 1652–53 and remained until 1662. Even in all three of the known Independent parishes such as St. James Garlickhithe, St. Pancras Soper Lane, and St. Thomas the Apostle, there were clearly Presbyterian civic leaders. In 1646–47, John Arrowsmith, Christopher Love, and possibly Anthony Burgess were invited to preach at St. Pancras Soper Lane. In 1648–52 the ministers chosen at St. James Garlickhithe were Jonathon Lloyd, Lawrence Wise, and Zachary Crofton. And in the parish of St. Thomas the Apostle, Matthew Sheppard, a colonel in the London militia, was undoubtedly a lay Presbyterian. So also were Andrew Neale and Thomas Lockington of St. Mary Magdalen Old Fish

Street.[172] The failure of the Second Classis in Puritan London clearly reveals the importance of economic and social factors for the Presbyterian church government in the City.

Fundamentally, of course, the Presbyterians had failed to have a truly strong Presbyterian church government established by parliamentary ordinances—much as they had wished and afterward regretted. When the London Provincial Assembly was founded, not only were four of the twelve classical presbyteries never formed but a number of the City parishes even within the constituted classes refused with impunity to join the Presbyterian church government. And with the Army's triumphant occupation of the City and the collapse of the Presbyterian faction in the City government, the future of the Presbyterian experiment in London was doomed. Presbyterianism in London after 1648 was "in a state of ever increasing internal decay," as William A. Shaw has long since well observed.[173] Yet all the initial weaknesses of the Presbyterian church government and its inevitable decline after 1648 notwithstanding, the strength of Presbyterianism in Puritan London was a truly formidable one. As observed earlier in this chapter, the confluence of eminent and influential Presbyterian divines in the City of London during the years of the Civil War was a unique phenomenon not only in their number but also in their religious and political persuasiveness. And as has also been seen in the selective analyses of Presbyterian civic leaders in the various London parishes, the broad appeal of Presbytarian church government and discipline not only to ordinary London tradesmen but also to prominent City Fathers was equally extraordinary. In a sense, London's counterrevolution against the Army in 1647 was not without a concrete and extensive basis in the City—a basis that was religious as well as political, though, needless to say, the London businessmen were no professional officers and the London militia was no match for the New Model Army. Yet, had it not been for the rebellion and triumph of the Army, the history of Presbyterianism in Puritan London could well have been different. The institutional deficiencies of the Presbyterian system could have been amended, and the economic predicaments of the City parish ministries improved.[174]

In any case, to the Presbyterian divines, their efforts in Puritan London were not totally fruitless. On 1 August 1655, in a sermon preached at the funeral of Thomas Gataker, Simeon Ashe must have looked back sadly to the Civil War period when there gathered in London a large group of eminent Presbyterian brethren, some of whom had now died and many others departed from the City, either to the Universities or to other places in the country. The death of Gataker, Ashe wrote in his epistle to the Presbyterian ministers within the Province of London, "may well minde us of the deaths of many more of our brethren, whose hearts, heads and hands, went along with us in the setting up and exercising of the Presbyterian Government in our respective Congregations, with mutual Assistance, Classical and Provinciall, both for the Ordination of Ministers, and the more pure administration of the Sacraments." Although "much contempt is cast upon us . . . as an inconsiderable number," Ashe insisted that there still were "three score Presbyterian Ministers within the precincts of our Province, who preach profitably, did live godly, who are not tainted with the erroneous tenets either of the Arminians, Antinomians or Anabaptists."[175] Of course, Ashe was yet to learn that many of them were to play an important role in the restoration of the monarchy in less than five years.[176]

NOTES

1. Clement Walker, *The Mysterie of the Two Ivnto's, Presbyterian and Independent* (London, 1647), pp. 3, 14.

2. Ibid.

3. A. H. Drysdale, *History of the Presbyterians in England: Their Rise, Decline and Revival* (London, 1889), p. 304.

4. For this historiographical debate among historians, see J. H. Hexter, "The Problem of the Presbyterian Independents," reprinted in Hexter, *Reappraisals in History* (New York, 1961), pp. 163–84; George Yule, *The Independents in the English Civil War* (Cambridge, 1958); David Underdown, "The Independents Reconsidered," *Journal of British Studies* 3 (1965): 57–84; Yule, "Independents and Revolutionaries," ibid., 7 (1968): 11–32; Underdown, "Independents Again," ibid., 8 (1968): 83–93.

5. See Valerie Pearl, "London Puritans and Scotch Fifth Columnists: A Mid-Seventeenth-century Phenomenon," in A. E. J. Hollaender and William Kellaway, eds., *Studies in London History* (London, 1969), pp. 313–31; Pearl, "London and the Counter-Revolution," in G. E. Aylmer, ed., *The Interregnum: The Quest for Settlement 1646–1660* (London, 1972), pp. 29–56; Michael Mahony, "Presbyterianism in the City of London, *1645–1647,*" *The Historical Journal* 22, no. 1 (1979): 93–114; Tai Liu, "The Founding of the London Provincial Assembly, 1645–47," *Guildhall Studies in London History* 3, no. 2 (1978): 109–34.

6. Firth and Rait, 1: 749–54, 870–74; Shaw, 2: 399–404; Surman, 2: 1–196.

7. This will be an interesting subject for further study. Cf. Shaw, 2: 300–364, *passim; W. R.,* pp. [42]–[63], *passim;* Surman, 1: 184–310, *passim;* Alex. F. Mitchell and John Struthers, eds., *Minutes of the Sessions of the Westminster Assembly of Divines* (London, 1874), *passim.*

8. Ibid.; W. M. Hetherington, *History of the Westminster Assembly of Divines* (Edinburgh, 1878), *passim;* S. W. Carruthers, *The Everyday Work of the Westminster Assembly* (Philadelphia, 1943), *passim;* Ethyn Williams Kirby, "The English Presbyterians in the Westminster Assembly," *Church History* 33 (1946): 418–28.

9. See chap. 7 below.

10. Firth and Rait, 1: 852–55. For the historical background see Liu, "The Founding of the London Provincial Assembly," pp. 115–16.

11. *Mercurius Elencticus* (London, 1649), p. 58; Baillie, 2: 362.

12. See Shaw, 2: 399–404.

13. See GLMS 4012/1, f. 179. For a different case, see Charles E. Surman, ed., *The Register-Booke of the Fourth Classis in the Province of London 1646–1659.* Publications of the Harleian Society (London, 1953), pp. 72, 80.

14. These ten parishes were St. Bride, St. Dunstan in the West, St. Katherine Coleman, St. Margaret Lothbury, St. Bartholomew Exchange, St. Mary Magdalen Milk Street, St. Michael Cornhill, St. Peter Cornhill, St. Peter Westcheap, and St. Olave Jewry. See GLMS 6554/2, ff. 35b–37; GLMS 3016/1, f. 280; GLMS 1124/1, no folio number, vestry minute, 26 July 1646; GLMS 4352/1, f. 178; GLMS 2597/1, f. 85; GLMS 4072/1, f. 178; GLMS 4156/1, f. 287; GLMS

642/1, no folio number, vestry minute, 19 July 1646; GLMS 4415/1, f. 132b; Freshfield, ed., *Vestry Minute Books of St. Bartholomew Exchange,* pt. 2, pp. xxvi, 19. The only recorded election of a ruling elder in later years was that of Maximilian Bard in the parish of St. Peter Westcheap. See GLMS 642/1, no folio number, vestry minute, 28 February 1651/52. It is to be noted that Roger Drake, one of the staunch Presbyterian divines in the City, was then minister of the parish.

15. For the maintenance of Puritan ministers in the City during the revolutionary period, see chap. 5 below.

16. See Jordan, p. 52; Pearl, pp. 162–63, 189; and chap. 1 above.

17. The value of tithes was given as £84 by the incumbent, John Lawson, in the survey of 1638, but the parish maintained that it was £88. 16s. 8d. In addition, there was a weekly sermon, which was worth £13. 6s. 8d. See Newcourt, 1: 245; Dale, p. 9; LPL MS CMVIII/37, f. [1]; Jordan, pp. 287–88; Hill, p. 260.

18. For Seaman, see *C. R., s. v.; D. N. B., s. v.;* Baillie, 2: 62, 67; Surman, 2: 196; 1: 276. For a contemporary view of Seaman's shifty position under the Commonwealth, see *Lazarus's sores licked . . .* (London, 1650), "To the Reader": "Truly . . . had he not been a Presbyterian and an eminent one, and by his open Apostacie, and impudent defence of a dangerous Errour both in Cambridge and London, scandalized his profession, reproached the Gospel, hardned the wicked, and perverted many, and grieved and made ashamed the rest of Gods faithful people . . . a most learned and pious Doctor . . . this relapsed Presbyterian Doctor, whose fall is so notorious." George Thomason identified Lazarus as Lazarus Seaman in his copy. See BL E.615. (19).

19. The children of Richard Turner were baptized in this parish church as late as 1650. A son of Francis West was baptized in the parish church in 1637, but as one of the Common Councilmen of the parish of St. Augustine in 1640, he was identified as "dwelling in Bread Street." See W. Bruce Bannerman, ed., *The Registers of Allhallows, Bread Street, and of St. John the Evangelist, Friday Street, London* (London, 1913), pp. 27, 31; GLMS 635/1, vestry minutes, 1640.

20. PRO SP19/78, ff. 60b, 60c; PRO SP19/78, f. 91b; Green, 1: 150.

21. CLRO J. Co. Co., 40, ff. 42, 44, 67, 128, 153, 193, 215b; Firth and Rait, 1: 928.

22. CLRO J. Co. Co., 40, ff. 153b, 174b; 41, ff. 43–44. For the identification of these lesser civic figures, see Bannerman, ed., *The Registers of Allhallows, Bread Street,* pp. 22–30, *passim;* Mahony, "Presbyterianism in the City of London," p. 105.

23. Pearl, "London Puritans and Scotch Fifth Columnists," p. 328; Mahony, "Presbyterianism in the City of London," pp. 94–95; Edmund Calamy, *The Righteous Mans Death Lamented. A Sermon Preached at St. Austins, London, Aug. 23, 1662. At the Funeral of that Eminent Servant of Jesus Christ, Mr. Simeon Ash. Late Minister of Gospel there* (London, 1662), p. 17. For Roberts, see *D. N. B., s. v.;* Surman, 1: 272. For Ashe, see *D. N. B., s. v.; C. R., s. v.;* Surman, 1: 184.

24. GLMS 635/1, vestry minutes, 1640.

25. Ibid., vestry minutes, 1641–60, *passim.*

26. PRO SP 19/78, f. 60b; CLRO J. Co. Co., 40, ff. 42, 215b; Firth and Rait, 1: 487, 842, 928.

27. Quoted in Mahony, "Presbyterianism in the City of London," p. 107. For Orlibear's career, see GLMS 635/1, vestry minutes, 1641–47, 1653–60 and list of feoffees at the end of the volume; Woodhead, p. 123, *s. v.* John Orlebar.

28. GLMS 635/1, vestry minutes, 1648, 1656–60 and list of feoffees at the end of the volume; *D. N. B., s. v.;* Woodhead, p. 19; Surman, 1: 188; Richard Baxter, *Faithful Souls shall be with Christ* (London, 1881); "The Wills of London Ministers" (transcripts at Dr. Williams's Library, London), pp. 37–39.

29. For Barton, see CLRO J. Co. Co., 40, ff. 153b, 174b; Mahony, "Presbyterianism in the City of London," p. 105; Surman, 1: 192. For Gellibrand, see CLRO J. Co. Co., 40, f. 302; *A Paire of Spectacles for the Citie* (London, 1648), p. 10 [12]; Surman, 1: 226; GLMS 635/1, list of feoffees at the end of the volume. Gellibrand, too, was an overseer for the will of Simeon Ashe.

30. Jordan, p. 52; chap. 1 above; chap. 6 below.

31. For Gower, see Surman, 1: 250. For the Harley family, see *D. N. B.*, *s. vv.* Sir Robert Harley and Brilliana Harley.

32. PRO SP 19/78, f. 60d; CLRO J. Co. Co., 40, ff. 44, 52b, 86–86b, 215b; Firth and Rait, 1: 928.

33. CLRO J. Co. Co., 40, ff. 42, 44, 86–86b.

34. See Thomas Edwards, *Gangraena: Or A Catalogue and Discovery of Many of the Errours, Heresies, Blasphamies and pernicious Practices of the Sectaries of this time* (London, 1646), p. 135. For Jeston [Jesson], see CLRO J. Co. Co., 40, ff. 128, 219; for Radcliffe, Toking, and Lee, see ibid., ff. 153b, 174b; Mahony, "Presbyterianism in the City of London," p. 105. Fox was Common Councilman in 1644–45 and probably also a Presbyterian. See CLRO J. Co. Co., 40, ff. 100, 128.

35. GLMS 1311/1, f. 143.

36. Shaw, 2: 400. In 1641–43, Browne had been elected Common Councilman in the parish of St. Dunstan in the West. In future years, Browne became one of the most important political figures in the City. A colonel in the London Militia, Browne was elected Sheriff in 1648–49 and, though imprisoned under the Commonwealth, chosen M. P. for London in 1656–58, 1659, and 1660–61. One of the City leaders who intrigued for the restoration of the Monarchy, Browne was knighted by Charles II and chosen Lord Mayor of London in 1660. See also CLRO J. Co. Co., 40, f. 22b; GLMS 3018/1, ff. 129b, 130, 130b; GLMS 3016/1, f. 235. For the future career of Browne, see *D. N. B.*, *s. v.;* Woodhead, pp. 39–40, *s. v.*

37. For Gouge, see *D. N. B.*, *s. v.;* Seaver, pp. 76–77, 98–99, 225–26; Isabel M. Calder, ed., *Activities of the Puritan Faction of the Church of England* (London, 1957), *passim;* William Jenkyn, *A Shock of Corn Coming in In Its Season. A Sermon Preached at the Funeral of that Ancient and Eminent Servant of Christ William Gouge* (London, 1654), p. 34.

38. The other five parishes of the First Classis in which the Presbyterian church government was more or less successfully established were St. Benet Paul's Wharf, St. Faith, St. John the Evangelist, St. Margaret Moses, and St. Mildred Bread Street. The six parishes of this Classis in which the Presbyterian system was probably never adopted were St. Andrew Wardrobe, St. Gregory by St. Paul's, St. Mary Aldermary, St. Mary le Bow, St. Matthew Friday Street, and St. Peter Paul's Wharf. Some of these parishes will be discussed in chaps. 3 and 4.

39. The eight parishes of the Third Classis in which the Presbyterian church government was adopted were Allhallows Lombard Street, St. Edmund the King, St. Mary Bothaw, St. Mary Woolchurch, St. Mary Woolnoth, St. Nicholas Acons, St. Stephen Walbrook, and St. Swithin. Yet it is doubtful that the Presbyterian system functioned either properly or very long in the parishes of Allhallows Lombard Street and St. Edmund the King. In the parish of St. Mary Bothaw, the ministry was never firmly settled. The four parishes of the Third Classis in which the Presbyterian church government was never established were Allhallows the Great, Allhallows the Less, St. Lawrence Pountney, and St. Mary Abchurch. See also chaps. 3 and 4.

40. GLMS 1012/1, f. 3; GLMS 1013/1, ff. 193, 199; CLRO J. Co. Co., 40, ff. 86–86b, 128, 215b; Firth and Rait, 1: 928, 957.

41. PRO SP 19/78, f. 60e; CLRO J. Co. Co., 40, f. 42; Firth and Rait, 1: 871; Shaw, 2: 400. Herring was churchwarden in 1642 and also a leading vestryman in future years. See GLMS 1013/1, f. 182b; GLMS 1012/1, ff. 1–3.

42. Surman, 1: 231, 240, *s. vv.*

43. CLRO J. Co. Co., 40, f. 302; *A Paire of Spectacles for the Citie*, p. 9 [11].

44. For Wheatley, see C. R., *s. v.;* Surman, 1: 299, *s. v.* Richard Ball was identified as Dr. Ball in 1661 in the churchwardens' account, but his later career is not known. See also GLMS 1012/1, ff. 6, 34; GLMS 1013/1, ff. 195b, 201b, 204b, 212–39b.

45. GLMS 593/4, no folio number, churchwardens' account, 1640–41; PRO SP16/492, f. 75.

46. Jordan, p. 52. In light of the parish register, the occupations of the parishioners of St. Stephen Walbrook were mostly grocers, skinners, druggists, and merchants. In fact, the parish regularly contributed £20 a year to the parish of St. Bride for the relief of the latter's poor people.

See GLMS 593/4, churchwardens' accounts, *passim;* W. B. & W. B. Bannerman, eds., *The Registers of St. Stephen's, Walbrook, and of St. Benet Sherehog, London,* 2 vols. (London, 1919–20), 1: 22–28.

47. Beaven, 1: 337, 339, 341, 347; 2: 65, 66, 79, 82, 83; Pearl, pp. 325–27; CLRO J. Co. Co., 40, ff. 81, 100, 128, 310–10b; 41, ff. 16, 64b; GLMS 594/2, ff. 37, 46, 84, 89; Steven J. Watson, *A History of the Salters' Company* (London, 1963), p. 145.

48. Sharp, 2: 266–67.

49. CLRO J. Co. Co., 40, f. 302; *A Paire of Spectables for the Citie,* p. 10 [12].

50. George Cokayne, *Divine Astrology. . . . Being the Substance of a Sermon Preached in Stephen Walbrook, Jan. 19, 1657. At the Funeral of the Hon. Colonel William Underwood, one of the Aldermen of the City of London* (London, 1658).

51. Shaw, 2: 400; Surman, 1: 295; 2: 3, 13; Firth and Rait, 1: 794.

52. Surman, 1: 289; 2: 30, 39, 78, 113, 141.

53. In a certain sense, it is modern historians who attempt to impose a more rigid ideological consistency upon the patterns of behavior among the Puritans in religion and in politics than what many of them chose and had to choose to follow under immediate historical circumstances, especially in an age of revolution and political crises.

54. GLMS 593/4, no folio number, churchwardens' accounts, 1647–48, 1658–59, 1659–60, 1660–61. For the traditional value of tithes in the parish, see Newcourt, 1: 538; Dale, p. 181; LPLMS CM VII/37, f. [4].

55. In the parish of St. Mary Woolnoth, the known ruling elders were Robert Sweet, Thomas Eyre, and Captain William Hubbard. In the parish of St. Swithin, John Sheffield was minister from 1647 to 1661 and the known ruling elders were George Willingham, William Bowe, and Robert English. For Sheffield, see *C. R., s. v.*

56. Surman, 1: 272, *s. v.; D. N. B., s. v.;* Simeon Ashe, *The Good Mans Death Lamented. A Sermon Preached at Mary Woolnoth in Lombard street London, June 18, 1655. At the Funerall of that Faithfull servant of Christ Mr. Ralph Robinson* (London, 1655), p. 26.

57. Beaven, 1: 343; 2:68; *D. N. B., s. v.;* Woodhead, p. 168; *s. v.;* Dorothy K. Clark, "A Restoration Goldsmith-banking House: The Vine on Lombard Street," in *Essays in Modern History in Honour of Wilbur C. Abbott* (Cambridge, Mass., 1941), pp. 3–47, *passim.*

58. See n. 56 directly above; Willianm Spurstowe, *Death and the Grave No Bar to Believers Happiness. Or, A Sermon preached at the Funeral of Lady Honor Vyner, in the Parish of Mary Woolnoth in Lombard Street* (London, 1656).

59. GLMS 4060/1, vestry minutes, 1642; GLMS 2050/1, f. 43; CLRO J. Co. Co., 40, f. 174; Beaven, 1: 339; 2: 66; Surman, 1: 188, *s. v.*

60. GLMS 4060/1, vestry minutes, 1639–48, *passim;* CLRO J. Co. Co., 40, ff. 39b, 81, 100, 128.

61. GLMS 4060/1, vestry minutes, 1649–53, *passim* (for Nicholas Skinner), 1654–61, *passim* (for Henry Gray); Beaven, 1: 347; 2: 99, 103; Woodhead, pp. 79 (*s. v.* Henry Gray), 150 (*s. v.* Nicholas Skinner); Watson, *A History of the Salters' Company,* p. 145.

62. For Peck and Meriton, see Surman, 1: 259 (*s. v.* John Meriton), 266 (*s. v.* Francis Peck); *A Serious and Faithful Representation of the Judgements of the Ministers of the Gospel Within the Province of London* (London, 1648/9), p. 19 (for Peck). It is to be noted that Meriton was apparently converted to the Anglican position at the end of the revolutionary era. He was identified as "Convert" in early 1661. See BL Add. MS. 36781, f. 33b.

63. The four parishes were St. Martin Orgar, St. Botolph Billingsgate, St. Benet Gracechurch, and St. Michael Crooked Lane. Cf. Surman, *The Register-Booke of the Fourth Classis, passim.*

64. The former three were St. Magnus, St. Margaret New Fish Street, and St. Leonard Eastcheap; the later two were St. Dionis Backchurch and St. Clement Eastcheap. For these parishes, see chaps. 3 and 4 below.

65. These five parishes were St. Michael Cornhill, St. George Botolph Lane, St. Mary at Hill, St. Peter Cornhill, and St. Andrew Hubbard.

66. It is rather surprising that with Bunce as one of the leading parishioners and Daniel Cawdrey and William Harrison as its ministers in the 1640s, the parish of St. Benet Gracechurch eventually failed to have the Presbyterian church government established. No elders were chosen in the parish during the entire revolutionary period. Partly this was because the civic leaders of the parish during the Civil War period were divided three ways: Sir Jacob Garrard was a Royalist; James Bunce, a political Presbyterian; and Thomas Foot, a political Independent. Partly, we may assume, the downfall of Bunce after 1647 must have been a terrible blow and an irreplaceable loss to the Presbyterians in the parish. See GLMS 4214/1, ff. 15–21. For Garrard, Bunce, and Foot, see Pearl, pp. 298–99, 313–14, 315–16.

67. GLMS 4072/1, ff. 177b, 178. A Mr. Ward was supplying the place of the ministry at that time. See ibid., f. 178b.

68. See Leona Rostenberg, "The New World: John Bellamy, 'Pilgrim' Publisher of London," in *Literary, Political, Scientific, Religious & Legal Publishing, Printing & Bookselling in England, 1551–1700* (New York, 1965), pp. 97–129; Tolmie, pp. 13–15.

69. *Mercurius Aulicus, A Divrnall, Communicating the intelligence and affairs of the Court to the rest of the Kingdome* (Oxford, 1642), p. 561.

70. The author of *Mercurius Aulicus* added: "the master of the Office great *Bellamie* himselfe having heretofore been a very painfull Preacher, till sedition and Treason grew so publique and common, that it was not worthy his private Revelation." In any case, Bellamy had become a leading Presbyterian civic figure in the City by 1645–46. See Tolmie, p. 128; John Price, *The City Remonstrance Remonstrated* (London, 1646); John Bellamy, *A Justification of the City Remonstrance and Its Vindication* (London, 1646); John Lilburne, *The Charters of London* (London, 1646).

71. PRO SP 19/78, f. 60b; CLRO J. Co. Co., 40, ff. 21b, 52b, 184, 193, 215b; GLMS 4069/1, ff. 221b–254, *passim;* GLMS 4069/2, f. 258b.

72. GLMS 4072/1, ff. 166b–198b, *passim,* especially ff. 179b, 198–198b. Cf. also Surman, 1: 194, *s. v.;* idem, ed., *The Register-Booke of the Fourth Classis,* p. 135, *s. v.*

73. PRO SP 19/78, f. 60b; CLRO J. Co. Co., 40, ff. 32b, 40b, 42, 86–86b, 128, 184, 215b.

74. Hooker was one of the London civic leaders found guilty of high misdemeanor in 1647 and committed to the Sergeant-at-Arms. See *C. S. P. D., 1645–47,* p. 601; *A Paire of Spectacles for the Citie,* p. 9 [11].

75. GLMS 1240/1, ff. 43b–51b, *passim;* GLMS 952/1, ff. 14b–15b. Cf. Surman, 1: 241, *s. v.;* idem, *The Register-Booke of the Fourth Classis,* p. 146, *s. v.*

76. GLMS 4069/1, ff. 218–67, 239. Rowell was appointed as assessor for parliamentary subscriptions in 1642, and he later reappeared as a Common Councilman in 1653–56. See PRO SP19/78, f. 60b; GLMS 4069/2, ff. 262–69. For Turlington, see GLMS 4069/2, f. 275b. Cf. also Surman, 1: 273, *s. v.* Rowell; idem, *The Register-Booke of the Fourth Classis,* pp. 149, *s. v.* James Martin; 153, *s. v.* Rowell; 156, *s. v.* James Tourlington, whose name was given as John Turlington in the parish records; 158, *s. v.* William Webb.

77. For Alston, see *D. N. B., s. v;* Pearl, "London Puritan and Scotch Fifth Columnists: A Mid-Seventeenth-Century Phenomenon," p. 321. For Lenthall, see PRO SP 19/78, f. 60b; CLRO J. Co. Co., 40, ff. 86–86b, 128; BL Add. MS. 36781, f. 85; Woodhead, p. 167, *s. v.;* For Harris, see Harvey, p. 2; Firth and Rait, 1:1129; Woodhead, p. 85, *s. v.* John Harris, where William Harris was given as a clothworker. Cf. also Surman, *The Register-Booke of the Fourth Classis,* pp. 133, *s. v.* Alston; 145, *s. v.* Harris; 148, *s. v.* Lenthall.

78. PRO SP 19/78, f. 60b; CLRO J. Co. Co., 40, ff. 176, 193, 215b; Firth and Rait, 1: 794, 871, 928. Cf. also Surman, 1: 224, *s. v.;* idem, *The Register-Booke of the Fourth Classis,* p. 143, *s. v.*

79. For Lusher, see GLMS 4165/1, ff. 260, 280, 282; CLRO J. Co. Co., 40, f. 21b; GLMS 4069/1, ff. 218, 220b; Pearl, pp. 137, 139, 150. For Meade, see PRO SP 19/78, f. 60b. For Pease and Cooling, see GLMS 4069/1, ff. 229b–37; CLRO J. Co. Co., 40, f. 153b; Woodhead, p. 128, *s. v.* Pease. For Robinson and Bromwich, see S. Pitt, *Some Notes on the Worshipful Company of Armourers and Brasiers* (London, 1930), p. 42. For Biker, see W. W. Grantham, comp., *List of*

the Wardens of the Grocers' Company (London, 1907), p. 29; GLMS 4165/1, ff. 260, 280, 331. Cf. also Surman, 1: 195 *s. v.* Lewis Bicar; 226, *s. v.* Pease; 272, *s. v.* Robinson; idem, *The Register-Booke of the Fourth Classis*, pp. 135, *s. v.* Biker; 140, *s. v.* Cooling; 150, *s. v.* Meade; 151, *s. v.* Pease; 152, *s. v.* Robinson.

80. Thomas Manwaring was Common Councilman in 1647, 1648, 1655–56, and 1656–57. Richard Best, who had residence both in the parish of St. Dionis Backchurch and in Stepney, was probably a merchant. Nehemiah Wallington has been well known to modern historians of this period for his journals and notes on contemporary events, and his brother, John, was warden of the Turners' Company in 1639 and 1643 and became the Company's master in 1647 and 1648. John Wallington was also appointed an assessor for parliamentary subscriptions in 1642. For Manwaring, see GLMS 4216/1, ff. 20, 40, 113, 123. For Best, see GLMS 4215/1, ff. 79, 82; Woodhead, p. 178, *s. v.* John Winn. For Nehemiah Wallington, see *D. N. B., s. v.* For John Wallington, see A. C. Stanley-Stone, *The Worshipful Company of Turners of London* (London, 1925), p. 291; PRO SP 19/78, f. 60b. Cf. also Surman, 1: 195, *s. v.* Best; 256, *s. v.* Manwaring; idem, *The Register-Booke of the Fourth Classis*, pp. 135, *s. v.* Best; 149, *s. v.* Manwaring; 157–58, *s. vv.* John and Nehemiah Wallington.

81. Edmund Calamy, *An Account of the Ministers . . . Who Were Ejected . . . in 1660* (London, 1713), p. 18; *D. N. B., s. v.; C. R., s. v.;* Surman, 1:248, *s. v.;* John Price, *The Pulpit Incendiary* (London, 1648), pp. 15, 20.

82. Pearl, "London Puritans and the Scotch Fifth Columnists," p. 327.

83. *D. N. B., s. v.;* Pearl, p. 167; Seaver, pp. 268–69; Surman, 1:255, *s. v.;* Christopher Love, *Englands Distemper* (London: 1645); idem, *Short and plaine Animadversions on some Passages in Mr. Dels Sermon* (London, 1646), "To His Excellence Sir Thomas Fairfax, Generall of the Army . . . ;" idem, *Works of Darkness Brought to Light* (London, 1647), pp. 8, 11, 12. Cf. also *A Modest and Clear Vindication of the Serious Representation, and late Vindication of the Ministers of London* (London, 1649). For John Hewson and William Dell, see *D. N. B., s. vv.; Biographical Dictionary, s. vv.* For Paul Hobson, see Tolmie, pp. 58–59, 158–59 and *passim, Biographical Dictionary, s. v.* For Roger Quarterman, see Tolmie, pp. 30–32, 34, 48. On the outbreak of the Puritan Revolution, Quarterman became one of the early radical iconoclasts in both Southwark and London, and he was to be appointed an agent for the Committee for the Advance of Money and chosen as the City Marshall in 1643. See *Mercurius Aulicus*, p. 113; *C. S. P. D.,* 1643, p. 289; CLRO J. Co. Co., 40, f. 73.

84. See n. 23 above. See also Calamy, *An Account*, pp. 1–2; Carruthers, *The Everyday Work of the Westminster Assembly*, p. 139; Pearl, "London and the Counter-Revolution," p. 51; Liu, "The Founding of the London Provincial Assembly," p. 115. Cf. also Simeon Ashe and William Rathband, *A Letter of many Ministers in Old England, requesting the judgement of their Reverend Brethren in New England concerning Nine Positions* (London, 1643); Samuel Rutherford, *A Free Disputation Against pretended Liberty of Conscience* (London, 1649), p. 264; Simeon Ashe, *Good Covrage Discovered and Encovraged* (London, 1642); idem, *A True Revelation, of the Most Chiefe Occurences, at, and since the late Battell at Newbery* (London, 1644); idem, *Religious Covenanting Directed, and Covenant-keeping persuaded: Presented, in a Sermon preached before the Right Honourable Thomas Adams Lord Major, and the Right Worshipfull the Sheriffs, and Aldermen his Brethren, and the rest of the Common-Councel of the famous City of London, January 14, 1645. Upon which day the solemn League and Covenant was renewed by them and their Officers, with Prayer and Fasting, at Michael Basing-shaw, London* (London, 1646).

85. Calamy, *An Account*, pp. 2–3; *D.N.B., s. v.; C.R., s. v.;* Surman, 1:261, *s. v.*

86. *D. N. B., s. v.; C. R., s. v.;* CLRO J. Co. Co., 40, ff. 151–53b; CLRO Letter Books, QQ, ff. 184b–87b; Liu, "The Founding of the London Provincial Assembly," p. 113.

87. For Heyrick, see *D. N. B., s. v.;* Surman, 1: 100–101. In fact, Heyrick was chosen minister in late 1649 in the parish of St. Mary Colechurch. See GLMS 41/1, f. 45b. For Jaggard, see Seaver, p. 275; Surman, 1: 246, *s. v.;* GLMS 1453/1, ff. 43, 47; GLMS 1455/1, churchwardens' account for 1650–51, for reference to Jaggard's imprisonment.

88. For Tuckney and Conant, see *D. N. B., s. vv.; C. R., s. vv.*

89. For Poole, see Calamy, *An Account,* pp. 14–15; *D. N. B., s. v.; C. R., s. v.;* Surman, 1: 267, *s. v.* For Barton, see *D. N. B., s. v.;* Hist. MSS. Comm., *Sixth Report,* Appendix, pp. 79, 108.

90. Surman, 1: 269, *s. v.;* Wilson, pp. 127n, 243, 247; *C. R.,* p. 553; *A serious and faithfull Representation of the Judgements of Ministers of the Gospell Within the Province of London* (London, 1640), p. 17; Liu, *Discord in Zion,* p. 163.

91. The two parishes in which the Presbyterian church government was not adopted were St. Olave Silver Street and St. Mary Staining. The former does not appear to have had a settled ministry during the revolutionary period, whereas the latter had Nathaniel Holmes, a future Fifth Monarchy man, as minister from 1643 to 1662. See chap. 3 below.

92. For the social conditions of these two parishes, see chap. 1 above.

93. They were Francis Ashe (Ald., 1648), Humphrey Bedingfield (Ald., 1651), John Perrin (Ald., 1654–56), William Daniel (Ald., 1651), and Nicholas Herne (Ald., 1657). Herne was a merchant tailor. See Beaven, 1: 343, 345; 2: 69, 75, 79, 84, 86; Dale, p. 60; W. R. Prideaux, *Memorial of the Goldsmiths' Company* (London, 1896), 1: 353; Woodhead, p. 89, *s. v.* Nicholas Herne; p. 103, *s. v.* William Knight (for William Daniel); p. 168, *s. v.* Thomas Vyner (for John Perrin).

94. CLRO J. Co. Co., 40, ff. 62b, 81, 128, 153b, 215, 215b; Firth and Rait, 1: 928, 930; *C. S. P. D., 1645–47,* pp. 380, 385. For Glyde, see also Surman, 1: 227, *s. v.*

95. For John Gellibrand, see PRO SP 19/78, f. 60a; GLMS 2050/1, ff. 43–45. For Edward Honeywood, see Firth and Rait, 1: 794, 871; Woodhead, p. 92, *s. v.;* John Nicholl, comp., *Some Account of the Worshipful Company of Ironmongers* (London, 1851), pp. 408–9. Cf. also Surman, 1: 225, *s. v.* Gellibrand; 241, *s. v.* Honeywood.

96. For Floyd and Overton, see GLMS 642/1, no folio number, vestry minute, 19 July 1646; CLRO J. Co. Co., 40, ff. 151b–53b, 174–74b; Mahony, "Presbyterianism in the City of London," p. 105. For Bard, see GLMS 642/1, vestry minute, 28 February 1652; Firth and Rait, 1: 975; 2: 365, 1455; Woodhead, p. 23, *s. v.*

97. For Hart, see Firth and Rait, 1: 794, 871; Edwards, *Gangraena,* pt. 1, p. 133. Perhaps this was the William Hart who was master of the Ironmongers' Company in 1636. See Nicholl, comp., *Some Account of the Worshipful Company of Ironmongers,* pp. 408–9. For Greenhill, see PRO SP 19/78, f. 60d; CLRO J. Co. Co., 40 ff. 22b, 40, 128; Surman, 1: 231, *s. v.* For Mills, see CLRO J. Co. Co., 40, f. 52b; Surman, 1: 260, *s. v.* Mills was the master of the Company of Tylers and Bricklayers in 1649–50 and 1659–60. See W. G. Bell, *A Short History of the Worshipful Company of Tylers and Bricklayers of the City of London* (London, 1938), p. 68.

98. For Vicars, see *D. N. B., s. v.* For Widmerpole, see CLRO J. Co. Co., 40, f. 302; *A Paire of Spectacles for the Citie,* p. 11: "A Gentleman of good Account and Quality, a very stout and valiant man, an able and knowing Souldier, one that hath been very active for the Parliament from the beginning of these troubles." Mahony also lists four other signatories of the 1645–46 petitions as of this parish: Anthony Bickerstaffe, Gervase Blackwell, John Jones, and Harmon Shease. Jones was probably Captain John Jones of St. Bartholomew by the Exchange and Shease was a parishioner of St. Mary le Bow in 1642. See Mahony, "Presbyterianism in the City of London," p. 105; PRO SP 16/492, ff. 88, 94. For Jones, see also n. 132 below; for Shease, see CLRO J. Co. Co., 40, ff. 310b–11; for Bickerstaffe, see Firth and Rait, 1: 957 and Surman, 1: 196, *s. v.;* for Blackwell, see Firth and Rait, 2: 1294.

99. For Sherman, see PRO SP 19/78, f. 60a; GLMS 2050/1, ff. 43b–46; Firth and Rait, 1: 794, 871; Alfred Plummer, *The London Weavers' Company* (London, 1972), p. 452. For Hamms, see GLMS 2050/1, ff. 42–43; CLRO J. Co. Co., 40, f. 55; Woodhead, p. 83, *s. v.* Stephen Hams. For Blackley, see Austin T. Young, *The Annals of the Barber-Surgeons of London* (London, 1890), pp. 8–9. For Nicasius, see *Register of Apprentices of the Worshipful Company of Clock-makers of the City of London* (London, 1931), pp. 324–25.

100. GLMS 2050/1, ff. 40b–45; CLRO J. Co. Co., 40, ff. 100, 128; PRO SP 19/78, f. 60a; Firth and Rait, 1: 794, 871. Johnson was identified as a merchant tailor in parish records. Although he appears to have been a substantial tradesman, Johnson held no office in his company. See GLMS

1455/1, f. 55. Cf. also Liu, "The Founding of the London Provincial Assembly," p. 124.

101. For Flesher, see PRO SP 19/78, f. 60a; GLMS 2050/1, ff. 43b–46, 47b–50; Woodhead, p. 70, *s. v.*

102. For Allen, see PRO SP 19/78, f. 60a; GLMS 2050/1, ff. 45b–51; Woodhead, p. 16, *s. v.*

103. For Yardley, see GLMS 2050/1, f. 45b; Guy Parsloe, ed., *Wardens' Accounts of the Wordhipful Company of Founders of the City of London* (London, 1964), pp. 306–66, *passim.* For Whitturne, see GLMS 2050/1, ff. 46, 47, 48b; Oliver Warner, *A History of the Innholders Company*, 2d ed. (London, 1962), list of masters. For Hutchinson, see GLMS 2050/1, ff. 42–43, 45, 47b–50; PRO SP 19/78, f. 60a. For Bromley, see GLMS 2050/1, ff. 48–51b; Woodhead, p. 33, *s. v.* For Glassbrooke, see CLRO J. Co. Co., 41, f. 64; Beaven, 1: 352; Jordan, p. 132.

104. GLMS 6554/1, ff. 11b–12, 26, 35b-37.

105. For the reorganization of the governmental structure of the parish, see chap. 6 below. The ten Common Councilmen were Joseph Parrott, Stephen Sedgewick, Thomas Lownes, Robert Russell, Thomas King, Joseph Holden, William Hancocke, John Alsopp, John Baker, and Valentine Fyge. See GLMS 6554/1, ff. 6–204, *passim,* in which the Common Councilmen of the parish for each year were identified.

106. Robert Russell was often identified as Major Russell in the parish records; John Alsopp was given as Major Alsopp in 1648–49 and as Lieutenant-Colonel in 1650–51. See GLMS 6554/1, ff. 68, 132b; GLMS 6552/1, ff. 180, 200.

107. They were respectively John Baker and Valentine Fyge in the former case and Joseph Parrott and John Alsopp in the latter event. See CLRO J. Co. Co., 40, ff. 151b–53b, 174–74b; GLMS 6554/1, ff. 98b, 132b; Mahony, "Presbyterianism in the City of London," p. 105.

108. GLMS 6554/1, f. 68.

109. Surman, 2: 108. Incidentally, Shaw did not include the 1652 returns from the Fifth London Classis in his treatment of the decay of Presbyterianism in London. See Shaw, 2: 108–10. Perhaps this is an appropriate place to give some further observations on the Presbyterian civic leadership in this parish. To be sure, not all the ruling elders of the parish were staunch and militant Presbyterians. In fact, Robert Russell, Thomas King, and Joseph Holden, all three of whom served as Common Councilmen in 1649–50, were apparently not among those men who had been involved in the Presbyterian agitation in the City during the previous years. Russell was probably associated with the Independents, too. For Russell, see *A Paire of Spectacles for the Citie,* p. 8; Woodhead, p. 142, *s. v.* Robert Russell (A). For Alsopp and Fyge, also see ibid., pp. 17, 74, *s. vv.*

110. Calamy, *An Account,* pp. 4–7; *D. N. B., s. v.; C. R., s. v.; Biographical Dictionary, s. v.;* GLMS 3570/2, f. 43b; CLRO J. Co. Co., 40, f. 160; Pearl, "London and the Counter-Revolution," p. 51; Smectymnuus [i.e., Stephen Marshall, Edmund Calamy, Thomas Young, Matthew Newcomen, and William Spurstowe], *An Answer to a Book entitled An Humble Remonstrance* (London, 1641); Edmund Calamy, *A Just and necessary Apology* (London, 1646), p. 9; John Price, *The Pulpit Incendiary,* pp. 6, 9, 11; *A Modest and Clear Vindication of the Serious Representation, and late Vindication of the Ministers of London* (London, 1649), p. 10. For Calamy's sermons on church polity during the Puritan era, see Liu, *Discord in Zion,* chaps. 1 and 2, *passim.*

111. Calamy, *An Account,* pp. 12–13; *D. N. B., s. v.; C. R., s. v.;* Wilson, pp. 240, 242, 245, 246, 247, 249; Price, *The Pulpit Incendiary,* pp. 14, 16; Thomas Jacomb, *Abraham's Death. The Manner, Time, and Consequent of it. Opened and Applied in a Funeral Sermon, Preached upon the Death of the Reverend Mr. Thomas Case* (London, 1682), p. 42. Cf. also Surman, 1: 204–5, *s. v.*

112. *C. R., s. v.;* Price, *The Pulpit Incendiary,* pp. 3–4.

113. Calamy, *An Account,* pp. 3–4; *D. N. B., s. v.; C. R., s. v.;* Surman, 1: 244–45, *s. v.*

114. Calamy, *An Account,* pp. 739–40; *D. N. B., s. v.; C. R., s. v.;* Pearl, "London and the Counter-Revolution," p. 51. It is to be noted that when Love was minister, Witham, who had probably been deprived of his ministry at St. Alban Wood Street, also served as lecturer in the parish of St. Lawrence Old Jewry. In this light, this must have been a strongly Presbyterian parish. See GLMS 2593/2, ff. 153, 176, 180, 202.

115. For Arrowsmith and Wallis, see *D. N. B., s. vv.;* Surman, 1: 187, 295, *s. vv.;* Shaw, 2: 401, 568. For Horton, see *D. N. B., s. v.;* GLMS 66/1, ff. 91b, 95b, 114b; GLMS 64/1, ff. 45, 53, 68b.

116. Seaver, pp. 50, 345–46, n. 64; Pearl, p. 166; GLMS 3570/2, ff. 45, 46, 49, 50, 52, 61, 62b; PRO SP 19/78, f. 60b; Beaven, 1: 346, 350; 2: 67, 80; Woodhead, pp. 97, *s. v.* James James; 124–25, *s. v.* Christopher Pack; 179, *s. v.* George Witham.

117. Green, 1: 1; GLMS 3570/2, ff. 48, 52b, 53; CLRO J. Co. Co., 40, ff. 86–86b, 193, 215b; Firth and Rait, 1: 795, 872, 928; Surman, 1: 198, *s. v.*

118. GLMS 3570/2, ff. 52b, 58.

119. GLMS 4415/1, f. 100b. For Wright and Gurney, see Pearl, pp. 302–3, 307–8, *s. vv.* For Tryon, see Harvey, p. 12; Green, 1: 135. For Neve, see GLMS 4415/1, ff. 103b, 109. Neve was replaced as Common Councilman by William Vaugham in 1642, and his name disappeared from the vestry records of the parish. He was apparently still alive and fined for the offices of both Alderman and Sheriff in 1651. See Beaven, 1: 345; 2: 75; CLRO J. Co. Co., 41, f. 61.

120. GLMS 4415/1, ff. 119, 122, 124, 133, 140, 189b. For Wollaston and Foot, see Pearl, pp. 315–16, 328–331, *s. vv.*

121. GLMS 4415/1, f. 132b. For Vaugham, see PRO SP 19/78, f. 60c; GLMS 4415/1, ff. 109, 120, 125, 135; Surman, 1: 290, *s. v.* For Mascall, see GLMS 4415/1, f. 129; Firth and Rait, 2: 1455; Woodhead, p. 113, *s. v.;* Surman, 1: 258, *s. v.* For Frederick, see Woodhead, p. 73, *s. v.*

122. GLMS 2590/1, f. 359; GLMS 2593/2, f. 33; Pearl, pp. 295–96, 297–98, *s. vv.*

123. For Bisbey, see PRO SP 19/78, f. 60c; Firth and Rait, 1:795, 872; J. Steven Watson, *A History of the Salters' Company* (London, 1963), p. 145. For Addams, see PRO SP 19/78, f. 60c; CLRO J. Co. Co., 41, f. 2; Beaven, 1:346; 2:71. For Hadley, see CLRO J. Co. Co., 41, f. 3b; Beaven, 1:339; 2:71.

124. Seaver, pp. 149–50, 153; Jordan, pp. 289, 290.

125. GLMS 2590/1, ff. 341, 348, 382, 390, 409, 431, 459; GLMS 2593/2, ff. 66, 75, 110, 160, 176, 179, 202, 254, 272, 288, 289, 309, 327, 340, 355.

126. GLMS 2597/1, ff. 50, 59, 67, 70–73, 77–78, 85, 114–18; GLMS 2596/2, ff. 87b–88, 95b–96, 133b–34, 137b–38. For Aldworth, see Harvey, p. 13 (where his name is given as Alsworth). For Story, see GLMS 2597/1, ff. 50, 75; CLRO J. Co. Co., 40, f. 100. Robert Story was master of the Clothworkers' Company in 1649. See Thomas Girtin, *The Golden Ram: A History of the Clothworkers' Company, 1528–1958* (London, 1958), pp. 326–27. For Waterhouse, see GLMS 2597/1, ff. 80, 85; CLRO J. Co. Co., 40, ff. 100, 128, 153b. For Webster, see GLMS 2597/1, ff. 83, 85, 92; CLRO J. Co. Co., 40, f. 128. Anthony Webster was master of the Ironmongers' Company in 1660. See Nicholl, comp., *Some Account of the Worshipful Company of Ironmongers*, pp. 408–9. For Brinley, see GLMS 2597/1, f. 85; PRO SP 19/78, f. 60c; Firth and Rait, 1:795, 872. Among these civic leaders of St. Mary Magdalen Milk Street, Brinley appears to have been an active and staunch Presbyterian, and he signed the citizens' petitions in 1645–46. See CLRO J. Co. Co., 40, ff. 153–53b, 174–74b. Cf. Surman, 1:199, *s. v.* For Robinson, see Woodhead, pp. 139–40, *s. v.* See also chap. 4 below.

127. GLMS 64/1, ff. 27, 27b, 28b, 38b, 39b; GLMS 66/1, ff. 86, 91b, 96b, 97b. For Towse, see Pearl, p. 325, *s. v.* Towse left a legacy of £50 to the parish for payment of the arrears for repairing the parish church. See GLMS 66/1, f. 111. For Pitchford, see GLMS 64/1, ff. 28b, 38b, 39b, 43; PRO SP 19/78, f. 60c. For Sleigh, see GLMS 64/1, f. 39b. Sleigh was to be elected Alderman in 1652–57. See Beaven, 1:337; 2:81; *A List of Some Eminent Members of the Mercers Company of London* (London, 1872), p. 31. Cf. also Surman, 1:279, *s. v.* For Jackson, see GLMS 64/1, f. 43; Woodhead, p. 97, *s. v.* Cf. also Surman, 1:245, *s. v.* For Manwaring, see Pearl, p. 323, *s. v.* For Shambrooke, Lawrence, and Lorymer, see W. S. C. Copeman, *The Worshipful Society of Apothecaries of London* (London, 1967), pp. 95–96.

128. For Christian, see GLMS 62/1, ff. 10, 14; CLRO J. Co. Co., 40, ff. 100, 128. For Haynes, see GLMS 1431/2, ff. 174, 181, 196; PRO SP 19/78, f. 60b. For Manwaring, see GLMS 6047/1, f. 10; PRO SP 19/78, f. 60c; CLRO J. Co. Co., 40, ff. 128, 215b; Firth and Rait, 1:795, 872, 928. For Winch, see Harvey, p. 12; Dale, p. 125; Beaven, 1:341; 2:89; A. H. Johnson, *The History of the Worshipful Company of the Drapers of London*, 5 vols. (Oxford, 1922), 4:137. For Bastwick, see *D. N. B., s. v.; Biographical Dictionary, s. v.;* Surman, 1:192, *s. v.*

129. *D. N. B., s. v.;* Firth and Rait, 1:186; Hist. MSS. Comm., *Sixth Report,* Appendix, pp. 67–68; GLMS 4425/1, ff. 35b–54a; Edwards, *Gangraena,* epistle to the reader by James Cranford; Price, *The Pulpit Incendiary,* p. 14; Pearl, "London Puritans and Scotch Fifth Columnists," pp. 520, 524. Cf. also Surman, 1:209–10, *s. v.*

130. *D. N. B., s. v.;* Price, *The Pulpit Incendiary,* pp. 11, 16. Cf. also Surman, 1:206, *s. v.*

131. Edwin Freshfield, ed., *The Vestry Minute Books of the Parish of St. Bartholomew Exchange in the City of London* (London, 1890), pt. 1, pp. 143, 146; pt. 2, pp. 5, 10; CLRO J. Co. Co., 40, ff. 22, 67; PRO SP 19/78, f. 60b; Firth and Rait, 1:223, 487, 842, 795, 872; John Vicars, *Gods Arke Overtopping the Worlds Waves, or The Third Part of the Parliamentary Chronicle* (London, 1646), p. 239. Cf. also Surman, 1:257, *s. v.*

132. Freshfield, ed., *The Vestry Minute Books of the Parish of St. Bartholomew Exchange,* pt. 2, pp. 4, 9, 10, 12, 15, 23, 24; PRO SP 19/78, ff. 60b, 60e; CLRO J. Co. Co., 40, ff. 153–53b, 184, 193, 215b; Firth and Rait, 1:928; *C. S. P. D., 1645–47,* p. 601. Cf. also Surman, 1:249, 290, *s. vv.*

133. PRO SP 19/78, f. 60d; Freshfield, ed., *The Vestry Minute Books of the Parish of St. Bartholomew Exchange,* pt. 2, pp. 72, 78; Beaven, 1:339; 2:84; Grantham, comp., *List of the Wardens of the Grocers' Company,* p. 28; William Herbert, *The History of the Twelve Great Livery Companies of London,* 2 vols. (London, 1834), 1:183–84.

134. PRO SP 19/492, f. 86; GLMS 4425/1, ff. 32a, 96–97. In November 1642, when contributions to the Parliament were collected in the City parishes, Richaut and Underwood were "out of town," while Middleton, Culling, and King were "not to be spoken with." In fact, in 1641/42, the election of William Middleton as Common Councilman had been challenged by the parishioners of St. Bartholomew by the Exchange and St. Benet Fink, who were in favor of Samuel Harsnett and James Story. Furthermore, at St. Christopher, after James Cranford was chosen lecturer in September 1641, all of these men refused to pay their contributions for the lecture. See CLRO J. Co. Co., 40, f. 22; GLMS 4423/1, churchwardens' accounts, 1641–42.

135. GLMS 4069/1, ff. 218, 220b, 225b, 227b, 229b, 233b, 234b, 237b; CLRO J. Co. Co., 40, ff. 55, 100, 128. Roberts was a leading vestryman in the parish. See GLMS 4425/1, ff. 32a, 35b.

136. *A Paire of Spectacles for the Citie,* p. 11; CLRO J. Co. Co., 40, f. 302. See also GLMS 4425/1, ff. 35b, 36a.

137. PRO SP 19/78, f. 60b; Firth and Rait, 1:795, 872; GLMS 4425/1, ff. 32a, 35b, 36a; W. A. D. Englefield, *The History of the Painter-Stainers' Company of London* (London, 1923), p. 223.

138. PRO SP 19/78, f. 60b; GLMS 4425, ff. 36b–42b; CLRO J. Co. Co., 40, ff. 215, 302; *A Paire of Spectacles for the Citie,* p. 9 [11]: Ruthworth, 7:788; Surnam, 1:290, *s. v.*

139. GLMS 2601/1, ff. 142, 153, 159, 164; CLRO J. Co. Co., 40, 26b, 31b, 32b; Pearl, pp. 126 n. 79, 147–48. See also chap. 4 below.

140. PRO SP 19/78, f. 60b; CLRO J. Co. Co., 40, ff. 193, 213, 215, 215b, 220b; Firth and Rait, 1:928. George Dunne was master of the Barber-Surgeons' Company in 1646, and Walter Pell was to be elected Alderman in 1648 and Sheriff in 1649. See Young, *The Annals of the Barber-Surgeons of London,* pp. 8–9; Beaven, 1:345; 2:69; CLRO J. Co. Co., 41, f. 15b. For Edwin Browne see also Woodhead, p. 39, *s. v.*

141. CLRO J. Co. Co., 40, ff. 86–86b, 184, 215, 215b, 220b; Firth and Rait, 1:795, 872, 928. For the life of Pack, see *D. N. B., s. v.;* Woodhead, p. 124, *s. v.* Cf. also Surman, 1:265, *s. v.* It may be worthy of notice that in early 1649, when Pack was appointed to take charge of raising money for the Army in both Cripplegate Ward Without and Cripplegate Ward Within, he laid down the following conditions: "if Common Councilmen or sufficient inhabitants will join me, else not" and "if as Common Councilman etc. Thomas Read will join me." The only other City leaders who made similar conditions for action were Lord Mayor Abraham Reynardson and Alderman Richard Chambers, both of whom were soon to be imprisoned for their refusal to recognize the new Commonwealth. See CLRO J. Co. Co., 40, ff. 310b–11. For Reynardson and Chambers, see Pearl, pp. 305–6, 314, *s. vv.* Cf. also Charles M. Clode, *London during the Great Rebellion. Being a Memoir of Sir Abraham Reynardson* (London, 1892).

142. James Story was chosen Common Councilman in a disputed election in 1641–42 and sat on a number of committees in the Common Council between 1643 and 1647. He was also appointed a lay trier for the Seventh Classis in 1645. See CLRO J. Co. Co., 40, ff. 22, 52b, 81, 190b, 193; Firth and Rait, 1:795, 872, 957. Cf. also Surman, 1:284, *s. v.* Robert Launt was appointed an assessor for parliamentary subscriptions in 1642 and a lay trier in 1645. He was in all probability the Robert Lant who became master of the Merchant Taylors' Company in 1658. PRO SP 19/78, f. 60b; Firth and Rait, 1:795, 872; Charles M. Clode, *The Early History of the Guild of Merchant Taylors*, 2 vols. (London, 1888), 2:348; Pearl, "London Puritans and Scotch Fifth Columnists," p. 521. Cf. also Surman, 1:252, *s. v.* The career of George Poyner as an important civic figure lay in the future. He became warden of the Ironmongers' Company in 1658 and master of the Company in 1662. In 1661 he was also elected Alderman. See Woodhead, p. 133, *s. v.*; Nicholl, comp., *Some Account of the Worshipful Company of Ironmongers*, p. 481. Cf. also Surman, 1:268, *s. v.* John Everett was appointed an assessor for parliamentary subscriptions in 1642 and was elected Common Councilman in the same year. In 1643 he sat on the committee for the fortification of the City. Although not a substantial tradesman, Evereet became a leading parishioner during the Civil War period and managed the parish affairs. See PRO SP 19/78, f. 60a; CLRO J. Co. Co., 40, ff. 55, 100, 128; GLMS 4526/1, ff. 54b–69a; GLMS 4524/2, ff. 58a, 77; Hist. MSS. Comm., *Sixth Report,* Appendix, p. 115.

143. GLMS 4352/1, f. 178. For Bedingfield, see David Underdown, *Pride's Purge; Politics in the Puritan Revolution* (Oxford, 1971), pp. 237, 367. For Corbet, see *D. N. B., s. v.; Biographical Dictionary, s. v.* Thomas Essington was probably not a regular inhabitant in this parish. In November 1642 William and Thomas Essington of St. Swithin contributed £50 to the Parliament. And Essington was still the leading vestryman in St. Swithin in 1647. Thomas Essington's name appeared in the parish records of St. Margaret Lothbury only in 1646. Perhaps the Essingtons had premises in both parishes. Thomas Essington was elected Alderman in 1651. See PRO SP 16/492, f. 73; GLMS 4352/1, ff. 176b, 178; GLMS 560/1, no folio number, vestry minutes, 1647; Beaven, 1: 341; Green, 1: 407. For Lowther, see CLRO J. Co. Co., 40, ff. 213b, 215, 219, 220b, 259b; Green, 2: 668. Lowther was also elected Alderman in 1650. See Beaven, 1: 341; 2: 74. Edward Chard was appointed an assessor for parliamentary subscriptions in 1642 and elected Alderman in 1661–62. See Woodhead, p. 45, *s. v.* Ralph Hugh was master of the Clothworkers' Company in 1643 and Common Councilman in 1644. See Girtin, *The Golden Ram: A History of the Clothworker's Company*, pp. 326–27; CLRO J. Co. Co., 40, f. 100. In 1657, a certain Hough was a delegate from the Seventh Classis to the London Provincial Assembly, but this might be Thomas Hough, a merchant tailor, who was churchwarden of the parish of St. Stephen Coleman Street in 1647–48. See GLMS 4458/1, ff. 154, 156, 158.

144. Jordan, p. 22; Hill, p. 296; Pearl, pp. 135, 163, 183; Seaver, pp. 147, 282–83, 286; David A. Kirby, "The Radicals of St. Stephen's, Coleman Street, London, 1624–1642," *The Guildhall Miscellany* 3. no. 2 (April 1970): 98–119; GLMS 4458/1, ff. 134, 135, 147; Surman, 1: 110. Cf. also chap. 3 below. For Taylor, see Calamy, *An Account,* p. 37, *s. v.; C. R., s. v.;* Surman, 1: 286, *s. v.*

145. For Pennington, see *D. N. B., s. v.;* Pearl, pp. 176–84, 198–206, 210–16, 218–21, 260–65 and *passim.* For Rowe, see *D. N. B., s. v.;* Pearl, p. 324, *s. v.* For Russell, see Pearl, pp. 324–25, *s. v.* For Ashurst, who was Common Councilman in 1651–58, see GLMS 4458/1, ff. 170, 179, 187, 208, 236; Kirby, "The Radicals of St. Stephen's Coleman Street, London, 1624–1642," p. 110 n.115.

146. GLMS 4458/1, f. 134.

147. CLRO J. Co. Co., 40, ff. 83b, 86–86b, 148, 176, 184, 190b, 193, 199, 213b. 215, 215b; GLMS 4458/1, ff. 127, 132; Beaven, 1: 345; 2: 67; Kirby, "The Radicals of St. Stephen's, Coleman Street, London," p. 111.

148. Thomas Barnardiston, a younger brother of Sir Nathaniel Barnardiston, was an Adventurer in the Providence Island Company and a friend of John Winthrop. He became Master of the Mint in 1649. He was very active in parish affairs between 1644 and 1649. It may be worth noticing that he was one of the signatories for the resolutions upon John Goodwin's return. See

GLMS 4458/1, ff. 129–61, *passim;* Kirby, "The Radicals of St. Stephen's, Coleman Street, London," pp. 110 n.125, 111. Kendrick, a mercer and merchant, was Common Councilman in 1645–47 and Alderman in 1651–52. See GLMS 4458/1, ff. 138, 141; Beaven, 1: 337; 2: 80; Woodhead, p. 101, *s. v.* Andrew Kendrick, son of the above. For Silbley, see GLMS 4458/1, ff. 187, 208; Woodhead, p. 149, *s. v.* Lucas was a plasterer and Fitzwilliams a glazier. Neither appears to have held offices beyond the parochial level. In 1642 Lucas contributed £5 to the Parliament, but Fitzwilliams only £2. See GLMS 4458/1, f. 156; Surman, 1: 223, *s. v.* Fitzwilliams; PRO SP 16/492, ff. 76–76b.

149. Kirby, "The Radicals of St. Stephen's, Coleman Street, London," pp. 114–15; Tolmie, pp. 36–37, 76, 81, 111–17 and *passim.*

150. An exception must be made to this general observation in the case of some parishes in Southwark, which had the presence of some staunch and militant Presbyterian civic leaders. See n. 162 below. Spurstowe was minister at Hackney from 1643 to 1662 and Manton was minister at St. Mary Stoke Newington from 1645 to 1656. Both men were prominent Presbyterian divines in seventeenth-century England. For Spurstowe, see Calamy, *An Account,* p. 471, *s. v.; D. N. B., s. v.; C. R., s. v.;* Surman, 1: 282, *s. v.* For Manton, see Calamy, *An Account,* pp. 42–43, *s. v.; D. N. B., s. v.; C. R., s. v.;* Surman, 1: 257, *s. v.*

151. Jordan, pp. 35, 36, 52. For Blackwell, see Surman, 1: 179, *s. v.* For Walker, see GLMS 6836, ff. 158, 173, 196, 203–4, 207; *D. N. B., s. v.;* Surman, 1: 293, *s. v.* For Barham, see GLMS 6836, ff. 203–4, 205, 207; GLMS 6844/1, ff. 3, 6, 12, 15; *C. R., s. v.;* Surman, 1: 191, *s. v.*

152. For Atkins, see Woodhead, p. 20, *s. v.*; Pearl, pp. 311–13, *s. v.* For Dethick, see Woodhead, p. 60, *s. v.* Chamberlain, Cullen, and Hawkins were all appointed in 1642 as assessors for parliamentary subscriptions, and Hawkins was one of the chief lenders to the Parliament. Cullen was to be created a Baronet in 1661. See PRO SP 19/78, f. 60d; Pearl, p. 259 n.90; Green, 1: 150; *Complete Baronetage,* 3: 209.

153. *Mercurius Aulicus,* p. 170; Pearl, pp. 253, 254, 260.

154. Only Thomas Hutchins of the parish was appointed to the subcommittee for parliamentary subscriptions in 1642 and a lay trier in 1645. Yet Hutchins does not appear to have taken an active part in parish affairs. See Firth and Rait, 1: 795, 872; Green, 1: 1. It is to be noted that among the civic leaders of the parish were Henry Spurstow and Nicholas Ponfoy, two future Aldermen, and John Lawrence, a future Lord Mayor of London. Besides, Abraham Cullen and Abraham Chamberlain appear to have had premises also in this parish. For Spurstow, see Woodhead, p. 155, *s. v.* Henry Spurtow. For Ponfoy, see ibid., p. 34, *s. v.* For Lawrence, see ibid., p. 106, *s. v.*

155. Only Charles Chadwick, minister of St. Ethelburga, and Thomas Bedford, minister of St. Martin Outwich, appear to have taken part in the London Provincial Assembly in the early part of the Puritan era; Zachary Crofton of St. Botolph Aldgate participated in the late 1650s. Neither Chadwick nor Bedford played an important role in the Presbyterian movement in the City. Crofton was a rather notorious figure. See Surman, 1: 193–94, *s. v.* Bedford; p. 209, *s. v.* Chadwick; pp. 210–11, *s. v.* Crofton.

156. John Bond was identified as Deputy in 1642. See GLMS 1196/1, f. 22. William Bond was Alderman in 1649–59. See Beaven, 1: 346; 2: 72; GLMS 1196/1, ff. 15b, 48. Both Owfield and Thompson were identified as Common Councilmen in 1643. Thompson was also appointed an assessor for parliamentary subscriptions in 1642, and Owfield might well be the John Oldfield who was elected Alderman in 1649. See PRO SP 19/78, f. 60a; Beaven, 1: 342; 2: 71; GLMS 1196/1, f. 23. Richard Chiverton was to become a very prominent City Father in the future: Alderman in 1649–79, Sheriff in 1650–51, and Lord Mayor in 1657–58. He was to be knighted by both Cromwell and Charles II. "He lived long after, and was called the *Father of the City,*" as John Strype later observed. See Woodhead, p. 46, *s. v.*; GLMS 1196/1, ff. 15, 23; Strype, 2: 61. Shute was a known radical in the City from the very beginning of the revolutionary period. See *Mercurius Aulicus,* p. 170; Pearl, pp. 174, 252, 253, 255, 260–61; Tolmie, pp. 140, 171.

157. For Richard Bateman, see Pearl, p. 121. It is to be noted, however, that Bateman

continued to be Common Councilman until 1647 and sat on a number of important committees during the years of the Civil War. Cf. CLRO J. Co. Co., 40, ff. 52b, 62b, 67, 86–86b, 128, 219. Wilson was a prominent member in the Long Parliament, a colonel in the London militia, and a known Independent in the City. See *D. N. B., s. v.;* Tolmie, pp. 104, 187. Richard Clutterbucke, who was appointed only a collector for the parliamentary subscriptions in 1642, was to become master of the Mercers' Company in 1650 and elected Alderman in the same year. See PRO SP 19/78, f. 60b; Beaven, 1: 337; 2: 74; Surman, 1: 208, *s. v.* William Vincent was Common Councilman during the Civil War period and in 1647 sat on committees for the decay of trade and for the nomination of the London militia committee. He was to become a leading figure in the City on the eve of the Restoration and played an important part in it. See CLRO J. Co. Co., 40, ff. 213b, 215; Woodhead, p. 168, *s. v.;* Surman, 1: 291, *s. v.;* BL Add. MS. 36781, f. 87; BL Sloane MS, f. 970. As to the other two men, Beale was elected master of the Clothworkers' Company in 1643 and fined for the offices of both Alderman and Sheriff in 1650, while Hunt was to become master of the Ironmongers' Company in 1655. See CLRO J. Co. Co., 41, f. 31b; Beaven, 1: 349; 2: 73; Girtin, *The Golden Ram: A History of the Clothworkers' Company,* pp. 326–27; Nicholl, comp., *Some Account of the Worshipful Company of Ironmongers,* pp. 408–9. For the presence of these men in parish affairs, see GLMS 11394/1, no folio number, churchwardens' accounts, 1645–46, 47–48, 48–49, 49–50.

158. Both men were identified as Common Councilmen. See GLMS 4241/1, vestry minutes for 1646–48, which are contained in this volume of churchwardens' accounts.

159. For the social composition of this special parish, see chap. 1 above. Only a certain Salloman Vanderbrooke was appointed to the subcommittee for parliamentary subscriptions in 1642; but his identification cannot be traced. Green, 1: 1.

160. See chap. 3 below.

161. For Rawlinson, see *C. R., s. v.;* Surman, 1: 270, *s. v.* For the Whitakers, see *D. N. B., s. vv.* For Jeremiah Whitaker, see also Simeon Ashe, *Living Loves Betwixt Christ and Dying Christians. A Sermon. . . . At the Funerall of that faithfull Servant of Christ, Mr. Jeremiah Whitaker* (London, 1654), pp. 50–67. For William Whitaker, see also *C. R., s. v.;* Samuel Annesley, *A Sermon Preached at the Funeral of Reverend Mr. Will. Whitaker* (London, 1672), p. 19. For Gataker, see *D. N. B., s. v.;* Simeon Ashe, *Gray Hayres Crowned with Grace. A Sermon. . . . At the Funerall of that Revered, eminently Learned and faithfull Minister of Jesus Christ Mr. Thomas Gataker* (London, 1655), pp. 41–54.

162. Ruthworth, 6: 788; Surman, 1: 190, 281, *s. vv.*

163. Norman G. Brett-James, *The Growth of Stuart London* (London, 1935), pp. 187–212; Pearl, pp. 11–12, 40. The inhabitants of the St. Gabriel Fenchurch, St. Olave Hart Street, and Allhallows Barking in 1638 included, respectively, the following: (1) William Courteen, Peter Fountain, George Franklin, John Rushaut, and William Langhorne; (2) Sir John Wolstenholme, Sir Abraham Dawes, Alderman John Highlord, and [Thomas] Burnell; and (3) Richard Carwarden, Marmaduke Rauden, and Thomas Crathorn. Some of these men were known Royalists, and none of them appeared to have been associated with the parliamentary and Puritan factions in the City. See Dale, pp. 3–4, 62, 66. For the Royalist connections of some of these men, see Pearl, *passim.*

164. The ministries at both St. Katherine Coleman and St. Margaret Pattens were vacant in 1648, and the ministry at Allhallows Staining was not firmly settled in most of the time during the Puritan era. See Shaw, 2: 103–4 n; GLMS 4570/2, ff. 165, 168, 170; GLMS 4956/3, churchwardens' accounts, 1645–46 to 1660–61, *passim.*

165. GLMS 4887, ff. 502, 504, 512, 547. Cf. also chaps. 3 and 6.

166. Cf. Brett-James, *The Growth of Stuart London,* pp. 127–49; London County Council, *Survey of London,* vol. 10: The Parish of St Margaret, Westminster, pt. 1 (London, 1926).

167. Brett-James, *The Growth of Stuart London,* pp. 214–22; GLMS 3016, ff. 206–573, *passim.* Cf. also chap. 6.

168. Jordan, pp. 286, 288, 289, 291; Hill, pp. 254, 259; Pearl, pp. 163, 165; Seaver, pp. 80, 123,

155. See GLMS 1045/1, no folio number, vestry minutes, 1648, 1649, 1654–59, for the elections of the six lecturers each year. For Offspring, see Surman, 1: 262, *s. v.*

169. The nine parishes were: St. John the Baptist, St. Mary Magdalen Old Fish Street, St. Mary Mounthaw, St. Mary Somerset, St. Nicholas Cole Abbey, St. Nicholas Olave, St. Pancras Soper Lane, St. Thomas the Apostle, and St. Benet Sherehog. See Shaw, 2: 103–4n.

170. The four parishes were: St. Michael Queenhithe, St. Mary Mounthaw, St. Nicholas Olave, and St. Benet Sherehog. See Jordan, p. 41n.

171. Four of these parishes were located on the northern bank of the River. They were St. Martin in the Vintry, St. James Garlickhithe, St. Michael Queenhithe, and St. Mary Somerset. The other eight near the bank were: St. John the Baptist, St. Thomas the Apostle, St. Michael Royal, Holy Trinity the Less, St. Nicholas Olave, St. Mary Mounthaw, St. Nicholas Cole Abbey, and St. Mary Magdalen Old Fish Street. St. Benet Sherehog was the second smallest parish in seventeenth-century London. Cf. also chap. 1 above, *passim.*

172. For Haviland, see *C. R., s. v.;* Surman, 1: 238, *s. v.;* GLMS 4835/1, no folio number, churchwardens' accounts, 1644, 1647–48. For Witham, see n. 112 above; GLMS 577/1, no folio number, churchwardens' accounts, 1652–53, 1654–55, 1661–62. For the cases of St. Pancras Soper Lane and St. James Garlickhithe, see GLMS 5018/1, churchwardens' accounts, 1646, 1647; GLMS 4813/1, ff. 74, 79b, 80, 87b, 90b. For Sheppard, see GLMS 662/1, f. 122; PRO SP 19/ f. 60e; *A Paire of Spectacles for the Citie,* p. 9 [11]; Woodhead, p. 147, *s. v.* For Neale and Lockington, see GLMS 1341/1, churchwardens' accounts, 1648, 1649, 1650–51; CLRO J. Co. Co., 41, ff. 43–44.

173. See Shaw, 2: 98–116.

174. For the plan of the Presbyterian civic leaders for improving the ministerial maintenance in the City, see Liu, "The Founding of the London Provincial Assembly, 1645–47," pp. 132–33.

175. Ashe, *Gray Hayres Crowned with Grace,* "To the Reverend, and my much Honoured Brethren, the Presbyterian Ministers of the Gospel within the Province of London."

176. See George R. Abernathy, Jr., *The English Presbyterians and the Stuart Restoration, 1648–1663. Transactions of the American Philosophical Society,* vol. 55, pt. 2 (Philadelphia, 1955); L. H. Carlson, "A History of the Presbyterian Party from Pride's Purge to the Dissolution of the Long Parliament," *Church History* 11 (1942): 83–122; Ethyn W. Kirby, "The Reconcilers and the Restoration, 1660–1662," in *Essays in Modern English History in Honor of Wilbur Cortez Abbott* (Cambridge, Mass., 1941), pp. 49–79.

3

The Independents in Puritan London

Any modern researcher who has studied closely the writings of Thomas Edwards and Robert Baillie during the years of the Civil War can still palpably feel their intense fear of the specter of Independency—a specter that haunted the minds of the Presbyterian clergy throughout the entire revolutionary era.[1] Perhaps more threatening than in any other part of the country, this specter of Independency loomed large in the City of London. The City, as has been pointed out by both contemporaries and modern historians, had undergone unprecedented expansion in the previous hundred years; it had a growing population of a quarter of a million people in the early seventeenth century.[2] Consequently, although the rich merchants and the well-to-do tradesmen of the London Livery Companies continued to control the government of the City, the social structure and composition of the inhabitants in early seventeenth-century London had become much diversified, as previously observed at the beginning of this study.[3] It should be emphasized, however, that this social diversification in early seventeenth-century London must not be understood merely in terms of an oversimplified dichotomy between the rich and the poor but rather in light of the changing and divergent perceptions, observable among both the rich and the poor, regarding religion, society, and government. While this changing intellectual mentality was not unconnected with the expansion in population, it was also the vitality and complexity of the life in the City that gave birth to new ideas. Furthermore, the outbreak of the Revolution undoubtedly created a condition favorable to popular radicalism in religion as well as in politics.[4] If religious Independency had been impossible, sociologically, in the City of London without the population growth and the diversification in its social composition, it would be equally inconceivable without the changing perceptions among its citizenry and the immediate political crisis. In the light of the convergence of all these historical circumstances, the following words of Roger Williams are revealing. Williams wrote:

> The church or companies of worshipers, whether true or false, is like unto a body or college of physicians in a city; like unto a corporation, society or company of East India or Turkey merchants, or any other society or company in London; which company may hold their courts, keep their records, hold disputations, and in matters concerning their society may dissent, divide, break into schisms and factions, sue and implead each other at the law, yea, wholly break up and dissolve into pieces and nothing.[5]

The main purpose of Williams's arguments was to show that the creation and dissolution of independent church societies, like all trade companies, would not in any way impair or disrupt the life and peace of the nation. Yet this very imagery of a church as an artificially gathered body of men and women, with the analogy drawn between churches and trading companies, while no doubt appealing to those who believed in gathered church congregations as true churches of the saints, must have sounded startling to the more traditionally minded men, whether parochial ministers or civic leaders, who still looked at social institutions, whether the church or a guild, as corporations embodied historically.[6] However that may be, this was the general historical context in which the successes and failures of the Independents in Puritan London ought to be examined.

According to Robert Baillie, the Independents were "the smallest of all the Sects of the time for number," and modern historians are often of the opinion that there was little difference between the Presbyterians and the Independents either in doctrine or in church polity.[7] Baillie's oft-quoted statement, however, must be understood in its proper historical context, for he was writing in response to the Dissenting Brethren and at this point had them in his mind only.[8] Similarly, modern historians have placed much emphasis, rather unwarily, on the "middle way" of the Dissenting Brethren, as was publicly proclaimed in their *Apologeticall Narration* of 1644.[9] At the same time historians have also imposed, perhaps unconsciously, a clearly delineated denominational structure upon the early seventeenth-century Puritan movement. Consequently, a sharp distinction has been drawn between the "middle way" Independents and men of other gathered churches. The latter are considered as sectarians far more radical in doctrine and reckless in action, with whom the "middle way" Independents had no association and from whom they were distinguishable.[10] While this may be true in the later years of our period, what is lacking in such judgments, however, is a full recognition of the undefined, complex, and changing positions of the Puritan groups, especially leaders of the gathered churches, during the twenty years of the Revolution.[11] In fact, both in principle and in association, the "middle way" Independents had intrinsic and close affinity with men of the gathered churches, at least in the early stages of the revolutionary era.[12] In this broader sense, the Independents, both the "middle way" group and their sectarian friends, constituted,in spite of Baillie's statement, an important group, in number as well as in influence.

Furthermore, it is to be noted that even the divisions between the Presbyterians and the Independents began to become hardened only when the Civil War was near its end. The open conflict between the Presbyterians and the Independents, which eventually broke out in 1645, must not conceal the fact that there had, indeed, existed a united Puritan brotherhood and alliance, strenuous as it might have been, at the beginning of the Revolution. As Hugh Peters once argued, what was an Independent "but an overgrown Puritan?"[13] It was only natural, therefore, that when the Revolution began, all Puritan groups—future Presbyterians, future "middle way" Independents, and future sectarians—were allies against a common enemy: the Laudian episcopate. It would be wrong, of course, to say that there was no difference either in doctrine or in polity between the Presbyterians and the Independents, for the leaders of both sides were well aware of their different positions in both areas. In fact, as early as 1641, Thomas Edwards, astute and staunch Presbyterian divine and polemicist, was already warning against the danger of Independency and called upon "all the Sonnes of Sion to endeavour in their places, the putting out of this fire, before it goe too farre."[14] Cassandra-like, Edwards's early warning was untimely. At that juncture the Independents—that is, both the "middle way" men and the so-called sectarians—were an essential part of a united Puritan front, because they were, indeed, praised, more often and more highly than not, in the writings of John Vicars, another Presbyterian pamphleteer and propagandist, who later joined Edwards in virulent attacks upon Independency and the Independents.[15] In spite of the warnings of Edwards in 1641, therefore, the leading Presbyterian and Independent divines in London concluded a written agreement for united action.[16] Both sides pledged that "(for advancing of the publicke cause of a happy Reformation) neither side should preach, print, or dispute or otherwise act against the other's way; And this to continue 'til both sides, in a full meeting, did declare the contrary."[17] Or, as Robert Baillie afterward put it, "we have to get determined to our mutual satisfaction, if we were ridd of Bishop."[18]

From the preceding account of the historical background, we shall perhaps be better able to understand the reasons why, all the later sound and fury against Independency notwithstanding, the Independents were allowed to procure a number of lectureships and ministerial positions in the City and thus to exercise their influences openly among the London inhabitants in the early years of the Revolution. What was more disturbing to the Presbyterians, of course, was the fact that, in the meantime, the Independents had formed and continued to form their own private gathered churches outside the parochial structure. Unfortunately, we have little concrete and substantial knowledge of these gathered churches in the City during the revolutionary period, for few of them have left their church records to posterity. A modern historian, after a systematic and nearly exhaustive search among contemporary sources, has identified thirty-nine such gathered churches in and about the City.[19] It is not unlikely, however, that other more obscure or more ephemeral gathered churches had also existed.[20] And some of these gathered congregations were probably rather extensive either in the number of their members or in the area they covered. Thomas Edwards later wrote that "every one of their particular Churches is not a Parish church but a Bishops Diocese, nay some of them are Archbishopricks and Provinces, far larger than the Presbyterian Provinces, reaching from *London* to *Dover,* as Dr. *Holmes,* who hath severall members there, going twice or thrice a year."[21] The case of Holmes might be unique, but there can be little doubt that a gathered church in the City could often draw its members not from a single parish but from a number of parishes of the City.

In the present chapter we are concerned with the Independents within the parochial structure of the City, for which we are fortunate to have the extant parish records and know considerably more. We shall examine to what extent and under what circumstances the Independents were able to attain the pulpits of the various London parishes, either as occasional preachers or as regular lecturers, or even, in a number of cases, as beneficed ministers. But before we proceed in this survey, let us once more turn to Thomas Edwards first, who for obvious reasons was particularly interested in searching out the activities of the Independents in the City in the early years of the Revolution. From his writings in 1644–46, we are able to gather the following account: Jeremiah Burroughes lectured or preached at Stepney, St. Giles Cripplegate, St. Michael Cornhill, and St. Mildred Bread Street; Sidrach Simpson, at St. Anne Blackfriars and St. Margaret New Fish Street; William Bridge, at St. Margaret New Fish Street and St. Magnus; [Thomas] Lamb, at St. Benet Gracechurch; Lawrence Clarkson, at St. Mary le Bow; Hanserd Knowles, at St. Christopher and St. Mary le Bow; and Hugh Peters, at St. Magnus, Allhallows Lombard Street, and Stepney, as well as the Three Cranes in the Vintry.[22] Thomas Goodwin is said to have held several lectureships in the City and "preached and published his opinion . . . at large," though the locations of Goodwin's lectureships and preaching are not given.[23] Philip Nye, Edwards admitted, had seldom preached in the City, for, since his return from exile, Nye had lived mostly in noblemen's houses and in Yorkshire; yet Edwards did not fail to add that Nye had acted "the state-parasite and played the politician more, dealing in private, underhand, and against the government of the Church of Scotland."[24] In short, in the eyes of Edwards, the extensive and perhaps insidious activities of the Independents in the City had helped spread their views all over London from Stepney in the east to Westminster in the west. He summarized:

> they do not, as we Ministers sit still expecting a call to places, but they are forward men, bestirring themselves to attain this place or that, getting such great mens Letters in their behalf, using such Ministers of note, and other persons of quality and power in parishes to make ways for them to come in, pretending to preach for nothing, &c. . . to times when few or no Lectures else are, as on the Lords day in the morning between six and

seven a clock, all those lectures at that time of the day from *Stepney* to *Westminster,* they either have possession of, or have laboured for them; yea, and to have set up others on the Lords days in the morning at Ludgate, Aldersgate, &c. if by themselves or all the friends they made, they could have effected it; and so the Lords day in the evening, when other sermons are done, they have gotten that Lecture at the *Three Cranes,* and so the Lecture on Monday night, when there is no Lecture else, besides the Exposition Lectures on week days in the severall parts and quarters of the City, and new Lectures in other eminent places of the City, which they have endeavoured to set up, if they could have obtained the Ministers consent.[25]

A closer look at the activities of the Independents in Puritan London from other contemporary sources would reveal that Edwards's descriptions, venomous as they are in intention and in characterization, hardly exaggerated the situation. After a general survey of the extant parish records and other sources, we find the presence of the Independents, at various times and in different capacities, in no less than forty-five parishes in the City of London during the revolutionary period. And, needless to say, this is by no means an exhaustive and complete list. It is to be noted, however, that the presence of an Independent in a London parish does not necessarily signify that the parish as a whole was Independent in its religious persuasion. In fact, as the cases of Henry Burton and John Goodwin will clearly show, Independents often met with strong opposition and suffered defeat even in unquestionably Puritan and radical parishes. And both Burton and Goodwin were famous and influential men, the former being known as one of the Laudian martyrs before the Revolution and the latter as "the great Red Dragon" of St. Stephen Coleman Street.[26] Nonetheless, the extent of the Independents' successes in intruding into the parochial structure of the City is impressive and far-reaching. It was undoubtedly one of the fundamental reasons for the failure of the Presbyterian experiment in Puritan London.

Contrary to the biased and disparaging characterization of Thomas Edwards, many of the Independents succeeded in obtaining their lectureships and ministerial positions in the City parishes not by insinuating themselves but rather through parliamentary appointment or parochial election, and this was true not only with the "middle way" Independents but with the so-called radical sectarians as well—at least in the early years of the Revolution. It is perhaps appropriate for us to look at the so-called sectarians first. In March 1642, for instance, John Simpson was appointed to a lectureship at St. Dunstan in the East and, a month later, to another at St. Botolph Aldgate.[27] It is interesting to note that John Simpson, who was to become one of the leading Fifth Monarchy men in London, must already have been a known radical sectarian, and it is inconceivable that his appointment to the lectureship at St. Dunstan in the East was not without the prior knowledge or even recommendation of at least some of the parishioners. We may recall that at the beginning of the revolutionary era, St. Dunstan in the East was a strongly Puritan parish with a group of known Puritan civic leaders such as

Maurice Thompson, Lawrence Bromfield, John Fowke, Robert Russell, George Hanger, William Allen, and Captain John Milton. And in November 1642 its parishioners made the largest contribution to the Parliament of all the London parishes.[28] Yet, perhaps because he was too radical a choice for most of the inhabitants, Simpson apparently did not hold the lectureship for long, for in the following May Walter Bridges, "an orthodox divine," was elected lecturer "by unanimous consent of the vestry."[29] On the other hand, Simpson's appointment to the lectureship at St. Botolph Aldgate proved to be long-lasting. One of the largest parishes outside the Wall at the east end of the City, the parish of St. Botolph without Aldgate was clearly divided religiously among its inhabitants, though in general it was a Puritan parish. During the revolutionary period, some of its civic leaders were probably political Independents and John Simpson must have had the support of these men as well as of a large number of its inhabitants in order to maintain his lectureship. In any case, in spite of Simpson's known antinomianism and millenarianism in future years and some heated controversies in the parish, he was able to continue in his lectureship in the parish until 1659.[30]

Similarly, Nathaniel Holmes, another future Fifth Monarchy man, was appointed lecturer at St. Michael Bassishaw in early 1642 and to the rectory of St. Mary Staining sometime in the following year.[31] Holmes's lectureship at St. Michael Bassishaw was, again, a brief one, but he maintained his ministry at St. Mary Staining even beyond the revolutionary years, until his ejection in 1662.[32] St. Michael Bassishaw, as we have seen previously in this study, was one of the old and substantial parochial communities in the City, and its inhabitants were understandably more conservative in their social outlook. Even though some of its civic leaders were clearly Puritan in their religious persuasion and active in political affairs in the City in the early years of the Revoltuion,[33] yet Holmes, who, as has been described earlier in this chapter, was a radical sectarian with his own gathered church congregations from London to Dover, was certainly too radical a choice for such a parish. In any case, we find no trace of him in the parish records.[34] On the other hand, St. Mary Staining, which was one of the poorest parishes in the City, appears to have had a group of Independent laymen among its inhabitants, for even long after the Restoration, Holmes was said to have been a "teacher to a Church lately meeting at St. Mary Stayning, London, according to the Order of the Gospel."[35]

Furthermore, some of the so-called sectarians appeared to have been actually chosen as preachers or lecturers by various parishes in the City. In 1641 at St. Olave Old Jewry, a certain Mr. Feake, "preacher of the word of God," was chosen "to read the divinity lecture every Sabbath day in the afternoon."[36] This was in all probability Christopher Feake, also a leading Fifth Monarchy man in London during the 1650s.[37] In the same period we find Simpson (probably John Simpson) preaching at St. Christopher and John Webster at St. Benet Gracechurch.[38] In 1643–44 Daniel Dyke was lecturer at

St. Martin Ludgate and, in the following year, both St. Matthew Friday Street and St. Vedast Foster Lane petitioned for Dyke's appointment as their minister.[39] John Tombes, too, served either as lecturer or as minister at St. Gabriel Fenchurch in 1644–45.[40]

As has been noted earlier in this chapter, the presence of Independents, especially sectarians, in a London parish is by no means sure evidence that the parish itself was Independent or radical in its general religious persuasion. In fact, almost all the parishes mentioned above were to turn out to be conservative or clearly Presbyterian parochial communities in future years during the Puritan era. In the parish of St. Olave Old Jewry, as we have seen, the Presbyterian church government was to be formally established in 1646, with William Vaugham, George Almery, John Frederick, and John Mascall as its ruling elders, all of whom were also prominent civic leaders in the City of London during the revolutionary period.[41] In light of this, it is all the more remarkable to know that Feake was once chosen lecturer of the parish, though its future regular ministers and lecturers were all Presbyterians such as Ralph Robinson, Immanuel Bourne, John Fathers, and John Wells.[42] St. Martin Ludgate was another London parish in which the Presbyterian church discipline was officially adopted by a general vestry in 1646, and in which Stanley Gower and Thomas Jacombe, both renowed Presbyterian divines, were to serve the cure successively.[43] Among its civic leaders were William Hobson, Thomas Arnold, William Jeston, and Matthew Fox, and four of its lesser inhabitants signed the 1645 petition for strong Presbyterianism.[44] Dyke's lectureship in this parish in 1643–44, therefore, is also noteworthy. St. Christopher, too, was to become a Presbyterian stronghold in the City. Simpson's presence must have been a brief one, for its ministry was soon to fall into the hands of James Cranford, one of the staunch and active Presbyterian clergymen in the City during the revolutionary era, and its civic leaders included two strongly Presbyterian laymen: William Williamson and Joseph Vaugham.[45] Even more surprising is the appearance of John Tombes in the parish of St. Gabriel Fenchurch in 1644–45, for there were in this parish a number of royalist or court-connected rich merchants: William Courteen, Peter Fountain, George Franklin, John Rushaut, and William Langhorne. Even the Puritan civic leaders of the parish, such as Stephen White, Joseph Newman, and Humiliation Hinde, were probably moderate Presbyterians.[46] Similarly, the parish of St. Vedast Foster Lane, had a concentration of rich merchants, especially goldsmiths such as Francis Ashe, William Daniel, Henry Bedingfield, and John Jerrin, none of whom was known for religious or political radicalism. In addition, Richard Glyde, a prominent Presbyterian civic leader in London during the Puritan era, and Nicholas Herne, whose sons were leading Troeis in the City after the Restoration, were also its leading parishioners.[47] Again, it is rather surprising to learn that this parish petitioned for the appointment of Daniel Dyke as its minister. Perhaps the most surprising case is the appearance of John Webster in the parish of St.

Benet Gracechurch, which had among its inhabitants two influential civic figures in the City in the early years of the Revolution: Sir Jacob Gerrard and James Bunce. And Bunce was a leading opponent of Independency in 1645–47.[48] Among these parishes, perhaps only St. Matthew Friday Street may be considered a radical parish. It had been traditionally Puritan, and Henry Burton had been reinstated as its minister after his release from imprisonment by the Long Parliament. Yet it is to be noted that, ironically, as we shall see, Burton had just been ousted from the parish because of his religious Independency.[49]

From the preceding analysis it becomes clear that even the so-called radical sectarian wing of the Independents fared well in Puritan London, especially in the early stage of the Revolution. They were not only tolerated but actually supported, either by certain members of the Parliament at Westminster or by some groups of the inhabitants in the various parishes of the City. The situation was radically changed, however, after 1645—the year when the Presbyterians in the City launched an intensive campaign both against Independency and for the establishment of a strict Presbyterian church government. During the following three years, the London Presbyterian divines maintained a concerted and sustained agitation, and this clerical Presbyterian faction, which gradually took shape, not only had the support of their Scottish brethren but almost won over to their position the civic leaders of the Corporation of the City of London.[50] It was during these years that two of the most important and influential Independent ministers, John Goodwin and Henry Burton, were expelled from their livings, and that even some of the lay Independent civic figures were threatened.[51] It is understandable, therefore, that with the exception of John Simpson as lecturer at St. Botolph Aldgate, and Nathaniel Holmes as minister at St. Mary Staining, the radical sectarian Independents disappeared from the parochial churches of the City. It is also during these years, however, that these men became far more radicalized in attitude as well as in action.[52] When they returned to the scene after the collapse of the Presbyterian movement in 1647–48, many of them became leaders of the Fifth Monarchy Movement, and two of the City parishes, Allhallows the Great and St. Thomas the Apostle, were turned into centers of religious and political radicalism. Allhallows the Great became not only the meeting place of John Simpson's gathered church congregation but also the chosen site for a national convention of Fifth Monarchy men.[53] And from 1650 to 1654 the pulpit of this City parish church was dominated by such men as Christopher Feake, Samuel Highland, John Spencer, Henry Jessey, Vavasor Powell, and John Simpson.[54] During these same years John Rogers became the minister of St. Thomas the Apostle in 1652–54.[55] In addition we find John Simpson, John Goodwin, Vavasor Powell, and John Canne serving either as preachers or as lecturers at St. Mary Abchurch in 1648–50;[56] Christopher Feake preaching at St. Pancras Soper Lane in 1649[57] and serving as minister at Christ Church in

1652;[58] John Webster preaching at Allhallows Lombard Street and possibly Hanserd Knowles at St. Mary Woolchurch in the same year;[59] and Nathaniel Holmes preaching at St. Michael Crooked Lane in 1654–55.[60]

More important than the activities and intrusions of these radical sectarians were the presence of, and the positions held by the "middle way" Independents, that is, the Dissenting Brethren and their close associates, who were patronized by parliamentary leaders, respected by the Puritan brethren, and finally supported by Cromwell. We may recall that according to Thomas Edwards, Jeremiah Burroughes lectured at St. Giles Cripplegate, St. Michael Cornhill, and St. Mildred Bread Street; Sidrach Simpson, at St. Anne Blackfriars and St. Margaret New Fish Street; and William Bridge, at St. Margaret New Fish Street and St. Magnus. In fact, the activities of the "middle way" Independents in the City parishes were far more extensive. Before we turn to the Independent incumbents in the City, let us briefly survey their activities either as occasional preachers or as elected lecturers. In 1642 George Cokayne was lecturer at Allhallows Barking, and in the same year the parish of St. Pancras Soper Lane sought to procure William Greenhill and William Carter to preach in its parish church. And Greenhill and Burroughes were also lecturers at Stepney.[61] In 1643 Walter Cradock, who had just fled to London from Wales, accepted a lectureship at Allhallows the Great; and Thomas Brooks was preaching or serving the ministry at St. Martin Orgar in 1643–45.[62] During the years of 1644–46, William Strong was elected lecturer at St. Dunstan in the West, Thomas Goodwin was probably lecturer at St. Benet Gracechurch, and Joshua Sprigg was chosen lecturer by the parish of St. James Garlickhithe.[63] In future years Thomas Brooks lectured at St. Thomas the Apostle in 1650–51;[64] Walter Cradock preached at Allhallows Lombard Street in 1650; Seth Wood was appointed vicar of Christ Church in 1654; and Philip Nye became a teacher at St. Bartholomew by the Exchange in 1656.[65] The parish of St. Michael Crooked Lane was a unique case. Its minister, Joseph Browne, who maintained his ministry throughout the Puritan era, was probably not a Puritan. Yet, we find Thomas Goodwin lecturing there in 1646–47, George Cokayne preaching there in 1648, William Carter lecturing there in 1650–58, and Thomas Mallory lecturing there in 1659–60.[66] As has been pointed out previously, this survey is by no means complete or exhaustive. In the late 1650s, for instance, Alderman Robert Tichborne founded a lectureship in the parish of St. Olave Silver Street,[67] and we can be almost certain that the men chosen for this lectureship could only be Independent ministers.

In actuality, some of the Independent divines became settled incumbents, at various times and for longer or shorter terms, in a number of the City parishes during the revolutionary period. In the preceding pages reference has already been made to John Goodwin at St. Stephen Coleman Street, Henry Burton at St. Matthew Friday Street, Nathaniel Holmes at St. Mary Staining, and John Rogers at Allhallows the Great. In addition, Independent ministers accepted parochial benefices in at least another fourteen parishes in the City: Joseph Caryl at St. Magnus; John Cardell at Allhallows Lombard Street; Matthew Barker first at St. James Garlickhithe and then at St. Leonard Eastcheap; William Strong at St. Dunstan in the West; Joseph Symmonds at St. Mary Abchurch; Thomas Brooks at St. Margaret New Fish Street; Henry Scudder at St. Mildred Poultry; George Cokayne at St. Pancras Soper Lane; Robert Bragge at Allhallows the Great; Samuel Dyer first at St. Nicholas Olave and then at Allhallows on the Wall; Samuel Lee at St. Botolph Bishopsgate; Sidrach Simpson and John Loder at St. Bartholomew by the Exchange; and Tobias Conyers at St. Ethelburga. We may now turn to some of these parishes for a closer look at the Independent ministries in Puritan London.

St. Magnus had been one of the traditionally Puritan parishes in pre-Revolutionary London. Its minister had been Cornelius Burgess, who was to become one of the most active and politically important Puritan clergymen both in the City and in national affairs during the Puritan era.[68] After Burgess left the cure, the parish apparently rejected an appointee of the Bishop of London, and finally Caryl became its minister in 1645.[69] Yet it appears that the general religious attitude of the parish was a moderate one, neither strongly Presbyterian nor extremely Independent. And Caryl himself was a moderate, or perhaps even a conservative, Independent; as such, he was probably the only Independent divine who ever participated in the Presbyterian church government in the City of London.[70] The triumph of Independency and the Independents in the parish of Allhallows Lombard Street more clearly reflected the changing course of the Revolution. John Cardell, who became a known independent in 1648, had been the curate of the parish before 1640. It is not clear whether he had been a Puritan. Yet, after the old incumbent of the parish had been sequestered, Cardell became its minister.[71] During the years of the Civil War, Allhallows Lombard Street was strongly Presbyterian in its civic leadership. Thomas Cullum, Richard Young, and Richard Waring were all leading civic figures from this parish.[72] It is not surprising, therefore, to find Cardell appointed a trier for the Third Classis of the London Presbyterian church system, and on at least one occasion he served as moderator.[73] With the collapse of the Presbyterian faction in the City in 1647–48, both Cardell and the parish became closely associated with the Independents. On 17 October 1648, for instance, the vestry adopted the resolution that "Mr. Thomas Goodwyn, minister of Gods Word shall be thankfully accepted to preach each other Lord's day the afternoon in our church and to administer the sacrament to his congregation at such times as his soe doinge may not preiudice us nor wee him."[74] How long Goodwin's congregation used the parish church of Allhallows Lombard Street is not known, but, as has been noted, Walter Cradock preached here in 1650 and in 1652, when Cardell was ill, John Webster was invited to supply the ministry for him.[75] However, in 1657–58, Cardell left the parish and Thomas Lye, who had been lecturer in the parish in the mid-1640s, returned to become its rector.[76]

The parish of St. Mary Abchurch appears to have had a group of Independent laymen among its inhabitants, though in the early years of the Civil War there was no clear sign of religious Independency. In fact, the living was sequestered in 1643 from Benjamin Stone first to John Rawlinson, a Presbyterian divine, and the parish took the Covenant in the same year.[77] Yet, when Rawlinson left the cure for the benefice at Lambeth in 1646, the parish chose Joseph Symmonds as its minister.[78] During the following three years, the pulpit in the parish church of St. Mary Abchurch was completely dominated by Independent divines: John Simpson, John Goodwin, John Canne, Vavasor Powell, and Joseph Symmonds.[79] In addition, John Goodwin also moved his own gathered congregation here sometime after he had been ousted from St. Stephen Coleman Street in 1645.[80] The predominance of the Independents in this parish, however, seems to have declined in the 1650s until John Kitchen, a Presbyterian minister, came to the cure in 1655.[81] Like St. Mary Abchurch, the parish of St. James Garlickhithe clearly had a group of Independent laymen among its parishioners, for Matthew Barker was chosen as its minister in 1643 and upon Barker's recommendation, Joshua Sprigg was elected lecturer in 1645.[82] Even after Barker publicly proclaimed his Independent principles concerning ministry and church discipline, his election was confirmed by the parish in 1646.[83] After Barker's departure from the parish in 1648, another Independent minister, John Onge, was alected in 1655,[84] though in the meantime Zachary Crofton, a controversial and quarrelsome Presbyterian clergyman, served the cure from 1651 to 1654. Crofton's ministry ended in a sordid conflict between him and the parish.[85] Another parish that had a strong lay Independent faction was St. Margaret New Fish Street. In 1646 William Bridge, as noted before, was chosen as its lecturer, and two years later Thomas Brooks was elected minister "with a full and free consent."[86] Upon his election, Brooks laid down several specific conditions under which he would accept the call to the ministry.[87] Apparently, he met with some opposition to his conditions in the parish, but he continued to serve the ministry until 1660.[88]

The parish of St. Dunstan in the West deserves special attention because it was undoubtedly one of the most radical parishes in the City from the very beginning of the revolutionary era.[89] In 1641, in a contested and perhaps manipulated election, the old civic leaders were ousted, and the new civic leaders in this parish during the revolutionary period included Alexander Normington, Richard Browne, William Perkins, Francis Allen, Matthew Hinde, John Halleywell, Anthony Webb, Gilbert Gynes, and Praise-God Barbone.[90] Yet, surprisingly, the parish appears to have been very moderate in its general religious persuasion, though some of its civic leaders were, indeed, very radical either in religion or in politics or in both.[91] In fact, it was one of the London parishes in which the Presbterian church government was officially established by the vestry in 1646, with Andrew Perne as minister and William Ball, Francis Allen, Thomas Scott, John Glover, Ralph Farmer, Alexander Normington, William Perkins, John Smith, Thomas Edwards, Edward East, Thomas Cooke, and John King as ruling elders.[92] It was upon the resignation of Perne in 1647 that William Strong, who had been lecturer in the parish from 1644, became its minister.[93] But Strong was a moderate, perhaps even a conservative, Independent.[94] What is more interesting is that Strong left the parish in the early 1650s exactly when the civic leadership fell into the hands of such men as Alexander Normington, Praise-God Barbone, and Gilbert Gynes.[95] And Strong's successors both as lecturer and as minister were two leading Presbyterian divines: Thomas Manton and William Bates.[96] Finally it may be added that Thomas Goodwin was consulted by the parish of St. Stephen Walbrook in 1646–47, when it was searching for a minister.[97] It appears, however, that Goodwin either declined to accept or failed to obtain the ministry at St. Stephen Walbrook.[98]

All in all, it seems certain that Independent ministries were established and accepted in seven of the parochial communities in the City before the collapse of the Presbyterian faction in 1647–48.[99] If we put these Independent ministries and activities in the City alongside those of the sectarians either as occasional preachers or as regular lecturers, we may easily see that to the Presbyterians the success of the Independents in the City of London during the years of the Civil War was indeed threatening.

It was also during these years, however, that, as was pointed out earlier in this chapter, two of the Independent ministers, Henry Burton at St. Matthew Friday Street and John Goodwin at St. Stephen Coleman Street, suffered unexpected defeat and were actually ousted from their benefices. It may be said that they were the victims of the Presbyterian agitation in the City in 1645–47, which has been discussed previously in various contexts.[100] Yet, a closer look at these two cases may further reveal the complex nature of religious life in Puritan London.

The parish of St. Matthew Friday Street had been a traditionally Puritan parochial community in the City with Henry Burton as its minister from 1621 to 1634.[101] After the suppression and imprisonment of Burton by Archbishop Laud, the ministry fell into the hands of two Anglicans, Joseph Browne and Robert Chestlin.[102] As might have been expected, the parish maintained its traditional Puritan attitude. In 1641 one hundred and nineteen of its parishioners took the Protestation, and in the following year, as noted before, thirty inhabitants in this parish contributed £588 to the Parliament with the addition of another £170 being brought in by "well-affected" young men.[103] After his release from imprisonment, Burton was first appointed as its lecturer and, upon the sequestration of Chestlin, became its minister.[104] But, surprisingly, in April and May 1645 the parish presented petitions against Burton to the Committee for Plundered Ministers and requested his sequestration.[105] The reason given by the parish was that Burton had refused to officiate in accordance with the Directory for Public Worship, which had been adopted by the Westminster Assembly and approved by the Parliament earlier in the year. To be sure, Burton, whose religious position had been one of radical Independency, would not be likely to accept a form of worship that had been formulated largely by the Presbyterians in the Westminster Assembly.[106] It is not known whether the petitions against Burton from the parish had been instigated by the Presbyterian faction in the City, but, given the fact that a strong Presbyterian campaign had been just launched in the City at this very juncture, it is not inconceivable that the two events were connected, at least indirectly. On the other hand, however, it is reasonably clear that the petitions against Burton were the work of certain Presbyterians in the parish.[107] Eventually, the case was settled when unpaid tithes from 29 September 1642 to 29 September 1645—a total of £89.15s.7d.—were collected and paid to Burton, on condition that upon receiving the money, he would return all the keys of the parson's house and give a written agreement under his own hand to "discharge the parishioners of all tithes, duties, and demands whatsoever."[108]

The expulsion of John Goodwin from the parish of St. Stephen Coleman Street was more tempestuous. Called by a modern historian "the Faubourg St. Antoine of London" in the English Revolution, the parish had long been a traditionally Puritan parochial community in the City of London, and in comparison was far more important than St. Matthew Friday Street, whether in wealth, in the social and political status of its civic leadership, or in terms of the number of its inhabitants.[109] And John Goodwin was certainly a far more influential Puritan divine than Burton, with more important political connections and a larger popular following. Yet, Goodwin, too, was ousted from his vicarage in 1645. Again, it is inconceivable that the defeat of Goodwin in his own parish was unconnected with the Presbyterian campaign in the City, though it was the concrete issue of the exclusion of parishioners from the sacrament of the Holy Communion which brought the conflict to a head. The issue had its origin in a general vestry meeting held on 12 and 14 December 1643, in which it was resolved that "all those that shall desire and be found worthy by Mr. Goodwin and such as he shall nominate in the parish or the major part of them and the parish approves of to partake of the sacrament in this parish shall submit to have their names writ downe in a book kept for that purpose by which they shall be accounted members of this church and Congregation."[110] Clearly, John Goodwin and his followers were attempting to turn the parish church into an Independent congregation, as the last clause of the above resolution unmistakably testifies. Whether or not this resolution was actually carried out is unknown, but there can be no doubt that such an attempt would meet strong opposition of the parishioners who did not belong to Goodwin's gathered church and faction and thus did not share his fundamental principle of religious Independency.

Consequently, a conflict had broken out between Goodwin and the parish by the summer of 1644, for on 15 August a committee was appointed to settle their differences.[111] The dispute apparently continued until the middle of 1645, when on 12 May the two sides—six men nominated by Goodwin and six men nominated by the parish—met in a final attempt to settle the dispute.[112] Unfortunately, the vestry minutes did not record the arguments from both sides. Again we may recall that this was the year of the Presbyterian campaign in the City and it is not surprising that Goodwin and his faction lost. By 1 August 1645 Goodwin had been sequestered and William Taylor, a Presbyterian divine, chosen minister of the parish.[113] Unlike Henry Burton, however, John Goodwin would have his revenge, for after the collapse of the Presbyterian faction in the City in 1647–48, not only was Goodwin reinstated as lecturer of the parish but his gathered church was officially recognized. In the vestry minutes for 11 November 1649, we read the following statement:

> fforasmuch as it hath pleased the All-wise God by the hand of the present supreme Authoritie of this Nation to reinstate his faithfull servant Mr. John Goodwin into his place in Coleman street Where he is willing to bestowe his labours soe it may bee without preiudice, to that Church of Christ, to whom he is united and with whome hee hath walked hitherto, is [*sic*] in annother place, Wherefore it is desired one behalfe of that Church, That they may have the same libertie and accomdacon in the publicke meetinge place of Coleman street.[114]

Alderman Isaac Pennington and Col. Owen Rowe were the leading signatories to this order, which included five particular conditions favorable to Goodwin's gathered church congregation.[115]

The collapse of the Presbyterian faction in London created, directly or indirectly, opportunities for the Independents within the parochial structure of the City, if they were willing to accept such ministerial charges. As has been observed, the preaching of the "middle way" Independents as well as their sectarian friends was greatly increased in the City during the early 1650s.[116] From 1648 to 1659, therefore, the Independent divines became parochial ministers in at least eight more parishes in the City of London.[117]

It should be noted, however, that the triumph of the Independents in these City parishes under the Commonwealth and the Protectorate was not in all cases directly related to the collapse of the Presbyterian faction in the City or, to put it more bluntly, with the purge of Presbyterian ministers. In fact, after Goodwin's triumphant return, William Taylor maintained his ministry at St. Stephen Coleman Street.[118] Only in three of the parishes, we may say, did the Independents succeed as a result of the collapse of the Presbyterian faction. In others the ministry had not been firmly established and now, perhaps with the fear of a Presbyterian conformity removed, the Independents were willing to accept the ministerial charges. One of these parishes had long been a radical parochial community, and the coming of the Independents was only a natural development.

The parish of St. Leonard Eastcheap was clearly Presbyterian during the 1640s, with Henry Roborough as its minister and Tobias Lisle, Nehemiah Wallington, and John Wallington its ruling elders.[119] It was after Roborough's death that Matthew Barker was chosen minister of the parish, and he served the cure from 1650 to 1661.[120] Although the Wallingtons continued to participate in the Presbyterian classical government,[121] it may safely be said that Barker's election is certainly a clear indication that the Presbyterian influences in the parish had declined. After all, the parish had a number of political Independents such as Stephen Estwick, Samuel Lee, Henry Bonner, Thomas Player, and Richard Waring, who could now exercise their influence in the election of the parish minister.[122] The parish of St. Pancras, Soper Lane, too, was clearly Presbyterian in the early years of the revolutionary period, though its ministry does not appear to have been firmly settled. Yet during the 1640s it was mostly Presbyterians who served either as occasional preachers or regular lecturers in the parish—George Smith, Christopher Goade, William Thomas, John Sedgwick, Humphrey Chambers, John Arrowsmith, Anthony Burgess, and Christopher Love.[123] It was with the collapse of the Presbyterian faction in the City and the radicalization of the Revolution in 1648–53 that George Cokayne became its minister, and the pulpit of the parish church was also made available to other Independent preachers such as Nicholas Lockyer, Christopher Feake, and John Rogers.[124] Unlike the parish of St. Leonard Eastcheap, however, the Independents were unable to maintain their position in this parish for very long, for after 1653 Presbyterian divines returned and sometimes even Anglican clergy were invited to preach here.[125] Even less successful was the presence of the Independents in the parish of St. Bartholomew by the Exchange, which resulted in a long and tempestuous controversy. And this might have been expected, for St. Bartholomew by the Exchange had been a very strongly Presbyterian parochial community not only in its ministerial association with the Presbyterian movement in the City but also in the political involvement of its civic leaders. In 1645 Thomas Cawton, one of the active and influential Presbyterian divines in the City, was chosen as minister, while among the Presbyterian civic leaders in the parish were Col. Samuel Harsnett, Captain Richard Venner, Captain John Jones, and William Webb.[126] And both Cawton and Jones wee deeply involved in the Presbyterian movement in the City in 1645–47.[127] Even after the collapse of the Presbyterian faction in the City, and especially after the flight of Cawton to Holland because of his involvement in Christopher Love's plot, the parish remained defiant in its religious attitude. In fact, in 1651–54, the parish actually twice elected an Anglican minister, George Hall, for the cure.[128] It was under such circumstances that Sidrach Simpson and John Loder were appointed to its ministry, and that Nye's gathered church congregation was also allowed to worship in the parish church.[129] But the presence of the Independents at St. Bartholomew by the Exchange led to long conflicts, first over tithes, then over the use of the parish church by Nye's congregation, and finally over Loder's title to the living.[130] Predictably, as the revolutionary era was drawing to a close, the Independents lost, and Loder was ordered to be kept out of the parish church, by force if necessary.[131]

The Independent ministries in the other five London parishes were less eventful. St. Nicholas Olave was a small parish in an overchurched area of the old City, with many poor people in it but few substantial or well-to-do tradesmen. Its ministry was never firmly settled during the revolutionary period. Samuel Dyer became its minister in 1654 only to leave it in the following year to serve the cure at Allhallows London Wall, where Andrew Janeway, probably an old Puritan of the prerevolutionary tradition, had been minister from long before the Revolution until his death in 1654 or 1655. And Dyer continued to serve the cure until 1660.[132] St. Botolph Bishopsgate was a large parish outside the Wall and its inhabitants consisted of mostly poor tenants. It also appears that there was some difficulty for tithes to be collected in the parish. In any case, its ministry was never firmly established until 1655, when Samuel Lee came to the cure. It was said that Lee was unwilling to accept the living, but he was personally solicited by Cromwell. He continued in the ministry until his resignation in 1659.[133] It is also known that Tobias Conyers, at one time a member of John Goodwin's congregation, became the minister of the parish of St. Ethelburga.[134]

The remaining parish to be discussed, Allhallows the Great, was one of the radical parishes in the City during the period of the Revolution. The parish of Allhallows the Great had very early contact with the Welsh Independents. In 1643, as has been noted, when the Llanvaches church fled to London, they worshiped in the parish church of Allhallows the Great, and the Llanvaches minister, Walter Cradock, accepted a lectureship here. Although during the 1640s John Downham, a Presbyterian divine, served as its minister, it is reasonably clear that Presbyterianism was never established in this parish.[135] On the contrary, the religious attitude in this parish became far more radicalized during the revolutionary era. In the early 1650s, as has been pointed out earlier in this chapter, it became the center of the Fifth Monarchy movement in the City of London.[136] It was also during these years that Robert Bragge was chosen as its minister. In spite of the rising tide against Puritanism, the vestry of Allhallows the Great courageously attempted to retain their Independent minister even after the Restoration. In their vestry minutes for 13 December 1660 we read the following resolution:

It was Ordered & agreed uppon That a Petition shalbee forthwth made and delivered to the Right Reverend Willm Archbishopp of Canterbury That Mr Robert Bragge whom (by Gods mercy) we have had experienced for about Eight yeares, of his being Sound in Doctrine, & of a holy Conversation, may be continued to be our Minister, & settled in the place for the time to come.[137]

The petition was, of course, presented in vain, and Bragge was to be ejected in 1662.[138] After all, the Puritan era was over.

In conclusion, it must be emphasized that the preceding survey of the Independent divines in Puritan London can hardly reveal the true historical significance of these men during the revolutionary era. As we shall see in another context, among the members of the Independent churches in Puritan London were some of the most prominent and influential civic leaders of the period.[139] More important it was the Independent divines who, when confronted with the threat of a new religious authoritarianism, dissented and ably defended their right to dissent, thus contributing significantly to the establishment of an important tradition for modern man—the tradition of the liberty of conscience.[140]

NOTES

1. See Thomas Edwards, *Reasons against the Independent Government of Particular Congregations: As also against the Toleration of such Churches to be erected in the Kingdom* (London, 1641); idem, *Antapologia: Or, A Full Answer to the Apologeticall Narration* (London, 1644); idem, *Gangraena: Or A Catalogue and Discovery of many of the Errours, Heresies, Blasphemies and pernicious Practices of the Sectaries of this time, vented and acted in England in the four last years* (London, 1646); Robert Baillie, *A Dissvasive from the Errours of the Time* (London, 1645); idem, *Letters and Journals.*

2. See Brett-James, *The Growth of Stuart London,* especially chap. 20: "Estimates of London's Population in the Seventeenth century."

3. See chap. 1 above.

4. Milton wrote in his *Areopagitica:* "Behold now the vast city, a city of refuge, the mansion house of liberty, the shop of war hath not there more anvils and hammers working, to fashion out the plates and instruments of armed justice in defence of the beleaguered truth, than there be pens and heads there, sitting by their studious lamps, musing, searching, revolving new notions and ideas, wherewith to present, as with their homage and their fealty, the approaching Reformation." Though idealized by Milton in the above passage, London was, indeed, a city of "new notions and ideas" during the English Revolution. The Thomason collection of tracts and pamphlets published mostly in London during the Revolutionary period testifies unmistakably to this point. See G. K. Fortescue, ed., *Catalogue of the Pamphlets, Books, Newspapers and Manuscripts Relating to the Civil War, the Commonwealth, and Restoration Collected by George Thomason, 1640–1660,.* 2 vols. (London, 1908).

5. Roger Williams, *The Bloudy Tenent of Persecution for Cause of Conscience Discussed in a Conference between Truth and Peace* (n.p. [London], 1644), reprinted in A. S. P. Woodhouse, ed., *Puritanism and Liberty. Being the Army Debates* (1647–49) *from the Clarke Manuscripts with Supplementary Documents* (London, 1966), p. 267.

6. For the Presbyterian clerical attitude, see Edmund Calamy, *England's Looking Glass* (London, 1642); idem, *An Indictment against England Because of her Self-Murdering Divisions* (London, 1645); Richard Vines, *The Impostvres of Seducing Teachers Discovered* (London, 1644); Simeon Ashe, *The Church Sinking* (London, 1645); John Brinsley, *The Araignment of the Present Schism of New Separation in Old England* (n.p., 1646); William Spurstowe, *The Magistrates Dignity and Duty* (London, 1654); Richard Vines, *Obedience to Magistrates, Both Supreme and Subordinate* (London, 1656).

7. *A Dissuasive from the Errours of the Time,* p. 53. The common view has been that the

only difference between the Presbyterians and the Independents was that between a centralized and a decentralized national church. For further analysis of their differences both in doctrine and in church polity, see Tai Liu, *Discord in Zion,* pp. 29–50; George Yule, *Puritans in Politics. The Religious Legislation of the Long Parliament 1640–1647* (London, 1981), chaps. 5, 6, 7.

8. Baillie wrote: "We hope shortlie to gett the Independents put to it to declare themselves either to be for the rest of the Sectaries, or against them. If they declare against them, they will be but a small inconsiderable companie." Baillie, 2: 299.

9. Woodhouse, *Puritanism and Liberty,* pp. [34], [45]–[46]; William Haller, *Liberty and Reformation in the Puritan Revolution* (New York, 1655), pp. 116–19.

10. Denominational church organizations became more clearly defined only after the Restoration. In the early seventeenth century, Independents, Baptists, and, to a certain extent, even the radical sectarians were often in close association and could not be separated. For their affinity in doctrine and in association, see Nuttall, *Visible Saints,* and Tolmie, *The Triumph of the Saints.*

11. See Liu, *Discord in Zion,* chaps. 3–5.

12. Ibid., chaps. 1–3.

13. Quoted in Edwards, *Gangraena,* p. 183: "And then . . . why pray may not an Independent be a Common Councel man? What is he, but an overgrown Puritan, or words to that effect?"

14. *Reasons against the Independent Government of Particular Congregations,* "To the Honourable the Knights . . . of the Commons House of Parliament."

15. See John Vicars, *God in the Mount. Or, England's Remembrancer* (London, 1641); idem, *God on the Mount, or, a Continuation of England's Parliamentary Chronicle* ([London], 1643); idem, *God in the Mount. Or, England's Parlaimentarie-Chronicle* (London, 1644). In these earlier pamphlets, Vicars praised Henry Burton as "that learned and pious Pastour, that faithfull servant and courageous witnesse of the precious Truth," John Lilburne as "that undaunted pious young Gentleman," and Isaac Pennington as "a most pious wise and active Gentleman." No attack on the Independents, lay or clerical, can be detected in these earlier writings of John Vicars.

16. See Edwards, *Antapologia,* pp. 240–43; W. R. [i.e., William Rathband] *A Brief Narration of Some Church Courses* (London, 1644), "Preface to the Reader;" John Vicars, *The Schismatick Sifted. Or, The Picture of Independents* (London, 1646), pp. 15–16; Baillie, *A Dissuasive,* pp. 130–31; idem, 1: 311; 2: 117.

17. Vicars, *The Schismatick Sifted,* pp. 15–16.

18. Baillie, 1: 311.

19. Cf. Tolmie, p. 245: "Index of Separate Churches in London."

20. For instance, there was clearly in existence during the 1650s a gathered church in the parish of Holy Trinity the Less. See GLMS 4835/1, churchwarden's accounts, 1655–58.

21. Edwards, *Gangraena,* pt. 1, p. 72.

22. For Burroughes, see Edwards, *Antapologia,* p. 216; idem, *Gangraena,* pt. 1, pp. 72, 111; pt. 3, p. 108. For Simpson, see Edwards, *Antapologia,* pp. 215–16; idem, *Gangraena,* pt. 2, pp. 16, 151. For Bridge, see Edwards, *Antapologia,* p. 216; idem, *Gangraena,* pt. 1, pp. 72, 103, 216. For Lamb, see Edwards, *Gangraena,* pt. 1, p. 120. For Clarkson, see ibid., pt. 2, p. 7. For Knowles, see ibid., pt. 1, pp. 215–16. For Peters, see ibid., pt. 1, pp. 182–83; pt. 3, p. 124. Strictly speaking, Clarkson, a Ranter, was not an Independent.

23. See Edwards, *Antapologia,* pp. 216–17; idem, *Gangraena,* pt. 1, p. 71.

24. Edwards, *Antapologia,* p. 217.

25. Edwards, *Gangraena,* pt. 1, p. 71.

26. The sobriquet is given in Edwards, *Gangraena,* pt. 2, p. 31.

27. Shaw, 2: 301 (22 March 1641/2), 302 (29 April 1642).

28. See chap. 1 above. The parish of St. Dunstan in the East was the birthplace of John Simpson, and a certain Fabian Simpson was one of the vestrymen in the early 1640s.

29. GLMS 4887, f. 497 (22 May 1642).

30. See J. A. Dodd, "Trouble in a City Parish under the Protectorate," *English Historical Review* 10 (1895): 43–44; Seaver, pp. 283–85.

31. *C. R., s. v.;* Shaw, 2: 301 (18 March 1641/2).

32. It is not known how long Holmes lectured in the parish of St. Michael Bassishaw, if he lectured there at all. Early in the following year the living was sequestered from John Gifford to Charles Newton. See *W. R.,* p. [48], *s. v.* John Gifford; Shaw, 2: 308; Hist. MSS. Comm., *Fifth Report,* Appendix, p. 75. For his ministry at St. Mary Staining, see GLMS 1542/2, f. 44–44b; BL Add. MS. 36781, f. 32b.

33. Among the civic leaders of the parish in the early years of our period were Robert Alden, Robert Gardner, Edwin Browne, George Dunne, Francis Greenway, Walter Pell, and Christopher Packe. Alden and Gardner were probably royalists, while the others were probably all religious or political Presbyterians in the 1640s.

34. Only the churchwardens' accounts of the parish for our period have survived, and no payment to Holmes either for the lecture or for preaching was recorded for the year 1642–43.

35. *C. R., s. v.*

36. GLMS 4415/1, f. 101b.

37. Christopher Feake was to become a leading figure of the radical Fifth Monarchy movement in the late 1640s and early 1650s, but he had already been included among the London sectarians in Edwards, *Gangraena,* pt. 2, p. 63. Given the fact that other future Fifth Monarchy men such as John Simpson and Nathaniel Holmes were appointed to London lectureships in the same period, the identification of this Feake as Christopher Feake may not be entirely off the mark. The lectureship was for six months, and Feake was succeeded by [Thomas?] Gibbs. Finally, Ralph Robinson, a future prominent Presbyterian divine in London, was chosen on 13 October 1642. See ibid., ff. 107b, 113b, 117b.

38. E. Freshfield, ed., *Accomptes of the Churchwardens of the Paryshe of St. Christofer's in London, 1575 to 1662* (London, 1885), p. 92 (Simpson preached four sermons in the year 1640–41); GLMS 1568, f. 628 (13s. 4d. was paid to Webster for a Fast day sermon). Again, the identifications in these two cases are tentative. The parish of St. Christopher was to become one of the strongly Presbyterian parishes in London; yet, we may recall, Thomas Edwards did mention Hanserd Knowles's preaching in this parish in the early years of the Revolutionary period. The parish of St. Benet Gracechurch, too, was basically a Presbyterian parish, especially in its civic leaders such as James Bunce. It is to be noted, however, that there must have been lay Independents in the parish, for Thomas Goodwin was to preach in this parish in 1644–45. See n. 22 above; GLMS 1568, f. 643.

39. This identification of Dyke in the parish of St. Martin Ludgate as Daniel Dyke is also tentative, but again, Thomas Edwards included Ludgate among the London parishes where Independent lectureships were established. The petitions of St. Matthew Friday Street and St. Vedast Foster Lane were both unmistakably for Daniel Dyke. See GLMS 1311/1, f. 140; GLMS 4214/1, f. 19; BL Add. MS 15669, ff. 76, 150b, 164b; see above, n. 25.

40. BL Add. MS. 15669, ff. 64b, 69. The parish sequestrators were ordered to collect tithes and pay John Tombes for his services before the appointment of John Wallis in November 1644 to the ministry of the parish.

41. See chap. 2 above.

42. GLMS 4415/1, ff. 107b, 119b, 124b, 128b, 133.

43. GLMS 1311/1, ff. 138b, 148b.

44. See chap. 1 above. Mahony, "Presbyterianism in the City of London, 1645–47," p. 105. The four were Walter Lee, Hugh Radcliff, Edward Toking, and Philip Combes. Mahony had included several other signatories of the 1645–46 petitions as of St. Martin Ludgate, but their identifications are uncertain. For the above four, see GLMS 1311/1, ff. 139b, 152–54; GLMS 1313/1, churchwardens' accounts for 1649–50 and 1651–52.

45. GLMS 4425/1, ff. 33b–34a, 35b; E. Freshfield, ed., *Minutes of the Vestry Meetings and Other Records of the Parish of St. Christopher le Stocks* ([London], 1886), p. 35. See also chaps. 1 and 2 above.

46. See. chap. 1 above; BL Add. MS 15669, f. 69: Sir Stephen White, Humiliation Hinde, Joseph Newman, Richard Little, and William Coleston were appointed sequestrators of the parish.

47. See chap. 1 above.

48. See chap. 1 above; the ministry of the parish appears not to have been firmly settled until William Harrison came to the cure in 1646. A certain Mr. Grey, Nathaniel Dyke, and Daniel Cawdry had been chosen as ministers in the previous years. See GLMS 4214/1, ff. 19, 21; GLMS 1568, ff. 631, 637, 643, 646, 651; *W. R.*, p. [56], *s. v.* William Quelch.

49. BL Add. MS. 15669, ff. 60b, 72, 80, 91, 96, 142; GLMS 3579, f. 77. It is interesting to note that while the Committee for Plundered Ministers did not act in favor of Burton, it appointed, on the other hand, Colonel John Venn to provide for the cure of the parish. Since Venn was a leading Independent both in the Long Parliament and in the City, the petition for Daniel Dyke and his appointment to the ministry of St. Matthew Friday Street were clearly not accidental. There must have been some political maneuvering behind the scenes. But it is not known whether Dyke actually came to the parish.

50. For a general discussion of this Presbyterian movement in the City of London, see Liu, "The Founding of the London Provincial Assembly, 1645–47," pp. 109, 134.

51. See below nn. 105–15; CLRO J. Co. Co., 40, ff. 166–66b.

52. See Liu, *Discord in Zion*, chaps. 3–4.

53. See Louise F. Browne, *The Political Activities of the Baptists and Fifth Monarchy Men in England during the Interregnum* (Washington, 1911), pp. 19, 21, 18.

54. Ibid., pp. 48, 67, 97, 114.

55. GLMS 622/1, ff. 149, 151b. Rogers was referred to either as minister or as rector in the churchwardens' accounts for 1652–53 and 1653–54.

56. GLMS 3891/1, no folio number, see churchwardens' accounts for 1648–49 and 1650. Though generally a moderate Presbyterian parish, there were apparently a number of Independents among its parishioners, including, indeed, Edmund Rozier, one of the lay pastors among the gathered churches in London. And, in 1647, Joseph Symonds became its minister. Both *D. N. B.* and Dr. G. F. Nuttall have identified Simpson as Sidrach Simpson, but it is doubtful that the latter would have been associated with John Goodwin, Vavasor Powell, and John Canne in these particular years. See *D. N. B., s. v.* Sidrach Simpson; Nuttall, p. 12. In any case, the ministry was officially considered vacant both in 1648 and in 1652. Shaw, 2: 103, 109.

57. GLMS, 5019/1, f. 135, vestry minutes for 30 October 1649.

58. Surman, 2: 108: "ye Eldership is incomplete & Mr. Feak is of another judgmt." Shaw did not include the returns of the 5th classis in 1652 in his work.

59. GLMS 4049/1, f. 17b [i.e., f. 31b]; GLMS 4051/1, f. 143; GLMS 1012/1, f. [22], vestry minute, 29 December 1652 (the name of Knowles was given as Hanellet[?] Knowles).

60. GLMS 1188/1, f. 363.

61. See n. 23 above; Shaw, 2: 304; GLMS 5019/1, f. 81; Nuttall, *Visible Saints*, pp. 12, 17.

62. Ibid., p. 35; GLMS 959/1, churchwardens' accounts for 1643 and 1644; *W. R.*, pp. [61]–[62], *s. v.* Brian Walton; BL Add. MS 15669, ff. 98, 116.

63. GLMS 3016/1, ff. 241, 263; GLMS 2968/3, f. 671; GLMS 2968/4, ff. 40b, 42b, 43b; GLMS 1568, f. 645; GLMS 4813/1, f. 68b.

64. GLMS 662/1, ff. 143, 145b.

65. Thomas Richards, *A History of the Puritan Movement in Wales* (London, 1920), p. 74; *C. R., s. v.* Seth Wood; Freshfield, ed., *The Vestry Minute Books of St. Bartholomew Exchange in the City of London* (London, 1890), pt. 2, pp. 59, 61–62, 73–74. In the case of Philip Nye, his position in the parish church was ambiguous. John Loder was appointed to the rectory of St. Bartholomew by the Exchange by Oliver Cromwell, and Nye assisted him as teacher. But they were never officially accepted by the parishioners, who claimed that they ministered only to their own gathered congregation in the parish church.

66. Surman, *Register-Booke of the Fourth Classis*, p. 61: "Michaels-Crookedlane, wher Mr. Browne is minister, have noe Elders, & doe refuse to make any Election of Elders . . . & he himselfe neglect to afford his due assistance by his presence." GLMS 1188/1, ff. 198, 309, 340, 344, 349, 358, 377, 387. In fact, Thomas Goodwin in 1648 requested permission to administer the Sacrament of the Holy Communion to his own gathered congregation in this parish church. The

churchwardens of the parish for that year reported the request to the classical meeting, and the request was naturally denied.

67. GLMS 1257/1, ff. 85, 96. We may also point out that at some time during the Revolutionary era Nicholas Lockyer was lecturer at St. Benet Sherehog. See *C. R., s. v.;* Tolmie, *Triumph of the Saints,* p. 103.

68. See *D. N. B., s. v.; C. R., s. v.*

69. GLMS 1179/1, ff. 28, 43, 53, 62. For Caryl, see also *D. N. B., s. v.; C. R., s. v.*

70. Surman, *Register-Booke of the Fourth Classis, passim.*

71. GLMS 4049/1, ff. 21b, 25b, 26; GLMS 4051/1, ff. 95, 111, 127.

72. For the civic leaders of the parish, see chap. 1 above. According to the churchwardens' accounts, the rectory was first sequestered to a Mr. [Samuel?] Fisher, who did not appear to have come to the cure. Although Cardell's admission to the ministry was as early as 1643, his induction to the rectory did not take place until sometime in 1647–48, after the death of the old incumbent. See Shaw, 2: 314; GLMS 4049/1, f. 2b; GLMS 4051/1, f. 127.

73. Shaw, 2: 400; Surman, 1: 203, *s. v.*

74. GLMS 4049/1, f. 27. Cardell preached before the House of Commons on 31 January 1648/49, the day after the execution of Charles I. See Cardell, *Gods Wisdom Justified, and Mans Folly Condemned . . . a Sermon Preached Before the Honorable House of Commons, Ian. 31, 1648* [i.e., 1649], (London, 1649).

75. See above, nn. 59, 65.

76. GLMS 4049/a, f. 26; GLMS 4051/1, f. 173.

77. *W. R.,* p. [58], *s. v.* Benjamin Stone; GLMS 3891/1, no folio number, see churchwardens' account for 1643. The parishioners appeared to be very conscientious about the parish church and its minister in 1643, when among other things, they spent £5. 18s. 6d. to repair the parson's house for Rawlinson and £90 to build new pews in the church.

78. Ibid., see churchwardens' account for 1646.

79. See above n. 56.

80. GLMS 4458/1, f. 161. In 1649, when John Goodwin and his Independent church returned triumphantly to St. Stephen Coleman Street, the vestry of the latter resolved that Goodwin and his congregation "may have the same libertie and accomodacon in the public meeting place of Coleman streete, as with readynes was granted them by the people in Abchurch lane parish."

81. GLMS 3891/1, see churchwardens' accounts for 1655–60; BL Add. MS. 36781, f. 33b; *C. R., s. v.* John Kitchin.

82. GLMS 4813/1, ff. 62, 68b.

83. Ibid., ff. 69b, 70.

84. Ibid., ff. 87b, 121–31. It appears that Onge served the ministry until 1658.

85. Ibid., ff. 113–19b. It was stated that Crofton "hath most ungratefully asperst & villified this p[ish] generally (that have bine soe gratefull to him)."

86. GLMS 1175/1, no folio number, see vestry minutes, 1 September 1646 and 8 April 1648.

87. *C. R., s. v.;* Surman, *Register-Booke of the Fourth Classis,* p. 82.

88. Brooks left the parish sometime in 1660, when he was succeeded by George Smallwood. GLMS 1175/1, see vestry minute, 22 January 1660/61; BL Add. MS 36781, f. 36b.

89. See chap. 1 above and chap. 6 below.

90. For these civic leaders, see GLMS 3016/1, *passim;* GLMS 3018/1, *passim.*

91. Praise-God Barbone, for example, was not only a lay pastor of a Separatist gathered church in London but also a radical leader in politics.

92. GLMS 3016/1, ff. 269, 280.

93. Ibid., ff. 291, 321, 322.

94. It appears that Strong was never associated with the radicals among the Independents. Cf. Liu, *Discord in Zion,* pp. 120–21, for Strong's rather conservative position in the early 1650s.

95. GLMS 3016/1, ff. 356, 369, 374.

96. Ibid., ff. 389, 399, 403.

97. GLMS 593/4, no folio number, see churchwardens' account for 1646–47.

98. Thomas Watson became the minister of St. Stephen Walbrook in 1648. See GLMS 593/4, churchwardens' account for 1647–48.

99. To these seven should be added, of course, John Goodwin at St. Stephen Coleman Street, Henry Burton at St. Matthew Friday Street, and Nathaniel Holmes at St. Mary Staining.

100. See above, n. 50.

101. For Burton's career, see *D. N. B., s. v.;* Nuttall, p. 52; Seaver, p. 249; Tolmie, pp. 94, 110.

102. GLMS 3579, f. 61; *W. R.,* p. [44],, *s. v.* Robert Chestlin.

103. GLMS 3579, f. 339. The list of those who took the Protestation in 1641 is placed at the end of this volume. It is rather interesting to observe that Robert Chestlin's name is among the signatories. See also chapter. 1 above.

104. Shaw, 2: 304; GLMS 3579, ff. 67, 70; Baillie, 1: 277; BL Add. MS. 15669, f. 72, where it is said that Burton was appointed to the ministry on 16 June 1643.

105. Ibid., ff. 60b, 63.

106. Ibid., ff. 72, 80, 87.

107. See above, n. 49, for the role of Colonel John Venn and the petition of certain parishioners for Daniel Dyke.

108. GLMS 3579, f. 77; BL Add. MS. 15669, ff. 142b, 164b–65.

109. See Pearl, p. 183; see also David A. Kirby, "The Radicals of St. Stephen's Coleman Street, London, 1624–1642," *The Guildhall Miscellany* 3, no. 1 (April 1970): 98–119.

110. GLMS 4458/1, f. 125. James Russell, Samuel Avery, Richard Ashurst, William Mountain, George Foxcroft, and a certain "Mr. Smith minister" were appointed to assist Goodwin on this matter.

111. Ibid., f. 129.

112. Ibid., f. 134. The six nominated by Goodwin were Colonel Owen Rowe, Mark Hildesley, Dr. [Nathan?] Paget, John Price, William Mountain, and Richard Ashurst. On the parish side were Samuel Avery, Thomas Fitzwilliams, Joseph Sibley, Edward Lucas, Andrew Kendrick, and Thomas Barnardiston.

113. Ibid., f. 135; BL Add. MS. 15669, ff. 66, 68b, 74, 169. John Goodwin was sequestered from the vicarage on 22 May 1645. Jeremiah Whitaker was first appointed to officiate in the parish church after Goodwin's sequestration.

114. GLMS 4458/1, f. 161.

115. Ibid. Other signatories included Mark Hildesley, Thomas Barnardiston, and Richard Ashurst.

116. See above, nn. 53–60.

117. This figure is based upon the extant London parish records and is therefore by no means a comprehensive one.

118. GLMS 448/1, ff. 164, 200, 254. Taylor was again officially chosen vicar in 1659, but he apparently left the parish in 1660. In early 1661 the name of the minister was "Alford," who was identified as an "orthodox." BL Add. MS. 36781, f. 34.

119. Surman, *Register-Booke of the Fourth Classis, pasim.*

120. *C. R., s. v.;* BL Add. MS. 36781, f. 33b, where Barker was mistakenly identified as a "Presbyterian."

121. Surman, *Register-Booke of the Fourth Classis,* pp. 157–58, *s. vv.* John Wallington and Nehemiah Wallington.

122. These names were included in the 1638 assessments of the parish. Since the records of the parish for our period have been lost, we have no way of knowing whether all these men remained in the parish until the 1650s. It may be assumed that not all of them had left. See Dale, pp. 88–89.

123. GLMS 5018/1, see churchwardens' accounts for the years of 1644–47; GLMS 5019/1, ff. 74, 75, 76, 90, 99, 102, 117, 119, 127.

124. GLMS 5018/1, see churchwardens' accounts for the years of 1648–50; GLMS 5019/1, f. 169.

125. GLMS 5018/1, see churchwardens' accounts for the years of 1654–58; GLMS 5019/1, f. 135.

126. Freshfield, *Vestry Minute Books . . . St. Bartholomew Exchange,* pt. 2, p. 11 and *passim.*

127. See Pearl, "London Puritans and Scotch Fifth Columnists," pp. 320, 323.

128. Freshfield, *Vestry Minute Books . . . St. Bartholomew Exchange,* pt. 2, pp. 40, 44, 48.

129. Ibid., pp. 73–74; Shaw, 2: 108, 268–70.

130. Freshfield, *Vestry Minute Books . . . St. Bartholomew Exchange,* pt. 2, pp. 59, 61, 62, 70, 72.

131. Ibid., p. 77.

132. *C. R., s. v.* Samuel Dyer; GLMS 5090/2, no folio number, see churchwardens' accounts for 1655–56 and 1657–58.

133. *C. R., s. v.* Samuel Lee. See Hist. MSS. Comm., *Sixth Report,* Appendix, pp. 6, 32, 35, 98, 115, for examples of the difficulty in collecting tithes in this parish during the Revolutionary era.

134. *C. R., s. v.* Tobias Conyers.

135. GLMS 819/1, ff. 135, 172; GLMS 818/1. No elders were mentioned.

136. See above, nn. 53–54.

137. GLMS 819/1, f. 200.

138. BL Add. MS. 36781, f. 34; *C. R., s. v.* On 12 March 1660/61, perhaps in anticipation of the return of an Anglican minister, the parish appointed twenty men as feoffees for the management of the rents and tenements of the parish. See GLMS 891/1, f. 201.

139. See chap. 7 below.

140. See Tai Liu, "In Defence of Dissent: The Independent Divines on Church Government, 1641–1646," *Transactions of the Congregational Historical Society* 21, no. 3 (May 1972): 59–68.

4

The Anglican Clergy in Puritan London

One of the most interesting and also intriguing subjects in a study of Puritan London is the fortunes, or rather the misfortunes, of the orthodox Anglican clergymen of the City parishes during the revolutionary era. Undoubtedly more vulnerable than the lay royalists as a social group, and more directly under the shadow of parliamentary power at Westminster and Puritan radicalism in the City, these men became the early victims of the Civil War. As many a contemporary Anglican writer observed, however prejudicial his views might be, the Anglican world was crumbling under the irresistible hostile forces from both above and below. From above, the Long Parliament, or rather the Puritan faction in it, issued an "imperious order" to encourage men to oppose established forms of worship;[1] from below, the zealous multitude, swept along by the rising tide of radicalism in the City, acted in rebellious and iconoclastic tumults in many London parishes.[2] Furthermore, parliamentary committees were created to receive and examine petitions and articles exhibited against the old incumbents by their discontented parishioners.[3] As a result, the so-called scandalous ministers were often molested, sequestered, and imprisoned, and as the Civil War proceeded, the orthodox Anglican clergymen in London were almost all replaced by Puritan ministers.[4]

There can be little doubt that in the early years of the revolutionary era, there surged a wave of Puritan radicalism in London, which, Hydra-like, showed its ugly heads in city parishes prior to and contemporaneous with the semi-legal proceedings in Parliament for future reformation. In 1648 Robert Chestlin, the sequestered rector of St. Matthew Friday Street, published a lengthy account of the sufferings of London Anglican clergymen. After having given a vivid description of how "in diverse Churches unheard of violences were offered to Ministers officiating in full congregations by a few Sectaries, yet scarce durst any man either rescue the Minister, or defend their own Religion," Chestlin listed, parish by parish, the names of the old incumbents who had been molested, abused, sequestered, or forced to resign.[5] Of course, Chestlin himself was one of the first London Anglican clergymen to suffer from the Puritan persecution. St. Matthew Friday Street had been traditionally a Puritan parish, with Henry Burton, one of the three famous Laudian martyrs in London and later a radical Independent, as its minister until he was silenced and prosecuted by Archbishop Laud. In early 1642 parishioners of St. Matthew Friday Street petitioned the House of Commons to order Chestlin to readmit Burton as a lecturer,[6] and a few months later Chestlin was arrested on the accusation made by the Lord Mayor, Isaac Pennington, for preaching against Parliament "with dangerous points tending towards the disheartening of the well-affected." Pennington must have been informed by the "well-affected" parishioners. And, according to Chestlin, he had been violently assaulted in his house before he was committed to the Compter and afterward sent to the Colchester jail in Essex.[7] In actuality, radical Puritan riots against old Anglican incumbents had taken place much earlier in some parishes in and about the City. The first incidents of parish tumult, so far as we know from official records, occurred in the churches of St. Olave and St. Savior in Southwark, and in St. Magnus at the City end of the London Bridge. Early in June 1641, as some orthodox parishioners from these Southwark parishes complained, "great disorders [had been] committed in these churches during the administration of the communion."[8] According to the curate of St. Olave, what happened there was that the radicals "insisted upon his administering the sacrament to them sitting after 500 had received it kneeling, and [they] threatened if he refused to drag him about the church by the ears."[9] At the same time, three church-wardens of St. Olave, who were obviously of the radical faction, presented a counterpetition. According to these men, "many hundreds of parishioners refused to come to the sacrament on account of the rails around the altar, and after having sought in vain the parson, Dr. Thomas Turner, for a remedy for the prevention of disorder, they quietly removed the rails and disposed of them for the benefit of the parish."[10] The fact was probably that the rails were pulled down by riotous mobs in these parishes. Similar riot also occurred at St. Paul's Cathedral in the very heart of the City.[11]

These incidents were not, of course, isolated cases. Such popular Puritan radicalism was soon to spread to other parishes in and about the City. At Lambeth, which had been turned into a prison, the soldiers who guarded the palace were instigated by Dr. Layton [Leighton], also one of the Laudian martyrs, and his zealous wife to break into the church, and they tore the Book of Common Prayer into pieces upon the communion table.[12] At St. Mary Woolchurch, some men, especially a certain Mr. Hunt, "defaced a very faire windowe, & other Emblems of antiquity in that church" shortly after the parliamentary order to remove "superstitious" monuments and images of "idolatry" from parish churches.[13] In Christ Church, the church organ was obstructed by Peter Mills, a bricklayer and churchwarden, who was to become a Common Councilman in 1642–43, by filling its pipes with brickbats.[14] To be sure, iconoclasm was to become a common feature of the Puritan reformation among the London parishes in the years to come, as clearly testified to by the churchwardens' accounts, which, in most cases, recorded, item by item, the expenses incurred by iconoclastic actions.[15]

This London Puritan radicalism found its most practical and perhaps also most effective outlet in presenting petitions and articles to parliamentary committees against the old Anglican parish clergy. Dozens of such petitions are known, and a number of them were also published.[16] The charges against the old incumbents are mostly typical of the Puritan attitude toward tradition in ceremony or doctrine, which had survived the English Reformation or which had been revived in the English Church during the Laudian supremacy. In short, the articles are usually concerned with things that were viewed as "Popish" in the eyes of the Puritans: "superstitious ceremonies," "idolatrous disciplines," "erroneous doctrines," "Popish tenets" as well as pluralities of benefice, lack of preaching, misconduct, and scandalous lives.[17] It will be unnecessary and perhaps pointless for a modern student of history to pass judgment on the validity of such charges. The intention of the Puritan petitioners was clear and unmistakable: they wanted to get rid of the old incumbents and to replace them with men of their own religious persuasion and their own choice.

What is surprising, however, is the fact that the tumultuous actions of the London radicals were left uncurbed and the triumph of London Puritan radicalism unchallenged. In light of this, one would have to reconsider the moderate position of the parliamentary leaders in the early years of the Revolution. However moderate John Pym and his group might be in their own political and religious policies, they apparently needed the London radicals as a visible and concrete basis of their own political power. Mob actions were surely not suppressed, if not purposely tolerated. Chestlin accused the House of Commons of "countenancing all those who oppose the established worship of God." Another contemporary writer claimed that "to further the rebellion intended," the London civic leaders, in alliance with leaders of the Parliament such as Lord Say and John Pym, "cause the very dregs and scum of every parish to petition against the orthodox clergy."[18] In the case of the London Anglican clergymen, it was perhaps even imperative for the parliamentary leaders to accept the position of the London radicals. After all, as we have observed, the pulpit had to be controlled. And as we shall see, the Anglican clergymen in London were certainly not far behind their Puritan brethren, wading in the muddied waters of politics to protect their vested interests or, to put it more favorably, to defend their own beliefs in church and state.

The opposition of London Anglican clergy to parliamentary policies ranged from passive noncooperation to public denunciation. Richard Owen,

Rector of St. Swithin, for instance, was accused by the churchwardens that when a parliamentary declaration was given him to be read in the church, he did so without saying anything further to stir up the people. And he refused to contribute a penny for the parliamentary cause at the vestry.[19] Similar charges were also made against Roger Warfield, curate of St. Benet Fink.[20] William Haywood, Rector of St. James in the Fields, was even worse in his demeanor. He had the parliamentary Protestation read in the church in such a ridiculous, absurd, and disdainful manner and with such scorn and jeering that those parishioners who were "forward and well-affected" toward the parliamentary cause because the target of laughter among their neighbors. Of course, Haywood would not say a word to encourage people to take the Protestation either at the pulpit or elsewhere, but much to the contrary.[21] Thomas Tuke, Vicar of St. Olave Old Jewry, simply refused to read parliamentary orders, and when he had one read by mistake without knowing its contents, he held up his hand and cried, "The Devils confound all Traitors, Rebels and turbulent Spirits." And he preached against those who had contributed money to parliament.[22] Robert Pory, Rector of St. Margaret New Fish Street, too, refused to read parliamentary orders and spoke openly against Puritans and the Scots.[23] Matthew Griffith, Rector of St. Mary Magdalen Old Fish Street and St. Benet Sherehog, was imprisoned as a delinquent by the House of Commons on the ground that he had inveighed against Parliament with statements "to the stirring up and fomenting of seditious divisions and Mutinies in [the City], hindering of the Public Defense of the Kingdom."[24] Timothy Hutton, Curate of St. Giles Cripplegate, was also charged with making contemptuous statements against parliamentary orders.[25] Bryan Walton, Rector of St. Martin Orgar, openly asserted that the M. P.s for the City of London had all been chosen for factious reasons: Thomas Soames for his refusal to pay ship-money, Samuel Vassall for his refusal to pay the king's customs, Isaac Pennington for his assistance rendered to silenced Puritan ministers, and Matthew Cradock for his assistance in sending some of the Puritans over to New England.[26] And John Squire, Vicar of St. Leonard Shoreditch, affirmed publicly in the pulpit that the Papists were indeed the king's best subjects.[27]

To be sure, the opposition of the London Anglican clergymen to Parliament was not confined merely to words alone. At the parochial level, the Anglican clergy could become a rallying point for a counterrevolutionary movement in the City, however futile such an attempt would be in the early years of the revolutionary era. In the parish of St. Giles Cripplegate, for instance, the selected vestry was called William Fuller's "conclave," who disposed the principal officers of the parish at their pleasure, preferring their friends and allies and keeping out the "godly" and the "well-affected," that is, of course, the Puritans.[28] At St. Giles in the Fields, divers of the vestry were called the "creatures" of William Haywood, none of whom took the Protestation in 1641 as had been directed by the Parliament.[29] And certainly in many a London parish, the old Anglican incumbent had his friends.[30] When the Civil War was coming, William Stamp, Vicar of Stepney, was taken into custody because he had violently interfered with the enlisting of volunteers in the Stepney churchyard on 22 July 1642 to serve in the parliamentary army under the Earl of Essex.[31] It was also reported that £500 with plate and muskets was found in the house of William Fuller and taken to the Guildhall.[32] And not a small number of the London Anglican clergymen later served as chaplains in the Royalist army, as did their Puritan brethren on the other side during the Civil War.[33] On the other hand, even a moderate man such as Thomas Fuller, the future famous church historian, was found to have been involved in a peace movement.[34]

In any case, as has previously been observed, the Parliament needed to control the pulpit in order to create a favorable climate of opinion, whereas the London Puritans wanted to replace the old incumbents in their parishes with ministers of their own religious predilection and their own choice. As a result, therefore, the London Anglican clergymen were, sooner or later, sequestered or forced to leave their places, "so that," as Chestlin put it in 1648, "at this day, there is not a true orthodox minister left, freely speaking his conscience, or exercising his ministry, in the whole city."[35] And all this was done in spite of the fact that many a parish in London was deprived of settled ministry either temporarily or, as we have seen in another place, throughout the Puritan era. Again according to Chestlin, when the Earl of Northumberland spoke to "Calamy and Pedant, of whom, indeed, even the nobility stand in awe," about supplying about fifty churches in London void of settled ministry with the sequestered Anglican clergymen, Calamy replied, "God forbid!"[36]

Chestlin has given a bleak picture of the London Anglican clergymen during the revolutionary period, and in general it is probably very close to truth, especially for the earlier years of the Civil War. After a thorough examination of the parish records of this period, however, it becomes clear, rather to the surprise of a modern researcher, that the Puritan victory was never complete in London. As we shall see, the activities of orthodox Anglian clergymen in Puritan London, however difficult and unlawful, and the resilience of the tradition of the Church of England, however tenuous and constantly under attack, indicate that loyalty to the Anglican tradition continued to be an important force in the City, which, under different historical circumstances, would reappear and regain its influence. The Puritan Revolution was, after all, one of the minority. It was perhaps no exaggeraton when it was claimed that in an out-parish of above 5,000 communicants, many of whom were noblemen, knights, gentlemen, and respectable citizens, the radicals could draw none of any quality.[37] Edward Finch, Vicar of Christ Church, asserted that the legal proceedings against him were incited only by one William Greenhill, "the Arch-incendiary of Christ Church parish."[38]

A closer look at the Anglican clergymen in Puritan London also shows that although in many London parishes, especially during the first few years of the Revolution, the old incumbents were often subject to molestation and abuse by radical parishioners, generosity and respect were not totally lacking. At St. Benet Gracechurch, for instance, a petition was first presented against its old incumbent, William Quelch, in December 1641 and several further actions were taken in 1643–44, when Samuel Foot and John Brett were churchwardens and when Nathaniel Dyke and Daniel Cawdrey were chosen as ministers. Nevertheless, Quelch apparently remained in the parish and received an annuity of £20, which was regularly paid until 1653–54 when he died.[39] At St. Michael Queenhithe, John Hill entered into an agreement with the parish, under which an annual allowance of £25 was taken from the tithes for a minister to serve the cure in his place. He thereby kept his living, and when he died in 1645, the parish spent £11. 5s. 10d. for his funeral.[40] At St. Bartholomew by the Exchange, parishioners contributed £13.11s. 5d. to John Grant in April 1643 as a gratuity in appreciation for his permission to allow them to choose John Lightfoot as lecturer on Sundays, though Grant had complained in the previous year that he was "very rudely opposed" by a group of church intruders when he tried to preach in the absence of Simeon Ashe, then lecturer. Even when he was finally forced to resign from the living in 1644, he negotiated successfully with the parish for a lease of the rectory for twenty-one years at £50 p.a.[41] Similarly, the parish of St. Swithin proposed to offer Richard Owen £70 if the latter would voluntarily resign his right and interests in the rectory to its patron, the Worshipful Company of Salters, though, as we have seen, articles against him had also been exhibited by some parishioners. Owen probably declined the offer and continued to collect his fifth after the sequestration.[42] At St. Bride, the vestry negotiated with James Palmer, who had offered to resign, and proposed to pay him £40, which had been due to him from the Dean and Chapter of Westminster for two and a half years' salary, if Palmer would go to the Committee for Plundered Ministers and resign because of "his infirmities that he was Ancient, his voice failed, and his hands shook."[43] At St. Lawrence Old Jewry, a parish that was always generous toward its ministers, the vestry voted £120 for Thomas Crane for leaving the charge, even though his sequestration had been ordered by Parliament. And the parish frequently continued to give gratuities to Crane.[44] When Ephraim Udal died in 1647, the parishioners of St. Augustine gave £10 toward his funeral, and Francis Roberts, the Puritan minister, offered to let him be buried in the parish church chancel and have a minister of his own choice to preach his funeral sermon, though the latter offer was declined.[45] Similarly, when John Grant died in 1654, the vestry of St. Bartholomew by the Exchange ordered his burial in the parish church chancel free of charge and £10 given to his wife as a gratuity. Shortly afterward, upon a petition of "the aged widdowe" of Grant, a group of twenty-eight parishioners promised to contribute "what everye man is pleased to spare towards such a good worke" for her maintenance during her life. And among the twenty-eight men were some of Puritan civic leaders of the parish.[46] In general, it may be added that a fifth of tithes was usually paid to sequestered ministers, and gratuities were frequently given toward the relief of their wives and children.[47]

More important, the orthodox Anglican clergymen were never completely silenced in Puritan London. In fact, as the Revolution proceeded, the Anglican voice was increasingly to be heard in the City. This was partly due to the lack of settled ministry in London parishes and also partly due to the revival of Anglican sentiments in the City either as a result of the decline of Puritan zeal or as a reaction to the rise of more radical Puritan sectaries. In some parishes Anglican clergymen were invited as occasional preachers; in others, they were elected as lecturers; in still others, they were chosen as ministers. In the middle of 1647, for instance, the Committee of Plundered Ministers learned that at St. Clement Danes, several "disaffected and sequestered persons have been enterteyned to officiate." Richard Vines, the Puritan minister, preached there only when attending the Assembly of Divines, and his colleague, a certain D. Evans, had left for the Isle of Wight.[48] On the other hand, the churchwardens of St. Alphage London Wall, were charged with allowing "malignant ministers" to officiate there with the Book of Common Prayer, while its Puritan minister, Samuel Fawcett, was driven away by the ill-affected.[49] Henry Hammond mentioned that Bruno Ryves preached in 1649 in the parish of St. Martin Orgar, which, as the Fourth Classis of the London Province had complained the year before, did not have a settled ministry and was "content with wandering ministers."[50] We also know that during the years of 1648–50 a number of ministers, many of whom were in all probability orthodox Anglican clergymen, preached at St. Mary Magdalen Old Fish Street.[51] During the years of 1650–51, we find John Piggott preaching at Allhallows Staining, Dr. Samuel Baker at St. Margaret Pattens, Humphrey Tabor at St. Lawrence Pountney.[52] In 1655–56 the parish of Allhallows London Wall, which had been traditionally a Puritan parish with Andrew Janeway as its minister, was warned by the Committee for Plundered Ministers of bringing in "scandalous" ministers to officiate in its church. And, even more significant, a strongly Puritan parish such as St. Dunstan in the East invited Anglican clergymen to preach in the late 1640s and the 1650s whenever the ministry was vacant.[53]

Before we proceed farther to the next two groups, we may first examine the social and religious circumstances in these nine parishes, under which the reappearance of Anglican clergymen during the Puritan era became possible. With the exception of St. Clement Danes, the other eight parishes were all located within the Wall in the old City and, generally speaking, had been strongly Puritan in the early years of the Revolution. It is at least safe to say that there had been active Puritan civic leaders in every one of these eight parishes. In fact, even the case of St. Clement Danes requires some explanation. Though an out-parish to the west of the city, St. Clement Danes was a parochial community with special political importance for both the City and the nation. Just outside Temple Bar, the parish, as some of its Puritan parishioners claimed, was "so considerable and populous a place, so near the City of London" and it had "more than ordinary influence into all parts of the kingdom by reason of many lodgers, and several Inns of Chancery in the parish." According to Jordan, it was a relatively rich parish, too.[54] Yet we may reasonably presume that, given its geographical location, the parishioners of St. Clement Danes probably comprised a fair number of lawyers and minor gentlemen, and its general religious climate was a rather conservative one. Now with the Puritan ministers failing to fulfill their duties, Anglican clergymen could well be invited to preach by some of its parishioners with Anglican or Royalist sympathies. As a result, the Committee for Plundered Ministers appointed sixteen men, including Colonel Silvanus Taylor and Colonel James Price, "to take especiall care that noe minister that is scandalous or disaffected or that hath been sequestred doe preach or officiate in the said Church."[55]

Among the eight City parishes, the appearance of Bruno Ryves in the parish of St. Martin Orgar was, though perhaps ironical, not at all surprising. As has been noted before, the parish of St. Martin Orgar had had a long anticlerical, if not necessarily Puritan, tradition. Many of its parishioners had refused to pay tithes to its old Anglican incumbent, Brian Walton, and some had been involved in a conflict with Walton over the issue of the communion table. Yet, during the Puritan era, the parish did not care to have a settled ministry. During the years of 1647–52, the religious life of the parish was clearly in disarray. Under such circumstances, without a settled ministry and probably with the old Puritan civic leaders gone, some parishioners could well turn to an Anglican clergyman for an occasional sermon. After all, one of the new civic leaders in the 1650s was William Peake, a future strong supporter of the restored monarchy and a future Lord Mayor of the City of London.[56] Similarly, the parish of St. Mary Magdalen Old Fish Street had never had a settled ministry after the sequestration of the old incumbent, Matthew Griffith, though some of its civic leaders such as Philip Owen, Andrew Neale, and Thomas Lockington were either religious or political Presbyterians. While Owen was not active in Puritan politics in the City, both Neale and Lockington were deeply involved in the Presbyterian-Independent confrontation during the years of 1647–51. They had subscribed to the engagement for a personal treaty with the King and consequently became disqualified for the Common Council, and Neale was also replaced as a major in the London Militia by Charles Doyly, "Tichborne's creature." It is no surprise, therefore, that Anglican clergymen such as [John?] Gwin, Dr. [Charles?] Sherwood, and Dr. [Charles?] Mason were invited to preach in this parish in 1649 and 1950.[57] The parish of St. Margaret Pattens, too, had never had a settled ministry after the sequestration of the old Anglican incumbent, James Megge. In addition, the Puritan civic leaders in this parish are few in number and they were divided. Lawrence Loe was probably a Presbyterian who subscribed for a personal treaty and thus became ineligible for the Common Council, and Richard Arnold had probably been already "a Congregational man." Again, it is no surprise that Dr. [Samuel?] Baker was invited to preach in 1650–51. In fact, in the late 1650s, Dr. Edward Hicks became the rector of the parish. Hicks was identified as an "orthodox" minister in 1661 and later conformed.[58]

The intrusion of Anglican clergymen in the other five parishes during the Puritan era is both unexpected and surprising. Three of these parishes had been traditionally Puritan, and they were among the small number of London parishes that had been able to maintain Puritan ministers before the Revolution: Elias Crabtree in St. Lawrence Pountney, Andrew Janeway in Allhallows London Wall, and Adoniram Byfield in Allhallows Staining. In a certain sense, the cases of Allhallows London Wall and Allhallows Staining may be looked upon as merely accidental aberrations. In the former, the Anglican intrusion probably happened between the death of Andrew Janeway and the settlement of Samuel Dyer; whereas, in the latter, it was between the departure of John After and the coming of Samuel Smith. Nevertheless, the political events in the City during the years of 1647–51 might well be a factor, too. The triumph of the Independents in the City probably led to the temporary eclipse and alienation of the more conservative or Presbyterian civic leaders in these two parishes: men such as Robert Haunch and Thomas Birkhead in Allhallows London Wall, and Thomas Bewley and Edmund Trench in Allhallows Staining.[59] On the other hand, the change of religious attitude in the parish of St. Lawrence Pountney was a lasting one. It appears that the general religious and political climate of St. Lawrence Pountney was a rather conservative one. Though not without wealthy tradesmen among its inhabitants, few of its civic leaders were actively involved in Puritan politics during the revolutionary period. Perhaps in actuality the radicalization of the Revolution antagonized these men—six of them were wardens and masters of the livery companies of London. Furthermore, in the 1650s, the leading man of the parish was Eliah Harvey, and the Harvey family had long had Royalist sympathies. Under such circumstances, it is understandable that Humphrey Tabor was ministering here in this parish in 1654–55, Benjamin Spencer in 1655–57, and Thomas Sutton in 1657–61, though none of them had been officially instituted.[60]

The remaining two cases are even more surprising. Both St. Alphage London Wall and St. Dunstan in the East had been strongly Puritan parishes in the early years of the Revolution, and the latter was one of the most important parishes in seventeenth-century London both in wealth and in civic leadership. In fact, the parish of St. Alphage London Wall, too, had some important civic leaders, though far fewer in number. William Hayes was Common Councilman in the years of 1642–47; John Blackwell, son-in-law of John Lambert, in 1649–51; and Edward Basse, an old friend of Stephen

Marshall, in 1652. Yet, in 1647, when a certain William Cam served as church warden, he, along with a group of his supporters, invited Anglican clergymen to preach in the parish church, and in a vestry meeting on 1 October a formal resolution was made that "there shall be a committee appointed to go to Mr. Fawcett . . . to demand the parish house." The Committee for Plundered Ministers first ordered Cam "to conform to the authoritie of Parliament" and "to give assistance to the sequestrators." And both Hayes and Blackwell were added to the sequestrators of the parish. It is to be noted, however, that the Committee did not press the case any further but hoped that "the differences hapning between the p[ishioners] of the said parish may be composed in a quiett & amicable way."[61] If the case of St. Alphage London Wall showed the limitation of the power of the Committee for Plundered Ministers, the intrusion of Anglican clergymen in the parish of St. Dunstan in the East proved that the influence of Puritan leaders even in a strongly Puritan parish was limited. In any case, in 1649–50 and again in 1655–56, when the Puritan zeal was waning and when the ministry was vacant, a number of Anglican clergymen, including Dr. Bruin Reeve and Dr. John Hewett, were invited to preach in the parish of St. Dunstan in the East, even though Puritan leaders such as John Fowke, Lawrence Bromfield, Robert Russell, and Major John Milton were still in power.[62]

In fact, some London parishes did actually attempt to have an orthodox Anglican clergyman chosen either as minister or as lecturer during the period of the Puritan triumph, though their efforts did not always succeed. As early as 1646, the vestry of St. Mary Aldermanbury decided to have Daniel Votier deliver a weekly exposition lecture,[63] and the parish of St. Peter Cornhill chose Dr. Richard Holdsworth as its lecturer.[64] In the same year the parish of St. Mary Somerset petitioned for the restoration of its old incumbent, John Cook, who had been sequestered two years before,[65] and the vestry of St. Edmund the King requested the appointment of William Launce as its minister, the sequestered rector of St. Michael le Querne.[66] In October 1647 the Committee for Plundered Ministers acted against John Jones for having officiated with the Book of Common Prayer at St. Benet Sherehog during the previous six months.[67] Philip Edlin was nominated for the ministry of St. Botolph Aldersgate, though he was not chosen in the election.[68] Samuel Baker was actually chosen at St. Michael Royal, but his election was vetoed by the Committee for Plundered Ministers, and certain parishioners were charged with bringing him in tumultuously.[69] In November 1648 Henry Hammond was chosen as parson at the vestry of St. Lawrence Old Jewry.[70] Perhaps more surprisingly, William Styles was elected minister in 1652 by the vestry of St. Michael Cornhill, which had been and still was dominated by strongly Puritan lay leaders such as John Bellamy, Richard Norton, and William Rowell.[71]

Once again the resurgence of an interest in Anglican clergymen either as ministers or as lecturers in these London parishes during the Puritan era calls for further examination of the circumstances surrounding it. With regard to these nine cases, some analyses and explanations are especially in order because, unlike the intrusions of Anglican preachers described above, the effort to have an established Anglican ministry or lectureship, either by petition or by election, represented not the sporadic actions of individual churchwardens or parishioners but the general opinion of at least a majority of the inhabitants of these parishes. And it should be noted that most of these nine parishes were unmistakably Puritan, with active and, in some cases, prominent civic leaders in power.

Of these nine parishes the cases of St. Benet Sherehog, St. Mary Somerset, and St. Michael Royal are perhaps easy to explain, and the fundamental reason was probably economic. All three parishes were undoubtedly poor benefices in early seventeenth-century London: one was the smallest parochial community within the Wall in the old city and the other two each had an overwhelming number of poor. They all belonged to the Second Classis of the Province of London, which was never formed, and none of them had a settled ministry during the entire revolutionary period. The parish of St. Benet Sherehog was by no means an impoverished parochial community, and it was not lacking in Puritan civic leaders either. In 1642, we may recall, twenty-one of its parishioners contributed £307 to the Parliament—a rather respectable amount for a parish of only twenty-eight or twenty-nine houses.[72] One of its parishioners had been appointed a lay trier for the Second Classis in 1645 and another had signed the petition for the establishment of high Presbyterianism in the following year.[73] Yet the parish was simply too small in size and its value of tithes too low to support a settled Puritan minister. Under such circumstances, it is understandable that in 1647 the church wardens and other "ill-affected" parishioners "brought in for the last six months one Mr. Jones, a sequestered minister who readeth the booke of Common Prayer abolished by p[liament]."[74] In fact, the point is not Jones's appearance in such a Puritan parish but rather the lengthy six months during which he was able to continue to officiate with the Book of Common Prayer in the City and in the very year when the Presbyterian movement was at its zenith in London. This could hardly have happened without the general approval or acquiescence of the parishioners generally.

The other two were clearly impoverished parochial communities in early seventeenth-century London. The parish of St. Mary Somerset had an overwhelming number of poor, and for their relief the parish probably often received contributions of poor money from other parishes such as St. Augustine, St. Martin in the Vintry, and St. Michael Queenhithe.[75] Its tithes, though not inadequate at £80 p.a., fell short of the usual expectations of a Puritan minister during the Revolutionary period, especially if their collection was not guaranteed.[76] It appears, therefore, that the Puritan minister, Anthony Downes, who had been appointed to the living, had returned to his benefice in the country. In the light of such conditions, it is perhaps no surprise that in 1646 the parish petitioned the Committee for Plundered Ministers for the restoration of John Cook, who had been sequestered two years before.[77] In the case of the St. Michael Royal, the value of tithes was about only £32 p.a., and it was clearly inadequate for the maintenance of a Puritan minister. Although sequestrators had been appointed by the Committee for Plundered Ministers to provide for the cure, the ministry of the parish remained vacant.[78] On 19 June 1647, therefore, the parishioners petitioned the Committee for the settlement of Samuel Baker in the parish church, in spite of the fact that "no Certificate is produced vnder the hands of any godly ministers testifyinge the pietie & desert of the said Mr. Baker but on the contrary there are sevall exceptions brought against him by the Sequestrators." However, when the parishioners' petition was denied, Baker was brought in "by force & in a tumultuous waie." And what is more surprising is that the Committee finally suspended the formerly appointed sequestrators and the conflict was "referred to the Vestrie of the said p[ish] to agree compose & settle the said differences among themselves in an amicable way."[79] The feelings of the Anglicans had to be respected in a parish in which the Puritan civic leaders were too few to manage the parochial affairs.

For the other six parishes under discussion, the election of an Anglican clergyman either as minister or as lecturer is rather unexpected. With the possible exception of St. Edmund the King, all these parishes had been strongly Puritan in the early years of the Revolution and, as has been noted before, the Prersbyterian church government was established in every one of them. The parish of St. Edmund the King appears to have been a rather conservative parish. Among its inhabitants of 1638 were Sir George Whitmore and Sir Nicholas Rainton, two of the leading Royalists in the City, though, on the other hand, two radical Puritan civic leaders, Sir David Watkins and Tobias Dixon, were also among its parishioners in the early years of the Revolution. Nevertheless, conservatives and moderates probably constituted the majority of the parishioners, and Watkins was soon to leave the parish.[80] In any case, upon the death of the old incumbent and the departure of the new Puritan minister, the parish petitioned in 1646 for the settlement of William Launce, who had probably been forced to leave the rectory of St. Michael le Querne. Although originally opposed by the Westminster Assembly of Divines as a person unfit for the appointment, Launce finally confessed his "former miscarriages" in 1648 and was willing to comply with the new church polity "in promoting God's Glory, the orthodox Faith, and the Peace of the Church."[81]

The invitation of Daniel Votier as lecturer at St. Mary Aldermanbury and the election of Dr. Richard Holdsworth as lecturer at St. Peter Cornhill, both in 1646, are rather intriguing events. The parish of St. Mary Aldermanbury, as noted on many occasions, was one of the most important Presbyterian parishes in Puritan London. With Edmund Calamy as minister and Matthew Newcomen as lecturer, the cure of the parish was well provided. Yet, on 4 March 1645/6, when some parishioners requested that "mr. Daniel Vocher . . . may have the liberty of our Church for an exposition lecture to be held upon Sunday weekly," it was "consented to by the major part of those present" at the vestry that day. And it should be noted that the vestry of St. Mary Aldermanbury had been made a general one a few years earlier.[82] The only explanation for allowing Votier to deliver the Sunday exposition lecture in this parish would be that he had been in sympathy with the Puritans in London before the Revolution, but he had been sequestered from the rectory of St. Peter Cheapside the year before. And on 29 September 1645 the House of Commons ordered to examine whether he had preached in any way against the Parliament in a sermon at Lincoln's Inn on the previous day.[83] In any case, this case indicated that even in a parish such as St. Mary Aldermanbury, there were not lacking moderate men with sympathies toward sequestered Anglicans. Similarly, in the parish of St. Peter Cornhill, there was clearly a conscious effort to choose the Anglican Dr. Richard Holdsworth as lecturer, though the parishioners were well aware of the fact that this was contrary to the position of the Parliament. In a vestry meeting on 26 March 1646, upon a proposal that a lecturer should be elected for the lecture on Sabbath days in the afternoon, Holdsworth "was by the most of then present chosen," though the vestry added: "so long as it should be approved of by the higher powers." Later in the year the parish even made the newly chosen Puritan minister declare "his willingness for the chosing of Dr. Holdsworth to be Lecturer . . . provided the Committee approved the same." It should be pointed out that during this same period the parish formally established the Presbyterian church government and elected their six ruling elders.[84] In fact, Holdsworth's election had been vetoed by the Committee for Plundered Ministers, which in "no way" would approve the petition of the parish to make him lecturer there.[85] In the light of these events, we may perhaps safely assume that there was still a strong Anglican sentiment in the parish.

The remaining three parishes actually attempted to elect Anglican clergymen as their ministers. St. Botolph Aldersgate had been undoubtedly a Puritan parish in the early years of the Revolution, and it was one of the London parishes that, as we shall see, had completely reorganized its parochial governmental structure. Yet, in an election of the parish minister in early 1647, Edlin was one of the four nominated candidates, and another nominee, a certain Mr. Sharpe, was probably also an Anglican clergyman.[86] Although neither Edlin nor Sharpe was chosen in this election, the very fact that they had been nominated in this parish is interesting. In the other cases, the Anglican ministers were actually chosen, though in neither case did the elected Anglican minister actually succeed in obtaining the living. After all, both parishes had been strongly Presbyterian in their clerical and civic leadership. In a sense both cases were immediate reactions against the triumph of the Independents in the City during the years 1647–51. It is to be noted, however, that there was probably a genuine strong Anglican sentiment in the parish of St. Lawrence Old Jewry. Sir John Cordell and Sir George Clarke had been leading parishioners of the parish. Under such circumstances, it is perhaps understandable that in a vestry meeting on 10 November 1648 Henry Hammond was chosen minister "by plurallity of Voyces (though much against the mind of some present)."[87] Similarly, at St. Michael Cornhill, in a vestry meeting on 12 July 1652, William Styles "was chosen at this vestry to come into the place of Minister in this parish." And ironically, the vestry directed the Puritan civic leaders such as John Bellamy, Richard Norton, and William Rowell to inform Styles of his election.[88] Of course, as has been observed, neither Hammond nor Styles actually came to these new charges. In the parish of St. Lawrence Old Jewry, Christopher Love was soon to be elected; whereas the parish of St. Michael Cornhill rescinded the previous election with the resolution that "none shall be propounded to officiate in the place of minister in this Church but such as are and shall be comfortable to the present Government, and performe all ministerial duties."[89]

These attempts were mostly unsuccessful; yet, in the historical context of the English Revolution, they were highly significant developments in Puritan London. And, furthermore, in a few London parishes, Anglican clergymen were successfully maintained, especially during the second half of the revolutionary era. In 1650, for instance, the vestry of St. Clement Eastcheap decided to invite Thomas Fuller to deliver a weekly lecture in the parish church, and the vestrymen went as far as to make a special resolution that accommodations should be provided for Fuller's friends and followers from other parts of the City, who would come to attend the weekly lecture at St. Clement.[90] During the following years other Anglican clergymen such as Pearson, Hall, and Hardy were all chosen as lecturers in this parish.[91] In the same years, Richard Goddard, Dr. Browning, and Dr. Gillingham had been chosen lecturers at St. Gregory by St. Paul's.[92] And John Evelyn heard the renowned Dr. Jeremy Taylor preaching there in 1654 and again Dr. Wild in 1655. No wonder Evelyn maintained that St. Gregory was the place in the City, where "the use of the old Liturgy &c." was connived at by "the Ruling Powers" of the Protectorate.[93] St. Gregory was admittedly a conservative parish in its general social composition, but St. Clement Eastcheap had been undoubtedly Puritan in the earlier years of the revolutionary era. The same was also true with the parish of St. Mary Magdalen Milk Street, where Dr. Hewet and Thomas Cartwright were chosen as ministers in 1656 after a whole decade of Puritan ministry and discipline under Thomas Case.[94] In fact, Philip Edlin had been appointed to the rectory of St. Michael Bassishaw in 1652 under the Great Seal of the Commonwealth.[95] The most recalcitrant Anglican parish in London during the Puritan era was probably that of St. Peter Paul's Wharf. As the London Provincial Assembly clearly recorded in

1652, its parishioners "cannot be induced to choose Elders nor to have a minister that may act in the government."[96] According to Evelyn, the Book of Common Prayer was openly in use there in March 1649, barely two months after the death of Charles I, and later in the year its continuous use caused a violent intrusion by soliders of the New Model Army.[97] The Anglican minister, John Williams, had been officiating in this parish, apparently with full support of the parishioners. In 1658 a special commission was created to investigate the sitation, and its report clearly stated that "the cure thereof is supplied with Constant Use of the Comon Prayer, and that the said Church is filled up with Persons from all Parts of Citty who are disaffected to Reformation." The commission suggested that it be combined with the neighboring parish of St. Benet Paul's Wharf.[98] Nothing seems to have happened, for both Williams and another Anglican clergyman, Robert Mossom, were still officiating there in 1660–61.[99]

The reasons for the successful intrusion of Anglican clergymen in these five parishes in Puritan London again varied from case to case. The parishes of St. Gregory by St. Paul's and St. Peter Paul's Wharf were clearly conservative or Anglican parochial communities in the City. St. Gregory was a large rich parish. Although it was by no means lacking in able and active Puritan civic leaders during the revolutionary period, these men appeared to have been unable to control the religious life of the parish. In fact, among its Puritan civic leaders were William Antrobus, Martin Brown, Henry Barton, and John Box, all of whom were active in politics in the City. Yet, perhaps partly because the parish church had been demolished and had to be rebuilt in the early years of the Puritan era and partly because the civic leaders were all political or religious Independents, the Presbyterian church government and discipline were never established in this parish. So in the 1650s, when the Puritan zeal began to decline, the parish turned to Anglican clergymen for service and preaching in the parish church. It is to be noted, however, that the Puritan civic leaders were still in power in the 1650s.[100] Once again, the limitation of the influence and power of the Puritan leaders in parochial life was evident. On the other hand, the parish of St. Peter Paul's Wharf was small and poor. The economic decay in the parish during the early seventeenth century was noted by Strype, and modern researches have confirmed Strype's judgment. We may safely assume, therefore, that the poverty of the parish was such that no settled Puritan ministry could be maintained.[101] As a result, the parish church, as with some of the other poor parishes in Puritan London, was open to Anglican clergymen. What is more surprising, however, is that the Anglican sentiment of the parishioners and their support for Anglican clergymen were unmistakably genuine and unexpectedly strong in such an impoverished parochial community.

The other three parishes had been all strongly Puritan in the early years of the Revolution. In the parish of St. Michael Bassishaw, six of its parishioners had been appointed in 1642 as assessors for contributions to the Parliament:

George Dunne, Walter Pell, Francis Greenway, Edward Parker, Edwin Brown, and Christopher Packe. All these men were probably religious Presbyterians. Other civic leaders of the parish during the revolutionary period included William Christmas, Abraham Church, William Flewellen, and John Rutter. With the radical developments in 1647–51, these men probably became alienated. In 1652 it was reported that the parish had "no minister, 2 elders, [who] scarce ever appear. Mr. Ashe as lecturer." When Ashe left in late 1652, Edlin was presented under the Great Seal.[102] It was possible that Edlin had taken the Engagement, but his appointment to and acceptance by such a Puritan parish is still interesting. Similarly, the parish of St. Clement Eastcheap had been Puritan in the early years of the revolutionary era and, indeed, had officially established the Presbyterian church government and discipline. Yet during the 1650s, while its ruling elders continued to participate in the proceedings of the classical government, the parish invited Anglican clergymen to be lecturers in the parish church.[103] In this case, we may assume that the change of religious attitude was a conservative reaction against the radicalization of the Puritan movement in the City with the triumph of the Independents after 1647–48. Even more Puritan and Presbyterian was the parish of St. Mary Magdalen Milk Street. It was one of the London Parishes, we may recall, that had its ruling elders officially elected in the vestry and their election recorded in the vestry minutes. And all the four ruling elders, George Cornish, Anthony Webster, Lawrence Brinley, and Francis Waterhouse, were prominent civic leaders in Puritan London. Yet, in 1649 its Puritan minister, Thomas Case, was sequestered, and its civic leaders were probably also affected by the changing events in the City. Furthermore, in the middle of the 1650s, John Robinson, a Royalist and a future Lord Mayor of London, became the leading parishioner in the parish. It is no surprise, therefore, that Anglican ministers such as John Hewett, Thomas Cartwright, and John Jones were chosen as lecturers between 1656 and 1658.[104]

Three other unique cases of the Anglican clergymen in Puritan London must be treated separately. Two of them are rather perplexing. Throughout the entire Puritan era, Dr. Robert Gell and Joseph Brown maintained their ministries in the parishes of St. Mary Aldermary and St. Michael Crooked Lane, respectively. They were clearly not Presbyterian divines, and both were, indeed, identified as "orthodox" ministers in 1661. Perhaps neither was truly orthodox Anglican. Christopher Hill has identified Gell as a Familist, and Brown apparently had received favorable testimonies on his behalf from Edward Ashe, a member of the Long Parliament, and possibly also from Thomas Edwards. It is to be noted, however, that some parishioners of St. Michael Crooked Lane did present articles against Brown in 1647, and those of the parish of St. Mary Aldermary were engaged in a long suit in 1645 to have Gell removed by the Committee for Plundered Ministers. Yet they both survived these Puritan or Presbyterian attacks.[105] In the case of Brown, it was probably because the parish was deeply divided among its inhabitants, and no group was powerful enough to sway the religious life of the parish in one direction—Anglican, Presbyterian, or Independent. St. Mary Aldermary was a rich parish, with a concentration of wealthy merchants most of whom were probably conservatives in both religion and politics. Robert Hanson, a future Lord Mayor of London, was one of the leading parishioners in our era.[106] Furthermore, it may be added that since both men held their livings legally, they could not be removed unless they openly disobeyed the ordinances of the Parliament.

The most interesting case in this survey of Anglican clergymen in Puritan London is undoubtedly that of Nathaniel Hardy, a minister of St. Dionis Backchurch. At the beginning of the revolutionary era, St. Dionis was unmistakably Puritan in its religious affiliations. In November 1642 the parishioners contributed £960 to the parliamentary cause, and during the early years of the period it also produced a number of active civic leaders in Puritan London.[107] In 1642–43, a series of trial sermons were held for the election of a lecturer until Nathaniel Hardy was finally chosen.[108] Hardy had been known for his Puritan beliefs and was an able preacher. In the meantime iconoclastic alterations were carried out in the parish church: its chancel where the high altar stood was changed and the cross on the church steeple was taken down.[109] In 1645–46, when the high Presbyterian movement reached its zenith in the City, the vestry of St. Dionis showed its support by ordering the Covenant framed and hung in the parish church.[110] Indeed, Hardy's reputation as a Prebyterian preacher in the City was such that, though relatively a younger man, he was chosen as one of the parliamentary ministers to attend the Uxbridge negotiations. Surprisingly, it was while at Uxbridge that Hardy was converted to the orthodox tenets of the Anglican tradition by Henry Hammond.[111] In spite of this unexpected turnabout on the part of Hardy, there is no evidence that the parish of St. Dionis ever tried to remove him.[112] It is true that Hardy continued to attend the Fourth Classis of the new Presbyterian church government in London, but it is also clear that he no longer preached on fast days, when usually an official purpose or theme was set, but, according to Anthony Wood, maintained a "loyal lecture" instead, at which monthly collections were made for sequestered orthodox clergymen, and also an annual sermon on the anniversary of the Royal Martyr.[113] Or, as Richard Meggott put it in his sermon at the funeral of Hardy of 1670:

> He showed that he was converted himself, after a while; by improving all opportunities for the strengthening of his brethren: Not only in Private but in Publick, with Courage and Faithfulness, reproving the Usurpation, Oppression, Perjury, Sacrilege, Hypocrisie, and the rest of the raigning Sins of those Times of Violence and Madness. I need not insist upon these things; they were not done in a Corner, but in the Heart of England's chieftest City.[114]

Indeed, by the middle of the 1650s, St. Dionis had probably become a center of Royalists in the City. In 1654, for instance, in a collection for the repairment of the parish church, the chief contributors included neo-Royalists such as Alderman Adams and Alderman Cullum.[115]

It is difficult to say whether any other Puritan ministers followed Hardy's route of conversion back to Anglicanism during the revolutionary period. In the light of the parish records we may presume that similar cases must have occurred in several other parishes, though not so dramatically as Hardy's at St. Dionis Backchurch. At the parish of St. Mary at Hill, where Hardy had served as lecturer in 1643, Thomas White was chosen as minister in 1647, when the parish was unmistakably Puritan with Edward Hooker, Thomas Lenthall, Francis Lenthall, and Nicholas Corsellis as leading civic figures. Yet by 1662 White had become an orthodox Anglican.[116] Similarly, at St. Martin Outwick, Matthew Smallwood became its minister in 1652–53, but he was identified as an orthodox Anglican in early 1661.[117] So also was Christopher Flower, who had been minister at St. Margaret Lothbury since 1652.[118] To be sure, many Anglican clergymen either regained or newly acquired benefices in London upon the collapse of the Puritan Revolution. From an incomplete list of the names of London parish ministers, which was compiled on 4 March 1661, we find at least forty-four ministers identified as orthodox Anglican clergymen.[119]

From the preceding analysis of the Anglican clergy in Puritan London, a few observations may be made with regard to both the Anglican tradition and the Puritan experiment in the City during the revolutionary era. First of all, it may not be entirely wrong to say that the strength of the Anglican tradition was much stronger than modern historians have realized. The extent of both the Anglican appeal and the activities of Anglican ministers in Puritan London went far beyond what Bosher's excellent study on this subject has indicated. Second, modern historians will have to be more careful about their generalizations regarding the strength and appeal of Puritanism even where it had been the strongest. The Puritan Revolution was, indeed, one of the minority. And, finally, in the light of the preceding analysis, the Restoration and its settlement will become more understandable. The Anglican tradition had reestablished itself in London long before the return of the Monarchy.

NOTES

1. Robert Chestlin, *Persecution Vndecima. The Chvrches Eleventh Persecution. Or, A Briefe of the Pvritan Persecvtion of the Protestant Clergy of the Church of England: More Particularly within the City of London. Begun in Parliament, Ann. Dom. 1641* (London, 1648), p. 20. It is not clear to which particular order of the House of Commons Chestlin was referring here. The Long Parliament was opened on 3 November 1640, and three days later it was resolved that a Grand Committee of the whole House for religion was to meet every Monday at two o'clock in the afternoon. On 25 November the Grand Committee for Religion took action against Edward

Layfield, Vicar of Allhallows Barking, for setting up the Communion Table altarwise and rails and images at the Altar. On 31 August 1641, the House of Commons formally adopted a resolution that "the Churchwardens of Every Parish church or Chapel, do forthwith remove the Communion-Table from the East End of the Church, Chapel, and Chancel, where they stand Altarwise, and place them in some convenient Place of the Church or Chapel; and take away the Rails, and level the Chancels, as heretofore they were before the late Innovations." On the following day, a series of more extensive and systematic resolutions were passed in the House and an order was issued accordingly. See *C. J.*, 2: 35, 278–79; *The Orders from the House of Commons for the Abolishing of Superstition, and Innovation, in the Regulating of Church Affairs* (London, 1641); S. R. Gardiner, *The Constitutional Documents of the Puritan Revolution 1625–1660* (Oxford, 1962), pp. 197–98.

2. *Mercurius Aulicus* (Oxford, 1845), pp. 97, 98, 99, 113. For further descriptions of these iconoclastic tumults and riotous actions among the London parishes in the early days of the Revolution, see below, nn. 8–11.

3. *C. J.*, 2: 54; Shaw, 2: 177–78.

4. Chestlin, *Persecution Vndecima*, pp. 47–49; *W. R.*, pp. [42]–[63].

5. Ibid., p. 20.

6. *W. R.*, p. [44], *s. v.* Robert Chestlin; Shaw, 2: 304. Cf. also GLMS 1016/1, f. 191: The churchwarden recorded the payment of 8s. 6d. for the "charges about Mr. Chestlin." It is interesting to note that Chestlin had taken the Protestation on 3 June 1641. See GLMS 3579, f. 339.

7. Chestlin, *Persecutio Vndecima*, p. 47.

8. His. MSS. Comm., *Fourth Report*, Appendix, p. 73.

9. Ibid., p. 74.

10. Ibid. The churchwardens were Cornelius Cooke, John Rose, and Robert Houghton. Rose was an obscure person, but both Cooke and Houghton were to become rather prominent figures in the Puritan era. For Turner, see *W. R.*, pp. [60]–[61], *s. v.* The curate was Oliver Whitby, who was later sequestered as Rector of St. Nicholas Olave. See ibid., p. [62], *s. v.* The case of St. Magnus perhaps requires some explanation. It had been a Puritan parish with the renowned Cornelius Burgess as its Rector, but, for some unknown reasons, Burgess was replaced in 1641 by Samuel Bordman, who had been appointed by the Bishop of London. We may assume that this was a rather belated attempt on the part of the Bishop either to remove Burgess or to control the pulpit of the parish church. To be sure, the parishioners were opposed to this appointment, which was probably one of the reasons for the riots in this parish. Cf. above, n. 8.

11. *Mercurius Aulicus*, p. 113.

12. Ibid., pp. 98–99.

13. *The Heads of Severall Petitions and Complaints* (London, 1641), p. 2; *Mercurius Aulicus*, pp. 98–99. Cf. also GLMS 1013/1, f. 184. The parish paid £12. 8s. 6d for this work, and the churchwarden was Michael Herring, a rather prominent figure in Puritan London.

14. *Mercurius Aulicus*, p. 712.

15. See, for examples, GLMS 4215/1 (St. Dionis Backchurch), f. 69 (£1. 18s. "for altering the Chancel where the high alter stood"); GLMS 2088/1 (St. Andrew by the Wardrobe), no folio number, churchwardens' account, 1643–44 (2s. "for the workman in pulling down of the crosses and putting up of the weathercock"); GLMS 4051/1 (Allhallows, Lombard Street), f. 111 (£2. 2s. 3d. "paid Mr. Turner Mason for demolishing of the Images"); GLMS 1013/1 (St. Mary Woolchurch), f. 184 (£3. 8s. 6d. for "altering the images" and another £9 for "taking away the superstitious Images," for "erasing superstitious inscriptions," and for "cutting others in their stead that are not offensive"). In the parish of St. Pancras, Sopher Lane, the surplices and tippet of the old incumbent as well as the rails around the altar and a stone in the church were all sold to some parishioners. See GLMS 5018/1, no folio number, churchwardens' account, 1643–44.

16. The first of such petitions against Anglican incumbents in London appears to be the one presented by some parishioners of Allhallows Barking against Dr. Edward Layfield, which was read in the House of Commons on 25 November 1640. Layfield was the son of Archbishop

Laud's half-sister. See *C. J.*, 2: 35; *W. R.*, p. [53], *s. v.* Edward Layfield. After the creation of the committee for removing scandalous ministers on 19 December 1640, such petitions were probably addressed to this committee; but from time to time, some parishes still presented their petitions directly to the House of Commons. See *C. J.*, 54, 65, 311.

17. For a typical petition against the old Anglican incumbent, see *The Petition and Articles Exhibited in Parliament against Dr. Fvller, Dean of Ely, and Vicar of Giles Cripplegate. With the Petition Exhibited in Parliament against Timothy Hutton, Curate of the said Parish. By the Parishioners of Saint Giles* (London, 1641).

18. Cf. Chestlin, *Persecutio Vndecima*, p. 20; *A Letter from Mercurius Civicus to Mercurius Rusticus*, reprinted in Sir Walter Scott, ed., *Somers Tracts* (London, 1750), 1: 594–95. Prejudiced as these writings might be, it is nevertheless true that few of the radicals were prosecuted.

19. Green, 1: 124; *W. R.*, pp. [54]–[55], *s.v.* The churchwardens' account for 1643–44 recorded the payment of £10. 19s. "towards the ousting of Mr. Owen & maintaining the privilege of the parish in choice of their minister." See GLMS 559/1, f. 45.

20. Green,. 1: 123; *W. R.*, p. [62], *s. v.*

21. *The Petition and Articles exhibited in Parliament against Doctor Heywood . . . By the Parishioners of St. Giles in the Fields* (London, 1641), p. 8. Heywood was also prebend of St. Paul's and Westminster. See also *W. R.*, p. [50], *s. v.*

22. *W. R.*, p. [60], *s. v.* We may recall that St. Olave Old Jewry was one of the strongly Puritan and Presbyterian parishes in Revolutionary London, with William Vaugham, George Almery, John Frederick, and John Mascall both as its civic leaders and as future ruling elders. Tuke's strong anti-puritan position could hardly be accepted by these men. He was soon to be sequestered. See GLMS 4415/1, f. 113b.

23. *W. R.*, p. [55], *s.v.* The parish spent £6. 1s. "in prosecuting the complaints against Mr. Pory at Westminster." See GLMS 1176/1, no folio number, churchwardens' account, 1642–43.

24. *W. R.*, p. [49], *s. v.; D. N. B., s. v.*

25. *W. R.*, p. [51], *s. v.; The Petition and Articles Exhibited in Parliament against Dr. Fvller. . . . With the Petition Exhibited in Parliament against Timothy Hutton;* Hist. MSS. Comm., *Fourth Report*, Appendix, p. 103.

26. *The Articles and Charge Proved in Parliament against Doctor Walton Minister of St. Martins Orgar in Cannon-street* (London, 1641), p. 12; *W. R.*, p. [61], *s. v.*

27. *Articles Exhibited in Parliament, Against Master Ihon Squire, Vicar of Saint Leonard Shoreditch* (London, 1641); *W. R.*, p. [58], *s. v.*

28. *The Petition and Articles Exhibited in Parliament against Dr. Fvller*, Article 8.

29. *The Petition and Articles Exhibited in Parliament against Doctor Heywood*, p. 8.

30. In the parish of St. Swithin, for example, Richard Owen's opposition to the Parliament and to contributions for the parliamentary cause "caused his friends to do nothing," whereas in the parish of Allhallows Barking, for another example, twenty parishioners and the churchwardens presented a counterpetition in favor of Edward Layfield. See Green, 1:124; Maskell, *Collections in Illustration of the Parochial History and Antiquities of the Ancient Parish of Allhallows Barking*, pp. 149–51.

31. *W. R.*, p. [58], *s. v.*

32. Ibid., p. [48],, *s. v.*

33. Ibid., pp. [51], [56]–[57], [62], *s. vv.* William Isaacson, Bruno Ryves, William Watts, and Oliver Whitby, respectively.

34. *D. N. B., s.v.* See also Thomas Fuller, *A Sermon of Reformation Preached at the Church of the Savoy, last Fast day, July 27, 1643* (London, 1643).

35. *A Letter from Mercurius Civicus to Mercurius Rusticus*, in *Somers Tracts*, 1:595.

36. Chestlin, *Persecutio Vndecima*, p. 42.

37. R. M., *An Answer to a Lawless Pamphlet entitled, The Petition and Articles . . . against Dr. Heywood* (London, 1641), pp. 6–7. For another similar case, see *W. R.*, p. [55], *s. v.* John Piggott.

38. *An Answer to the Articles Preferd against Edward Finch, Vicar of Christ Church, by some*

of the Parishioners of the same (London, 1641), p. 13.

39. GLMS 1568, ff. 639, 645–86, *passim.*

40. GLMS 4825/1, ff. 56, 57b, 60b, 65b, 71b.

41. Freshfield, *The Vestry Minute Books of the Parish of St. Bartholomew Exchange,* pt. 2, pp. 1, 8, 10; *W. R.,* p. [48], *s. v.*

42. GLMS 560/1, no folio number, vestry minutes, 28 March 1648 and 8 January 1656. Owen returned to the parish in 1661.

43. GLMS 6554/1, ff. 9–9b.

44. GLMS 2590/1, f. 341; GLMS 2593/2, ff. 89, 160, 217.

45. *W. R.,* p. [61], *s. v.* Ephraim Udal.

46. Freshfield, *The Vestry Minute Books of the Parish of St. Bartholomew Exchange,* pt. 2, p. 48.

47. It should be pointed out that the fifth was legally due to the sequestered minister or his family, and the Committee for Plundered Ministers, upon petitions either by the sequestered minister or by his wife, would see to it that it was to be paid. See BL Add. MSS. 15669, ff. 49, 72b, 99b; 15670, ff. 17b, 35b, 123, 172; 15671, f. 53. For free gifts and gratuities, see, for examples, GLMS 587/1, ff. 83, 93, 98, 100; GLMS 4051/1, f. 127.

48. Hist. MSS. Comm., *Sixth Report,* Appendix, p. 201.

49. BL Add. MS. 15671, ff. 226, 234; *W. R.,* p. [50], *s. v.* James Halsey; GLMS 1431/2, f. 194.

50. *W. R.,* pp. [56]–[57], *s. v.* Bruno Ryves.

51. GLMS 1341/1, no folio number, churchwardens' accounts, 1648–50.

52. GLMS 4956/3, f. 149; GLMS 4570/2, f. 173; GLMS 3907/1, no folio number, churchwardens' accounts, 1653–57.

53. GLMS 5090/2, no folio number, churchwardens' account, 1655–56; GLMS 7882/1, ff. 373–74, 544–52, *passim.*

54. Hist. MSS. Comm., *Sixth Report,* Appendix, p. 201; Jordan, p. 42.

55. BL Add. MS. 15671, ff. 144b–45.

56. The parochial structure of the parish was clearly disrupted during the years 1648–52, when the churchwardens' accounts were discontinued. For William Peake, see GLMS 959/1, ff. 216b, 227; Woodhead, p. 128, *s. v.*

57. GLMS 1341/1, no folio number, churchwardens' accounts, 1648–50; CLRO J. Co. Co., 41, ff. 43–44; *A Pair of Spectacles for the Citie,* p. 11; Woodhead, pp. 110 (*s. v.* Thomas Lockington), 119 (*s. v.* Andrew Neale).

58. CLRO J. Co. Co., 41, ff. 43–44; Hist. MSS. Comm., *Popham,* p. 167; GLMS 4570/2, f. 173; GLMS 4571/1, f. 42; BL. Add. MS. 36781, f. 33b; *C. R., s. v.* Edward Hicks.

59. In the case of Allhallows London Wall, Andrew Janeway died sometime in 1654 and Samuel Dyer was admitted in March 1655; whereas, in the case of Allhallows Staining, John After left the parish sometime in 1649 and Samuel Smith was instituted sometime in 1652. See GLMS 5090/2, no folio number, churchwardens' accounts, 1653–54, 1655–56; GLMS 4956/3, ff. 127, 149, 157.

60. Among the civic leaders of the parish were Charles Snelling, Ellis Cunliff, Thomas Thorold, Robert Mead, Thomas Starkey, and George Downes. See GLMS 3908/1, no folio number, vestry minuters, 1639–52, *passim;* GLMS 3907/1, no folio number, churchwardens' accounts, 1653–54, 1654–55, 1656–57, 1657–61.

61. GLMS 1431/2, f. 194; BL Add. MS. 15671, f. 234.

62. GLMS 7882/1, ff. 373, 544, 547, 549, 552.

63. GLMS 3570/2, f. 54. Votier had been sequestered from the rectory of St. Peter Cheapside the year before. It is doubtful, however, that Votier actually ever held the lectureship at St. Mary Aldermanbury, and he died later in the same year. See also *W. R.,* p. [61], *s. v.*

64. GLMS 4165/1, f. 284.

65. BL Add. MS 15670, f. 112b; *W. R.,* p. [45], *s. v.*

66. Shaw, 2: 332, 353; *W. R.,* pp. [52]–[53], *s. v.*

67. BL Add. MS. 15671, ff. 240b, 262; *W. R.,* p. [52], *s. v.* The parish was wrongly identified as "Bennet Shoreditch" in the Add. MS. on both occasions.

68. GLMS 1453/1, f. 43.

69. BL Add. MS. 15671, ff. 74b, 76b.

70. GLMS 2590/1, f. 377.

71. GLMS 4072/1, f. 196b; *W. R.*, p. [399], s.v.

72. PRO SP 16/492, f. 19. For the social composition of this parish see chap. 1 above.

73. These two men were James Hayes and Robert Wilding. See Shaw, 2:400; CLRO J. Co. Co., 40, f. 153b.

74. Newcourt, 1:303; LPLMS CM VIII/37, f.[1]; LPLMS CM VIII/43, f.1; LPLMS CM IX/58; BL Add. MS. 15671, ff. 240b, 262.

75. For the social composition of the parish, see chap. 1 above; for poor relief contributions from other parishes, see GLMS 5714/1, no folio number, churchwardens' account, 1646–47.

76. Newcourt, 1:454; LPLMS CM VIII/37, f. [3]; LPLMS CM VIII/43 f. 2; LPLMS CM IX/58.

77. BL Add. MS. 15670, ff. 124b, 186b.

78. Newcourt, 1:492; LPLMS CM VIII/43, f. [3],; LPLMS CM IX/58; Dale, p. 155.

79. BL Add. MS. 15671, ff. 59, 87–87b.

80. Dale, 53; Pearl, pp. 304–5, 306–7.

81. Alex. F. Mitchell and John Struthers, eds., *Minutes of the Sessions of the Westminster Assembly of Divines* (Edinburgh and London, 1874), pp. 5213–24; *W. R.*, pp. [52]–[53] (*s. v.* William Launce), p. [55] (*s. v.* Ephraim Paget).

82. GLM 3570/2, ff. 43, 46b, 48b, 54.

83. *A Letter from Mercurius Civicus to Mercurius Rusticus*, in *Somers Tracts*, 1:582; *W. R.*, p. [61], *s. v.*

84. GLMS 4165/1, ff. 284, 285, 286, 287. The newly chosen minister was William Blackmore. Blackmore's consent to Holdsworth's lectureship was given in a vestry meeting on 4 December 1646, and in the same vestry, the date for the election of ruling elders was decided upon. The six ruling elders were elected on 30 December.

85. *W. R.*, [51], *s. v.* Richard Holdsworth. The veto of Holdsworth's election to the lectureship by the Committee for Plundered Ministers had been given on 12 November.

86. GLMS 1453/1, f. 43. Mr. Sharpe was probably Geoffrey Sharpe (*W. R.*, [57], *s. v.*). For the reorganization of the parochial governmental structure in St. Botolph Aldersgate, see below, chap. 6.

87. GLMS 2590/1, ff. 359, 377.

88. GLMS 4072/1, f. 196b.

89. GLMS 2590/1, 382; GLMS 4072/1, f. 197b.

90. GLMS 978/1, no folio number, vestry minute, 5 September 1651.

91. Ibid., vestry minutes, 18 August 1654 and 28 September 1655; GLMS 977/1, no folio number, churchwardens' accounts, 1651–57.

92. GLMS 1336/1, ff. 34, 37b, 38.

93. John Evelyn, *The Diary of John Evelyn*, ed. William Bray (London, 1870), p. 228; Robert S. Bosher, *The Making of the Restoration Settlement: The Influence of the Laudians, 1649–1662* (London, 1957), p. 12; Seaver, pp. 277, 279.

94. GLMS 2597/1, ff. 111, 114, 118; GLMS 2596/2, ff. 137–38b, 140b–41, 143b–44.

95. *W. R.*, p. 46, *s. v.*;GLMS 2601/1, no folio number, churchwardens' accounts, 1652–55; Seaver, p. 179.

96. Surman, 1:110; Shaw, 2:109.

97. Evelyn, *The Diary of John Evelyn*, p. 119; *W. R.*, pp. [53]–[54], *s. v.*, Edward Marbury.

98. LPLMS Comm. XIIa/20, ff. 5, 6; BL Add. MS. 15671, ff. 237b, 252.

99. BL Add. MS. 36781, f. 33; *W. R.*, p. [261], *s. v.* Robert Mossom.

100. GLMS 1336/1, vestry minutes, 1643–60, *passim*. The names of the Common Councilmen from this parish were regularly recorded each year. For the social composition of the parish, see chap. 1 above.

101. Jordan, p. 40. Cf. also Willoughby A. Littledale, ed., *The Registers of St. Benet and St. Peter, Paul's Wharf, London* (London, 1906), pp. 165–75. The occupations of the parishioners

were identified; they were mostly of minor crafts.

102. PRO SP 19/78, f. 60b; GLMS 2601/1, no folio number, churchwardens' accounts, 1638–62, *passim*.

103. Surman, ed., *Register-Booke of the Fourth Classis, passim*.

104. GLMS 2597/1, ff. 85, 114; GLMS 2596/2, ff. 115b, 124; *C. R.*, p. 104, *s. v.* Thomas Case.

105. BL Add. MS. 36781, ff. 33, 34; Christopher Hill, *Milton and the English Revolution* (New York, 1979), p. 34; Surman, ed., *Register-Booke of the Fourth Classis*, pp. 9, 10, 16 and *passim*; BL Add. MS. 15669, ff. 25b, 46b, 63b, 66b, 72 and *passim*; BL Add. MS. 15670, f. 23.

106. GLMS 1188/1, churchwardens' accounts, 1646–58, where the names of both Prersbyterian and Independent ministers who preached in the parish church were recorded.

107. PRO SP 19/78, f. 91. Among the civic leaders of this parish during the revolutionary era were Thomas Manwaring, James Church, Richard Best, Richard Hill, John Archer, Thomas Bludworth, Thomas Turgis, and Henry Davy.

108. GLMS 4215/1, ff. 68, 69.

109. Ibid., ff. 69, 73.

110. Ibid., f. 80.

111. *D. N. B., s. v.;* Seaver, p. 278.

112. It appears that after his conversion back to the Anglican position, Hardy declined to preach on Fast Days, which were, of course, usually appointed by the Parliament. The parish paid other ministers who preached in his stead. See GLMS 4215/1, ff. 82, 86.

113. Bosher, *The Making of the Restoration Settlement*, p. 12.

114. Richard Meggott, *A Sermon Preached at St. Martins in the Fields, at the Funeral of the Reverend Doctor Hardy, Dean of Rochester, June 9, 1670* (London, 1670), pp. 24–25.

115. GLMS 4215/1, f. 102.

116. GLMS 1240/1, f. 51b; BL Add. MS. 36781, f. 33b (where his name was given as Wayte). Cf. GLMS 1240/1, vestry minutes after 1662.

117. GLMS 11394/1, no folio number, churchwardens' account, 1652–53.

118. GLMS 4352/1, f. 202b; BL Add. MS. 36781, f., 33b.

119. BL Add. MS. 36781, ff. 32b–34, *passim*.

5

The Puritan Clergy and the Parish

It has long been recognized both by contemporaries and by modern historians that the City of London was a main center of the Puritan movement in pre-Revolutionary England, and during the period of the Revolution, as we have seen in earlier chapters of this study, the Anglican incumbents of the London parishes were, with few exceptions, sequestered from their livings and replaced, wherever settled ministries were reestablished, by Puritan clergymen. In a certain sense, the Puritans were indeed now in power in the City, both in its civic institutions and in its parochial churches. One may wonder, therefore, what the relationship was like between the Puritan ministers and their faithful flocks in the various London parishes under the new circumstances—with the bishop gone, the Anglican incumbents sequestered, the ecclesiastical courts abolished, and the threat of religious conformity and persecution removed. How were the Puritan ministers instituted? What was now the nature of the relationship between the Puritan minister and his parishioners? And, above all, how were the Puritan ministers maintained in the various London parishes?

Among these questions, the economic conditions of the Puritan ministers in London during the Revolutionary period is perhaps the most important, for the economic problems of the English Church, as Christopher Hill has long since told us, had been at the root of the Puritan opposition to both the Mitre and the Crown in England.[1] This had been, of course, a national issue, but the leaders in the Long Parliament, though they had intended to solve it, failed to carry out their plans for a better maintenance of the national ministry.[2] Owing to the contingencies of the Civil War and the consequent financial burdens of the national government, the church lands, which would have been used for the betterment of religion and the ministry, were eventually sold for the maintenance of the war and the army. The desultory payments of augmentation to individual ministers were too limited in nature to constitute a systematic policy.[3] In fact, the Puritan leaders in the City government, too, did once try to solve the economic problems of the London parochial ministries as a whole. On 13 August 1646, the Court of the Common Council was informed that divers parishes of the City were without a minister. For want of competent maintenance, many godly ministers had left the City and gone into the country; others intended to go away likewise. If no action was taken to amend the situation immediately, the City, the Common Council was warned, "will be destitute of Godly and faithful ministers to instruct the people."[4] In response to this appeal, the Common Council created a special committee to "advisedly Consider of the best way and meanes how the Ministers of this Citie may bee Compleatly provided for."[5] And, after some consideration, the committee attempted a noble solution. On 2 October it introduced a comprehensive proposal into the Court of the Common Council. First, the committee recommended that, in lieu of tithes, an annual City tax be levied upon all the houses within the City and suburban precincts. Second, all former church lands and properties within the City and the Liberties were to be procured from the Parliament. Finally, the committee advised that a comprehensive survey be conducted of the true value of every house in the City.[6] During the subsequent debate in the Common Council, the survey was to be extended to cover almost all categories of property as well: "all halls, shopps, warehouses, store houses, Die howses, Brew howses, Sellars, Stables, Keyes or Wharfes with Cranes belonging to the same, Tymber yards and Gardens."[7]

There can be no doubt that this plan, if successfully executed, would completely have changed the economic life of the London parish churches. In fact, a precept was issued by the Lord Mayor to the Alderman, his Deputy, and the Common Councilmen of every Ward, who were commanded to make the survey and to certify the returns of the results to the Lord Mayor by 12 October.[8] Obviously, the task involved in such a comprehensive survey was too complicated to be accomplished within the prescribed time of ten days. Several weeks were to elapse without any sign of the returns being rendered. On 3 November another order was issued by the Common Council, once more commanding that "returnes be made by all the severall Wards of this Cittie to the Lord Maior, according to the true intent & meaneing of the said Percept" within a week.[9] It is not known to what extent the survey was actually carried out. It appears, however, that it was done at least in some of the Wards of the City, and that returns had been submitted to the Lord Mayor by 1 March 1647, when "the bookes already brought in to the Lord Maior from severall Wards of the value of the houses &c." were delivered to the committee.[10]

In 1647, however, the religious concern of the City Fathers was soon to be lost in a gathering storm of larger political questions. In what Valerie Pearl calls London's counterrevolution, the lay Presbyterian leaders of the City government consolidated their control of the London militia and thus brought the City into a dangerous confrontation with the army.[11] The outcome of this contest of strength between the City and the army was predictable; and with the collapse of the political Presbyterian faction in the City government, this grand design of the London Puritan rulers was never to be heard of again.[12] Nevertheless, it should be pointed out that the significance of the episode lies not so much in the plan's ill success as in its initiation. The very attempt at such a plan signified the intention on the part of the City's Puritan leaders to improve the economic life of the London parish churches. The thoroughness of the plan went far beyond what Archbishop Laud and the Anglican clergy had ever attempted in their efforts to solve the economic predicament of the English Church in the 1630s.[13]

In any event, neither the national plans of the Long Parliament nor the noble design of the City of London had a chance of being put into execution. Without a general scheme to reconstruct the economic structure of the English Church, many of the old problems remained unresolved both in the nation and in the City. Yet, at least in the City of London, some new practices were introduced into the economic relationship between the Puritan minister and his parishioners. Although the situation was bound to vary from parish to parish, yet, as we shall see, a few basic patterns do emerge to throw some light upon the economic conditions of the Puritan ministers in the City.

The most satisfactory and perhaps also the most prevalent practice the London parishes now adopted in dealing with the economic problem of the ministry was the substitution of stipends for tithes. This meant primarily a mutual agreement between the minister and the parish on a certain fixed annual stipend, which the parish would pay for the service of the minister instead of traditional tithes. The stipend was, of course, nothing entirely new for the Puritans; it had been the usual form of payment for a Puritan lecturer before 1640, when the Anglican incumbent received the tithes. Occasionally, also, a minister had received a fixed stipend in cases where the parishioners were the impropriators and chose this method of renumeration.[14] This precedent of stipendiarian lectureship undoubtedly made the acceptance of a similar ministry a natural development, since the Puritan minister, unlike his predecessor, was wont to serve as lecturer as well. In some cases there was a direct transition from the one to the other. At St. Bartholomew Exchange, for instance, John Lightfoot was chosen as Sunday lecturer early in 1643, while John Grant, the incumbent, was still in possession of the rectory.[15] Lightfoot had an annual stipend of £60. A year later, the parishioners of St. Bartholomew obtained a lease of the rectory from the incumbent for twenty-one years at £50 a year. At the same time, they chose Thomas Cawton as minister with a yearly salary of £100 plus the house of the parsonage.[16]

The amount of the annual stipend paid by a London parish for the service of a minister varied. It depended naturally upon the relative wealth of the parish and, not unreasonably, also upon the reputation and the ability of the minister. At St. Mary Aldermanbury, a leading London Presbyterian divine, Edmund Calamy, had a yearly salary of £160 voted for his maintenance by the vestry as early as 27 May 1639. This was probably the highest annual stipend a London minister received so early in this period, though later in the 1650s Richard Vines and Edward Reynolds had a stipend of £180 a year at St. Lawrence Old Jewry.[17]

An exception must be made for Cornelius Burgess, whom the Parliament appointed as a Sunday lecturer at St. Paul's Cathedral in 1642 with a salary of £400 a year. But Burgess's appointment was a special case. A political activist, Burges was not an ordinary parish minister; nor was St. Paul's Cathedral an ordinary London parish.[18] At the other end of the scale, we find that John Paul received £15 a quarter at St. George Botolph Lane, and John Hoffman, £6 a month at St. Mary Woolchurch.[19] At St. Lawrence Pountney, Thomas Palmer agreed to serve six months for £35 only; whereas at St. Benet Gracechurch, Daniel Cawdrey, a rather prominent Presbyterian minister, supplied the place of the parson for one year at a salary of £60.[20]

In general, the annual ministerial stipends paid by the London parishes to their ministers during the revolutionary period ranged from £100 to £150; the most commonly used figure appeared to be £120. It is difficult to judge whether such stipends were higher or lower than the total values of tithes, glebes, and other ministerial accruements of those parishes in which fixed stipends were substituted, for the traditional clerical revenues depends upon the actual collections each year. It has been well known that tithes had never been popular; their collection was always a precarious business.[21] Furthermore, in case of an impropriation or pluralism, the tithes had been kept by the impropriator or the absentee rector, and only a small fee was given to the vicar or the curate. In the light of this precarious nature of traditional parochial livings, the fixed stipend was clearly an improvement. In some of the London parishes, the stipends during the Puritan era were clearly equitable. At St. Bride, for instance, where the parishioners had leased the Impropriation from the Dean and Chapter of Westminster at £130 a year, while the Dean and Chapter had paid the vicar £16 a year, it is doubtful whether the Anglican vicar had had any other income beyond the casualties and a gratuity of £50.[22] In 1646, when John Dicks was elected minister of the parish, his annual stipend was £140: £16 for him as vicar, £104 as lecturer, and £20 for a house.[23] It is clear that Dicks now enjoyed almost the total value of the benefice. At St. Bartholomew Exchange, the living had consisted of about £75 from tithes and £25 from the glebe. In 1644, as noted, when Thomas Cawton was chosen minister, the parish offered him a yearly salary of £100 and the house of the parsonage. At St. James Garlickhithe, the yearly value of tithes had been estimated at £92, whereas in 1646 the annual stipend for the parson, Matthew Barker, was £100.[24] Similarly, the tithes of St. Michael Cornhill had been estimated at £116. 6s. 4d.[25] In 1646, four leading parishioners agreed to undertake a yearly salary of £120 for the support and maintenance of a minister.[26]

While the instances given above do not indicate any increase in the value of the benefice, there were substantial increases in some other cases. At St. Swithin, the tithes had been valued at £75 per annum.[27] During the Interregnum, when John Sheffield was Rector from 1647 to 1661, the annual stipend was £120 and obviously guaranteed. On 20 September 1648, when it was reported at the vestry meeting that £6. 15s. 7d. had not been collected for Sheffield, the vestry ordered the balance to be paid out of the parish stock. A month later, at another meeting on 20 October, it was again unequivocally ordered that "30li a quarter should be paid down by the Parish to Mr. Sheffield according to a former agreement."[28] At St. Benet Gracechurch, the increase in the value of the living was much more impressive. The tithes of the parish had been worth approximately £55 annually.[29] Although Daniel Cawdry served one year in 1644 for merely £60, the parish in later years of the period always made efforts to pay a yearly salary of £100 to its ministers.[30] And this was done in spite of the fact that the full value of the tithes was never collected and the parish regularly paid £20 a year to the sequestered rector, William Quelch, until his death in 1654.[31] Similarly, there was a large increase at the parish of St. Mary Woolchurch, though it was not until after a reorganization of the feoffees in 1648 and the sequestrators in 1650.[32] The annual value of the tithes had been estimated at £50. 16s. 6d., while the glebe of the parish was worth £22. 13 s. 4d.[33] In 1645, as has been pointed out, the parish paid no more than £6 a month to its minister; yet, after the reorganization of the feoffees, the minister, Richard Ball, received regularly from 1653 onward £128 a year—£100 as stipend and £28 for a house.[34] The most impressive increase of all is to be found in the parish of St. Stephen Walbrook, where the tithes had been worth only £40 per annum. During the Interregnum, the parish first paid £100 a year to Humphrey Chambers and then £120 to Thomas Watson. In 1658–59, Watson's annual stipend was raised to £150.[35]

Perhaps the real advantage of a fixed annual stipend for a London minister during the revolutionary period was not so much its amount as its certainty. In one case the minister was willing to accept less than the full value of the benefice as long as it was guaranteed. At St. Botolph Billingsgate, as the vestry minutes recorded, the tithes of the parish with the house of the parsonage were worth £135, yet Jacob Tice was "content to accept out of the above said sum £120 a year" and out of the £120, Tice was to pay the wife of the sequestered rector "the whole 5% of so much as Alderman Atkins and Alderman Andrewes shall agree unto." The only advantage in the arrangement was that the vestry promised to make good the £120 to Tice.[36] The minister's point of view on this matter was best expressed by Anthony Harford in his correspondence with the parish of St. Michael Cornhill upon his election as minister. His conditions about maintenance were, in the order he himself put them, "1. fixed, 2. competent, 3. unburthensome."[37] John Bellamy, one of the leading vestrymen, answered each point at length. Since Bellamy's letter vividly reveals the economic matters of the parochial ministry in Puritan London, it deserves full quotation:

ffirst, for the fixednes, ours being a sequestration, there will be Collectors appointed by the Sequestrators to collect the duties from every house,

And the Minister coming in by order of the Committee of Parliament, if
any shall refuse to pay their duties, the Sequestrators are usually upon
Complaint made by them to the Committee presently inabled to recover
them for the use of the minister. 2dlie, for the Competency, it is one
hundred pounds a year or somewhat better arising from the certaine duties
payable by each severall house—besides ancient gift sermons and other
casulties by funerall sermons, &c. And a convenient dwelling house for
the Minister. ffor the 3d viz. unburthensome. I know not well your mean-
ing, whether you intend it to be unburthensome to your selfe or to the
pparishioners, if to yourself, I say the care hitherto hath bin such as to free
the minister from all taxes levied for the maintenance of the Army, and I
doubt not but it will be soe for the future also, and then it will be
unburthensome unto you.[38]

And Bellamy added that when the sequestered rector died and if Harford was
then with the parish, the parishioners "will endeavour to doe thir best to
procure the presentation for you" from the Drapers' Company, which had the
patronage of the living.[39] Surprisingly, Harford declined the offer because, as
he wrote, "your maintenance is neither fixed, nor competent, that I might live
as a Christian, and a minister."[40]

If Harford's argument was at all justified, we may better appreciate the
economic problems of those poorer parishes in London where no substantial
stipend could be guaranteed and tithes continued to be the main basis of the
ministers' maintenance. And there is no evidence that tithes were more fully
collected in Puritan London than they had been under Episcopacy. In fact, a
few instances indicate that rather the contrary was the case.[41] At St. Martin
Orgar, for instance, Brian Walton, the Anglican incumbent and a future
Bishop of Chester, had received £73. 7s. 10d. a year from the parish.[42] In
truth, Walton should have been congratulated for what he had obtained, for
later in 1647 when the parson's duties were collected, they amounted to no
more than £46. 2s. 6d.[43] Similarly, at St. Mary Magdalen Old Fish Street, the
tithes had been estimated at £80 per annum; whereas, in 1648, only £47. 9s.
10d. were collected.[44] A more striking example can be cited from the parish
records of St. Michael Queenhithe. The annual value of tithes of the parish
had been estimated at £90,[45] and it appeared that the whole worth had been
usually received by the incumbent, John Hill, who, in 1641, agreed to give an
allowance of £25 a year for a minister to serve the cure for him. The allowance
was regularly paid until 1644.[46] Yet, in 1648–49, when £36. 10s. were collected
to pay ministers for their preaching, £29. 9s. 6d. were voluntary contributions, while only £7. 0s. 6d. came from tithes.[47]

This does not mean, however, that no efforts were made by the poorer
London parishes to improve their ministerial maintenance. As early as 1641
the parishioners of St. George Botolph Lane raised a stock of £33. 15s. 10d.
for the recovery of the land given to the parish by James Monford and his
wife.[48] In 1643–44, they also attempted to pay their minister a salary as much
as £20 a quarter.[49] Still, their annual receipts of church duties were hardly

enough so that, in 1648, the parish presented a petition to the Committee for Plundered Ministers, which was in all probability for an augmentation to its ministerial maintenance.[50] At St. Lawrence Pountney, a committee was appointed by the vestry on 20 October 1644 to petition the Parliament for certain houses in Ebb-gate Lane, which had belonged to the Dean and Chapter of St. Paul's Cathedral, to be settled upon the minister of the parish for better maintenance.[51] A few months later, another committee was set up to look into the legal documents concerning the impropriation of the parsonage and to have legal counsel how means might be raised for a competent maintenance of a minister.[52] In the 1650s, the parish did manage to pay its minister about £60 a year, with contributions as well as tithes.[53] Similarly, the parish of St. Austin Watling Street presented a petition to the House of Lords in 1643 requesting that the rent of certain houses in the parish belonging to the Dean and Prebends of Windsor be annexed to its minister's maintenance.[54] Perhaps the most telling story was the proceedings at the vestry of St. Clement Eastcheap in 1648. At first the vestry examined the records of tithes previously paid to the last three rectors of the parish. Obviously, in an effort to have the full worth of the tithes collected, the vestry had all the names of the fifty parishioners who had paid tithes and the amount each paid recorded in its minutes. Yet the total value of the tithes was only £10. 8s. 2d. quarterly and £41. 12s. 8d. a year; this was not only inadequate for a settled minister but also insufficient even for the payment of occasional preachers during the year.[55] It was resolved, therefore, at the vestry meeting on 8 October that in the vacancy of the living, the rent of the parson's house should be used toward the payment of preaching.[56] It was probably for the same purpose that the vestry of St. Lawrence Pountney decided in 1652 to have the cellar of the parish church let for twenty-one years either by way of fine or by yearly rent.[57]

All such efforts probably produced no significant result. The truth is that unless the tithes structure was reconstructed or a new way of maintenance was created, the economic problems were simply insoluble for the poorer benefices in the City. It was under such circumstances that another new practice emerged among the parish churches in Puritan London. It appeared that a number of the London parishes simply abandoned the hope of a settled ministry. Instead, individual ministers were hired to preach on Sundays and other Fast or Thanksgiving days. It is to be noted, however, that, in most cases, the lack of settled ministry by no means meant the decline of religious life in the various London parochial communities, though preaching without settled ministry or lectureship was bound to become more and more anomalous. We shall now look at some of these parishes.

At Allhallows the Less, there was no settled ministry for almost six years from 1646 to 1652, and it is evident that the parish did not trouble to solve the problem, though the parishioners later claimed that they had at their own cost maintained a minister to supply the place of the parson.[58] The truth is

that during these six years, the parishioners of Allhallows the Less frequently invited a minister to preach, and all such occasions were recorded in
the Churchwardens' Accounts.[59] It is interesting to observe that at the
beginning of these six distressful years, the date, the name of the preacher,
and the amount paid for each sermon were clearly registered, but gradually
the names of the preaching ministers no longer figured in the accounts.
Preaching was treated, so to speak, as merely a piece of merchandise. In fact,
one item in the accounts for the year 1650 reads that £3. 6s. 8d. were paid to a
certain minister for eight sermons at 8s. 4d. "a peece."[60] It may also be added
that although Allhallows the Less usually paid 10s. for a sermon, it could
pay as low a price as 6s. or even 5s. for two sermons on a Sunday.[61]

The situation of Allhallows the Less was, perhaps, a peculiar one. The
living of Allhallows the Less had been an Impropriation, valued at £65 a
year with only £8 to the curate, and it was clearly one of the poorest benefices
in the City.[62] In other places this new practice was maintained with a certain
degree of regularity. At St. Michael Queenhithe, we may recall, the incumbent agreed in 1641 to make an allowance of £25 a year out of his tithes, when
a certain Mr. Percival was employed to serve the cure. But Percival evidently
left the parish either in late 1643 or early in 1644, and for almost eight years
there was no settled ministry in the parish until 1651.[63] Yet it cannot be said
that preaching or religious edification of the parishioners was neglected
during these years. In four months alone from June to October in 1647, for
instance, twenty-six payments were made to individual ministers for their
preaching in the parish church. In 1648 £36. 10s. were spent on preaching; in
the following year £35. 14s. 10d.[64] If we use the commonly accepted fee of 10s.
a sermon as the basis of calculation, it is clear that seventy-two sermons were
preached in the latter year, with an average of six sermons a month.

Similar practices can be detected in the records of other parishes, such as
St. John the Baptist, St. Clement Eastcheap, and St. Thomas the Apostle. At
St. John the Baptist, where the living was in vacancy for six years, from 1646
to 1652, payments to individual preachers were regularly recorded each year,
though the amounts varied greatly—from a high £36. 13s. 4d. in 1648–49 to a
low £6 in the following year.[65] At St. Clement Eastcheap, while there was no
settled ministry from 1646 to 1651, £44. 13s. 4d. were paid for preaching in
1647–48, £22 during a period of five months from 12 November 1648 to 2 April
1649, and £54. 10s. for one whole year from 15 April 1949 to 2 April 1650.[66] At
St. Thomas the Apostle, with the exception of two short intervals in 1650–51
and 1653–54, there was no minister from 1646 to 1655. Yet payments to
individual preachers were made in 1646–47, 1649–50, 1651–52, and 1652–53,
though the situation at St. Thomas the Apostle appeared to be less consistent
than the other instances given above.[67]

It should not be suggested, however, that the two new practices described
above had completely replaced the traditional form of ministerial maintenance in all the London parishes. In actuality, in a number of the London

parishes, in which tithes were not only adequate but could be more or less fully collected, the ministry continued to be maintained by tithes during the years of the Puritan Revolution. We shall examine a few cases in this category.

At All Hallows Bread Street, the annual value of tithes had been estimated at £84. In addition, there was also a legacy of £13. 6s. 8d. for a sermon on every Sunday during the year, and in 1632 a yearly stipend of £20 had been allocated to a lecturer chosen by the parishioners.[68] During the Interregnum, Lazarus Seaman, who probably received all of these without much trouble, remained at All Hallows from 1643 to his ejection in 1662.[69] At St. Mary at Hill, the tithes had been worth £125 per annum, while the glebe of the parish was estimated at £24. Furthermore, Sir John Leman, a fishmonger and a past Lord Mayor, had left in 1632 a legacy of £1,000 to secure an annual stipend of £40 for a "learned lecturer of honest and good life and conversation" to preach a divinity lecture on every Thursday from nine to twelve in this parish.[70] In 1643 a prominent Presbyterian divine, John Ley, became the minister, and when Ley moved to the wealthy parsonage of Brightwell in Berkshire, Thomas White succeeded him at St. Mary at Hill. White stayed until 1662 and probably conformed.[71] At St. Mary Aldermary, to cite one more example, although the annual value of tithes had been estimated at only £63, the glebe was worth £100. Besides, there was a permanent gift sermon during the winter quarter, carrying £20 a year.[72] In 1641 Robert Gell, a future friend of John Milton's, became the rector of this parish church and here he, too, stayed until after the Restoration.[73] And it may also be safe to assume that even in those parishes where adequate tithes remained the main source of the living, their collection was probably assured. In the parish of St. Martin Ludgate, when Thomas Jacombe was chosen minister in 1650, the vestry promised that "the parish should take care to gather the tythes quarterly without putting him to any trouble therein"; whereas in the parish of St. Benet Gracechurch, tithes were clearly supplemented. In the parish of St. Lawrence Old Jewry not only was the stipend of £180 guaranteed by a committee but tithes were also supplemented by subscriptions each year.[74]

In addition to the economic aspects of the parochial ministries in Puritan London, other changes also took place in the new relationship between the Puritan minister and the parish during this revolutionary era. Above all, the minister was no longer to be imposed, either by the bishop from above or by a lay patron from without. He was mostly to be elected freely by the vestry and, in a number of cases, by the parishioners in general. And the ministerial elections of the London parishes in this period were perhaps the most progressive in seventeenth-century England in view of the property qualifications, corporate restrictions, and aristocratic influences in other parliamentary or municipal elections of the period.

A few specific features of the process of the ministerial elections in Puritan London stand out prominently and deserve further consideration. First, the ability of the candidate, particularly as a preacher, was often carefully tested by trial sermons. Occasionally, a parish would consult with other eminent divines about a prospective candidate. Only after such scrutiny was a minister to be chosen. Second, almost in all cases, more than one candidate was nominated in an election. Third, insofar as one can judge from the language of the parish records, the elections appear to have been freely and equitably conducted—either by hand, or by subscription, or, at least in one recorded case, by secret ballot. And, last but by no means the least important, the elected minister and the parish would come into a sort of contractual agreement, mostly, as we have seen, upon a fixed annual stipend but, in some cases, upon other ministerial and parish matters as well. To be sure, the election of a minister was not a business transaction, and the contractual agreement was but a mutual understanding. Again, at least in a few recorded cases, written contracts were, indeed, made. Now we may turn to the parish records for some concrete examples for each of these points.

The preaching of a trial sermon before the election of the minister was probably not a new practice for the Puritan communities in London. It must have been used before 1640 by the Puritan parishes of the city in selecting their lecturers. During the Puritan era, however, this practice was generally adopted and perhaps became more sophisticated. At the parish of St. Dionis Backchurch, for instance, five payments were made for trial sermons for the election of a lecturer in 1641–42 and 1642–43, though apparently none was chosen.[75] At St. James Garlickhithe, for another instance, when Matthew Barker recommended Joshua Sprigg for the lectureship in 1645, it was pointed out that the parishioners had heard him preaching three times previously. Sprigg was "accepted unanimously by hand."[76] At the parish of St. Bride Fleet Street, after the sequestration of the living in October 1645, four ministers were invited to preach before an election in the month following.[77] In 1658, when the ministry at St. James Garlickhithe became vacant, it was ordered that six ministers be procured to preach on six Sabbath days, obviously as trial sermons for an election of a future minister.[78]

The number of candidates in a ministerial election varied from case to case. In some cases only the minister elected is mentioned in the records—such as the election of Stanley Gower at St. Martin Ludgate in 1643;[79] Matthew Haviland at Holy Trinity the Less in 1644;[80] Thomas Cawton at St. Bartholomew by the Exchange in 1645;[81] and Thomas Brooks at St. Margaret New Fish Street in 1648.[82] Yet, even in these cases it is possible that more than one candidate was actually considered. At Holy Trinity the Less, Matthew Haviland was clearly chosen along with other nominations, because the parishioners "voted and gave a large majority" to him.[83] In an election at St. Peter Cornhill in 1646, William Blackmore was chosen minister, but it is clear from its vestry minutes that another minister, [Mark or Anthony?] Downes, also had been nominated in the election.[84]

In most recorded elections, the names of all candidates are given in the parish records. In 1643 John Crosse was elected a Wednesday lecturer at St.

Bartholomew by the Exchange with three other candidates also nominated in the election: Arthur Bramley, Richard Gibson, and George Newton.[85] At St. Bride, Fleet Street, as has been noted, when the ministry became vacant in 1645, four ministers who had preached there were nominated for the election. They were Dr. [Faithful?] Tate, [Thomas?] Porter, [Walter?] Bridges, and [Thomas] Coleman.[86] And since the elected minister, Coleman, and the alternate, Porter, both declined the offer, another election was conducted early in the following year with three candidates nominated: John Dix (Dicks), [John?] Reeve, and [Isaac?] Bedford. Finally, Dicks was chosen and he accepted the charge.[87] Sometimes there were as many as five, six, or seven candidates in one election. In an election in 1647 at St. Swithin, the parish procured five nominees: [Francis?] Peck, [Isaac?] Knight, [William?] Bethell, [Edward?] Bennet, and John Sheffield. The choice, as would be expected, went to Sheffield, a renowned divine in the City.[88] At St. Martin Ludgate, in an election in early 1650, six ministers were nominated as candidates: [T.?] Harward (Harwood), [William?] Eyre, [Samuel?] Slater, Thomas Jacombe, [Joseph?] Church, and [Lawrence?] Wise. Again, expectedly, the choice went to Jacombe, also one of the leading divines in London.[89] At St. James Garlickhithe, to cite one more example, there were four nominees (Dr. [Roger?] Drake, Jonathan Lloyd, [Samuel?] Slaughter [Slater?] the younger, and [John?] Williamson) in an election in 1648, three ([Philip?] Gardner, John Shute, and Lawrence Wise) in another in 1650, and a total of seven (though in this case, with only the chosen minister's name given) in still another election in 1655. Lloyd, Wise, and John Onge were chosen respectively in these elections.[90]

The most fascinating aspect of the ministerial elections in Puritan London is the various forms in which an election was conducted. It appears that election by consent was probably more traditional and clearly most frequently used when only one minister was nominated. Thus, we find that in a meeting of the vestry of St. Botolph Billingsgate on 23 May 1647 thirty-seven parishioners "gave their ascent [*sic*] for Mr. Jacob Tyce" to be their minister and parson.[91] Similarly, in a vestry meeting at St. Margaret New Fish Street on 18 April 1648, Thomas Brooks was chosen minister "with a full and free consent."[92] And, sometime in early November 1649, James Nalton was "by a very full and general consent" elected minister at St. Martin Ludgate, though "for reasons best known to himself," as the vestry minutes observed, Nalton did not accept the charge.[93] More formally, and particularly when more than one candidate was nominated, election by hand was used. As we have seen, Sprigg's election to the lectureship at St. James Garlickhithe in 1645 was "unanimously by hand."[94] In another election in the same parish on 10 September 1650 Lawrence Wise was "fairly and clearly chosen and elected" among the three candidates.[95] In an election at St. Martin Ludgate early in 1650, Thomas Jacombe was chosen out of six candidates nominated, and as the vestry minutes further added, "ther nott beinge one hand in the negative."[96] In some cases the number of votes each candidate received is clearly recorded. In the election at St. James Garlickhithe in 1648, for instance, twenty-three hands were for Lloyd, one each for Drake, Slaughter the younger, and Williamson respectively.[97] And, to cite another example, in a general meeting of the parish of St. Margaret New Fish Street on 19 September 1654 "for the choice of a lecturer to supply the ancient lecture on Monday nights for the winter half year," two candidates—Thomas Brooks and Ralph Robinson—were nominated. Because both nominees were prominent divines in the City, one being Independent and the other Presbyterian, the election was expectedly a close one; for the parish clerk made fourteen crosses for Brooks on a line next to his name, thirteen for Robinson.[98] It was in the election at St. James Garlickhithe in 1655 that the choice of John Onge as minister, out of seven candidates nominated, was made, as was clearly noted in the vestry minutes, "by ballot."[99]

Among the London parishes, St. Martin Ludgate probably had one of the best structured ministerial elections during the revolutionary period. In November 1640 the parish created a committee of sixteen parishioners for the choice of a lecturer. And the sixteen were chosen, out of forty-eight men nominated, equally from the two separate areas of the parish—eight from within the gate and eight from without. In 1643 a similar committee of fourteen—seven from within the gate and seven from without—was created "to make choice of an able divine to supply the cure of this parish in the room of Dr. Jermin who was lately voted from the place."[100] It is also reasonable to believe that the committee must have considered and possibly presented more than one candidate before Stanley Gower was elected. And the vestry minutes of St. Bride, Fleet Street, have preserved a vivid account of the most elaborate, if not the most typical, procedures of an election day of this period. For the election of a minister on 12 November 1645 a general meeting of the parish was ordered by the vestry. From eight o'clock on till nine in the morning, the great bell of the parish church would ring continuously to call all the parishioners to the meeting. At the meeting three "books" of paper were prepared, with the names of the candidates written in several separate columns in each. After the parishioners had gathered in the parish church and, in all probability, after prayers had been said, each of them would subscribe his name in the column under the name of the minister of his choice. Upon the completion of the process of subscription, the names in each column of the books were counted, and the minister who had received the largest number of subscriptions won the election. In this case, apparently, two of the candidates, Thomas Coleman and Thomas Porter, each had the same number of names subscribed. They were therefore put to another election, "by hande in a free choice." Eventually, Coleman was chosen.[101]

Now with ministers mostly elected and their maintenance provided either in stipends or with voluntary subscriptions to supplement their tithes, it is perhaps only natural that the new relationship that gradually emerged between the Puritan minister and his parishioners during the revolutionary period was basically contractual in nature. Although in most cases, as has been noted, the contractual agreement between the Puritan minister and the parish was chiefly concerned with the economic conditions of the ministry, it should be emphasized that the settlement of the ministry was not just a business transaction, and the ministerial maintenance not the only concern. To the Puritan minister, the conditions of religious life in a parish were certainly one of his foremost concerns before acceptance of the charge; whereas, to the parish, the ministerial duties needed to be specified in the agreement.[102] In fact, as in the case of the negotiations between Anthony Harford and the parish of St. Michael Cornhill, Harford wanted to know, first and foremost, "the rightnesse of y^{or} order in Church matters" as well as the economic conditions of the ministry to which I have referred earlier in this chapter.[103] Or, as in the cases of Matthew Barker and Thomas Brooks, upon their election to the ministeries of St. James Garlickhithe and St. Margaret New Fish Street, respectively, they publicly declared their principles or conditions for coming to the office.[104] Since Harford was a Presbyterian minister and St. Michael Cornhill a Presbyterian parish, no fundamental differences existed. But both Brooks and Barker were Independents, and there were naturally clear differences between their Independent position and the conditions in a parochial church. Brooks, for instance, proposed six specific conditions upon which he would accept the charge: "(i) that you which bee Elders shall wholly lay downe your offices as Elders; (ii) that ye godly partie gather themselves together, and they owne one anothers graces, in a way of conference; (iii) that you receive all strangers into you, though something differing in opinion, as you find them fitt; (iv) that then if you please you may choose officers; (v) that you admitt ye Church for them to receive in; (vi) and [that] then I will give you ye sacrament and baptise your children, and none else but ye body."[105] In most cases the contractual agreement was probably no more than a mutual understanding between the two parties involved; yet in some cases, such as that between John Dicks and the parish of St. Bride and that between Richard Vines and the parish of St. Lawrence Old Jewry, a written contract was actually drawn up and its articles were either recorded in the vestry minutes or engrossed on a separate document.[106] Indeed, Dicks had to seal a bond of £300 to the parish and promise not to leave the ministry without the approval of the lawfulness of his departure by four godly ministers, two to be chosen by Dicks himself and two by the parish.[107]

Closely related to this new contractual relationship was the growth of parochial independence and lay control in parish affairs. This sense of parochial independence was, of course, greatly encouraged by the unique political and ecclesiastical conditions of the revolutionary period. In the early years of the Revolution, as the Episcopacy had been under attack, the rights of patronage of the old ecclesiastical authorities, whether the Archbishop of

Canterbury or the Bishop of London or the Dean and Chapter of St. Paul's, were often challenged.[108] Afterward, as the City benefices were nearly all in sequestration, the rights of lay patrons were also ignored, as long as the sequestered incumbents were still alive and no new presentation was necessary.[109] But these topics lie outside the scope of this chapter. Insofar as the relationship between the Puritan minister and the parish is concerned, it is also clear that any possible challenge to this independence by a minister was strongly resisted. This was apparently the case with Matthew Barker at St. James Garlickhithe in 1646. Barker, as an Independent, wanted to declare that his ministry in a traditional parish was in no way contradictory to his own beliefs in religious Independency. It seems that Barker's Independent beliefs did not concern the parishioners so much as his declaration itself. It might be misinterpreted as the minister's claim to independence of the parish. In a vestry meeting on 28 September 1646, therefore, while the vestry publicly and unanimously reconfirmed their former choice of Barker as pastor and teacher, they likewise announced that it was "only at his request" that they had allowed him "more freely to declare himself unto them his own satisfaction touching his call by them unto the said charge." They made it clear that they "will not by any means relinquish their right and interest which they conceive they have on him."[110]

In certain other cases the minister was requested to sign a written document concerning the rights and privileges of the parish. In 1654, for instance, upon his resignation from the ministry at St. Benet Paul's Wharf, Allen Geare signed a written statement "fully and freely [to] resigne and put up unto the hands of the parishioners . . . in general all the right title and interest I have or had in the Rectory of the said parish."[111] Similarly, in the parish of St. Antholin, after some controversy over a disputed election, Stephen Watkins eventually signed a written document in which he did "freely acknowledge and declare that there is a Power and good Authority in the Minister, Churchwardens and Parishioners . . . and their successors yearly to Elect their weekly morning lecturers and every [one] of them and yearly to determine such elections at their own judgment and pleasure."[112] Perhaps the classical example of the growth of lay control in parish affairs during this period is the conflict between the parishioners of St. James Garlickhithe and the minister, Zachary Crofton, over the lease of parish land. The triumph of the parishioners in this case was clear when in 1655, after Crofton had left and John Onge was chosen minister, Onge promised, as was so noted in the minutes of the vestry, "not to meddle with the lands and tenements of the parish."[113]

This increasing lay control in parish affairs, however, must not be misinterpreted as anticlericalism. The Puritan divines, as we have seen in many respects during this period, played a very influential role in the City. Preaching now became a constant feature of religious life in the London parish churches, and most parishes, as we have seen, tried their best to provide a secure and adequate maintenance for their ministers. Within some individual parishes, a disciplined religious life was also maintained, through cooperation between the minister and the civic leaders, in catechizing and in the examination of the parishioners before admission to the sacrament of Holy Communion.

Godly discipline was, of course, one of the fundamental principles of Puritanism. It would be interesting to see how this discipline was actually carried out and practiced in the London parishes during the Puritan era. In this respect the parish records are regrettably too sketchy to provide a detailed picture, and only a rudimentary outline can be reconstructed by piecing together indirect, fragmentary information gleaned from the vestry minutes. We do know, for instance, that in certain parishes, such as St. Christopher and St. James Garlickhithe, the minutes of the vestry clearly recorded the request of the minister and the consent of the parishioners in regard to the catechizing of children and servants both at home and on Sundays in the parish church.[114] And it is reasonable to presume that this was generally practiced in those London parishes in which settled ministries were established. The most significant innovation in religious life during this period was probably the examination of parishioners prior to admission to the Lord's Supper. It was, in the eyes of the Puritan divines, one of the most crucial and fundamental conditions for the success of godly discipline.

It is to be noted, however, that the examination of the lives of parishioners and the exclusion of those found unfit for the Sacrament of Holy Communion were also controversial issues in Puritan London, and this was especially true in those parishes in which profound religious differences existed. As was seen in an earlier chapter, such practices in the parish of St. Stephen Coleman Street led first to the conflict between John Goodwin and the parishioners and eventually to Goodwin's expulsion.[115] Similarly, in the parish of St. Dunstan in the East, shortly after the new vestry committee ordered that "Mr. Henry Wilkinson our Minister shall forbeare administering the Sacrament until the Committee shall . . .," the order was rescinded. We find a "memorandum" that reads: "this order being not set down according to the intent and sense of this Committee, is therefore by a full consent to be void and struck and rased out." And four lines of the old order were indeed obliterated and are no longer legible.[116] The real reason was, in all probability, that some of the Independent civic leaders of the parish, such as John Fowke and Maurice Thompson, were opposed to the order.[117] Sometimes, even in a strongly Presbyterian parish such as St. Mary Aldermanbury, difficulties could also arise, though in such a case the minister would have the full support of the civic leaders of the parish.[118] Yet, in spite of such conflicts and difficulties in certain parishes and on certain specific occasions, this Puritan experiment was not a total failure. In the parish of St. Stephen Coleman Street, for instance, after Goodwin was ousted and William Taylor chosen minister, it was reestablished in early 1646.[119] Again, it may be safely assumed that this practice was instituted in most of the London parishes where the Presbyterian divines held the office of the ministry, and in a number of parishes the churchwardens' accounts recorded the purchase of tokens to be issued to those parishioners who had successfully passed their examination for participation in the Sacrament of Holy Communion.[120]

We may wonder how this examination was actually conducted in the various London parishes. Was it rigidly maintained in its almost inquisitorial scrutiny of the virtues and vices of men and women as, in view of the conventional image of the Puritan, we would expect? Or, to use an analogy of what we all know in our contemporary academic world, was there an inflation of the holy grace in these examinations, now that they had to be given to the populace in general, not just to the saints who had experienced their conversion? What were the feelings of ordinary men and women toward this new discipline? In all these respects, once more, the parish records were silent. Only in the vestry minutes of St. Michael Cornhill do we get an indirect glimpse of the situation. We may recall that upon his election as minister, Anthony Harford wanted to know "the rightness of y^{or} order in Church matters." In his answer to Harford's inquiry, John Bellamy, one of the ruling elders of the parish, described in some detail what the religious life was like in Puritan London. For five years in the past, when John Wall was parson, said Bellamy, the sacrament of the Lord's Supper had been regularly administered to the parishioners. The younger people were all examined before their admittance by the minister, either in the presence of the ruling elders or in their absence. And when children grew up or new servants came into the parish and desired to be admitted to that ordinance, they had to submit themselves to the minister's examination in advance. But for the old inhabitants of the parish, who had been usually admitted to the Lord's Supper before the establishment of the Puritan discipline, allowances apparently had to be made. Some were willing to come to the vestry to be examined by the minister in the presence of the ruling elders. Others, "through bashfulnesse or otherwise," were unwilling to be questioned before these laymen. In such cases, the minister would see them individually in the vestry and the meeting took the form either of examination or simply an informal conversation. If by such meetings the parishioners satisfied the minister and, through him, the elders, "in the sufficiencie of their knowledge," they were admitted to the sacrament. And, Bellamy concluded, "I conceive all those that have bin received to communion will expect to be continued in communion."[121] As St. Michael Cornhill was one of the prominent Puritan parishes in the City, we may consider Bellamy's description typical of the general situation in London. In any case it is refreshing to know that there was not lacking a certain human touch even in the godly discipline under the rule of the Puritans.

In conclusion we may say that, as far as the new clerical-lay relationship was concerned, the Puritan experiment in the City of London signified a unique period of parochial life. The election of the minister by the parishioners themselves, instead of the imposition of one either by a bishop or a lay patron, led both to a growing independence of the London parishes and to a corresponding increase in the consciousness of the parishioners about their own interests and their responsibilities in parochial affairs. And the various forms and procedures of the ministerial elections were, as I have suggested, perhaps far more democratic and rational in nature in comparison with contemporary parliamentary and municipal elections in seventeenth-century England. The contractual relationship between the Puritan minister and the parish also reveals a certain sign of the new social mentality. The ministry was no longer considered an unquestioned part of the social hierarchy but a kind of social service like many other services in a composite society. All these new developments, it is to be emphasized again, did not necessarily lead to the decline of religion. It is true that the Puritan civic leaders in the City failed to work out a systematic solution to improve the economic conditions of the City parish churches, but that was, after all, beyond their power. And even in this respect, the substitution of an annual stipend for the precarious tithes was certainly an improvement for many, if not all, of the parish churches in the City during the Puritan era. It may be pointed out, too, that there is surely a historical connection between these precedents during the revolutionary period and the provisions in 22 and 23 Car. II. c. 15, which allotted stipends ranging from £100 to £200 a year, in lieu of tithes, to fifty-one London parochial livings after the Restoration. These ministerial stipends were to be raised by rates in the City.[122] In a sense, the post-Restoration solution of the economic problems of the London parish churches was a belated but eventually successful realization of the earlier plans and experiments in Puritan London.

NOTES

1. See Christopher Hill, *Economic Problems of the Church from Archbishop Whitgift to the Long Parliament* (Oxford, 1956).
2. See Shaw, 2: 202–26.
3. See ibid., pp. 496–600.
4. CLRO J. Co. Co., 40, f. 190b; CLRO Letter Books, QQ, f. 234.
5. To be sure, this committee was composed mostly of the lay Presbyterian leaders in the City, especially among the Common Councilmen of the committee. They were: Alderman John Wollaston, Mr. Recorder [i.e., John Glynne], Alderman John Langham, Alderman John Fowke, Alderman James Bunce, Alderman John Kendrick, Alderman Samuel Avery, Alderman John Bide, Alderman George Witham, Deputy Christopher Pack, Walter Boothby, Thomas Steane, William Kendall, Captain John Jones, Colonel John Bellamy, Nathaniel Hall, Colonel Edward Hooker, Captain Richard Venner, George Dunne, James Story, Lieutenant Colonel Lawrence Bromfield, John Gase, Deputy Alexander Jones, Stafford Clare, and Lieutenant Colonel Nathaniel Campfield.
6. The report was written and reported by sixteen of the above committee: Wollaston,

Bunce, Avery, Bide, Venner, Bellamy, Boothby, Gase, Bromfield, Kendall, Campfield, Hall, Clare, Story, Steane, and Dunne.

7. CLRO J. Co. Co., 40, f. 193; CLRO Letter Books, QQ, ff. 237–37b.

8. Ibid.

9. CLRO Letter Books, QQ f. 245.

10. Ibid., f. 255.

11. See Valerie Pearl, "London's Counter-Revolution," in Aylmer, ed., *The Interregnum: The Quest for Settlement 1646–1660,* pp. 29–56. For a study of the Presbyterian movement in the City during the years of the Civil War, see Liu, "The Founding of the London Provincial Assembly, 1645–47," *Guildhall Studies in London History,* 3, no. 2: 109–34.

12. In 1648, after an investigation of the vacancies among the parochial ministries in the City, the City government petitioned the Long Parliament for better maintenance of ministers. It appears that the Parliament suggested the uniting of smaller parishes in the City so that adequate maintenance could be raised for ministers. The Common Council resolved against such a plan. See CLRO J. Co. Co., 40, ff. 297–97b. It is interesting to note that such a plan was to be adopted in the City after the Great Fire in 1666.

13. The London clergy's petition in 1635–38 had been primarily an attempt to increase the value of tithes to an equitable amount based upon the moderate rents of the houses in each parish. This plan of the City government in 1645 was actually to levy an annual tax in the City, and presumably to pay fixed stipends in lieu of tithes. More important, of course, the London clergy's petition in 1635–38 was strongly opposed by the City government, whereas this new plan was initiated and supported by the City leaders themselves.

14. See Seaver, pp. 150–53, 162–65.

15. GLMS 4384/1, f. 562; Freshfield, ed., *The Vestry Minute Books of the Parish of St. Bartholomew Exchange in the City of London, 1587–1676,* pt. 1, p. 146; Seaver, p. 273. It does not appear that Lightfoot ever possessed the rectory of the parish as Seaver has suggested.

16. GLMS 4384/2,, f. 36; Freshfield, *The Vestry Minute Books . . . of St. Bartholomew Exchange,* pt. 2, p. 11.

17. GLMS 3570/2, f. 43; GLMS 2590/1, f. 408; GLMS 2593/2, ff. 309, 340, 355. It should be pointed out that when Matthew Newcomen was chosen as lecturer at St. Mary Aldermanbury in 1643 with a stipend of £52 a year, £30 of it was to be paid by Calamy. See GLMS 3570/2, f. 48b.

18. For Cornelius Burgess, see *D. N. B., s. v.; C. R., s.v.* For contemporary opinions of Burgess, see *A Letter from Mercurius Civicus to Mercurius Rusticus,* in Scott, ed., *Somers Tracts,* 4:585.

19. GLMS 951/1, ff. 119, 120; GLMS 1013/1, f. 192b. St. George Botolph Lane was one of the small parishes in the City. In 1644, the total receipts from both tithes and contributions amounted to only £53, 13s. 5½d., and the churchwardens were ordered to take up £10 at interest in order to pay the minister. GLMS 951/1, f. 122. The parish of St. Mary Woolchurch did manage to pay as much as £25 a quarter to its minister, Richard Ball, in the 1650s. See GLMS 1013/1, ff. 215–15b.

20. GLMS 3908/1, no folio number, see vestry minutes, 24 November 1644; GLMS 4212/1, f. 21. These were obviously temporary agreements. St. Lawrence Pountney was an impropriation in the hands of the parishioners, and the curate's stipend had been only £11. 6s. 8d. In 1638 the incumbent's total income was £38. 17s. See LPLMS CM IX/58; Dale, p. 86. Dale probably mistook the figure of income in 1638 as the total value of tithes. St. Benet Gracechurch was also one of the small parishes in the City, and the total value of tithes of the parish was estimated at £50 or £60 a year. See n. 29 below.

21. See Dale, pp. 21, 26, 48, 52, 54, 81, 120, 168, 235. With the exception of St. Giles Cripplegate, which was one of the largest parishes and in which, as William Fuller reported, the loss of tithes could amount to as much as £100 a year, the reported losses ranged from £1 to £10. For a detailed account of tithes in arrears, see LPLMS CM VIII/16, ff. [1–3]. In any case, the fact remains that tithes could not be totally collected even under ordinary circumstances.

22. Dale, p. 201, LPLMS CM VIII/37, f. [4]. Strictly speaking, the legal independent income for the incumbent was only £16. See LPLMS CM IX/58.

23. GLMS 6554/1, f. 25. In this case the total value of tithes was probably much higher than the stipend, because St. Bride was a large parish. The figures recommended by the London clergy in 1638 for St. Bride were £250 and £260. See LPLMS CM VIII/4, f. [4]; LPLMS CM IX/82.

24. The values of tithes and glebe, if any, in the various London parishes were always estimated differently, and the actual income of the incumbent again varied from year to year. In my presentations of these figures, the following symbols are used: T = value of tithes, G = value of glebe, C.R. = clear revenue. For the parish of St. Bartholomew Exchange the figures are: T: £75, G: £23 (Newcourt, 1:291); T:£88. 16s. 4d., G:£19. 10s. (Dale, p. 36); T: £78, G: £30 (LPLMS CM VIII/37, f. [1]); C. R.: £89. 1s. 4d. (LPLMS CM VIII/43 f. [1]), £109. 19s. 4d.(LPLMS CM IX/58). For St. James Garlickhithe, T: £92 (Newcourt, 1:366); T: £92. 10s. 8d. (Dale, p. 75); T: £100, G: £28 (LPLMS CM VIII/37, f. [2]); C.R.: £56. 10s. 2d. (LPLMS CM VIII/43, f. [2],) £81. 3s. 10d. (LPLMS CM IX/58). See also n. 16 above; GLMS 4810/2, f. 70. It should be noted that the parish of St. James Garlickhithe was deeply in debt and had again borrowed £600 for repairing the parish church and its steeple in the year before. See GLMS 4813/1, f. 68; GLMS 4810/2, ff. 116, 118.

25. The various estimates for the value of tithes in St. Michael Cornhill are: T: £116. 6s. 4d. plus £4. 10s for sermons (Newcourt, 1:481); T: £117. 15s. (Dale, p. 146); T: £114. 14s. 5d. (LPLMS CM VIII/37, f. [3]); C.R.: £97. 7s. 4d. (LPLMS CM VIII/43, f. [2]), £98. 12s. 2d. (LPLMS CM IX/58).

26. GLMS 4072/1, f. 179b. The four parishioners were William Rowell, James Martin, Thomas Harris, and John Bellamy.

27. The various estimates for the value of tithes in the parish of St. Swithin are: T: £75 plus £14 for sermons (Newcourt, 1:542); T: £80 (LPLMS CM VIII/37, f. [4]); C.R.: £63. 4s. 6d. (LPLMS CM VIII/43, f. [4]); £64. 1s. 11-½d. (LPLMS CM IX/58).

28. GLMS 560/1, no folio number, see vestry minutes, 20 September and 20 October 1648. It should also be noted that when Sheffield received £7.10s. from William Gouge for the lectureship in early 1649, the vestry ordered that the same amount was to be deducted from Sheffield's salary.

29. The various estimates for the value of tithes in the parish of St. Benet Gracechurch are: T: £55 (Newcourt, 1:300); T: £57. 18s. 6d. (Dale, p. 40); C.R.: £50 (LPLMS CM VIII/43, f. [1]); £60 (LPLMS CM IX/58).

30. GLMS 1568, ff. 651, 657, 661, 665, 670, 682, 686, 692, 698, 706, 710. The ministers during this period were William Harrison, George Kendall, and Samuel Smith. The stipend consisted of both tithes and subscriptions. Sometimes the parish simply chould not live up to its promise, but it tried very hard indeed to keep it.

31. In 1650–51 only £52. 3s. 8d. were collected from tithes, while in 1653–54 only £48. 2s. 10d. were collected. GLMS 1568, ff. 670, 685. For the annual payment to William Quelch, see ibid., from 1644–45 to 1653–54.

32. GLMS 1013/1, f. 199b; GLMS 1012/1, f. [14]). Among the new feoffees were Colonel Thomas Gower, Thomas Brace, Matthew White, Francis Clay, and Lieutenant Colonel Robert Thompson.

33. The various estimates of the value of tithes and glebe in the parish of St. Mary Woolchurch are: T: £50. 16s. 6d., G: £22 (Newcourt, 1:460); T: £50. 8s. 6d., G: £10 (Dale, p. 122); T: £50. 19s. 6d., G: £10 (LPLMS CM VIII/37, f. [3]); C.R.: £58. 8s. (LPLMS CM VIII/43; f. [3]), £56. 15s. (LPLMS CM IX/58).

34. GLMS 1013/1, ff. 226, 230b, 232b.

35. The various estimates of the total value of tithes and glebe in the parish of St. Stephen Walbrook are: T: £40 (Newcourt, 1:538); T: £39. 10s. (Dale, p. 181); T: £39. 10s., G: £24 (LPLMS CM VIII/37, f. [3]); C.R.: £42. 10s. 8d. (LPLMS CM VIII/43, f. [3]); £47. 10s. (LPLMS CM

IX/58). See also GLMS 593/4, no folio number, churchwardens' accounts for 1644–45, 1645–46, 1647–48, 1658–59.

36. GLMS 943/1, no folio number, vestry minute, 2 April 1650. Tice had been minister of the parish from 1647–48. Apparently he preferred a fixed stipend to the precarious and difficult collection of tithes. See GLMS 942/1, no folio number, churchwardens' account for 1647–48.

37. GLMS 4072/1, f. 198.

38. Ibid., f. 198b.

39. Ibid.

40. Ibid., f. 199. Harford's decision to decline the offer was probably because neither a fixed stipend nor guarantee was given by Bellamy about his maintenance. In fact, as has been noted, when John Wall was chosen minister of the parish, the parishioners had resolved that £120 a year "shall for three years from his coming hither be assured unto him in lieu of tithes." Ibid., f. 179b. See also n. 26 above.

41. It appears that the Puritan ministers in sequestered livings in the City had no legal right to tithes, though either the minister or the parish sequestrators could always petition the Committee for Plundered Ministers against those who refused to pay them. See Hist. MSS. Comm., *Sixth Report,* Appendix, p. 115: "Affidavit of Robert Harris that he is informed by his counsel that he has no legal remedy against those who refuse to pay." For complaints about people who refused to pay tithes, see BL Add. MS. 15669, ff. 136, 190; Add. MS. 15670, ff. 8, 194b; Add. MS 15671, ff. 16b, 128, 192, 196b, 237b, 253, 256b.

42. The various estimates of the value of tithes in the parish of St. Martin Orgar are: T: £77 (Newcourt, I. 417); T: £80, 7s. 1d. (Dale, p. 130); T: £80 (LPLMS CM VIII/37, f. [3]); C.R.: £64. 16s. 8d. (LPLMS CM VIII/43, f. [3]); £76. 12s. ½d. (LPLMS CM IX/58). Walton's figure for clear revenue in 1638 is £71. 12s. 1 ½d. (Dale, p. 130). See also Hill, *Economic Problems,* pp. 277–78. Hill says that the true value of tithes was estimated at £1,600. Apparently, he mistook the total value of the moderate rents of the houses in 1638 as the estimated total value of tithes. It should also be noted that the parish maintained: "the Incumbent hath another livinge worth 200-li: p. ann. & 1000-li: in estate & vpwards havinge noe charge but himselfe & his wife." LPLMS CM VIII/37, f. [3].

43. GLMS 959/1, f. 204. As I have noted, the parish had no settled ministry in these years and was "content . . . with wandering ministers."

44. The various estimates of the value of tithes in the parish of St. Mary Magdalen Old Fish Street are: T: £80 (Newcort, 1:472); T: £101. 18s. 8d. (Dale, p. 139); T: £110 (LPLMS CM VIII/37, f. [3]); C.R.: £74. 16s. 7d. (LPLMS CM VIII/43, f. [3]); £92. 13s. 10d. (LPLMS CM IX/58). While the incumbent complained in 1638 that "there is no glebe that I know of, now belonging to this Church though it appears by divers records that above 40 houses were given unto it and enjoyed in right of it heretofore" (Dale, p. 140), the parish maintained that the value of tithes had been only £70 fourteen years before. (LPLMS CM VIII/37, f. [3].)

45. The various estimates of the value of tithes in the parish of St. Michael Queenhithe are : T: £90 (Newcourt, 1:487); T: £91. 3s. 4d. (Dale, p. 151); T: £93 (LPLMS CM VIII/37, f. [3]); C.R.: £47 [£97?]. 4s. (LPLMS CM VIII/43, f. [3]); £99. 10s. (LPLMS CM IX/58).

46. GLMS 4825/1, ff. 56, 57b, 60b, 65b.

47. Ibid., ff. 84–86b. Even after 1650–51, when the ministry was settled with Thomas Dawkes coming to the cure, only £30. 3s. 10d. were collected in 1650–51 and £56. 1s. 8d. in 1651–52. See ibid., ff. 92, 100.

48. GLMS 951, f. 104.

49. Ibid., f. 114.

50. Ibid., f. 135. Thomas Hinchman had been instituted as rector of the parish in 1647–48. The total value of tithes in the parish of St. George Botolph Lane was, indeed, very low. The various estimated figures are: T: £55 (Newcourt, 1:352); T: £58. 5s. (Dale, p. 64); T: £58 (LPLMS CM VIII/37, f. [2]); C.R.: £53. 3s. (LPLMS CM VIII/43, f. [2],); £60. 15s. 8d. (LPLMS CM IX/58).

51. GLMS 3908/1, no folio number, see vestry minute, 20 October 1644.

52. Ibid., see vestry minute, 26 January 1644/45. See also n. 20 above. This resolution of the

vestry clearly indicated the willingness of the parish to improve its ministerial maintenance in spite of the fact that the parish had been an impropriation.

53. GLMS 3907/1, see churchwardens' accounts for the years of 1654–60.

54. Hist. MSS. Comm., *Fifth Report,* Appendix, p. 119a. In fact, the value of tithes in the parish of St. Augustine appears to have been adequate. The various estimated figures are: T: £96 (Newcourt, 1:287); T: £98. 14s. 7d. (Dale, p. 35); T: £100 ("Within 40 years ye tithes were not 40 li p. an. There hath since been an increase of 60 li p. ann.") (LPLMS CM VIII/37, f. [1]); C.R.: £88. 3s. 8 ½d. (LPLMS CM VIII/43, f. [1]); £89. 14s. 3d. (LPLMS CM IX/58). A 1655 copy of the rates of tithes for ninety-two inhabitants in the three precincts of the parish gave the quarterly value at £24. 12s. 3 ½d. GLMS 635/1, at the end of the volume.

55. GLMS 978/1, no folio number, see vestry minutes, 1648. Ten years before, in 1635–38, the value of tithes in the parish of St. Clement Eastcheap had been estimated ast £40. (Newcourt, 1:326; Dale, p. 46; LPLMS CM VIII/37, f. [1]). And the clear revenue of the incumbent had varied from £25. 7s 2½d. (LPLMS CM VIII/43, f. [1]) to £34. 15s. (LPLMS CM X/58).

56. GLMS 978/1, vestry minute, 8 October 1648.

57. GLMS 3908/1, vestry minute, 21 March 1651/2.

58. GLMS 824/1, no folio number, vestry minute, 29 February 1651/2.

59. GLMS 823/1, no folio number, see churchwardens' accounts for the years of 1646–50.

60. Ibid., churchwardens' accounts for 1650.

61. Ibid., churchwardens' accounts, from 7 July to 3 October 1647.

62. Although the total value of tithes was given as £64 or £65, the stipend for the curate was only £8. So the minister had been mainly maintained by the parish. See Newcourt, 1:250; Dale, p. 14; LPLMS CM VIII/37, f. [4]; LPLMS CM IX/58.

63. The ministry was not settled until Thomas Dawkes came to the cure sometime in 1650–51. GLMS 4825/1, see churchwardens' accounts for the years of 1644–51.

64. Ibid., ff. 83, 86b, 91b. Only in 1647–48 and 1648–49 were the names of the individual preachers recorded.

65. GLMS 577/1, no folio number, see churchwardens' accounts for the years of 1646–52. The lack of preaching in 1649–50 was probably due to the repairing of the parish church in that year, on which the parish spent £1,160. 13s. 3d.

66. GLMS 977/1, no folio number, see churchwardens' accounts for these various years.

67. GLMS 662/1, ff. 130, 139b–40, 145b, 148. It has been said that Thomas Brooks was preacher at St. Thomas the Apostle in 1648 *(C.R., s.v.),* yet neither preaching nor any preacher's name was recorded in that year. In fact, Brooks appeared to be the minister of the parish in 1650–51. GLMS 662/1, f. 143.

68. The value of tithes and glebe in the parish of Allhallows Bread Street was estimated as follows: T: £84, G:£13. 6s. 8d. (Newcourt, 1:245; Dale, p. 9); T: £88. 16s. 6d. (LPLMS CM VIII/37, f.[1]); C.R.: £60. 16s. (LPLMS CM VIII/43, f. [1]); £80. 2s. 8d. (LPLMS CM IX/58). See also Hill, *Economic Problems,* p. 260.

69. For Lazarus Seaman, see *D. N. B., s. v.; C.R., s. v.*

70. The various estimates of the value of tithes and glebe in the parish of St. Mary at Hill are: T: £125, G: £24 (Newcourt, 1:450); T: £122, G(plus casualties): £42 (Dale, p. 1125); T: £122 G: £22 (LPLMS CM VIII/37, f.[3]); C.R.: £117. 15s. 10d. (LPLMS CM VIII/43, f. [2]); £149. 16s. 4d. (LPLMS CM IX/58). See also Jordan, *Charities of London,* p. 288.

71. GLMS 1240/1. ff. 46, 51b, 70b. It was said that Thomas White was ejected in 1662 from a lectureship at St. Bride, but White's name continued to appear in the vestry book of St. Mary at Hill until the 1670s. See *C. R., s.v.* Cf., perhaps, *D. N. B., s.v.* Thomas White (1628–98), a future bishop of Petersborough. For Ley, see *C. R., s.v.; D. N. B., s. v.*

72. The various estimates of the value of tithes and glebe are as follows: T: £63, G: £100 (Newcourt, 1:435); T: £64. 17s. 8d, G: £96. 8s. 8d. (Dale, p. 108); T: £65, G: £105, plus a lectureship of £20 (LPLMS CM VIII/37, f. [2]); C. R.: £127. 12s. 8d. (LPLMS CM VIII/43, f. [2]); £161. 2s. 10d. (LPLMS CM IX/58).

73. GLMS 4863/1, f. 19, where he signed as rector for the churchwardens' account, 1641–42.

Gell was clearly not a Presbyterian and refused to participate in the London Presbyterian system. Hill has described Gell as a Familist, but he was identified in 1661 as an "orthodox" minister in the City. However, he was for religious toleration. In any case, some parishioners of St. Mary Aldermary attempted in 1645 to get rid of Gell but, for unknown reasons, he survived, whereas, we may recall, even such prominent Independents as John Goodwin and Henry Burton were forced out of their livings in the same year. See BL Add. MS. 15669, ff. 25b, 46b, 63b, 66b, 72, 75b, 90, 96b, 142, 161, 177b, 192, 218b; Add. MS. 15670, f. 23; Add. MS. 36781, f. 33; Surman, 2:110; Shaw, 2:109; Hist. MSS. Comm., *Seventh Report,* Appendix, p. 148; Christopher Hill, *Milton and the English Revolution* (New York, 1979), p. 34. For Gell, see also *D. N. B., s.v.,* where he is mistakenly identified as rector of St. Mary Aldermanbury.

74. GLMS 1311/1, f. 149; GLMS 1568, ff. 170, 685; GLMS 2590/1, f. 410; GLMS 2593/2, ff. 250–51, 302, 304.

75. GLMS 4215/1, ff. 68, 69.

76. GLMS 4813/1, f. 68b.

77. GLMS 6554/1, ff. 11b–12.

78. GLMS 4813/1, f. 132b.

79. GLMS 1311/1, f. 138b.

80. *L. J.,* 6: 495; Hist. MSS. Comm., *Sixth Report,* Appendix, p. 9.

81. GLMS 4384/2, f. 36; Freshfield, ed., *Vestry Minute Books. . .St. Bartholomew Exchange,* pt. 2, p. 11.

82. GLMS 1175/1, no folio number, vestry minute, 18 April 1648.

83. Hist. MSS. Comm., *Sixth Report,* Appendix, p. 9.

84. GLMS 4165/1, f. 285.

85. GLMS 4384/2, f. 11; Freshfield, ed., *Vestry Minute Books. . .St. Bartholomew Exchange,* pt. 1, p. 4.

86. GLMS 6554/1, f. 11b.

87. Ibid., ff. 12–12b, 24b. Bedford and Reeve "had not above 2. or 3. hands a peice;" whereas Dicks "had many score hands."

88. GLMS 560/1, no folio number, vestry minute, 7 November 1647.

89. GLMS 1311/1, f. 148b.

90. GLMS 4813/1, ff. 74, 87b, 121.

91. GLMS 943/1, no folio number, vestry minute, 23 May 1647.

92. GLMS 1175/1, no folio number, vestry minute, 18 April 1648.

93. GLMS 1311/1, f. 148.

94. See n. 76 above.

95. GLMS 4813/1, f. 87b.

96. GLMS 1311/1, f. 148b; *C. R., s. v.*

97. GLMS 4813/1, f. 74.

98. GLMS 1175/1, no folio number, vestry minute, 19 September 1954.

99. GLMS 4813/1, f. 121.

100. GLMS 1311/1, ff. 134b, 138.

101. GLMS 6554/1, ff. 11b–12.

102. In most cases the agreements were concerned with ministerial and preaching obligations. See GLMS 3570/2, f. 43; GLMS 1453/1, ff. 43, 47.

103. GLMS 4072/1, f. 198.

104. GLMS 4813/1, f. 696; *C. R., s. v.* Thomas Brooks.

105. Ibid.

106. GLMS 6554/1, f. 25; GLMS 2590/1, f. 418.

107. GLMS 6554/1, ff. 46b–47.

108. See GLMS 1179/1, ff. 22, 29 and BL Add. MS. 15669, f. 55 (for a case between the parish of St. Magnus and the Bishop of London); Hist. MSS. Comm., *Fifth Report,* Appendix, p. 47 (for a case between the parish of Allhallows Bread Street and the Archbishop of Canterbury); ibid., p. 110 (for another example between the parish of St. Alphage London Wall and the Bishop of

London); *W. R., s. v.* Oliver Whitby (for a case between the parish of St. Nicholas Olave and the Dean and Chapter of St. Paul's).

109. See GLMS 593/4, no folio number, churchwardens' accounts, 1642–43 and Hist. MSS. Comm., *Fifth Report,* Appendix, p. 23 (for a case between St. Stephen Walbrook and the Grocers' Company). In other cases, the parish simply chose their ministers without procuring either permission from or presentation by the patrons. See GLMS 4072/1, ff. 179b, 189b (for the case between the parish of St. Michael Cornhill and the Drapers' Company) and GLMS 560/1, no folio number, vestry minute, 10 November 1647 and *C. R., s. v.* John Sheffield (for the case between the parish of St. Swithin and the Salters' Company).

110. GLMS 4813/1, f. 69b.

111. GLMS 877/1, f. 141.

112. GLMS 1045/1, f. 63.

113. GLMS 4813/1, f. 127. For the Crofton-parish conflict, see ibid., ff. 104–19b.

114. GLMS 4425/1, f. 43b; E. Freshfield, ed., *Minutes of the Vestry Meetings and Other Records of the Parish of St. Christopher le Stocks* ([London], 1886), p. 39; GLMS 4813/1, f. 90b.

115. See chap. 3 above.

116. GLMS 4887, f. 512.

117. Among the signatories following the minutes concerning this episode are John Fowke [whose name, for some unknown reason, was also crossed out], George Hanger, Maurice Thompson, John Milton, Lawrence Bromfield, Gilbert Keate, Thomas Stubbins, and Robert Foote.

118. GLMS 3590/2, f. 58.

119. GLMS 4458/1, ff. 147–48.

120. Ibid., For the use of tokens for admission to the Sacrament of Holy Communion in Puritan London, see Victoria History of the Counties of England, *London* (London, 1909), p. 355 and n.407.

121. GLMS 4072/1, f. 198b.

122. Hill, *Economic Problems,* p. 288.

6

The Parish as a Civic Institution

In the preceding chapters we have studied the parochial communities in the City of London during the period of the English Revolution mainly from the religious perspective. We have seen that in some parishes Presbyterianism and the Presbyterian church discipline were officially established during the Puritan era; in others the Independents appeared at various times and in different capacities either as occasional preachers, regular lecturers, or parochial incumbents; and in still others the ministry was never settled or, more interesting, Anglican clergymen returned to the scene in spite of the opposition of the civic leaders in a Puritan parish or actually by invitation of the inhabitants in parishes that either were conservative in their general religious attitude or had been disillusioned by the radicalization of the Revolution. It is clear, therefore, that as far as religion is concerned, Puritan London was far from being a city of harmonious religious unity during the twenty years of the Revolution. In this chapter we shall reexamine the London parochial communities from a different angle, that is, as civic institutions for the governance of secular affairs, and a new set of questions will be raised. We may ask, for instance, to what extent and in what ways the traditional structure of government of the London parishes was changed, if at all, during the period of Revolution. And, second, did the tradition of parochial governmental structure collapse in its civic functions in any of the City parishes as it clearly did, in some of them, in its religious and ministerial affairs? In this respect, the system of poor relief will serve as the focus of our study.

In an age of political revolution and with Puritanism as a reform movement, it would have been inconceivable that the parochial structure of the parishes in the City of London, the center of both the political crisis and the Puritan movement, would remain unaffected. To be sure, the English Revolution, unlike revolutions in the twentieth century, was one limited to the upper stratum of society and government, and, in spite of some cries in the wilderness and radical revolutionary rhetoric, few of the leaders of the Revolution, if any, intended and attempted "to turn the world upside down,"[1] and, of course, few of them could have, even if they had tried.[2] We can hardly expect, therefore, that there was a total reconstruction of the parochial governmental structure in the City of London during the revolutionary era, and most of the City parishes probably remained basically what they had been in their fundamental system of governance. Nonetheless, in some of the parishes of the City, changes did occur during the Puritan period, and it will be appropriate to look more closely at these changes in order to have a proper understanding of their nature and circumstances.

It is to be noted, first and foremost, that not all the changes in the parochial governmental structure among some of the London parishes were the result of political or religious radicalism, though the latter was undoubtedly one of the main forces for change. In some cases changes were made in the parochial governmental system either as a natural result of social progress in economic status and in literacy among the inhabitants in general or for the purpose of a more rational and better management of parish affairs. For the former case, the parish of St. Mary Aldermanbury may be cited as example. Both as a civic institution and as an ecclesiastical organization, St. Mary Aldermanbury, as we have seen on many occasions in this study, was one of the most important parishes in the City during the revolutionary period. Edmund Calamy, its minister, was a renowned Presbyterian and, as such, a conservative, and its civic leaders such as Simon Edmonds, George Witham, Gabriel Newman, William Methwold, John Holland, and Walter Boothby were all substantially wealthy merchants in the City. And the parish was well governed in religious as well as civil affairs. It is significant to note, however, that a complete reorganization of the parochial governmental structure took place in this parish, and, for that matter, it was the first and most thorough reorganization among all the London parishes during the revolutionary period. On 19 April 1642 a general meeting of the parishioners was called, and "by consent of the generality," it was resolved that "the selected vestry should be abolished and made void and upon all occasions should be a general meeting." More interesting, it was further agreed upon that "the former order which was that no man should be chosen into office but such as could both read and write . . . shall be disanuled and of none effect."[3] Given the social composition and the internal governmental structure of the parish, we may safely assume that such democratic changes were the result of neither factional struggle among the rich nor radical agitation from below. The fact might simply be that the select vestry and the literacy requirement for parochial officials had both become totally obsolete in such a parish as St. Mary Aldermanbury by the middle of the seventeenth century.[4]

In some other cases, the efforts to change the traditional parochial structure were clearly for better governance. St. Botolph Aldersgate, for example, was a large parish outside the Wall to the northwest of the old City. Its traditional vestry was select in composition and, as such, hardly representative in nature either socially or geographically. Its membership had no bearing with an equitable, geographical distribution, and in a large parish such as St. Botolph Aldersgate, this structural impediment of its traditional vestry must have been obvious. On 23 September 1645, therefore, "for the agitating and managing of all the civil matters and affairs of the parish," the parishioners of St. Botolph decided to change the composition of its vestry; and it was resolved that in future each of the four precincts of the parish was to choose six men to compose a new vestry and that the twenty-four men with the two churchwardens, or any nine of them as a quorum, were to govern the parish.[5] It is clear that this reorganization of the parochial governmental structure signified no radical social revolution or change. Even when sometimes a "convention" of the whole parish was convened, the governance and management of the parish affairs in this period were always maintained by such men as John Johnson, John Terry, James Russell, Miles Flesher, John Allen, Ralph Hutchinson, and Lawrence Blomley.[6] Religiously, too, the parish was Presbyterian; its ministers during the Puritan era included Elidad Blackwell, John Conant, and Thomas Jaggard.[7] In fact, in the late 1650s, as we have seen, an orthodox Anglican, George Hall, became its minister.[8] In short, St. Botolph Aldersgate was clearly a conservative parish. Like St. Botolph Aldersgate, the parish of St. Bride was also a large parochial community outside the Wall to the west of the old City. We may recall that St. Bride had a huge number of poor families and hundreds of poor children.[9] The reorganization of its parochial governmental structure was therefore clearly a necessity for the better management of parish affairs. It was, in fact, for the better management of the poor relief in the parish that early in 1647 the Lord Mayor issued a precept for the election of fifty men as supervisors of the poor, who were to be divided into five groups with ten in each group.[10] This new system of overseers of the poor must hve functioned well, for three months later the parish vestry decided to reorganize itself similarly.[11] It is to be noted that, again, this reorganization was by no means a radical change, for it was clearly stated that only ninety-eight parishioners who had served lower offices in the parish were eligible for election as vestrymen. And St. Bride was also a strongly Presbyterian parish. In actuality, even in an extremely radical parish such as Allhallows the Great and at the zenith of the Fifth Monarchy movement in the City, reforms in the parochial governmental structure were not necessarily radical in nature. In early 1653 the vestry of Allhallows the Great adopted a resolution that in future years six men were to be chosen from each of the three precincts of the parish as assistants to the two churchwardens for the management of all affairs of the parish from Easter to Easter every year.[12] And the men chosen for the year of 1653 reveal no radical change in the social composition of the civic leadership in the parish.[13] It appears that while the parishioners of Allhallows were not hostile toward the millenarian movement, the civic leaders of the parish never lost their sense of social responsibility, and the parish was well governed throughout the radical years.[14]

In the light of our analyses of the cases cited above, it becomes clear that in Puritan London changes and reforms in parochial governmental structure did occur in rather conservative parishes and for pragmatic reasons. We do have to be guarded, therefore, against believing that all changes and reforms among the London parishes during the Puritan era were radical in nature or inspired by radical aspirations. Having said this, however, I shall have to hasten to add that during this revolutionary period as an age of crisis in religion as well as in politics, radicalism in one form or another was bound to appear at the parochial level and become a potential force for change. In some London parishes it prodded men into action and brought about changes. We may now turn to such cases.

Among all the London parishes in which radical and democratic agitations took place and, indeed, prevailed during the Puritan era, the parish of St. Dunstan in the West deserves special attention. It was in this parish that the radical agitation to change the parochial governmental structure not only occurred very early in the revolutionary period but was also most successful, and it happened at a time when a constitutional crisis in both the national and City governments was being evolved. In all probability the action of the radical faction in the parish of St. Dunstan in the West was inspired, if not actually directed, by national and municipal leaders.[15] In any case, in December 1641 the old civic and parochial leaders of the parish, that is, those "who have borne offices" and thus constituted the select vestry, had elected Francis Kemp, Richard Wotton, and Robert Meade as Common Councilmen for the ensuing year, but when they were presented at the wardmote meeting held in the parish church of St. Sepulchre on 21 December, their elections were challenged. In the meantime the radical faction had elected their own candidates in the persons of Alexander Normington, Richard Browne, and William Perkins. In this disputed election the Alderman who presided over the wardmote would play a decisive role, and Sir John Wollaston, Alderman of Farringdon Ward Without, apparently manipulated the process in favor of the radical faction.[16] If this contest for the election of Common Councilmen in 1641 was then a struggle between two factions of similar social status, the inhabitants of the parish in general were soon to press further for their own rights as well in the election of parochial officials. Thus we learn from the parish records that in a similar meeting of the wardmote at the parish church of St. Sepulchre in 1642, "by occasion of the great accesse of ye generallity there was such a disturbance by reason of the greate multitude of people then assembled" that the Alderman—in this case Alderman William Gibbs—had to postpone the meeting to a later date at the Quest House in the parish of St. Dunstan in the West.[17] The issue in question now in 1642 was apparently the election of such parochial officials as Questmen, Constables, and Scavengers. While "divers of the ancient men" of the parish said that it had been the custom of the parish that "those only who have borne office ought to have the nomination and choice," those of "the generality" then present insisted that "they ought not to be barred but they have a right to give their voice at the election."[18] Although it appears that, unlike Wollaston in the previous year, Gibbs intended to give a fair hearing of the reasons from both sides and a debate was to have been held, it is probably safe to assume that the general inhabitants eventually won.[19] In any case the democratic agitation at St. Dunstan in the West continued until late in 1646, when it was resolved in a general meeting that "each person of the vestry should be put to the vote" by the inhabitants of the parish.[20] In fact, the parish affairs of St. Dunstan in the West had been conducted mostly in general meetings during these years.[21]

Reorganizations of the parochial governmental structure can also be traced in the parish records of St. Martin Ludgate and St. Dunstan in the East. Though perhaps less radical in nature than the democratization of the governance in the parish of St. Dunstan in the West, the structural changes in these two parishes are of special significance, for, in appearance if not in reality, the traditional vestry was actually abolished and replaced by a committee. In the parish of St. Martin Ludgate this change came early but gradually. First, when the lectureship in the parish became vacant in 1641, a special committee was created for the election of a lecturer, and this committee was to be composed of sixteen men, with eight from within the gate and eight from without.[22] Like the changes in St. Botolph Aldersgate, there was clearly a concern for equal geographical distribution and representation of the membership on this committee. Then, with the outbreak of the Civil War, factional conflict within the old vestry broke out, and we find that in October 1643 two of the old vestrymen were officially purged from the vestry, and, in the following month, after the sequestration of the incumbent, another special committee was formed for the election of a minister.[23] Thus, step by step, the governance of the parish passed from the vestry to special committees until, early in 1644, the vestry itself was reorganized accordingly. The new body now consisted of thirty men, with fifteen from within the gate and fifteen from without.[24] At St. Dunstan in the East, the change came as a result of a disputed election of churchwardens in 1643. The traditional form of electing churchwardens by the vestry "without the consent of the rest of the inhabitants," though "customary," was now considered as "illegal" by the "major part" of the inhabitants of the parish. The latter, in the meantime, had met separately on the same day and made choices of their men. More significant, when this dual, disputed election was presented to the House of Commons, the House, perhaps not unexpectedly, gave its verdict in favor of the general election as the valid one.[25] Under such circumstances, it is no surprise that the parishioners also elected "a committee consisting of thirty persons," who "instead of the vestrymen," were "to govern the affairs of the parish and church" in the future.[26]

The above cases of structural changes in parochial governance among the parishes in Puritan London, whether conservative and pragmatic or radical and democratic, are the ones for which we can gather enough information from the extant parish records to be able to describe the circumstances and the nature of such changes. As is well known to students of London history, not all parish records provide such detailed but invaluable information. It is clear, of course, that similar changes occurred in other London parishes as well. Yet, in some of these cases, we learn it only from a brief but tantalizing statement, whereas, in others, we can only draw inferences from conservative reactions years later against earlier radical or democratic changes. In 1644 the parishioners of St. Margaret Pattens clearly wished to assert their rights in the election of parochial officials. If they failed to change the traditional vestry, they were at least successful in achieving a favorable compromise; for, as was recorded in its vestry minutes, "divers others of the parishioners" moved that "the vestry should nominate, and the generalitie of the parish choose the parish officers."[27] Similarly, the vestry minutes of St. Botolph Aldgate recorded a protestation of the parishioners in 1647 that in future "the election of churchwardens should be publicly announced in the church."[28] In the vestry minutes of the parish of St. James Garlickhithe, we read on one occasion in early 1645, "It was enacted by the parishioners. . . ," and, on another in late 1649, "Ordered and agreed by the parishioners. . . ." In light of such statements, we may by reasonable inference conclude that general meetings of the parishioners were frequently called in the parish on important occasions, if the traditional vestry had, indeed, survived.[29] It is also in this parish, we may recall, that the election of a minister in 1655 was actually voted by ballot.[30] Perhaps the most interesting case can be deduced from the parish records of St. Margaret Lothbury. Perhaps alone among the records of the London parishes, the vestry minutes of St. Margaret Lothbury recorded the names of its parishioners who had been recipients of poor relief from the parish each year. Rather surprisingly, one of those on poor relief, Valentine Overton, was on several occasions listed among the candidates for parish offices and was at least once actually elected.[31]

In addition, we also learn from later conservative reactions that radical and democratic changes in parochial governmental structure during the Puritan era also took place in such parishes as Allhallows the Great, St. Clement Eastcheap, St. Margaret New Fish Street, and St. Giles Cripplegate.[32] This is perhaps the appropriate point to turn to the other side of our story in an examination of the London parishes in their efforts to preserve the traditional parochial governmental structure during the Puritan era. Although, as was pointed out earlier in this chapter, not all the changes and reforms among the London parishes in our period were radical in nature, there can be little doubt that many of them were, and, as is often the case in modern revolutions, radical changes simply did not work and, instead, confusion resulted. Consequently, when the revolutionary fervor died out in the 1650s, a number of parishes attempted and succeeded in the restoration of the old tradition.

It is to be noted that, in some of the London parishes, efforts had actually been made to forestall such radical tendencies in the early years of the Revolution. St. Botolph Billingsgate, for instance, was basically a conservative parish, even though, at the beginning of our era, its old civic leaders were ousted because of their royalist leanings.[33] Yet, rather unexpectedly, on 12 April 1642 the vestry of the parish was made a select one with no more than thirty-one men, and it was clearly proclaimed that only those who were placed in the thirteen highest pews of the parish church were eligible for election to the vestry. Also a parchment was ordered to register all names of the parishioners "according to their orderly placing in the said church."[34] It appears, however, that even such a conservative parish as St. Botolph Billingsgate could not prevent the impact of radicalism during the revolutionary period; for, as we have learned from the parish records, four years later, in 1646, twenty-six men where chosen "for vestrymen, or a Comittee for the orderinge affaires of ye Parish."[35] It is not clear, given the perhaps deliberately ambiguous language of the vestry minutes, whether the old vestry was abolished and replaced by a committee or whether this was merely an aping of the revolutionary rhetoric. What is clear is that the composition of the new vestry or committee appeared to be the same as that of the old vestry. The parochial governance remained in the hands of the substantial inhabitants of the parish.[36]

The parish of St. Margaret Pattens offers another example of the basic conservative attitude of the London parishes toward possible radical changes at the parochial level in the early stage of the Revolution. A rather small parish with one-third of its inhabitants being poor, the governance of the parish affairs was in the hands of a small group of well-to-do tradesmen. In early 1640 the vestry adopted a resolution that in future the churchwardens were to be chosen out of the vestrymen and the number of the vestrymen was not to exceed thirteen, "beinge a custome therein long contained."[37] To be sure, with the rise of the radical agitations in the City during the years of the Revolution, this conservative attempt to make the governance of the parish almost closed to new men was bound to be challenged. In early 1644, as noted earlier in this chapter, the general inhabitants of the parish at least won their rights in the process of the election of parish officials, even if the nomination of candidates remained in the hands of the vestry. In fact, it was resolved in the same meeting that "the vestry should continue to manage all other business concerning the parish, according to their ancient custome & not to exceed 14 in number nor to be less than Ten."[38] The conservative position of the vestry of St. Margaret Pattens appeared to be well maintained in later years, for in 1652 another resolution of its vestry clearly stated that no member of the vestry "shall hence forward declare or divulge (out of the vestry) any passages or matters in question that hath bin debated on concerning the parish business to either a vestry man or other person whatsoever." A fine of five shillings was to be imposed for every violation of this resolution.[39] The vestry again attempted to make itself a closed body.

The two cases of St. Botolph Billingsgate and St. Margaret Pattens are perhaps exceptional. We may presume that usually the conservative reaction began to prevail only after the radical forces had spent themselves. It was in the mid-1650s, as we have seen in other contexts, that a general conservative reaction appeared to gather more and more of its force in religion as well as in politics in the City. It is also in these years, therefore, that even some of the radical parishes began to retreat from their previous radicalism. Thus, on 2 January 1655 the parish of St. Margaret New Fish Street thought it "very Necessary and convenient" to restore "the Ancient custome wch for some few yeares hath bine layde asidde, wch is a Select vester [*sic*] of the Number of 27."[40] In the same year the vestry minutes of the parish of St. Clement Eastcheap recorded that "Whereas there have [*sic*] been a custom for some years past to make a general call of the whole parish to ye vestry," it was now found not only "inconvenient" but "contradictory" to the former order of the parochial governmental structure. Consequently, the vestry was again made a select one and it was ordered that "only those who had served as churchwardens or sidemen in this parish or in any other parish" were to be "admitted to be vestrymen."[41] In April 1656 "at a meeting of the Parishioners payable to ye poor" in the parish of Allhallows the Great, it was ordered that "a Vestry should be chosen consistinge of :32: men according to the ancient Custome for the managinge of the affairs of the Parish with the Churchwardens for the good of the same, & soe to be continued from time to time." A table of the names of the vestry was set up in the vestry room of the parish church.[42] It is significant to observe that while St. Clement Eastcheap was clearly Presbyterian in its general religious persuasion in the 1640s, the parish of St. Margaret New Fish Street was unmistakably Independent in the late 1640s and the early 1650s, and Allhallows the Great, we may recall, became the center of the Fifth Monarchy movement between 1651 and 1654.[43] Clearly, this conservative reaction to restore the old traditional institution of parochial governance was a common and widespread phenomenon in the City, and basically it was a civic action. We may presume, therefore, that similar actions must also have taken place in other parishes as well, but as was the case with the radical changes in earlier years, the parish records in most cases remain silent. Only by dint of inference may conjectures be made.[44] However, at least in one parish, the restoration of the traditional parochial governmental structure was so well explained that it might not be totally irrelevant to quote the passage *in toto*. In the vestry minutes of St. Giles Cripplegate for 1659 we read the following resolution:

> Whereas, formerly there was a Vestry held in this Parish of St. Giles, Without Cripplegate, as occasion required, consisting only of the Vicar, Churchwardens, and all that had passed the place and office of Churchwardenshipp, Overseers of the Poor, Surveyors for the Highwayes, Clerke and Sexton, as also for the letting of leases and several other business of concernment for the good of the Parish. But because of some discontented

parties in these troubles inhabitants of this Parish who were enemies to the ancient government of the same, caused the Vestry to be dismist and so made choyce of the above said officers by the generality of the inhabitants of this Parish, they being so numerous there could be no business conveniently debated in that multitude although it might much produce to the losse and damage of the Parish. The inconveniences thereof being seriously considered by divers of the Parish, it was moved on Monday in Easter week, being the third day of April, 1659, at a General Meeting of the whole Parish in our Church to settle a Vestry again; being put to the question, it was clearly carried by hands, ffor settlement thereof, in that anncient way as was used in the year—1640 and tyme out of memories before.[45]

After having described both the radical attempts to alter the old parochial governmental structure and the conservative reaction to restore the traditional institutions of the parish in the City, we may ask whether, in actuality, the civic life in some of the London parochial communities was substantially changed, as the radicals had wished or expected in the early years of the revolutionary era, or was seriously damaged, as the conservatives later claimed in the last few years of the Revolution. In other words, did the old parish organization lose its institutional continuity, or the parochial community its social stability, as a result of the radical changes during the period of the Revolution? In order to answer these questions, we shall again have to turn to the extant parish records. Although neither the vestry minutes nor the churchwardens' accounts would speak directly to such questions, yet, as they recorded the transactions of parochial affairs year by year, they do reveal, clearly albeit indirectly, the functions of the London parochial institutions. Sometimes, the condition of these records themselves—their consistency or interruption, clarity or confusion—could be helpful evidence. In these respects, if such a method of indirect historical inference may be allowed, we can reasonably conclude that, in general, most of the London parishes well maintained their institutional continuity and social stability during the revolutionary era.[46] Of course, in an age of both political and religious conflicts in the nation, it would be inevitable that changes of leadership in local governments became necessary for or were actually dictated by the changing authorities in the nation, and this was probably more so with the Common Councilmen in the City of London. But such changes, though in some parishes rather frequent, seldom disrupted the continuity of the parish as a civic institution.[47] Even in those parishes in which the radical factions were successful in their attempts to alter the old parochial structure of governance, changes, as we shall see, were more apparent than real.[48]

This is not to say that there were no disruptions in the civic life among the London parochial communities. In certain particular London parishes, whose civic leaders were deeply involved in political events of the nation, and especially during the years 1647–53, when the lay Presbyterian leaders in the City were engaged in a fatal but clearly futile confrontation with the Independents in the Army and the gathered churches, there appear to have been obvious signs among the parish records that the civic functions of some of the London parishes were, indeed, disrupted, at least partially. The following cases may be cited as examples. In the parish of St. George Botolph Lane, the recording of the annual election of Common Councilmen was suddenly discontinued for the years 1647–49;[49] in St. Augustine, for the years 1649–51;[50] and in Allhallows the Less, for the years 1650–51 and again for 1653.[51] During the same period the parish of St. Martin Orgar had no churchwardens' accounts laid out for the years 1648–52;[52] St. Pancras Soper Lane apparently lumped two years' transactions for 1648–50 together retrospectively;[53] and St. Benet Gracechurch had no vestry minutes recorded for the years 1648–51.[54] In the light of such disruptions in these parish records, we may presume that the civic functions of these parishes must have been affected by the political events of those years.

It is to be noted, however, that all these cases were rather exceptions to what we have observed as the general pattern among the London parishes during the revolutionary period. The case of St. George Botolph Lane can be easily understood. From 1641 to 1646, the Common Councilman recorded in the vestry minutes of St. George Botolph Lane had been Edward Hooker, one of the active and strongly Presbyterian civic leaders in the City and a colonel in the London Militia. Though also a parishioner and perhaps inhabitant in the neighboring parish of St. Mary at Hill, Hooker had also been a vestryman in the parish of St. George Botolph Lane and participated in its parish affairs.[55] As a leading figure in the London Militia, he must have been deeply involved in the dangerous confrontation between the City and the Army in 1647.[56] With the collapse of the military posture of the London Militia and the occupation of the City by the Army later in the year, Hooker's position as a Common Councilman must have been threatened. In any case, when the vestry minutes resumed the recording of the election of Common Councilman in 1650, Hooker was replaced by George Cony.[57] Similarly, in the parish of St. Augustine, the Common Councilmen from 1641 to 1647 had been Richard Turner and John Orlibear, both of whom were, like Edward Hooker, Presbyterian civic leaders in the City, though perhaps more moderate or less conspicuous than the latter. And Turner had also been a colonel in the London Militia. More important, the parish of St. Augustine, with Francis Roberts as its minister, was one of the strongly Presbyterian parishes in the City, and Roberts was in close association with the Scottish clerical commission in London. Again, it is understandable that both the religious life and the civic affairs of the parish would be affected by the events of these tempestuous years.[58] Although Turner was to reconcile himself with the new authorities both in the City and in the nation, Orlibear did not return to the scene until late in 1653, after the radical years were over.[59] The case of Allhallows the Less was less clear, though John Greene and William Coulson,

who had been Common Councilmen from at least 1644 to 1647, were probably political Presbyterians, and Coulson, too, had been a captain in the
London Militia.[60] In any case, the interruptions of the election and recording
of the Common Councilmen during these years could not have been accidental, and when the recording of the vestry minutes resumed its full traditional
form in 1654, Coulson was again recorded as Common Councilman and
continued to hold that position until 1658.[61]

Among the other three cases, the parish of St. Martin Orgar probably had
never had a broad and firm group of Puritan civic leaders, though the
parishioners, and some of their civic leaders in particular, were clearly and
highly anticlerical.[62] And during the entire period of the Revolution, its
ministry was never firmly settled and the parish, as we heard in another
context, contented itself "with wanderinig ministers."[63] Perhaps, given the
situation in the City between 1647 and 1650, the internal weakness of the
parish was further confounded by the cross-currents of those tempestuous
years, and both its religious and its civic affairs were no longer effectively
and orderly conducted.[64] On the other hand, the interruption in the parish of
St. Pancras Soper Lane was clearly caused by the political events in the City.
The predominant civic figure in the parish had been John Jurin, Common
Councilman and one of the lay Presbyterian leaders in the City.[65] It appears
that in 1647 the parish itself was deeply divided religiously.[66] No churchwardens were chosen for that year, and in one of the vestry meetings in early
July, the minutes could not be recorded because one of the parishioners had
kept the vestry book to himself.[67] With the fall of the Presbyterian faction in
the City, the ministry of the parish fell into the hands of George Cokayne in
1648 and its lectureship, into the hands of Nicholas Lockyer.[68] In the meantime Christopher Feake was invited to preach in the parish church.[69] It is
undoubtedly due to these changing events and the religious divisions that the
churchwardens' accounts were interrupted. Perhaps the most revealing case
was that of the parish of St. Benet Gracechurch. Although a very small
parish, it had a large number of prominent civic leaders in the City during the
revolutionary period; and, in the 1640s James Bunce was the predominant
figure.[70] It is not clear whether Bunce was a religious Presbyterian, though he
had been appointed a lay trier in 1645 for the founding of the Presbyterian
church government.[71] It is clear, however, that he played an important role in
1647 in the City in opposition to the Independents and the Army.[72] And, of
course, with Bunce, there were other Presbyterian civic leaders in the parish
such as William Beake and Robert Dycer, who were also involved in the
political events in the City.[73] It is no surprise, therefore, that with the collapse
of the Presbyterian faction in the City and the fall of Bunce, Dycer, and
Beake from power, the parish was greatly affected, and with the leading
vestrymen now all gone or alienated, the vestry was seldom called, if at all.[74]

From the previous analyses of the six parishes in which disruptions of civic
life occurred during the years 1647–53, we may reasonably conclude that,

with the possible exception of the parish of St. Martin Orgar, these disruptions were caused by political events and forces from without rather than by changes or reorganization from within. The issues involved during the years between 1647 and 1653 were, by nature as well as in stature, national rather than parochial ones, though some London parishes were, as we have seen, directly or indirectly affected. If we examine closely the London parochial communities in general or those parishes in which radical institutional reorganizations actually took place, we not only find few disruptions or disorders but, in fact, seldom detect any substantial changes either institutionally or socially. In order to explain this institutional and social stability among the London parochial communities during the revolutionary period, we may do well to set aside our perceptions of a radical revolution in the twentieth century and try to understand the parochial communities in Puritan London from historical perspectives.

First, it is appropriate to note that seventeenth-century English society was still a world in which deference to seniority and status was a "natural" attitude among men and the general pattern of behavior. And such a social attitude and behavior may at least partly explain the institutional continuity and social stability among the London parochial communities during the revolutionary period. In the parish of St. Pancras Soper Lane, for instance, Alderman Thomas Soames had been a leading figure on the vestry in the early 1640s, but a group of new men was soon to appear as active civic leaders in the parish. Yet, in 1644, when certain parish affairs were conducted in a vestry apparently without either his presence or knowledge, Soames's approval was sought and he wrote beneath the item "I doe very well approue hereof."[75] Similarly, in the parish of St. Benet Paul's Wharf, Edmund Harrison had been a predominant figure before the revolutionary era. Probably a royalist, he was replaced as Common Councilman in 1641 and disappeared from the vestry. Yet he apparently remained an influential figure in the parish, for underneath the vestry minutes for the election of parish officials in 1647 we read "Approved by Edm. Harrison."[76] Another revealing case can be found in the parish records of Allhallows Lombard Street. In 1648 the prominent old civic leaders of the parish such as Thomas Cullum, Richard Young, and Richard Waring, who had probably all been Presbyterians in the City during the previous years, were no longer in power, and the parish, as we have seen, was moving toward an Independent position. It was also at this juncture, we may recall, that Thomas Goodwin's gathered congregation was accepted to worship in the parish church.[77] When this resolution was taken, Cullum and three others were apparently absent from the vestry. Yet their approval was later solicited, and they "affirmed to give consent."[78] Perhaps this social deference as a general pattern of behavior was best demonstrated in the arrangement of pews in a parish church, and it was clearly maintained in the Puritan era. In the parish of St. Margaret New Fish Street, after the Independent divine Thomas Brooks was chosen minister in April 1648, a new chart of pews was drawn up. It is unmistakably clear that all members of the parish were properly placed in the traditional order.[79] It may be added that women, too, enjoyed this social deference in the church, for, as the vestry minutes of St. Peter Westcheap put it in the same period, they should be "placed according to there husbands Antiquity and bearing office."[80]

Second, the English Revolution in the seventeenth century, as is well known to historians of the period, was not a conflict between social classes. This was true at the parochial level no less than in the national arena. In spite of the institutional reorganizations and the frequent changes in civic leadership in some of the London parishes, it was still men of substantial or at least moderate wealth who actually governed the parochial communities. In this respect the parish of St. Martin Ludgate can be cited as a revealing example. In 1643, before the reorganization of the parish vestry, two old vestrymen were officially voted out of the vestry, and, after the reorganization, a few men of the old vestry were indeed excluded.[81] Yet it is to be noted that the leading men on the new vestry, both those from within the gate (e.g., Deputy William Hobson and Common Councilman William Jeston) and those from without the gate (e.g., Deputy Thomas Arnold and Common Councilman Matthew Fox) were unmistakably either more substantial in wealth or more prominent in social status than most men on the old vestry.[82] Similarly, in the parish of St. Dunstan in the East, when the new vestry of thirty was chosen in the middle of 1644, it included John Fowke, Gilbert Keate, George Hanger, William Batemen, Robert Foote, Thomas Stubbins, Maurice Thompson, Lawrence Bromfield, John Milton, and John Pettiward, all of whom were, in their various capacities, important civic figures in the City.[83] Even in a radical parish such as St. Dunstan in the West, no noticeably radical changes can be detected in the vestry of 1648, that is, a vestry chosen in a radical year, with each vestryman voted in individually by the general meeting of the parish.[84] In fact, it included both Francis Kempe and Robert Meade, two of the Common Councilmen who had been ousted in 1641.[85] Among others were Alexander Normington, Francis Allen, William Perkins, Matthew Hind, John Hallywell, and Henry Davy.[86] In the light of the parish records, one may indeed wonder whether even in those parishes in which the select vestry was abolished and a general one was established, there was ever in actuality a general participation of all the parishioners. For, on the one hand, parochial offices were probably as much a financial burden as a social privilege,[87] whereas, on the other, there always appeared to have been a bottom line, officially stated or customarily understood, to exclude the multitude. The case of St. Mildred Poultry is quite revealing in this regard. When it established "a general vestry of the whole parish" in 1644, it clearly stated that "noe parishioner shalbe a vestryman in the said parish vestry but such as doe pay unto the poor," and, obviously in practical consideration, made it a quorum that "there shalbe ten parishioners at every vestry besides the parson and the two churchwardens."[88] The general vestry was after all not really general.

And last, but by no means least important, there was the civic spirit among the London citizens, who, in spite of all their religious or even political differences, would, if called upon, serve the civic offices and fulfill their social responsibilities. In this regard the poor relief will serve as a focus of this study. But before we look more closely at poor relief among the London parochial communities during the revolutionary era, it is perhaps appropriate to explain what may have appeared an anomaly to modern historians of the gathered churches in this period: the participation of gathered church members in parochial affairs. A gathered church is usually understood as a body of believers who separated themselves from the traditional parish, and religiously this was undoubtedly the case. Yet it is to be noted that some members of the gathered churches in London were noted citizens in the City, and most of them, if not all, were inhabitants of the various London parochial communities. Unfortunately, no membership list of the London gathered churches in our period has survived, and only random cases can be studied. In the parish of St. Stephen Coleman Street, for instance, it is clear that a number of the parishioners who obviously belonged to John Goodwin's gathered church accepted and served in parochial offices.[89] In the parish of St. Martin Outwich, for another instance, Rowland Wilson, a member of George Cokayne's gathered church, was one of the auditors for the Churchwardens' accounts from the beginning of our era until his death in the early 1650s, and, as such, he must have served on the vestry of the parish as well.[90] In addition, we find that Richard Wollaston served on the vestry of St. Peter Cornhill in the early 1640s;[91] Richard Shute, on the vestry of St. Katherine Cree during the years 1644–46;[92] Richard Arnold on the vestry of St. Margaret Pattens from 1642 to 1655;[93] and James Russell, at various times, on the vestries of St. Stephen Coleman Street, St. Antholin, St. Nicholas Acons, and St. Botolph Aldersgate throughout the period of the Revolution.[94] And in the parish of Holy Trinity the Less, a certain Francis Emerson, a cloth-worker, in whose yard a gathered church of [John?] Rogers met to worship in the 1650s, must have been himself a member of the congregation; yet, he had been churchwarden of the parish in 1640–41, 1641–42, and 1643–44, had served on the vestry for the entire revolutionary period, and, in 1658–59, contributed £5 for the repairing of the parish church.[95] If the identifications in these cases are not all certain and perhaps prone to error, there can be no doubt in the cases of Praise-God Barbone and Edmund Rozier, both of whom were, indeed, lay pastors of gathered churches in London themselves. In 1646 Rozier contributed £8 for the repairing of the parish church of St. Mary Abchurch, and in 1655 even served as churchwarden of the parish.[96] Barbone, to be sure, has earned, justly or unjustly, notoriety as a fanatic in history, and his appearance in the parish affairs of St. Dunstan in the West from 1648 was clearly connected with the rise of the Independents in the City. He was chosen a Common Councilman first for 1649–51 and later again for the years 1657–59.[97] But he did not decline to sit on the vestry of the parish and on several occasions served as one of the auditors for the churchwardens' accounts. In fact, Barbone continued to participate in the meetings of the vestry until 1661.[98] Moreover, we may recall, Robert Tichborne, who was himself a member of George Cokayne's gathered church in London, founded, in the late 1650s, a lectureship in the parish of St. Olave Silver Street.[99] John Goodwin's gathered congregation, after their triumphant return to the parish church of St. Stephen Coleman Street, agreed to share half of their collections for the poor on Fast Days and Thanksgiving Days with the parish "for the use of their poor,"[100] and "Rogers' people" in Holy Trinity the Less regularly contributed, for several years in the 1650s, when the ephemeral existence of the congregation lasted, 10s. each year for the relief of the poor in that parish.[101] All these incidents, insignificant as some of them were, point to the conclusion that even men of the gathered churches in London, separated as they were from the traditional parishes in religious worship, never abandoned completely their civic obligations and social responsibilities toward the parochial communities in which they lived.

Of course, the civic spirit among the London citizens in general was undoubtedly one of the most important factors for the social stability in the City during the years of the Revolution, and nothing else can better illustrate this aspect of the civic life in Puritan London than the work of poor relief in the various London parishes. For some decades in the past, historians have had a persistently critical and harsh conception, or rather misconception, about the Puritans in regard to their attitude toward the poor. It has been the common belief that the Puritans were hard-hearted, face-grinding exploiters of poor people, and it has been asserted that the traditional poor-relief system collapsed during the rule of the Puritan saints.[102] Not until very recently have some historians begun to correct this misconception.[103] The fact is, as we find from a closer look at the extant parish records, that neither the amount nor the quality of poor relief in the London parishes declined during the Puritan era.

It is to be noted, first and foremost, that neither in the extant vestry minutes nor in the extant churchwardens' accounts of the various London parishes have we detected any signs of a hardened attitude toward the poor. The work of poor relief appears to have been maintained with consistency and, in certain aspects, we have sufficient reason to say, with magnanimity as well. And this was true of almost all the London parishes, large or small, substantial or impoverished, conservative or radical, with a settled ministry or without it. It is, for example, in the parish of St. Stephen Coleman Street, the most radical parochial community and one of the traditionally Puritan parishes in the City, that, as we read in its vestry minutes for 1643–44, its minister, John Goodwin, was requested specifically to preach in his sermons so as "to stir up his auditors to contribute liberally to the poor."[104] In the same period, for another example, in the parish of St. Mary Aldermanbury, perhaps a more conservative parochial community but certainly also one of the traditionally Puritan London parishes, when, at one time, £15 had to be drawn from the poor's stock to make up the stipend for the parish minister, Edmund Calamy, it was almost at once ordered to be paid back from the parish stock so that "the stock for the poor may not bee diminished."[105] In fact, in this respect, the poor money was often supplemented instead by the parish stock for actual relief work in most parishes, occasion after occasion, year after year. In 1646 the parish of St. Dunstan in the East ordered £20 to be given to the poor "against the time of Christmas," but when £4. 3s. 6d. was still lacking after all the money from legacies and collections on two Fast Days was put together, the balance was made up by the parish stock.[106] In 1651–52, St. Mary Aldermanbury spent on the poor £22. 16s. 7d. more than was actually collected.[107] Before we proceed to look at the collections for and the expenditures on the poor in the various parishes, it must be mentioned that during the period of the Revolution there were often, from time to time, extraordinary expenses for poor relief: collections for injured soldiers in the years of the Civil War, for evicted poor ministers from the country under the forces of the King, for the poor in Ireland and the northern counties. Occasionally, collections were made even for the poor in foreign lands.[108] In 1655 the parish of St. Stephen Coleman Street collected £155. 2s. for the poor Protestants in Savoy;[109] and, three years later, in 1658, it again contributed another £36. 14s. 3d. for the poor Protestants in Poland.[110]

If we look closely at the collections for, and the expenditure on, poor relief in some of the London parishes during the revolutionary period, we shall have sufficient reason to believe that there was no decline in either aspect of the poor relief work among the City parochial communities when the Puritans were in power. In fact, rather to the contrary, there appears always to have been some increase in both in spite of the political conflicts, the Civil War, and, as has been noted, the extraordinary expenses for the poor sometimes far beyond the traditional and geographical bounds of the individual London parishes. It lies outside the main focus of this study to pursue a comprehensive and statistical study of the poor funds in Puritan London, but the following examples may clearly testify to this basic assumption. Let us look at the collections first. In the parish of St. Peter Westcheap, £27. 7s. 6d. were collected for the poor in 1638–39, that is, the year before the outbreak of the Revolution. Seven years later, after the triumph of the Puritans in the Civil War and especially when the Puritan discipline had been established in the City, the amount collected for the poor in the parish was increased to £30. 14s. 6d. in 1646–47 and £36. 18s. 8d. in 1647–48.[111] Similarly, in the parish of St. Martin Outwich, £30. 12s. 10d. were collected in 1638–39; £30. 3s. 7d. in 1641–42; £33. 19s. 2d. in 1645–46; £38. 11s. 4d. in 1646–47; £40. 1s. 8d. in 1647–48; and £38. 4s. 10d. in 1649–50.[112]Clearly, neither the Civil War nor the turbulent years of 1647–50 adversely affected the collection of the poor money. And, in some cases, the increase was far greater. In the parish of St. Michael le Querne, £27. 14s. were collected in 1640–41; £51. 15s. 3¼d. in 1641–42; and £57. 13s. 11d. in 1642–43.[113]

In the parish of St. Helen, £55. 8s. 4d. were collected in 1639–40; and although, in 1646–47, the amount went down to £46. 13s., it was increased to £70 in 1649–50.[114] And in the parish of St. Olave Old Jewry, to cite one more example, £41. 11s. 10d. were assessed for the poor in 1643, and the amount was increased to £56. 8s. 10d. in 1650.[115]

Nor were the expenditures on the poor in the various London parishes diminished in the Puritan era. The parish of Allhallows the Great, which was, we may recall, one of the radical centers in the City, spent £20. 17s. for the poor people and £27. 12s. 4d. for nursing children in 1641–42; £24. 2s. 1d. for the poor people and £38. 5s. 6d. for nursing children in 1645–46; and £33. 8s. 5d. for the poor people and £41. 8s. 10d. for nursing children in 1648–49.[116] In the parish of Allhallows London Wall, to look at the poor relief work from another angle, £14. 0s. 8d. were given to monthly pensioners and £10. 8s. to weekly pensioners in 1639–40; £11. 12s. 6d. to monthly pensioners and £25. 9s. 6d. to weekly pensioners in 1650–51; and £16. 15s. to monthly pensioners and £12. 19s. 8d. to weekly pensioners in 1653–54.[117] And it is to be pointed out that even in a truly impoverished parish such as St. Mary Staining, with a radical Fifth Monarchist such as Nathaniel Holmes as minister, and especially during the tempestuous years of 1647–50, the work of poor relief was neither interrupted nor slighted. The parish gave £9. 12s. to pensioners and spent £14. 5s. 5d. for nursing children in 1647–48; £10. 2s. to pensioners and £11. 18s. 2d. for nursing children in 1648–49; and £10. 2s. to pensioners and £14. 12s. for nursing children in 1649–50.[118] Although there is no way to know whether the increase either in the amount collected for the poor or in the amount spent on the poor actually meant better poor relief, yet at least the evidence cited above clearly indicates that the work of poor relief was well maintained in the City during the period of the Revolution. And it is significant to note that in the vestry minutes of St. Sepulchre, augmentations of old pensions and approvals of new pensioners were recorded in the 1650s.[119]

Perhaps what is most fascinating about the poor relief in the City of London, at least to a modern student and one from another cultural world, was not the amount of money yearly collected for and spent on the poor, though, of course, this was what really counted, but rather the contents of the work of relief for the poor. It is to be emphasized that the work of poor relief in a London parochial community consisted of far more than merely the distribution of a few pence or of bread at the church door on the Lord's day or on special holy days, though this was its popular common feature and frequently done. As we have seen from the expenditures in poor relief earlier in this section, pensions were given to old poor people, and poor infants were sent to nursing women at the cost of the parish. In the latter case, we should add, schooling was always stressed for the raising of the children.[120] In addition, the poor youth were put to apprenticeship with tradesmen to learn skills for their future livelihood, with fees, provisions, and other charges all paid by the parish.[121] In winter charcoal and seacoal were purchased by the parish to be distributed to the poor, free or at a reduced price.[122] The poor sick were frequently sent to the hospital also at the cost of the parish, and, at least on one occasion, we learn that the parish paid the bill of a doctor for the treatment of the poor people.[123] In the parish of St. Giles Cripplegate, twice a year, at Allhallowtide and at Good Friday, new clothes were made especially for the poor. In its churchwardens' accounts we find that all the costs, item by item from the purchase of material, the dressing and dying of the cloth, hiring women and tailors for the cutting and making of shirts and smocks, gowns and coats, to the buying of stockings and shoes, were meticulously recorded.[124] All this, perhaps, had been a traditional practice in the parish, but, again, such a tradition was kept intact even in the turbulent years of 1648–50.[125] If there was anything that was possibly new in poor relief in Puritan London, it was, perhaps naturally, a new emphasis on religion. In several parishes, for example, Bibles were given to the poor children each year,[126] and one may wonder whether they were also given instructions in catechism and Scripture reading.[127] In the parish of St. Benet Paul's Wharf, when additional alms houses were built for the parish poor in 1649, new regulations were added to the old rules governing the inmates.[128] One of the new regulations required that the inmates "endeavour to serve God in a holy and Christian like manner, and frequent the parish church of St. Bennetts pauls wharfe above said, att service and sermons duelye and daylye as often, as it shall bee there, reade, and taught."[129]

After having looked at the civic life in the London parochial communities from various perspectives, we may conclude that the City parishes, as civic institutions, demonstrated a remarkable resilience in an age of social crisis, and that the London citizens, in spite of their political and religious differences, never abandoned their civic spirit and their sense of social responsibility. And we may ask whether, in modern historical scholarship, we have not placed too much emphasis upon the radical side of the English Revolution in London as well as in the nation.

NOTES

1. Derived from biblical passages, this concept undoubtedly affected the mind and the rhetoric of the radical groups in the English Revolution. See Christopher Hill, *The World Turned Upside Down: Radical Ideas during the English Revolution* (Harmondsworth, Middlesex, England, 1975). Hill admits that his approach in this work is "the worm's eye view," that is, seeing the English Revolution from below rather than from the top. It is to be noted, however, that in spite of their radical rhetoric, few of the radical men actually wanted to have the world turned upside down, as the quotation from Henry Denne's *Mercy and Peace* (1645) at the beginning of Hill's book clearly testifies. In 1653, during the heated debate over law reform both

within and outside of Barebone's Parliament, John Rogers, one of the leading Fifth Monarchy men, protested that "there is no man so *irrational* as to deny the due use of *Civil Discipline,* and (for the well ordering of *civil affairs*) of *sound Lawes. . . ."* See John Rogers, *Sagrir. Or Doomes-day drawing nigh* (London, 1653), p. 42.

2. On the national level, the suppression of the Levellers in 1649 and the expulsion of the radical sectarians at the end of Barebone's Parliament in 1653 are in both cases clear evidence. In fact, neither group was to turn the world upside down.

3. GLMS 3570/2, f. 46b.

4. I owe this interpretation to Dr. Christopher Hill, who suggested that the abolition of the literacy requirement was probably due to the high level of literacy among the inhabitants of this parish.

5. GLMS 1453/1. ff. 36–41, especially vestry minutes, 23 September 1645 and 28 December 1646.

6. Ibid. After 1650, some of the old civic leaders of the parish disappeared, but there is no sign of a radical change in its parochial governmental structure.

7. GLMS 1453/1, see vestry minutes, 8 September 1643, 7 December 1643, and 5 January 1646/7; GLMS 1453/2, see vestry minutes, 9 April 1652 and 21 June 1652; GLMS 1455/1, see churchwardens' accounts for 1652–53 and 1653–54. For Blackwell, see Surman, 1:197; for Conand, see *D. N. B., s. v.; C. R., s. v.;* for Jaggard, see Surman, 1: 246. See also Seaver, pp. 275–76.

8. See chap. 4 above.

9. See chap. 1 above.

10. GLMS, 6554/1, f. 42, vestry minute, 5 January 1646/7.

11. Ibid., f. 45, vestry minute, 21 April 1647. At first various numbers for the new vestry, from thirty to sixty men, were suggested. The vestry first agreed upon the number of forty, but finally the number of fifty was chosen, obviously after the new system of overseers of the poor. It is also to be noted that in the same vestry meeting it was clearly stated that only the ninety-eight men "who had borne offices" were eligible for election to the new vestry.

12. GLMS 819/1, f. 184, vestry minute, 26 January 1652/3. For the association between the parish of Allhallows the Great and the Fifth Monarchy movement in the City, see Louise Fargo Brown, *The Political Activities of the Baptists and Fifth Monarchy Men in England during the Interregnum* (Washington, 1912), pp. 19, 21, 28, 48, and *passim.* It is rather intriguing to note that the minister of Allhallows the Great from 1639 to 1652 had been John Downham [Downame], a moderate Presbyterian. For Downham, see *D. N. B., s. v.;* Surman, 1: 215.

13. GLMS 819/1, f. 185.

14. Cf. the vestry resolutions concerning parish affairs, such as attendance at the vestry meetings, audit of churchwardens' accounts, supervision of irregular inmates in the parish, etc. See ibid., ff. 172, 176, 189; GLMS 818/1, churchwardens' account for 1651–52. In light of this, the new parochial governmental system was adopted, in all probability, as a rather conservative action to maintain a better management of parish affairs.

15. For a broader view of the historical background, see S. R. Gardiner, *History of England from the Accession of James I to the outbreak of the Civil War,* 10 vols. (London, 1883–84), vol. 10; Pearl, *London and the Outbreak of the Puritan Revolution.*

16. GLMS 3018/1, f. 129b. The entire event was recorded in the parish register book of officers, but this memorandum was obviously written by the old conservative civic leaders of the parish. The signatories to the memorandum were George Sparkes, Richard Mawdett, Humphrey Drake, John Mason, Henry Davy, Thomas Paulson, and Robert Dering. In fact, Kemp, Wotton, and Meade had been Common Councilmen in the previous year.

17. GLMS 3016/1, f. 229, vestry minute, 21 December 1642. Another meeting was appointed five days later on St. Stephen's Day (26 December) at St. Dunstan's Quest (i.e., Inquest) House.

18. Ibid., vestry minute, 26 December 1642.

19. The radical faction's representatives were Alexander Normington, Captain [Richard] Cuthbert, Francis Allen, and Thomas Tutt. Names of the representatives from the other side

were not recorded, and it is not certain that any conference between the two sides ever took place.

20. Ibid., f. 288. It should be pointed out that Kemp, Meade, Mawdett, and Davy were all included in the lists of the vestrymen chosen for this year.

21. Ibid., ff. 269, 282, 315, vestry minutes, 16 December 1645; 23 April 1646; and 1 March 1647/8.

22. GLMS 1311/1, f. 134b, vestry minute, 25 January 1640/1.

23. Ibid., f. 138, vestry minute, 13 October 1643. The two old vestrymen involved were Gilbert Whitehead and Nicholas Banister.

24. Ibid., f. 139b. The leading figures on this committee were Thomas Arnold from outside the gate and William Hobson from within the gate.

25. GLMS 4887, f. 500. According to the vestry minutes the disputed election took place on 9 April 1643, and the verdict of the House of Commons was given on 27 April.

26. Ibid. In the meantime, a committee of thirty had been formed. See also ibid., f. 504, for another list of such a committee elected on 5 May 1644. Members on the latter committee included Alderman John Fowke, Gilbert Keate, Robert Foot, Maurice Thompson, Lawrence Bromfield, Captain John Milton, George Hanger, William Bateman, John Bond, and Stafford Clare.

27. GLMS 4571/1, f. 23, vestry minute, 23 April 1644.

28. GLMS 5234/8, f. 272, vestry minute, 30 April 1647. Again, it is to be pointed out that this was not necessarily a radical change, for it was made clear that only "all the inhabitants who have had the right in the choice may be present and give their consent." What the protestation did mean, however, is that since the parish of St. Botolph Aldgate was a large one, the election of parish officials should no longer be manipulated by a small group of men.

29. GLMS 4813/1, ff. 65, 79b, vestry minutes, 14 January 1644/5 and 7 November 1649. In the light of the vestry minutes in earlier years, the vestry had been a select one. Cf. ibid., ff. 52, 54b, vestry minutes, 26 February 1636/7 and 1 January 1640/1

30. See chap. 5 above.

31. GLMS 4352/1, ff. 162, 167, 170, 179b, vestry minutes, 23 April 1644; 12 April 1645; 7 April 1646; and 26 April 1647. In most of these years Overton was listed among the poor of the parish. See ibid., ff. 148b–149, 175b. In 1648 he desired to be excused from serving in the office of churchwarden, and in 1650 he was actually elected. See ibid., ff. 183b, 189.

32. See nn. 40–45 below.

33. GLMS 943/1, no folio number, see vestry minutes for the years 1638–43. Thomas Austin and Andrew Hawes, who had been Common Councilmen before 1640, had both lost their elections by the end of 1642. In 1642, however, these men were still leading figures of the vestry.

34. Ibid., vestry minute, 12 April 1642.

35. Ibid., vestry minutes, April 1646.

36. A comparison between the list of the new vestry or "committee" and earlier vestry lists shows no radical change in the composition of the vestry except, of course, for the disappearance of the names of Austin and Hawes, as noted above.

37. GLMS457/1, f. 1, vestry minute, 6 April 1640.

38. Ibid., f. 23. See also n. 27 above.

39. Ibid., f. 36b, vestry minute, 4 May 1652.

40. GLMS 1175/1, no folio number, vestry minute, 2 January 1654/5.

41. GLMS 978/1, no folio number, vestry minute, September 28, 1655.

42. GLMS 819/1, f. 195, vestry minute, 23 April 1656.

43. The parish of St. Clement Eastcheap had become more and more Anglican in its ministerial associations in the 1650s; in the parish of Allhallows the Great, the voices of radical sectarians had been silenced by 1655; yet Thomas Brooks continued to be the minister of St. Margaret New Fish Street until the end of our period. Cf. above, chaps. 2, 3, and 4.

44. In May 1644, for instance, the vestry in the parish of St. Mildred Poultry was made a general one for the year following. It is unknown whether this new experiment was continued

after 1645 or was soon to be abandoned. The vestry minutes are silent on the matter. See GLMS 62/1,f. 14.

45. GLMS 6048/1, f. 1. In light of the vestry minutes, this change was made while the civic leaders of the Puritan era were still all in power and the parish minister was Samuel Annesley, a prominent Presbyterian. See ibid., f. 4b, vestry minute, 23 April 1660.

46. This is clearly the general impression one obtains in reading the London parochial records of the Revolutionary era; such an interpretation is also borne out by an analysis of the poor relief in Puritan London later in this chapter.

47. See, for example, nn. 19 and 20 (St. Dunstan in the West) and nn. 34 and 35 (St. Botolph Billingsgate) above.

48. See, for example, nn. 25 and 26 (St. Dunstan in the East) and nn. 37 and 38 (St. Margaret Pattens) above.

49. GLMS 952/1, ff. 15b–16. The elections for other parish officials such as churchwardens, sidemen, and collectors for the poor were still recorded.

50. GLMS 635/1, no folio number, see vestry minutes of these years. Again, the elections for churchwardens, collectors, auditors, constables, and assessors were all recorded.

51. GLMS 824/1, no folio number, see vestry minutes of these years. In 1649 over half of the elected parish officials declined to serve and paid a fine.

52. GLMS 959/1, ff. 204–5b.

53. GLMS 5018/1, no folio number, see churchwardens' accounts for 1648–50.

54. GLMS 4214/1. The last recorded vestry minute in 1648 was under the date of 28 May, and henceforth no vestry minute was recorded for three years. It is to be noted, however, that the churchwardens' accounts of the parish were kept for these years, though not so well written as they had been in the past. See GLMS 1568, ff. 655–68.

55. GLMS 952/1, ff. 14b–15; GLMS 1240/1, ff. 43b–51b. Edward Hooker was a leading civic figure in both parishes.

56. For Hooker and the London Militia in 1647, see CLRO, J. Co. Co., 40, f. 215b; CLRO Letter Books, QQ, ff. 269b–70; Ruthworth, 6: 472; Firth and Rait, 1: 928. Hooker was described by a contemporary pamphleteer as "a valiant prudent godly and faithful Captain" and as "a man that stood up with the first and acted with the best, for the safety of King, Parliament, Kingdome and City." See *A Paire of Spectacles for the Citie*, p. 9 [11].

57. GLMS 952/1, f. 16, vestry minute, 21 December 1650.

58. GLMS 635/1, no folio number, see vestry minutes, 1641–47. For Turner and the London Militia in 1647, see CLRO J. Co. Co., 40, f. 215b; CLRO Letter Books, QQ, ff. 269b–70; Ruthworth, 6: 472; Firth and Rait, 1: 928. For Francis Roberts's association with the Scottish commissioners in London, see Pearl, "London Puritans and Scotch Fifth Columnists: A Mid-Seventeenth Century Phenomenon," in A. E. J. Hollaender and William Kellaway, eds., *Studies in London History*, p. 528. For Roberts, see also *D. N. B.*, *s. v.*

59. It may be interesting to observe that Turner had perhaps invested too much in the Revolution not to go along with the victorious army. It was said in early 1644 that Turner and his son, along with Maurice Gethin, William Hawkins, and Tempest Milner, had jointly lent £42,929.12s.8d. to Parliament. See Green, 1: 150. For Orlibear, see BL Add. MS. 36781, f. 84b, where Orlibear is identified as deputy of the Bread Street Ward in early 1661; Woodhead, p. 123, *s. v.* Orlebar.

60. GLMS 824/1, see vestry minutes, 1644–47. Both Green and Coulson had been assessors for contributions to Parliament in 1642. In 1644 Coulson's military title was captain, and when his name reappeared in 1654, his title was major. See also PRO SP 19/78, f. 60d; Harold A Dillon, "On a MS List of Officers of the London Trained Bands in 1643," *Archaeologia*, sec. ser., 2 (1890): 137.

61. GLMS 824/1, see vestry minutes, 1654–58.

62. There had apparently been a long conflict between some of the parishioners of St. Martin Orgar and the rector, Brian Walton, from the pre-Revolutionary years. See *The Articles and*

Charge Proved in Parliament Against Doctor Walton, Minister of St. Martins Orgar in Cannon-street, pp. 1–3. The civic leaders of the parish in the early years of the Revolution included William Gore, Michael Styles, and William Peake. Styles did not appear to have played any role in parish affairs, whereas Peake became an important figure only in the late 1650s. Gore's career was a rather strange one. He had been a leading opponent of Walton before the Revolution, but in 1644 he was first arrested for not having paid his assessment to Parliament and was later declared "a delinquent" for having "deserted the Kingdom." For Gore, see Green, 1: 126, 127; for Peake, see Woodhead, p. 128, *s. v.* In any case, it is clear that the civic leaders of the parish did not constitute a firm coherent group for the management of parish affairs.

63. See chap. 5 above.

64. It is interesting to note that according to Henry Hammond, Bruno Ryves, the sequestered Anglican rector of St. Martin Vintry and royalist propagandist during the Civil War, preached in the parish on 20 May 1649.

65. GLMS 5019/1, ff. 94, 102, 109, 118, 128, 137. Since the Second Classis, of which St. Pancras Soper Lane was one of the component parishes, was never formed, it is unknown whether Jurin was a religious Presbyterian. What is clear is that during the years of 1650–54, Jurin was replaced by Jeremy Rawston as Common Councilman from the parish. Jurin reappeared as Common Councilman after 1655. See ibid., ff. 138, 170, 176, 182, 186, 198. See also Woodhead, p. 100, *s. v.*

66. GLMS 5019/1, ff. 123, 127; GLMS 5018/1, no folio number, see churchwardens' account, 1647. George Cokayne, Anthony Burgess, and Christopher Love were all invited to preach in the parish church in 1647. While Cokayne was a radical Independent, Burgess and Love were prominent Presbyterian ministers in the City.

67. The churchwardens' account for 1647 noted that "here follows certain accounts of the yeare 1647 when nobody was chosen churchwarden wherein divers parishioners received and paid money." A marginal note in the vestry book for a vestry meeting on 2 July 1647 stated that "this vestry could not be written in the book when it was made because Mr. Dew [i.e., Arthur Dewe] keeps the book, the original of it in the keeping of John Jurin." See GLMS 5019/1, f. 126; GLMS 5018/1, churchwardens' account, 1647.

68. GLMS 5019/1, ff. 132, 135; GLMS 5018/1, churchwardens' accounts, 1648–50.

69. GLMS 5019/1, f. 135, vestry minute, 3 October 1649.

70. In the early 1640s, the leading civic figures of the parish were Sir Jacob Garrard, James Bunce, and Thomas Foote. While Garrard was a royalist, Bunce was to become a staunch political Presbyterian in the City, and Foote, a political Independent. For Garrard, Bunce, and Foote, see Pearl, pp. 298–99, 313–14, 315–16.

71. Shaw, 2: 401.

72. See CLRO, J. Co. Co., 40, f. 215b; CLRO Letter Books, QQ, ff. 269b–70; Ruthworth, 6: 472; Firth and Rait, 1: 928.

73. William Beake was Common Councilman during the years 1643–47, and Robert Dycer was also Common Councilman in 1645. See GLMS 3461/1 (Bridge Ward Within Wardmote Minute Book), lists of ward officials for these years; CLRO J. Co. Co., 40, ff. 52b, 128.

74. Given the fact Garrard had become a Royalist and Bunce had been impeached and imprisoned by the end of 1647, the governance of the parish must have been greatly affected. In addition, Thomas Foote had apparently moved to St. Olave Old Jewry. It is to be noted, however, that the churchwardens' accounts of the parish were regularly kept during these years. See Ruthworth, 7: 821; GLMS 4415/1, f. 140; GLMS 1568, ff. 655–75.

75. GLMS 5910/1, f. 104.

76. GLMS 877/1, f. 107. The Common Councilmen from this parish in the pre-Revolutionary years had been Edmund Harrison and Matthew Benson, who were replaced in 1641 by Thomas Gee and Thomas Kirton. See ibid. ff. 87, 92.

77. GLMS 4049/1, f. 27a, vestry minute, 17 October 1648. For a fuller description of the background, see chap. 3 above.

78. GLMS 4049/1, f. 27a. In fact, Cullum had also been one of the Aldermen charged with high treason in the previous year. See Ruthworth, 7: 821; Pearl, pp. 314–15.

79. GLMS 1175/1, no folio number, see the chart of pews drawn up after the election of Thomas Brooks on 18 April 1648. Several other charts of pews in the parish church were also recorded during the Revolutionary period.

80. GLMS 642/1, no folio number, see chart of women's seats in the pews drawn up on 31 December 1648. Incidentally, it may be added that while in the parish of St. Margaret New Fish Street the minister, Thomas Brooks, was a leading Independent, the minister of St. Peter Westcheap was Roger Drake, a leading Presbyterian divine in the City. Obviously, there was little difference between them in this respect.

81. GLMS 1311/1, ff. 135b–36, 138, 139b. Gilbert Whitehead and Nicholas Banister were officially ousted from the vestry in 1643, and several others of the old vestry were also conspicuously absent from the vestry elected in 1644. Nicholas Banister's name reappeared in the vestry in the late 1650s. Ibid., f. 154b.

82. In the 1638 assessments of the parish, the estimated values of the moderate rents of these men were: Hobson (£37.10s.), Jesson [Jeston] (£33.15s.), Arnold (£30), Fox (£9). The moderate rents for the two ousted vestrymen were: Whitehead (£9) and Banister (£12). See Dale, pp. 126–28. More important, the four new men were all more or less prominent civic figures in the City during the Revolutionary period.

83. See below Appendix B, for other parochial leaders.

84. GLMS 3016/1, f. 315 (1 March 1647/8). This was almost always the case since the adoption of the new rule in 1646.

85. Ibid.

86. Ibid. It should be noted, of course, that the elections of the Common Councilmen in this parish were always influenced by the political events in the City as well as in the nation. Praise-God Barbone was to be chosen Common Councilman from this parish in 1649–50 and again in 1657–59. See ibid., ff. 353, 356, 377, 449, 527, 554. For other parochial leaders of the parish, see Appendix B below.

87. Usually one would have to pay a fine in order to excuse oneself from such parochial obligations.

88. GLMS 62/1, f. 14.

89. There is no official list of the members of John Goodwin's gathered congregational church. We may infer, however, with reasonable certainty from the vestry minutes of the parish, that the following parishioners of St. Stephen Coleman Street were either members or unmistakable supporters of Goodwin's gathered church: Owen Rowe, Mark Hildesley, Richard Ashurst, William Mountain, Thomas Alderne, John Price, and possibly Isaac Pennington, James Russell, and Thomas Barnardiston. With the exception of John Price all of these men participated regularly in the management of parish affairs. See GLMS 4459/1, ff. 134, 161, for the making of the above list.

90. GLMS 11394/1, no folio number, see churchwardens' accounts, 1645–46, 1649–50, and 1652–53; Tolmie, pp. 104, 187.

91. GLMS 4165/1, ff. 160, 268. After 1645–46, when the parish of St. Peter Cornhill became more Presbyterian and conservative in its general religious stance, Wollaston probably withdrew from participation in parish affairs. See also Tolmie, pp. 150, 171.

92. GLMS 1196/1, ff. 27, 28, 31; Tolmie, pp. 140, 171.

93. GLMS 4571/1, ff. 23, 28, 31, 29; Tolmie, p. 115.

94. See n. 89 above; GLMS 1453/1, see vestry minutes, 28 Dec. 1646 and January 1647; GLMS 1041/1, see vestry minutes, 20 December 1649 and 19 December 1650; GLMS 4060/1, see vestry minutes, 1651; 14 April 1653; 4 November 1655. There was also a James Russell who served as churchwarden of St. Olave Silver Street in the years 1644–45 and 1645–46. See GLMS 1257/1, ff. 46, 47. Although we cannot be certain that all these instances refer to the same James Russell, yet it is possible that with the exception of the one in the parish of St. Olave Silver Street, all the others were the same man. In all these other cases, when the name of James

Russell showed up in the records of a parish, he always appeared to be a leading man of the vestry.

95. GLMS 4835/1, see churchwardens' accounts, 1640–41, 1641–42, 1643–44, 1658–59, and the lists of auditors for each year's account. For the references to the Separatist congregation in this parish, see ibid., churchwardens' accounts, 1655–56, 1656–57, 1657–58. Incidentally, this gathered church is not included in Tolmie, *Triumph of the Saints.*

96. GLMS 389/1, no folio number, see churchwardens' accounts for 1646 and 1655.

97. GLMS 3016/1, ff. 353, 356, 377, 499, 527, 554.

98. Ibid., ff. 293, 343, 584.

99. GLMS 1257/1, ff. 55, 96.

100. GLMS 4459/1, f. 161.

101. GLMS 4835/1, see churchwardens' accounts, 1655–56, 1656–57, 1657–58.

102. Cf. E. M. Leonard, *The Early History of English Poor Relief* (Cambridge, 1900); Sidney and Beatrice Webb, *English Local Government: English Poor Law History,* pt. 1: *The Old Poor Law* (London, 1927); R. H. Tawney, *Religion and the Rise of Capitalism* (London, 1926); Margaret James, *Social Problems and Policy during the Puritan Revolution, 1640–1660* (London, 1930); Christopher Hill, "Puritan and the Poor," *Past and Present* 2 (November 1952): 32–50.

103. Cf. Ronald W. Herlan, "Poor Relief in the London Parish of Antholin's Budge Row, 1638–1664," *Guildhall Studies in London History* 2, no. 4 (April 1977): 179–99; *idem,* "Poor Relief in the London Parish of Dunstan in the West during the English Revolution," ibid., 3, no. 1 (October 1977): 13–35; Valerie Pearl, "Puritans and Poor Relief. The London Workhouse, 1649–1660," in Donald Pennington and Keith Thomas, eds., *Puritans and Revolutionaries. Essays in Seventeenth-Century History Presented to Christopher Hill* (Oxford, 1978), pp. 206–32.

104. GLMS 4458/1, f. 128.

105. GLMS 3570/2, f. 52b.

106. GLMS 4887, f. 319. It may also be interesting to note that even a highly radical and Puritan parish such as St. Dunstan in the East would not or could not abandon the old tradition of social life in celebrating Christmas.

107. GLMS 3556/2, see churchwardens' account for 1651–52.

108. For examples of such payments, see GLMS 4415/1, churchwardens' account, 1643; GLMS 4241/1, churchwardens' accounts, 1642–44; GLMS 1542/2, churchwardens' account, 1644; GLMS 4524/2, churchwardens' account, 1643–44; GLMS 4214/1, f. 15b; GLMS 590/1, f. 185b; GLMS 878/1, f. 292b; GLMS 1391/1, churchwardens' account, 1641–42; GLMS 559/1, churchwardens' account, 1641–42.

109. GLMS 4458/1, f. 200.

110. Ibid., f. 238. See also GLMS 3579, f. 221b.

111. GLMS 645/2, no folio number, see churchwardens' accounts for these years.

112. GLMS 11394/1, no folio number, see churchwardens' accounts for these years.

113. GLMS 2895/2, no folio number, see churchwardens' accounts for these years.

114. GLMS 6836, ff. 155–56, 201, 206. In the years 1649–50 the churchwardens stated that only £7. 9s. were not collected.

115. GLMS 4415/1, ff. 115b, 157.

116. GLMS 818/1, no folio numbers, see churchwardens' accounts for these years.

117. GLMS 5090/2, no folio number, see churchwardens' accounts for these years.

118. GLMS 1542/2, ff. 40, 41, 43.

119. GLMS 3149/1, ff. 6–7, 32–33, 35.

120. Cf. GLMS 2895/2, no folio number, see churchwardens' account, 1642–43; GLMS 6836, ff. 201, 204.

121. Cf. GLMS 4524/2, ff. 164, 186b; GLMS 4525/2, no folio number, see churchwardens' account for 1653; GLMS 2593/2, f. 110; GLMS 645/2, no folio number, see churchwardens' account for 1642–43.

122. Cf. GLMS 1432/4, no folio number, see churchwardens' accounts for 1640–41 and 1646–47; GLMS 4525/2, no folio number, see churchwardens' acounts for 1651–52 and 1652–53.

123. GLMS 3556/2, no folio number, see churchwardens' account for 1651–52.

124. GLMS 6047/1, ff. 11–13, 30–33, see churchwardens' accounts for 1648–49 and 1649–50. The vivid detailed descriptions of this poor relief work are both informative and fascinating.

125. As we have seen earlier in this chapter, the political events in both the City and the nation affected the religious as well as the secular life of many a parish in London. In fact, the ministry of St. Giles Cripplegate had never been firmly settled during the Civil War period and was still vacant in 1648.

126. See GLMS 11334/1, no folio number, see churchwardens' accounts for 1647–48; GLMS 3149/1, ff. 4–5, 14–15, 30–31, 37–38; GLMS 4524/2, ff. 206, 263; GLMS 6047/1, f. 12 [11b].

127. Although the parish records seldom recorded procedures of catechism for the children of the poor, we may presume that biblical instruction must have been given along with the Bibles. For catechism, see GLMS 4813/1, ff. 90b, 97; GLMS 3016/1, ff. 269–70.

128. GLMS 878/1, ff. 191–92.

129. Ibid.

7

Conclusion

One of the main purposes of this study is to explore whether there was any correlation between the religious and the social configurations among the inhabitants of the City of London during the period of the English Revolution. Or, to put the question more plainly, was there any relationship between, on the one hand, the social conditions of the various parishes in the City and, on the other, their general religious affiliations during the revolutionary era—whether Anglican, Presbyterian, or Independent? For this purpose I have devoted the first chapter of this study to a series of descriptions and analyses of the general social compositions of the City parishes on the eve and during the years of the Revolution; in the three ensuing chapters, the religious affiliations of the London parishes are examined. What has emerged from these inquiries and analyses is a rather complex socioreligious picture that would deny any simple and broad generalizations. It is to be noted, however, that although no concise overall pattern can be delineated, some subsidiary patterns do appear to be discernible in spite of the complexity of the socioreligious configurations in Puritan London. With caution and with necessary qualifications, these patterns may cast some light on the subject of the correlation between religion and society in the City during the revolutionary era.

In the light of this general survey of the Presbyterians in Puritan London, it is reasonably clear that the parishes in which the Presbyterian church government was more or less successfully established during the Puritan era were, in most cases, substantial parochial communities in the City. Or, to set forth the circumstances more accurately, it was mostly in those parishes in which there was a concentration of wealthy merchants and well-to-do tradesmen that the Presbyterian church government appears to have had a tangible and firm social foundation. As natural civic leaders in the parochial communities of the City, these men were a vital and indispensable force for the

197

founding and functioning of the Presbyterian church government and discipline. As was often observed in the second chapter of this study, a coalescence of clerical and civic Presbyterian leadership almost invariably provided the most favorable condition for the success of the Presbyterian church Government in a London parish during the revolutionary period. The following examples may be cited from each of the constituted classes in the City: Allhallows the Great, St. Augustine, and St. Martin Ludgate of the First Classis; St. Mary Woolnorth and St. Mary Woolchurch of the Third Classis; St. Michael Cornhill and St. Mary at Hill of the Fourth Classis; St. Vedast Foster Lane, St. Peter Westcheap, and St. Botolph Aldersgate of the Fifth Classis; St. Mary Aldermanbury, St. Lawrence Old Jewry, and St. Mary Magdalen Milk Street of the Sixth Classis; St. Bartholomew by the Exchange, St. Christopher, and St. Michael Bassishaw of the Seventh Classis; and St. Helen and St. Andrew Undershaft of the Eighth Classis.[1]

It appears, therefore, that there was indeed an unmistakable correlation between the establishment of the Presbyterian church government in a London parish during the Puritan era and the presence of an adequate number of substantial merchants and well-to-do tradesmen in that parochial community. Yet how shall this correlation be interpreted or characterized? Various questions can more easily be raised than answered. Was this relationship between the establishment of the Presbyterian church government and the presence of substantial merchants and well-to-do tradesmen socioeconomic in nature? Or, was it a religious one? And did the Presbyterian church government as an ecclesiastical polity appeal exclusively or primarily to the rich and the well-to-do in the City?

First of all it is to be noted that while the Presbyterian church government was established mostly in the substantial parochial communities of the City, not all substantial parishes in Puritan London adopted the Presbyterian church government and discipline. In the First Classis, for example, the Presbyterian church government apparently failed to establish itself in six of its fifteen constituent parishes. Among these six parishes, only two, that is, St. Andrew by the Wardrobe and St. Peter Paul's Wharf, were truly impoverished parochial communities, whereas the other four, namely, St. Gregory by St. Paul's, St. Mary Aldermary, St. Mary le Bow, and St. Matthew Friday Street, were all relatively substantial parishes in early seventeenth-century London.[2] We may recall that in spite of the presence of a number of wealthy and unmistakably Puritan civic leaders, the parish of St. Gregory by St. Paul's was to become one of the strongholds of Anglican clergymen in the City in the latter part of the revolutionary era and that St. Matthew Friday Street, one of the traditionally Puritan parishes in London, failed to have the Presbyterian church government established even after its radical Independent minister, Henry Burton, had been forced to leave the parish in 1645.[3] It may also be useful to have a closer look at the parishes of St. Mary Aldermary and St. Mary le Bow.

According to Jordan, both parishes were among the twenty-two rich parochial communities in early seventeenth-century London in which there was a concentration of substantial merchants. In fact, St. Mary Aldermary was one of the five London parishes that together contributed well over a fourth of the total charitable contributions in the City between 1480 and 1660. It had, to quote Jordan, "a remarkable concentration of eighteen great merchants . . . drawn from the Merchant Taylors, while there were also thirty-three lesser merchants who were the members of the great livery companies," and "the immense generosity" of these men "excited the civic pride of Stow."[4] This characterizatiion of the social composition of St. Mary Aldermary can be verified by the known parochial and civic leaders of the parish during the revolutionary period. Among its churchwardens between 1640 and 1660 were six merchant tailors, three skinners, three drapers, a grocer, a vintner, a haberdasher, a barber-surgeon, and an apothecary.[5] Although the parish did not produce truly prominent City Fathers during the revolutionary era, some of its civic leaders were relatively important figures in the City and deserve some discussion.

Francis Peck, for example, was an active parliamentarian and, as Common Councilman, sat on a number of important committees in 1641–42: committees for the safety of the City, for the disputed elections of Common Councilmen, and for the composition of a counterpetition against the peace movement in London. Although Peck was appointed to the committee for church government in 1644, he had long been associated with men such as Stephen Estwick and Thomas Player, and was clearly not a staunch Presbyterian.[6] Nathaniel Hall, another leading parishioner, was appointed an assessor for parliamentary subscriptions and assessments in November 1642, and was also a Common Councilman, sitting on the committee for the maintenance of ministers in the City in 1646. Hall was clearly a religious Presbyterian and served as delegate to the London Provincial Assembly between 1650 and 1657.[7] Among its other civic leaders, Robert Deane was a captain of the Red Regiment in 1648, Thomas Chester was a captain of the Blue Regiment in 1661, and Robert Hanson was deputy of Cordwainer Ward in 1660–64, Alderman of Bassishaw Ward in 1664–80 and the Lord Mayor of the City in 1672.[8] Yet, in spite of the fact that Hall himself participated in the London Provincial Assembly, there is no sign that the Presbyterian church government was ever established in the parish. Robert Gell, the parish minister during the Puritan era, apparently refused to take part in the Presbyterian system in the City.[9]

The parish of St. Mary le Bow, too, was composed mostly of well-to-do tradesmen, and in the first three years of the Revolution, it had two active civic leaders of the city—Captain Francis Roe and Theophilus Ryley. Roe continued his support of the parliamentary faction in the City and became a colonel in the London militia in 1646.[10] The career of Ryley was, on the other hand, tortuous and revealing. Clearly a parliamentarian in the Common

Council in 1642–43, he was appointed an assessor for parliamentary subscriptions and assessments in 1642 and sat on a number of important committees in the Common Council—committees for the examination of "malignant, scandalous and seditious ministers," for the composition of a counterpetition against the peace movement in the City and for the London militia. Indeed, he was praised by a contemporary Puritan pamphleteer as one "who had the name and reputation of an honest and religious man." Yet, in 1644, Ryley abandoned the parliamentary cause and was implicated in a Royalist plot in the City.[11] The civic leaders of the parish were clearly divided among themselves. More interesting, the parish minister, Thomas Rutton, who was identified as a Presbyterian in 1660–61, appears to have also declined to act in the Presbyterian church government in the City.[12]

Similar exceptions can also be discerned in St. Lawrence Pountney of the Third Classis, Allhallows Honey Lane of the Sixth Classis, and St. Martin Outwich of the Eighth Classis. Again, none of these three parishes was an impoverished parochial community. The parish of St. Lawrence Pountney had a number of substantial merchants and tradesmen, though among its inhabitants in 1638 there appears to have been a higher proportion of the poor and the meaner sort of people.[13] Yet, as has been noted in an earlier chapter, among its civic leaders were at least six masters of the livery companies of the City: Thomas Thorold, master of the Ironmongers' Company in 1634, 1644, and 1645; Charles Snelling, master of the Ironmongers' Company in 1640 and 1646; George Downes, master of the Clothworkers' Company in 1658; Thomas Starkey, master of the Saddlers' Company in 1652; Robert Meade, master of the Salters' Company in 1652; and Ellis Cunliff, master of the Grocers' Company in 1661. In addition, Cunliff was chosen Alderman in 1658, and Eliah Harvey, another civic leader of the parish, was elected Alderman in 1649.[14] If Harvey, brother of the renowned William Harvey, was probably a Royalist, the other civic leaders of the parish appear to have been associated with the parliamentary faction in the City. Thorold was appointed an assessor for parliamentary subscriptions and assessments in the City in 1642; Snelling was appointed to a parliamentary commission in 1645; and Meade, also an active Common Councilman, was appointed a lay trier for the Third Classis in 1645.[15] Yet none of these men seem to have participated in the Presbyterian church government in London. In fact, the ministry of the parish was never firmly settled during the revolutionary era.[16]

Allhallows Honey Lane and St. Martin Outwich were, admittedly, small parishes in the City, and the former was considered by Jordan, rather mistakenly, as one of the impoverished parochial communities in early seventeenth-century London.[17] In actuality, these two parishes were by no means lacking in substantial merchants and well-to-do tradesmen. Among the civic leaders of Allhallows Honey Lane, for instance, were Edward Claxton and Daniel Waldoe. Claxton was master of the Clothworkers' Company in 1634 and elected Alderman in 1648, and Waldoe, Claxton's son-in-law, was master of the Clothworkers' Company in 1655 and elected Alderman in 1653. Furthermore, Claxton was appointed a commissioner and governor of the Excise Office, and Waldoe was appointed an assessor for the parliamentary subscriptions and assessments in the City in 1642. Waldoe was possibly also a Common Councilman during the years of the Civil War, though he does not appear to have been deeply involved in Puritan politics in the City.[18] In addition, a Dr. Ent of this parish was in all probability Dr. George Ent, who had published in 1641 *Apologia pro circuitione sanguinis* in vindication of Willian Harvey's discovery. And Ent was to become the President of the Royal College of Physicians in 1670–75, 1682, and 1684.[19] It appears, however, that the Presbyterian church polity was never adopted in this parish.

In comparison, the civic leaders in the parish of St. Martin Outwich were more numerous and influential. In the early part of the revolutionary period, the leading figures of the parish were Richard Bateman and Rowland Wilson. Bateman was master of the Skinners' Company in 1643–44 and a substantial merchant in both the East India Company and the Levant Company. Although of the conservative faction in the City in 1641, Bateman was an active Common Councilman between 1642 and 1647, and he sat on a number of important committees: committee for the fortification of the City, committee for the London militia, committee for church government, and the like. In 1648 he was elected Alderman and, in the following year, Sheriff of London.[20] Wilson was one of the most influential Independent civic leaders in Puritan London. A member of George Cokayne's congregation, he was called by a contemporary pamphleteer "an *Antinomian,* a Man that hath more Money then Wit and Valour." Colonel of the Orange Regiment in the London militia in 1645–50 and also a member of the Long Parliament in 1646–50, Wilson was elected Alderman of the City in 1648, and in 1649–50 he was appointed a member of the Council of State under the new Commonwealth.[21] Among the other civic leaders of the parish were John Beale, master of the Clothworkers' Company in 1643 and Alderman in 1650; Richard Clutterbuck, master of the Mercers' Company and Alderman in 1650; Samuel Harrison, master of the Apothecaries' Company in 1650–51; and Henry Hunt, master of the Ironmongers' Company in 1655.[22] Furthermore, in the latter part of the revolutionary period, the leading civic figure of the parish was William Vincent, who was elected Alderman in 1658 and Sheriff of London in the following year. In 1660 he was both an M. P. for London and colonel of the Blue Regiment of the London Militia. Also a prominent merchant in both the East India Company and the Levant Company, Vincent was master elect of the Grocers' Company in 1661.[23] Again, in spite of the presence of all these substantial merchants and tradesmen, the Presbyterian church government does not appear to have been well established in this parish.

The preceding analyses may serve as a necessary qualification to the basic pattern with regard to the correlation between the Presbyterian church government and the substantial parochial communities in Puritan London. I have elaborated on this point because these exceptions give warning against a rigid Marxist interpretation of the Puritan experiment in London in terms of socioeconomic classes. The temptation of selective evidence and simplified generalization is tantalizing, but with a closer and fuller view of the complex socioreligious configurations in Puritan London, one becomes increasingly aware that religious beliefs and church polities cannot be defined simply in socioeconomic terms.

Indeed, it may be further observed that the Presbyterian church government was by no means a monopoly of the rich and the well-to-do. As was noted in the second chapter, it was well established in a number of the poorer parishes in the City. In this respect the following cases may be cited as examples: St. Anne Blackfriars and St. Benet Paul's Wharf of the First Classis; St. Anne and St. Agnes Aldersgate, St. Leonard Foster Lane, St. Bride, and Christ Church of the Fifth Classis; and St. Alban Wood Street and St. Michael Wood Street of the Sixth Classis. In none of these parishes can we find great merchants or substantial tradesmen during the revolutionary period, and in most of these parishes the number of the poor and the meaner sort of people was overwhelming.[24] Yet almost all these parishes became strongholds of the Presbyterian movement in the City during the years of the Civil War. As was often noted in the second chapter, the success of Presbyterianism in these parishes was derived primarily from the leadership and influence of their ministers: William Gouge at St. Anne Blackfriars, Allen Geare at St. Benet Paul's Wharf, Christopher Love at St. Anne and St. Agnes Aldersgate, James Nalton at St. Leonard Foster Lane, Simeon Ashe at St. Bride, William Jenkin at Christ Church, Arthur Jackson at St. Michael Wood Street, and Peter Witham at St. Alban Wood Street.[25] The impact of these men on their parishioners through their sermons, lectures, and personal persuasion can hardly be denied. "The judgment of God," as Edward Dering well observed, "pierces deeply into the hearts of true believers, and the word that they hear, it worketh mightily in them, more sharp than a two-edged sword."[26]

Similarly, the Independents and the Anglicans in Puritan London cannot be characterized in socioeconomic terms. It is true that the separatist Independent churches in the City were composed mostly of the meaner sort of people—at least contemporary Presbyterian pamphleteers often so maintained. Unfortunately, few of the Independent congregations of this period have left their church books to posterity, so that we have no concrete information with regard to the general picture of the social composition in these gathered churches. It is to be noted, however, that the presence of known Independent ministers in such City parishes as St. Magnus, St. Mary Abchurch, St. James Garlickhithe, St. Pancras Soper Lane, St. Dunstan in the West, and St. Stephen Coleman Street clearly indicates that religious Independency, too, had its appeal to well-to-do tradesmen and wealthy merchants in the City.[27] Indeed, among the known lay Independents in

Puritan London were some of the most important civic leaders during the revolutionary period—men such as Isaac Pennington, Rowland Wilson, Owen Rowe, Robert Tichborne, John Ireton, Stephen Estwicke, Mark Hildesley, William Underwood, and William Steele.[28] In the case of the Anglicans in Puritan London, we find them both in substantial parochial communities such as St. Gregory by St. Paul's and St. Dionis Backchurch and in one of the most impoverished parishes of the City, namely St. Peter Paul's Wharf.[29]

These necessary qualifications once made, we may now come to understand the nature of this correlation between the Presbyterian church polity and the substantial parochial communities in the City during the revolutionary period. Such a correlation does, after all, appear to have existed. What, then, is the nature of this correlation? First of all, it may be pointed out that the Presbyterian church government was based on the traditional parish churches, the ministries of which were, in turn, maintained by the tithes and subscriptions of the individual parochial communities. Only in those substantial parishes in which the value of tithes was more or less adequate could a settled ministry be secured. Furthermore, the value of tithes even in a substantial parish was often less than enough, given the amount of annual income a minister usually expected and often received in the City during the revolutionary era.[30] The collection of tithes had never been easy, and there is no sign that it was more effectively enforced by the Puritan leaders when they were in power. Consequently, as was noted before in this study, tithes were usually supplemented by subscriptions for ministerial maintenance, even in some of the richest parishes of the City.[31] Needless to say, the subscriptions to supplement tithes came from the rich and the well-to-do parishioners of the various parishes. In this light it may perhaps be said that the correlation between the establishment of the Presbyterian church government and the substantial parochial communities in the City was economic in nature.

Even in this limited sense, however, it should be noted that the continuing reliance upon the traditional parochial structure for the Presbyterian church government was more of a religious and social consideration than an economic one. For the Presbyterian divines who, at least until their forced exodus from the Church of England in 1662, had never questioned the ecclesiastical polity of a national church and had never intended to separate themselves from the parochial churches, a national Presbyterian church government, with the parish churches as its natural constituent-church congregations, was what they believed in. After all, it was their creation in the Westminster Assembly. To the lay Presbyterian civic leaders in London, the parochial structure was a fundamental institution in traditional local government. It was, indeed, one of the cornerstones upon which the whole civic edifice of the City was founded.[32] To say this is not to imply that these men, lay Presbyterians as they were, did not have religious concerns about church polity. In any case, paying both in tithes and in subscriptions, these men clearly did not have any economic advantage in support of the Presbyterian church government in Puritan London.

Another main question is whether, and if so in what ways, the triumph of Puritanism in the City changed the parochial life of the various London parishes. It is in this respect that some of the developments in Puritan London are fascinating and significant. First, now with the bishop gone and the old episcopal hierarchy destroyed, the parochial ministers were in many cases chosen by the parishes themselves instead of being imposed from above by a higher authority. And we may recall that in some of the parishes the various forms of ministerial election were far more liberal and democratic than either the municipal elections in the City or the parliamentary elections in the country as a whole.[33] Second, as a consequence of such elective process, the relationship between the minister and the parish became contractual in nature with regard to the ministerial maintenance as well as ministerial duties, and in a few cases a written contract was actually drawn up.[34] Third, in some of the parishes, the old select vestries were opened up, at least in principle, to all parishioners, whereas in others they were reorganized like committees to ensure a more equitable representation and a more effective governance of parochial affairs.[35] Also noticeable was a growing sense of parochial independence, not only from the old episcopal jurisdiction in the early years of our period but, in later years, from lay patrons as well.[36] To be sure, none of these new practices and developments were commonly adopted by all the parishes in the City, and exceptions can easily be detected. Nevertheless, among the City parishes, rich or poor, big or small, such practices and developments were numerous and unmistakable. There can be little doubt that in many of the parishes in Puritan London, the conduct of parochial affairs, civil as well as religious, was veering, unmistakably though not invariably, from the old norm based on tradition and custom to a new one that was more rational and contractual in nature.

It seems that this evidence can be used plausibly to support Max Weber's interpretation of Puritanism and the modern rational and contractual social behavior in Western society. Perhaps so. It is to be emphasized, however, that in history continuity is as significant a feature as change. Seventeenth-century society, even in Puritan London, continued to be one of social status. In spite of all the organizational or institutional changes in the various parishes of the City, there was no fundamental disintegration or change in the traditional social structure of the parochial community. Again, as was often observed in an earlier chapter of this study, the vestry, open or select, in committee form or as a co-optative group, was always composed of the substantial and well-do-do inhabitants of the parish.[37] And social deference remained the basic principle of social relationships among men. A study of the pew charts in the parochial records of our period further confirms this observation.[38] And with the exception of a few special cases, the governance of the City parishes was never disrupted in spite of all the radical revolutions at Westminster or in the City government itself.[39] The traditional form of poor relief continued to be well maintained in almost all the City parishes during the revolutionary period.[40] In short, the social fabric of the City remained intact during the period when the Puritans were in power. From a longer historical perspective, continuity was probably a more prominent force than change in the parochial life in Puritan London.

At this juncture we should perhaps address ourselves to the question of identifying the civic leaders in Puritan London in terms of church polity, especially the Presbyterian civic leaders discussed in chapter 2 with regard to the founding of the Presbyterian church government in the various parishes of the City. It is to be noted, however, that many of them continued to serve either in the municipal government or in national offices after the collapse of the Presbyterian faction in the City in 1647–48. Indeed, some of them openly cooperated with the Army after the latter had marched on London. Were they truly religious Presbyterians? Or, should we call them political Presbyterians or political Independents? Or, to put it more bluntly, should we conclude that these names were meaningless labels and ought to be discarded in modern studies? Yet their involvement in the Presbyterian movement in the City before 1647 and, in some cases, their continuous participation in the Presbyterian church government after 1648 made them unquestionably religious Presbyterians. Contemporaries could and did charge them with trimming their sails to the political wind of each moment without any principle:

> Theres *Bateman, Water-house,* and *Chamberlain*
> Who otherwise imploy'd were honest men.
> Theres Edwin Browne as moderate as they,
> And *Francis West,* but much I cannot say.
> . . . .
> Theres *Iackson, Player,* both their parts can *play,*
> On either side that beares the greatest *sway.*
> Theres *Glyde* a busie *knave* of *Weavers* Hall
> That thinks himselfe the wisest of all.
> Theres *Arnold, Hall,* two *Bellamyes,* and Jesson,
> Have all took out the *Independent-Lesson.*
> Yet can at pleasure it againe forget
> And Presbyterians be when they think fit.
> . . . .
> Theres *Kendall* a brave *Button-seller,* hee
> On all *occasions* can *new-molded be.*
> And Mr. *Gaze,* a Reverend *Turner* too
> His *Occupation* shewes what he can doe.[41]

Farther removed from the scene and with more historical sympathy, a student of Puritan London in the twentieth century would prefer a kinder judgment. To be sure, in any age, especially in an age of revolution, there are men of great hypocrisy and deceit, whose actions are motivated and guided solely by self-interest. For many of the civic leaders in Puritan London, however, the inconsistency between their pronounced religious belief and their changing political positions was of a different nature. As religious Presbyterians, they fought for the establishment of the Presbyterian church government when there was hope; yet, as civic leaders, they had to fulfill their civic responsibilities to maintain peace and stability in the City when they were needed. This sense of civic responsibility can also be seen in the seemingly anomalous activities of the Independents in Puritan London, who, on the one hand, had joined separatist gathered congregational churches for religious worship but, on the other, continued to participate in the parochial institutions, either as vestrymen or as churchwardens or as auditors, over civic affairs. In this respect, the activities of Mark Hildesley in St. Stephen Coleman Street, Rowland Wilson in St. Martin Outwich, William Underwood in St. Stephen Walbrook, Samuel Eames in St. Margaret Lothbury, Robert Tichborne in St. Olave Silver Street, and especially the lay pastors of gathered churches such as Praise-God Barbone in St. Dunstan in the West and Edmund Rosier in St. Mary Abchurch are all most revealing.[42] No explanation other than their sense of civic duty to their respective parochial communities in which they lived can better elucidate their willingness to hold such offices.

Finally, it may not be inappropriate to point out that this monograph is a study of London during the Puritan era from a single historical perspective. It is *not* a history of the City and the Puritan Revolution. Students of the history of this great City who have read either John Stow's *Survey of London,* published at the beginning of the seventeenth century, or James Howell's *Londinopolis,* written at the end of the revolutionary period, know well the magnitude and the breadth of London's political and economic importance in the nation. Only when we remember the total picture of the City and the far-reaching radiations of her economic wealth and political power can we fully understand the place of London in the history of the Puritan Revolution. And only in this light can we say that what happened in the City within her own Walls assumed the character of national significance. It is hoped, therefore, that this monographic study, which is based primarily upon the parochial records of the City during the Puritan era, may contribute, however slightly, to our understanding not only of the Puritan experiments in the parochial communities of the City but also of greater issues as well.

"It is no exaggeration to say," Thomas B. Macaulay wrote in the nineteenth century, "that but for the hostility of the City, Charles I would never have vanquished, and that without the help of the City, Charles II could never have been restored."[43] In this study we have observed, directly or indirectly, the strength of Puritanism in the various parishes of the City at the beginning of the revolutionary period. On the outbreak of the Civil War it was the Puritans in the City who contributed large sums of money for the creation and maintenance of a parliamentary army, or supplied men and horses to be maintained by themselves. With the triumph of the Independents in 1647 and 1648, the Presbyterian leaders in London, lay as well as clerical, began to retreat from the revolutionary movement. And, as we have also seen in this study, Anglican clergymen reappeared in many parishes of the City in the 1650s long before the return of the monarchy in 1660. Perhaps, London's importance in the Puritan Revolution has been most eloquently expressed by one of the Puritan divines of the City in a sermon he preached in early 1647 before the House of Commons:

> I shall desire you seriously to commune with your own hearts, of *What London hath done for you. London* the mirrour and wonder of Love, Zeal, Constancy, and Bounty to you and your Cause: *London,* the Arke that hath kept you safe, in the deluge of bloud that hath overflowed the Nation: *London,* your *Ophir* and *Indies* that hath supplyed you with masses of Money and Plate in all your wants: *London,* your banke and stock of men and hearts: *London,* your so much, that you have not been what you are, if it had not been for *London:* London, that under a Parliament hath preserved a Nation: and London, that under God hath preserved a Parliament. Was it ever seen, or could it ever be related, that any City under heaven ever did, as *London* hath done in love and kindnesses to your Cause and you? What one among you can look into his owne heart, but he must needs find *London* written there?[44]

Or, to quote the words of another famous divine, who spoke more transcendently to the citizens of London in 1658:

> As *Athens* was called the *Greece* of *Greece,* so may *London* be stiled the *England* of *England.*[45]

NOTES

1. For the social conditions in all these parishes, see chap. 1 above. For the founding of the Presbyterian church government in these parishes, see chap. 2 above.

2. For the social conditions of these parishes, see chap. 1 above.

3. For the parish of St. Gergory by St. Paul's, see chap. 4 above; for St. Matthew Friday Street, see chap. 3 above.

4. See Jordan, pp. 35, 52.

5. See GLMS 4863/1, ff. 16b–36, where the occupations of the churchwardens for each year are identified.

6. Peck was the leading signatory of the auditors for the churchwardens' accounts in 1649–50, 1650–51, and 1655–56. See also CLRO J. Co. Co., 40, ff. 5, 11, 16, 23, 44, 86–86b; Hist. MSS. Comm., *Fifth Report,* Appendix, p. 100; Pearl, p. 323.

7. Hall was churchwarden in 1640–41. See also PRO SP 19/78, f. 60c; CLRO J. Co. Co., 40, ff. 193, 259b; Firth and Rait, 1: 1138; Surman, 1: 233, *s. v.*

8. Deane was churchwarden in 1653; Chester was churchwarden in 1657. See also CLRO J. Co. Co., 40, f. 302; BL Add. MS. 36781, f. 89. Hanson was one of the leading auditors for churchwardens' accounts in 1647–48, 1649–50, and 1652–53. For Hanson, see Woodhead, p. 84, *s. v.*

9. See chap. 4 above.

10. For Francis Roe, see PRO SP19/492, f. 88; Firth and Rait, 1:842.

11. For Ryley, see PRO SP16/492, f. 88; PRO SP 19/78, f. 60c; CLRO J. Co. Co., 40, ff. 32b, 42, 44, 62b, 67, 79, 81; Pearl, p. 259n.

12. Hist. MSS. Comm., *Sixth Report,* Appendix, p. 5; CLRO J. Co. Co., 40, f. 153; CLRO Letter Books, QQ, ff. 186–87; BL Add. MS. 36781, f. 32b; Surman, 2: 110; Shaw, 2: 109.

13. For the social conditions in St. Lawrence Pountney, see chap. 1 above.

14. See Nicholl, comp., *Some Account of the Worshipful Company of Ironmongers,* pp. 408–9; J. W. Sherwell, *The History of the Guild of Saddlers of the City of London* (London, 1937), Appendix: "Masters of the Company"; Girtin, *The Golden Ram: A History of the Clothworkers' Company,* pp. 326–27; Grantham, comp., *List of the Wardens of the Grocers' Company from 1345 to 1907,* p. 29; Charles R. Rivington, *The Records of the Worshipful Company of Stationers* (Westminster, 1883), pp. 46–48; Watson, *A History of the Salters' Company,* p. 145; Beaven, 2: 70, 78, 182; Pearl, p. 150; GLMS 3908/1, vestry minutes, no folio number. For Meade, see also CLRO J. Co. Co., 40, ff. 100, 128; PRO SP 19/78, f. 60e.

15. See PRO SP 19/78, f. 60c; Firth and Rait, 1: 733; Shaw, 2: 400.

16. See GLMS 3907/1, churchwardens' accounts, no folio number, in which payments to individual preachers in the various years are recorded.

17. See chap. 1 above; Jordan, p. 41.

18. Beaven, 2: 68, 83, 185; Firth and Fait, 1: 203; CLRO J. Co. Co., 40, f. 128; PRO SP 19/78, f. 60c. Beaven identified Waldoe as the brother-in-law of Claxton, but see Woodhead, p. 169, *s. v.* Edward Waldo.

19. For Ent, see *D. N. B., s. v.* For all three men mentioned see also GLMS 5026/1, churchwardens' accounts, "A List of parishioners [who] promised to maintain 34 men for 3 months at 4s. 8d. a week," 16 November 1642.

20. CLRO J. Co. Co., 40, ff. 52b, 62b, 67, 86–86b, 128, 129; Beaven, 2: 69, 182. See also Pearl, p. 121.

21. See *D. N. B., s. v.,* Beaven, 2: 69, 182; Firth and Rait, 1: 990, 1007, 1261.

22. Beaven, 2: 73, 74; W. S. C. Copeman, *The Worshipful Society of Apothecaries of London. A History 1617–1967* (London, 1967), pp. 95–96; Nicholl, comp., *Some Account of the Worshipful Company of Ironmongers,* pp. 408–9.

23. Beaven, 2: 89, 186; Woodhead, p. 168, *s. v.* For all the men mentioned in this paragraph, see GLMS 11394/1, churchwardens' accounts, no folio numbers, auditors' names for each year.

24. For the social conditions in these parishes, see chap. 1 above.

25. For the establishment of the Presbyterian church government in these parishes, see chap. 2 above.

26. Quoted in Seaver, p. 14.

27. For these parishes, see chap. 3 above.

28. Pennington was Prime Warden of the Fishmongers' Company in 1640, Alderman in 1639–57, and Lord Mayor in 1642–43; Wilson has been discussed earlier in this chapter. Tichborne was master of the Skinners' Company in 1650, Alderman in 1651–60, and Lord Mayor in 1656–57; Ireton was master of the Clothworkers' Company in 1652, Alderman in 1651–60 and Lord Mayor in 1658–59; Estwicke was an active Common Councilman during the years of the Civil War and Alderman in 1650–57; Hildesley was master of the Vintners' Company in 1650 and Alderman in 1649–51; Underwood was Colonel of the Blue Regiment in the London Militia in 1645 and Alderman in 1651–58; Rowe was also an active Common Councilman during the years of the Civil War and Colonel of the London militia; and Steele was appointed Recorder of the City in 1649. It is to be pointed out that only their major civic positions are given here, but the importance of these men in Puritan London can hardly be indicated even by such prominent positions.

29. See chap. 4 above.

30. See chap. 5 above.

31. Ibid.

32. For the Presbyterian divines' defense of the national church, see Liu, *Discord in Zion,* pp. 35–36, 43–46, 52–55; for a succinct treatment of the parochial institutions in the City of London, see Frank Freeman Foster, *The Politics of Stability: A Portrait of the Rulers of Elizabethan London* (London, 1977), chap. 3: "Local Officers and Local Institutions," pp. 29–53.

33. See chap. 5 above.

34. Ibid.

35. Ibid.

36. Ibid.

37. See chap. 6 above.

38. Ibid.

39. Ibid.

40. Ibid.

41. *Mercurius Elencticus,* no. 26 (May 17–24, 1648), p. 203.

42. See chaps. 3 and 6 above; GLMS 4352/1, ff. 189b, 191b, 197b, 206–12, 217b.

43. Thomas B. Macaulay, *The History of England from the Accession of James II,* 5 vols. (Philadelphia, n. d.), 3: 324.

44. John Lightfoot, *A Sermon Preached Before the Honourable House of Commons* (London, 1647), p. 26.

45. Nathaniel Hardy, *The Olive-Branch. Presented to the Native Citizens of London. In a Sermon preached at St. Paul's Church, May 27, being the Day of their Yearly Feast* (London, 1658), p. 28.

Appendices

Appendix A

The figures contained in this table are based upon the following documents:

(a) LPLMS CM VIII/4, ff. 4–5.
(b) LPLMS CM VIII/43, ff. 1–4.
(c) LPLMS CM IX/58.
(d) LPLMS CM IX/82.
(e) LPLMS CM IX/41 and LPLMS CM IX/80.
(f) Dale, *The Inhabitants of London in 1638*.

Name of the London Parishes	Number of Houses or Assessment Entries	Number of Communicants	Value of Rents (total) (£-s.-d.)	Value of Tithes (£-s.-d.)	Tithes Recommended (£-s.-d.)	Tithes or income 1636/1638 (£-s.-d.)
(1) Allhallows Barking	300(a) 300(e) 443(f)	1200(a)	4000(b) 4891(c) 4891-10-0(f)	542(b) 672-10-3(c)	290-0-6(a) 290-0-0(d)	107-18-1(b) 165-10-2(c) 206-5-6(f)
(2) Allhallows Bread Street	66(a) 66(e) 74(f)	300(a) 300(e)	2560(b) 1807(c) 1807(f)	352(b) 248-9-3(c)	140-2-3(a) 130-0-(d)	60-16-0(b) 80-2-8(c) 84-0-0(f)
(3) Allhallows the Great	260(a) 260(e) 246(f)	1232(a) 1232(e)	2201(b) 1976(c) 1976-18-0(f)	312-12-9(b) 264-16-0(c)	200-1-3(a) 180-0-0(d)	100-3-4(b) 120-15-2½(c) 132-17-0(f)
(4) Allhallows Honey Lane	34(a) 32(e) 37(f)	200(a) 200(e)	1363(b) 1000(c) 1000(f)	187-8-3(b) 137-10-0(c)	95-0-3(a) 95-0-0(d)	35-5-1¾(b) 40-9-0(c) 42-1-0(f)
(5) Allhallows the Less	120(a) 120(e) 103(f)	600(a)	1549(b) 1429(c) 1429(f)	212-19-9(b) 196-9-9(c)	120-0-9(a) 110-0-0(d)	8-0-0(c) 64-0-0(f)
(6) Allhallows Lombard Street	64(a) 64(e) 66(f)	370(a) 370(e)	2500(b) 2000(c) 2813-10-10(f)	343-15-0(b) 275(c) 386-13-9(f)	150-0-3(a) 160-0-0(d)	108-4-10½(b) 88-1-6(f)
(7) Allhallows London Wall	154(a) 154(e)	600(a) 600(e)	1810(b) 1653(c) 1653(f)	248-17-6(b) 227-5-9(c) 237-4-11(f)	120-0-9(a) 120-0-0(d)	69-10-10-(b) 80(c) 86-5-0(f)
(8) Allhallows Staining	140(a) 140(e) 201(f)	500(a)	1550(b) 1351(c) 1653(f)	213-2-6(b) 185-15-3(c) 237-4-11(f)	120-0-9(a) 120-0-0(d)	8-0-0(c) 81(f)

Church						
(9) Christ Church	---	6500(a)	4500(c)	618-15-0(c) 600(f)	450-0-9(a) 440-0-0(d)	52(b) 300(f) 40(c) 40(f)
(10) Holy Trinity the Less	94(a) 94(e) 90(f)	400(a) 400(e)	1003(b) 978(c) 978(f)	137-18-3(b) 134-9-0(c)	90-1-3(a) 90-0-0(d)	66-1-9(b) 72-0-11(c) 11-5-8(f)
(11) St. Alban Wood Street	140(a) 140(e) 134(f)	600(a)	1600(b) 1500(c) 1500(f)	220(b) 206-5-6(c) 206-5-0(f)	150-0-3(a) 150-0-0(d)	90 (b) 102-16-4(c) 106-11-4(f)
(12) St. Alphage	157(a) 157(e)	512(a)	1378(b) 1500(c)	220(b) 206-5-6(c)	150-0-3(a) 150-0-0(d)	90(b) 102-16-4(c)
(13) St. Andrew Hubbard	100(a) 100(e) 93(f)	304(a) 304(e)	1200(b) 1294(c) 1294(f)	165(b) 171-1-0(c)	85-5-0(a) 85-5-0(d)	49-7-8(b) 72-17-8(c) 68-16-0(f)
(14) St. Andrew Undershaft	206(a) 206(e) 199(f)	900(a) 900(e)	4037(b) 2974(e) 2974(f)	550(b) 402-0-6(c) 407(f)	220-0-0(a) 210-0-0(d)	137-0-10½(b) 140(c) 155(f)
(15) St. Andrew by the Wardrobe	172(a) 172(e) 242(f)	820(a)	1700(b) 2030(c) 2030-2-8(f)	223-15-0(b) 276-2-6(c) 283-5-0(f)	140-2-3(a) 130-0-0(d)	61-0-0(b) 83-17-6(c) 80-1-8(f)
(16) St. Anne & St. Agnes Aldersgate	141(f)	400(a)	4000(b) 1605(c) 1605(f)	412-10-0(b) 220-13-9(c)	120-0-9(a) 120-0-0(d)	77-0-6(b) 80-0-0(c) 76-15-8(f)

(17) St. Anne Blackfriars	200(a) 190(e)	1456(a)	3000(b) 3000(c)	412-10-0(b) 412-10-0(c)	150-0-3(a) 140-0-0(d)	100(c)
(18) St. Antholin	61(f)	---	1300(b) 1353(c) 1353(f)	180(b) 186-0-9(c)	80-0-6(a) 80-0-0(d)	37-8-0(b) 49-0-0(c) 38 & some s.(f)
(19) St. Augustine	106(f)	497(a)	2500(b) 1700(c) 1700(f)	347(b) 233-15-0(c) 233-5-0(f)	170-1-9(a) 160-0-0(d)	88-3-8½(b) 89-14-3(c) 98-14-7(f)
(20) St. Bartholomew by the Exchange	86(a) 86(e) 96(f)	400(a) 400(e)	2700(b) 2044(c) 2044-10-0(f)	370-15-0(b) 281-1-0(c) 281-2-4½(f)	140-2-3(a) 140-0-0(d)	89-1-4(b) 106-19-4(c) 88-16-4(f)
(21) St. Benet Fink	100(a) 100(e) 110(f)	350(a)	1500(b) 1175(c) 1175(f)	206-5-0(b) 161-10-9(c) 151-11-3(f)	140-2-3(a) 120-0-0(d)	16-1-4(b) 26-13-4(c) 55-5-6¼(f)
(22) St. Benet Gracechurch	36(a) 36(e) 42/46(f)	240(a) 180(e)	820(b) 1200(c) 1200(f)	112-15-0(b) 165(c) 165(f)	95-0-3(a) 95-0-0(d)	50(b) 60(c) 57-18-6(f)
(23) St. Benet Paul's Wharf	162(a) 162(e)	700(a) 700(e)	1690(b) 2000(c)	232-7-0(b) 275-0-0(c)	140-2-3(a) 120-0-0(d)	57(b)
(24) St. Benet Sherehog	29(a) 29(e) 28(f)	132(a)	650(b) 613(c) 613(f)	89-7-6(b) 84-5-9(c)	61-1-9(a) 65-0-0(d)	33-10-4(b) 35-13-4(c) 31-5-8(f)

Parish						
(25) St. Boltolph Billingsgate	110(a) 110(e) 94(f)	430(a)	1800(b) 1405(c) 1405(f)	247-10-0(b) 193-3-9(c)	150-0-3(a) 155-0-0(d)	112-14-10(b) 118-19-6¾(c) 122-0-0(f)
(26) St. Christopher le Stocks	73(a) 73(e) 62(f)	250(a) 250(e)	1994(b) 1242(c) 1242(f)	274-7-6(b) 193-3-9(c) 170-15-6(f)	150-0-3(a) 155-0-0(d)	112-14-10(b) 118-19-6¾(c) 69-1-4(f)
(27) St. Clement Eastcheap	43(a) 42(e) 49(f)	312(a) 312(e)	800(b) 1008(c) 1008(f)	110(b) 138-12-0(c) 138-12-0(f)	80-0-6(a) 80-0-0(d)	25-7-2½(b) 34-15-0(c) 40-0-0(f)
(28) St. Dionis Backchurch	140(f)	----	2400(b) 2617(c) 2617(f)	330(b) 359-16-9(c) 417-8-0(f)	150-0-3(a) 140-0-0(d)	87-18-8(b) 58-9-8(c) 98-2-4(f)
(29) St. Dunstan in the East	270(a) 266(f)	1300(a)	5000(b) 4506(c) 4506(f)	687-10-0(b) 619-11-6(c)	300-0-6(a) 300-0-0(d)	86-19-2½(b) 109-14-11(c) 136-6-4-(f)
(30) St. Edmund Lombard Street	80(a) 80(e) 75(f)	350(a) 350(e)	2000(b) 1562(c) 1562(f)	275-0-0(b) 206-10-6(c) 214-15-6(f)	150-0-3(a) 150-0-0(d)	83-7-8(b) 86-14-5(c) 86-19-4(f)
(31) St. Ethelburga	100(a) 100(e) 110(f)	550(a) 550(e)	1649(b) 1172(c) 1172(f)	214-6-1(b) 170-2-6(c)	100-2-6(a) 100-0-0(d)	58-6-9(b) 69-0-0(c) 65(f)
(32) St. Faith	160(a) 160(e) 131(f)	500(a) 500(e)	3400(b) 2500(c)	467-10-0(b) 343-15-0(c) 358-10-6(f)	200-1-3(a) 180-0-0(d)	40-0-0(b) 60-0-0(c) 73-18-1(f)

(33) St. Gabriel Fenchurch	71(a) 71(e) 76(f)	264(a)	1200(b) 1007(c) 1007-10-0(f)	158-16-5(b) 138-9-3(c)	110-0-0(a) 110-0-0(d)	76-15-8½(b) 87-1-6(c) 67-17-4(f)
(34) St. George Botolph Lane	39(a) 39(e) 39(f)	120(a) 120(e)	800(b) 963(c) 963-10-0(f)	110-0-0(b) 132-7-9(c) 131-15-0(f)	90-1-3(a) 90-0-0(d)	53-3-0(b) 60-15-8(c) 58-5-0(f)
(35) St. Gregory by St. Paul's	204(f)	---	1346(b) 3742(c) 3742-10-0(f)	261-1-5(b) 514-10-6(c) 500(f)	200-1-3(a) 180-0-0(d)	10(c) 80(f)
(36) St. Helen	103(a) 103(f)	530(a)	1947(b) 1732(c) 1732(f)	261-12-2(b) 238-3-0(c)	140-2-3(a) 120-0-0(d)	13(b) 20(c) 63-13-0(f)
(37) St. James Duke's Place	140(a) 140(e) 163(f)	500(a) 500(e)	1144(b) 1213(c) 1213-10-0(f)	159-6-0(b) 159-18-3(c)	100-2-6(a) 100-0-0(d)	38-11-4(b) 46-0-0(c) 60-17-0(f)
(38) St. James Garlickhithe	140(a) 140(e) 123(f)	500(a) 500(e)	1560(b) 1648(c) 1648(f)	214-5-0(b) 226-12-0(c)	150-0-3(a) 150-0-0(d)	56-10-2(b) 81-3-10(c) 92-10-8(f)
(39) St. John the Baptist	90(a) 80(e) 112(f)	465(a)	1000(b) 1040(c) 1040(f)	137-10-0(b) 143-0-0(c) 143-0-0(f)	95-0-3(a) 95-0-0(d)	66-5-0(b) 67-7-6½(c) 72-9-6½(f)
(40) St. John the Evangelist	24(a) 22(e) 24(f)	140(a) 140(e)	800(b) 671(c) 671(f)	110-0-0(b) 92-4-9(c) 92-5-3(f)	70-2-6(a) 70-0-0(d)	52-1-4(b) 67-9-4(c) 44-10-0(f)

(41) St. John Zachary	118(f)	----	1100(b) 1300(c) 1300(f)	168-5-0(b) 178-15-0(c) 178-15-0(f)	90-1-3(a) 100-0-0(d)	63-19-1½(b) 61-9-8(c) 64-2-4(f)
(42) St. Katherine Coleman Street	150(a) 150(e) 168(f)	500(a) 500(e)	1600(b) 1500(c) 1500(f)	220-0-0(b) 206-5-0(c)	150-0-3(a) 140-0-0(d)	99-2-0(b) 104-3-1(c) 87-15-1(f)
(43) St. Katherine Creechurch	--	----	1499(b) 2000(c)	206-3-3(b) 275-0-0(c)	160-1-0(a) 140-0-0(d)	3-0-0(b) 8-0-0(c) 60-0-0(f)
(44) St. Lawrence Jewry	143(f)	----	2400(b) 2019(c) 2019(f)	330-0-0(b) 277-12-3(c)	160-1-0(a) 160-0-0(d)	23-11-11½(b) 25-8-0(c) 80-15-8(f)
(45) St. Lawrence Pountney	100(a) 100(e) 100(f)	400(a)	1200(c) 1134(c) 1134-10-0(f)	165-0-0(b) 159-18-6(c) 155-18-6(f)	100-2-6(a) 110-0-0(d)	14-0-0(b) 11-6-8(c) 38-17-0(f)
(46) St. Leonard Eastcheap	60(a) 60(e) 65(f)	200(a) 200(e)	820(b) 1216(c) 1061(f)	112-15-0(b) 145-17-3(c)	90-1-3(a) 90-0-0(d)	49-9-8(b) 43-0-0(c) 63-13-8(f)
(47) St. Leonard Foster Lane	219(a) 219(e) 256(f)	758(a)	2786(b) 3116(c) 3116(f)	383-8-6(b) 428-9-0(c) 428-9-0(f)	160-0-3(a) 150-0-0(d)	95-0-0(b) 90-0-0(c)
(48) St. Magnus the Martyr	94(a) 90(e) 95(f)	470(a) 470(e)	2000(b) 2092(c) 2092(f)	275-0-0(b) 287-12-6(c) 287-12-0(f)	184-16-0(a) 160-0-0(d)	57-14-8½(b) 68-6-1½(c) 81-12-8(f)

Parish						
(49) St Margaret Lothbury	113(a) 113(e) 108/98(f)	340(a) 390(e)	1638(b) 1514(c) 1514(f)	225-0-0(b) 208-3-6(c)	130-1-6(a) 130-0-0(d)	59-7-6(b) 61-14-0(c) 72-2-8(f)
(50) St. Margaret Moses	50(a) 50(e) 53(f)	200(a) 200(e)	1574(b) 1482(c) 1482(f)	216-4-6(b) 203-15-6(c)	100-0-0(d)	32-15-4$^{3}/_{4}$(b) 37-11-3/4(c) 62-6-8(f)
(51) St. Margaret New Fish Street	81(a) 81(e) 94(f)	350(a)	1507(b) 1200(c) 1200(f)	205-14-3(b) 158-2-6(c)	130-1-6(a) 120-0-0(d)	90-2-4(b) 78-17-8(c) 70-0-0(f)
(52) St. Margaret Pattens	42(a) 42(e) 60(f)	220(a) 200(e)	800(b) 563(c) 763(f)	110-0-0(b) 77-7-9(c) 104-8-3(f)	80-0-6(a) 80-0-0(d)	34-13-0(b) 48-12-8(c) 44-17-8(f)
(53) St. Martin Ironmonger Lane	39(f)	200(a)	900(b) 606(c) 606(f)	123-15-0(b) 83-6-6(c)	80-0-6(a) 80-0-0(d)	58-15-7(b) 52-17-0(c) 40-3-0(f)
(54) St. Martin Ludgate	217(a) 217(e) 227(f)	900(a)	4050(b) 3346(c) 3346-12-6(f)	554-17-6(b) 460-1-6(c) 460-2-10(f)	210-1-0(a) 200-0-0(d)	117-7-2(b) 124-0-0(c) 126-0-0(f)
(55) St. Martin Orgar	90(a) 80(e) 97(f)	400(a) 400(e)	2000(b) 1600(c) 1600(f)	224-15-0(b) 220-0-0(c)	150-0-3(a) 150-0-0(d)	64-16-8(b) 76-12-½(c) 80-7-1(f)
(56) St. Martin Outwich	54(a) 48(e) 54(f)	257(a) 350(e)	1012(b) 1012(c) 1012(f)	139-1-0(b) 139-3-0(c)	80-0-8(a) 100-0-0(d)	39-19-0(b) 74-0-0(c) 57-17-2(f)

Church						
(57) St. Martin Vintry	230(a) 230(e) 260(f)	1100(a) 1100(e)	2200(b) 2080(c) 2080(f)	302-10-0(b) 286-0-0(c) 286-0-0(f)	200-1-3(a) 180-0-0(d)	83-19-2(b) 81-5-4(c) 115-0-0(f)
(58) St. Mary Abchurch	122(a) 120(e) 111(f)	480(a) 480(e)	1820(b) 1410(c) 1657(f)	264-0-0(b) 195-17-6(c) 227-16-0(f)	130-1-6(a) 130-0-0(d)	81-0-5(b) 75-12-7(c) 86-0-0(f)
(59) St. Mary Aldermanbury	103(e)	---	2000(b) 1800(c)	200-0-0(b) 247-0-0(c)	150-0-3(a) 160-0-0(d)	8-0-0(c)
(60) St. Mary Aldermary	96(a) 96(e) 90(f)	400(a)	1500(b) 1490(c) 1490(f)	206-5-8(b) 204-17-6(c)	120-0-9(a) 110-0-0(d)	127-12-8(b) 161-2-10(c) 62-4-4(f)
(61) St. Mary Bothaw	47(a) 44(e) 45(f)	240(a) 240(e)	974-10-0(b) 828-0-0(c) 828-5-0(f)	133-19-0(b) 113-17-0(c)	80-0-6(a) 85-0-0(d)	45-12-4(b) 41-10-4(c) 41-10-4(f)
(62) St. Mary le Bow	92(f)	---	2900(b) 1905(c) 1905(f)	400-10-0(b) 261-18-9(c) 262-1-3(f)	160-0-3(a) 160-0-0(d)	85-9-4½(b) 94-2-4(c) 89-2-6(f)
(63) St. Mary Colechurch	48(a) 48(e) 48(f)	200(a) 220(e)	1000(b) 800(c) 816(f)	137-10-0(b) 110-0-0(c)	80-0-6(a) 80-0-0(d)	33-14-0(b) 33-4-0(c) 44-0-0(f)
(64) St. Mary at Hill	100(a) 100(e) 113(f)	400(a) 400(e)	2224(b) 1486(c) 1486(f)	308-0-0(b) 204-11-6(c) 204-11-6(f)	170-1-9(a) 165-0-0(d)	117-15-10(b) 149-16-4(c) 122-0-0(f)

Parish						
(65) St. Mary Magdalen Milk Street	45(a) 45(f)	235(a)	850(b) 1233(c) 1233(f)	116-17-6(b) 169-10-9(c)	100-2-6(a) 110-0-0(d)	58-7-3(b) 60-0-0(c) 74-0-3(f)
(66) St. Mary Magdalen Old Fish Street	120(a) 172(f)	560(a)	2000(b) 1888(c) 1888(f)	275-0-0(b) 259-12-0(c)	160-0-3(a) 150-0-0(d)	74-16-7(b) 92-13-10(c) 101-18-8(f)
(67) St. Mary Mounthaw	45(a) 45(e) 56(f)	180(a)	500(b) 392(c) 392-3-4(f)	68-15-0(b) 53-18-0(c)	51-1-3(a) 50-0-0(d)	43-6-6(b) 43-9-8(c) 26-10-8(f)
(68) St. Mary Somerset	126(a) 126 & the waterhouse(e) 143(f)	600(a) 600(e)	1300(b) 1303(c) 1303-10-0(f)	178-15-0(b) 179-3-3(c)	110-0-0(a) 110-0-0(d)	83-14-6(b) 78-11-4(c) 80-0-0(f)
(69) St. Mary Staining	46(a) 46(e) 44(f)	190(a) 190(e)	510(b) 406(c) 900(f)	70-0-0(b) 55-0-0(c) 58-0-0(f)	45-2-0(a) 50-0-0(d)	28-10-0(b) 31-12-4(c) 21-12-4(f)
(70) St. Mary Woolchurch	77(f)	390(a)	1699(b) 1830(c) 1830(f)	225-16-9(b) 251-12-6(c)	130-1-6(a) 130-0-0(d)	58-8-0(b) 56-15-0(c) 50-8-6(f)
(71) St. Mary Woolnoth	80(a) 80(e) 87(f)	300(a) 300(e)	1900(b) 1963(c) 1963(f)	253-15-0(b) 269-17-9(c)	140-2-3(a) 140-0-0(d)	77-18-8(b) 84-5-0(c) 84-4-0(f)
(72) St. Matthew Friday Street	45(a) 45(e) 54(f)	235(a) 300(e)	1020(b) 1178(c) 1183-10-0(f)	140-5-0(b) 162-13-3(c) 162-14-7½(f)	95-0-3(a) 100-0-0(d)	46-8-4¾(b) 48-8-7¼(c) 49-14-0(f)

(73) (73) St. Michael Bassishaw	180(a) 180(e) 197(f)	----	2700(b) 2590(c) 2590-6-8(f)	360-0-0(b) 356-2-6(c) 354-16-6(f)	190-0-6(a) 190-0-0(d)	111-0-0(b) 99-10-9(c) 132-11-6(f)
(74) St. Michael Cornhill	140(a) 140(e) 161(f)	723(a) 723(e)	3200(b) 2528(c) 2528(f)	441-10-0(b) 374-12-0(c) 346-10-0(f)	210-1-0(a) 200-0-0(d)	97-7-4(b) 98-12-2(c) 117-15-0(f)
(75) St. Michael Crooked Lane	115(a) 115(e) 115(f)	401(a) 404(e)	1654(b) 1280(c) 1280(f)	225-15-6(b) 176-0-0(c)	130-1-6(a) 120-0-0(d)	64-16-10½(b) 86-12-7(c) 80-0-0(f)
(76) St. Michael Queenhithe	130(f)	560(a)	1500(b) 1401(c) 1401(f)	206-5-0(b) 192-12-9(c)	120-0-9(a) 120-0-0(d)	47-4-0(b) 99-10-0(c) 91-3-4(f)
(77) St. Michael le Querne	100(f)	----	1400(b) 1241(c) 2241-10-0(f)	192-10-0(b) 170-12-9(c)	100-2-6(a) 120-0-0(d)	48-13-1(b) 54-8-3(c) 54-8-3(f)
(78) St. Michael Paternoster Royal	93(a) 93(e) 90(f)	336(a) 336(e)	938(b) 873(c) 873-19-0(f)	134-0-0(b) 120-0-3(c)	80-0-6(a) 80-0-0(d)	32-0-6(b) 26-10-3(c) 33-2-10(f)
(79) St. Michael Wood Street	113(a) 113(e)	500(a) 500(e)	1583-10-0(b) 1600(c)	204-0-0(b) 220-0-0(c)	110-0-0(a) 110-0-0(d)	35-15-4(b) 38-2-4(c)
(80) St. Mildred Bread Street	68(a) 68(e) 86(f)	257(a) 120(e)	1300(b) 614(c) 614(f)	178-15-0(b) 84-8-6(c) 84-8-6(f)	90-1-3(a) 90-0-0(d)	51-4-9½(b) 51-17-5(c) 51-17-5(f)

(81) St. Mildred Poultry	80(a) 80(e) 98(f)	350(a)	2000(b) 1917(c) 1917-15-0(f)	275(b) 263-11-9(c) 263-13-9(f)	140-2-3(a) 135-0-0(d)	82-19-6(b) 86-1-4(c) 89-8-2(f)
(82) St. Nicholas Acons	53(a) 42(e) 51(f)	230(a) 230(e)	1169(b) 1018(c) 1018(f)	160-14-9(b) 139-19-6(c) 139-19-6(f)	95-0-3(a) 90-0-0(d)	64-16-2(b) 54-14-0(c) 68-18-0(f)
(83) St. Nicholas Cole Abbey	136(f)	400(a)	1342(b) 1224(c) 1224(f)	184-10-6(b) 168-6-0(c)	110-0-0(a) 105-0-0(d)	67-6-8(b) 75-14-0(c) 72-12-2(f)
(84) St. Nicholas Olave	60(a) 60(e) 62(f)	200(a)	821(b) 804(c) 804(f)	107-18-5(b) 110-11-0(c) 113-1-8(f)	65-0-9(a) 80-0-0(d)	42-12-10½(b) 31-12-9(c) 45-9-8(f)
(85) St. Olave Hart Street	210(a) 210(e) 181(f)	800(a)	3000(b) 2746(c) 2746(f)	412-10-0(b) 347-11-6(c)	190-0-6(a) 180-0-0(d)	102-17-7(b) 119-16-9(c) 133-18-8(f)
(86) St. Olave Old Jewry	60(a) 60(e) 62(f)	320(a)	1400(b) 1142(c) 1142(f)	192-10-0(b) 157-0-6(c)	100-2-6(a) 100-0-0(d)	65-13-11¼(b) 75-8-3¼(c) 53-1-10(f)
(87) St. Olave Silver Street	100(a) 100(e) 121(f)	400(a)	830(b) 1004(c) 1004-15-0(f)	109(b) 137-11-0(c) 138-3-0(f)	70-2-6(a) 80-0-0(d)	49-13-5(b) 59-12-10(c) 58-12-6(f)
(88) St. Pancras Soper Lane	39(a) 39(e) 42(f)	193(a) 193(e)	1220(b) 968(c) 968(f)	197-0-0(b) 133-1-6(c)	80-0-6(a) 90-0-0(d)	28-14-2(b) 51-0-0(c) 36-17-4(f)

(89) St. Peter Westcheap	80(a) 82(e) 89(f)	390(a)	2275(b) 1894(c) 1894(f)	312-0-0(b) 260-8-6(c)	140-2-3(a) 140-0-0(d)	59-1-5(b) 65-18-7(c)
(90) St. Peter Cornhill	123(a) 123(e) 160(f)	600(a) 600(e)	3300(b) 3190(c) 3190(f)	453-15-0(b) 438-2-6(c)	200-1-3(a) 180-0-0(d)	135-13-0(b) 164-16-0(c) 100-0-0(f)
(91) St. Peter Paul's Wharf	90(a) 90(e) 77(f)	350(a) 350(e)	1060(b) 1185(c) 1185(f)	145-10-0(b) 162-18-9(c)	90-1-3(a) 90-0-0(d)	42-1-6(b) 36-11-2(c) 47-10-2(f)
(92) St. Peter le Poor	84(a) 84(e)	464(a) 464(e)	2200(b) 2000(c)	302-10-0(b) 274-0-0(c)	140-2-3(a) 140-0-0(d)	48-8-0(b) 34-17-6(c)
(93) St. Stephen Coleman Street	---	----	2999(b) 2500(c)	453-12-3(b) 343-15-0(c)	160-1-0(a) 180-0-0(d)	12-0-0(c)
(94) St. Stephen Walbrook	55(a) 99(49?)(e) 48(f)	300(a)	1750(b) 1200(c) 1200(f)	230-0-0(b) 165-0-0(c)	120-0-9(a) 110-0-0(d)	42-10-8(b) 47-10-0(c) 39-10-0(f)
(95) St. Swithin	95(a) 95(e)	300(a) 300(e)	1314(b) 1350(c)	181-3-0(b) 185-12-6(c)	110-0-0(a) 110-0-0(d)	63-4-6(b) 64-1-11½(c)
(96) St. Thomas the Apostle	114(a) 114(e) 112(f)	500(a) 500(e)	1327(b) 1387(c) 1387(f)	182-9-3(b) 190-14-3(c)	120-0-9(a) 120-0-0(d)	71-7-6(b) 78-9-8(c) 85-9-0(f)

(97) St. Vedast Foster Lane	128(f)	----	3380(b) 2702(c) 2702(f)	464-15-0(b) 371-10-6(c) 371-5-4(f)	190-0-6(a) 180-0-0(d)	66-18-1(b) 67-5-3(c) 96-7-3(f)
(98) St. Andrew Holborn	894(f)	5000(a)	6000(b) 10297(c) 10297-13-4(f)	825-0-0(b) 1415-16-9(c) 1415-16-9(f)	450-0-9(a) 480-0-0(d)	251-8-8(b) 346-0-0(c) 360-0-0(f)
(99) St. Bartholomew the Great	---	----	----	"a special custom"(b)	100-2-6(a) 100-0-0(d)	53-1-4(b)
(100) St. Bartholomew the Less	109(f)	----	1000(b) 1286(c) 1286-10-0(f)	137-10-0(b) 176-16-6(c)	80-0-6(b) 80-0-0(c)	23-6-8(b) 20-0-0(c) 20-0-0(f)
(101) St. Botolph Aldersgate	568(f)	1250(a)	4500(b) 3000(c)	618-15-0(b) 412-0-0(c) 1000(f)	350-1-6(a) 240-0-0(d)	48-0-0(b) 51-16-8(c) 200-0-0(f)
(102) St. Botolph Aldgate	1202(f)	----	6900(b) 6900(c) 6910(f)	948-15-0(b) 945-15-0(c)	500-1-9(a) 400-0-0(d)	39-0-0(b) 58-0-0(c) 388-17-0(f)
(103) St. Botolph Bishopsgate	337(f)	7000(a)	6800-0-0(b) 4891(c) 4891(f)	935-0-0(b) 672-9-0(c) 672-4-9(f)	500-1-9(a) 320-0-0(d)	235-17-4(b) 240-15-0(c) 224-5-8(f)
(104) St. Bride	---	3000(a)	7000(b) 4000(c)	962-10-0(b) 550-0-0(c)	250-2-3(a) 260-0-0(d)	22(b) 16-0-0(c) 50-0-0(f)

(105) Bridewell Precinct (extra parochial)	67(f)	---	900(b) 1055(c) 1055-10-0(f)	123-15-0(b) 145-1-3(c)	80-0-6(a) 80-0-0(d)	32-13-4(b) 32-13-4(c)
(106) St. Dunstan in the West	500(a) 270(e) 459(f)	3000(a)	6200(b) 8985(c) 3985(f) 9855(f)	852-10-0(b) 1235-8-9(c)	340-0-9(a) 300-0-0(d)	235-17-4(b) 264-4-½(c) 217-0-4½(f)
(107) St. Giles Cripplegate	---	7000(a)	7977(b) 8415(c) 8415(f)	1000(b) 1157-10-0(c) 1124-10-0(f)	500-1-9(a) 480-0-0(d)	343-18-6(b) 310-18-6(c) 400-0-0(f)
(108) St. Olave Southwark	---	---	1200(b) 6300(f) 330(f)	165(b)	---	70-0-0(b) 40-0-0(b) 325-16-0(f)
(109) St. Sepulchre	600(a)	7500(a)	6700(b) 10000(c)	921-5-0(b) 1374-0-0(c)	550-1-3(a) 540-0-0(d)	150-0-0(b) 200-0-0(c)
(110) Whetefriars Precinct (extra parochial)	---	---	---	---	---	---

Appendix B

A Selective List of Civic and Parochial Leaders in the City Parishes

(1) Allhallows Barking
   Marmaduke Rawden
   John Fowke
   John Wood
(2) Allhallows Bread Street
   Morris Gething
   William Kendall
   Tempest Milner
   John Box
   John Mellish
   Richard Turner
   Francis West
(3) Allhallows the Great
   Henry Cleaver
   William Bromskill
   John Harborne
   Thomas Bromley
(4) Allhallows Honey Lane
   Edward Claxton
   Daniel Waldoe
(5) Allhallows the Less
   John Greene
   William Coulson
   Richard Stocke
   Roger Lazenbye
   Richard Smith
   George Waterman
   John Ramsey
(6) Allhallows Lombard Street
   Thomas Cullum
   Richard Waring
   Ralph Imgram
   Joshua Woolnough
   Richard Young
   William Ellwood
   Joshua Foote
   John Travel
   Nicholas Crispe
   George Snell
   John Holiday

Thomas Stocke
(7) Allhallows London Wall
Robert Haunch
Thomas Birkhead
(8) Allhallows Staining
John Jacob
John Kendrick
William Methwold
Edmund Trench
Thomas Bewley
Henry Sweet
(9) Christ Church
William Hart
William Greenhill
Peter Mills
John Ireton
William Steele
(10) Holy Trinity the Less
Richard Beale
Nicholas Clegate
James Cooke
(11) St. Alban Wood Street
Ralph Yardly
Hugh Wood
Anthony Biddulph
(12) St. Alphage
William Haynes
John Blackwell
Edward Basse
(13) St. Andrew Hubbard
John Gace
Robert Wood
Cornelius Mountney
John Blunt
(14) St. Andrew Undershaft
Thomas Atkins
Abraham Chamberlain
Abraham Cullen
John Dethick
William Hawkins
Thomas Mead
John Smith
Robert Gayer
Anthony Abdy

Christopher Cletherow
(15) St. Andrew by the Wardrobe
Christopehr Nicholson
Luke Lee
Henry Coles
(16) St. Anne and St. Agnes
Aldersgate
John Sherman
Josiah Hammes
Stephen Hammes
John Nicarius
Henry Blackley
(17) St. Anne Blackfriars
Richard Browne
Issac Ash
Jacob Ash
Gideon Delaune (?)
John Lufkin
(18) St. Antholin
Francis Taylor
Thomas Newman
Thomas Bromfield
John Mayo
James Russell
Isaac Legay
George Mayo
(19) St. Augustine
Richard Turner
John Orlibear
Henry Ashurst
Ralph Harrison
William Kendall
Samuel Langham
Christopher Meredith
Ozias Churchman
George Nodes
William Isard
(20) St. Bartholomew by the
Exchange
Samuel Harsnett
Stephen Burton
John Jones
Richard Venner
Thomas Colwell

John Lawson
Martin Dallison
Edward Carlton
William Ihans
William Webb
George Smith
Thomas White
(21) St. Benet Fink
James Fenn
James Story
John Smart
(22) St. Benet Gracechurch
Jacob Gerrard
James Bunce
Thomas Foote
Robert Dycer
Samuel Foote
Anthony Lawrence
John Brett
Robert Newton
John Cutler
(23) St. Benet Paul's Wharf
Edmund Harrison
Thomas Gee
Thomas Kirton
John Cole
John Wynn
Robert Carter
Nathaniel Lukins
Joseph Gillman
(24) St. Benet Sherehog
James Hayes
Thomas Bowater
(25) St. Botolph Billingsgate
Robert Child
Randalph Baskerville
Thomas Soame
Thomas Austin
(26) St. Christopher
William Middleton
Peter Richaut
John Roberts
Gilbert Morewood
Joseph Vaughan

Thomas Bolton
William Williamson
John Brett
(27) St. Clement Eastcheap
Baldwin Hamey
Richard Piggot
Benony Honeywood
Martin Hall
Robert Gale
Robert Bullock
(28) St. Dionis Backchurch
Richard Hill
Thomas Manwaring
John Archer
Thomas Bludworth
Henry Davy
Thomas Turgis
Nathaniel Owen
(29) St. Dunstan in the East
John Fowke
Mauris Thompson
Lawrence Bromfield
Robert Russell
John Milton
George Hanger
William Bateman
Anthony Bateman
John Pettiward
Oliver Reynolds
Thomas Stubbins
Robert Cheslin
Gilbert Keate
(30) St. Edmund Lombard Street
George Whitmore
Nicholas Rainton
David Watkins
Edward Watkins
Tobias Dixon
(31) St. Ethelburga
Richard Hardmet
William Eveleigh
Thomas Beare
Richard Pym
(32) St. Faith

Christopher Meredith
Roger Quartermain
George Thomason
Richard Burgess
(33) St. Gabriel Fenchurch
William Courteen
Samuel Cranmer
Stephen White
Humiliation Hinde
(34) St. George Botolph Lane
Edward Hooker
George Cony
Arnold Beake
Ephraine Payne
Francis Lodwick
(35) St. Gregory by St. Paul's
William Antrobus
George Ward
Robert Newman
Thomas Cole
Martin Browne
John Wall
Henry Barton
John Box
(36) St. Helen
Nicholas Bonfoy
Timothy Cruso
Abraham Chamberlain
John Lawrence
(37) St. James Duke's Place
Sallomon Vanderbrooke
(38) St. James Garlickhithe
John Coke
George Bromley
George Langham
Christopher Gore
Robert Gore
(39) St. John the Baptist
Alexander Jones
Isaac Rutton
John Ellis
Thomas Cox
Walter White
(40) St. John the Evangelist

William Hitchcock
(41) St. John Zachary
John Wollaston
Alexander Jackson
William Haslefoot
Richard Gibbs
Josiah Demoris
Thomas Noell
James Noell
Richard Morell
(42) St. Katherine Coleman
Henry Isaacson
Philip Parker
(43) St. Katherine Cree
John Bond
John Owfield
William Thompson
Richard Chiverton
Richard Shute
(44) St. Lawrence Old Jewry
John Cordell
George Clarke
William Addams
William Bisley
Thomas Stons
Jasper Chapman
George Hadley
Thomas Astill
William Justice
Hugh Nettleship
(45) St. Lawrence Pountney
Charles Snelling
Thomas Thorold
Robert Meade
Thomas Starkey
George Downes
Ellis Cunliff
Eliah Harvey
William Dugard
(46) St. Leonard Eastcheap
Richard Waring
Stephen Estwick
Thomas Player
Tobias Lisle

John Wallingham
Nehemiah Wallingham
Henry Bonner
Samuel Lee
(47) St. Leonard Foster Lane
William Gibbs
Mathew Jumper
(48) St. Magnus
Edward Bellamy
William Greene
John Greene
William Adis
Stephen Beale
Lawrence Markman
(49) St. Margaret Lothbury
Myles Corbett
Anthony Bedingfield
Ralph Hugh
Edward Chard
Thomas Essington
Robert Lowther
Samuel Eames
(50) St. Margaret Moses
Robert Smith
Stephen Iles
(51) St. Margaret New Fish Street
Nicholas Houghton
Abraham Babington
Thomas Andrews
Francis Warner
William Wyberd
Anthony Silby
Peter Smith
(52) St. Margaret Pattens
Lawrence Loe
Richard Arnold
Giles Vandeput
(53) St. Martin Ironmonger Lane
Hugh Smithson
Robert Winch
William Webb
(54) St. Martin Ludgate
Thomas Arnold
William Hobson

William Jesson (Jeston)
Matthew Fox
John Clarke
(55) St. Martin Orgar
William Gore
Michael Styles
George Winn
William Peake
Russell Alsop
(56) St. Martin Outwich
Rowland Wilson
Richard Bateman
Samuel Harrison
Richard Clutterbuck
Henry Boothby
John Beale
William Vincent
(57) St. Martin Vintry
Capt. Hackett
(58) St. Mary Abchurch
Zouch Watson
Edmund Rosier
(59) St. Mary Aldermanbury
Simon Edmonds
Humphrey Onby
Bartholomew Edwards
Gabriel Newman
George Witham
John Holland
James James
Walter Boothby
William Methwold
Samuel Foote
(60) St. Mary Aldermary
Nathaniel Hall
Richard Coysh
Francis Peck
Robert Deane
Robert Hanson
(61) St. Mary Bothaw
Sir Edward Bromfield
Thomas Man
Francis Heath
(62) St. Mary le Bow

Francis Roe
Francis Dashwood
Harman Shease
Theophilus Ryley
Thomas Waterhouse
(63) St. Mary Colechurch
John Towse
Randall Mainwaring
William Pitchford
Edmund Sleigh
Thomas Jackson
James Edwards
Theophilus Biddulph
Henry Box
William Shambrooke
John Lorrymor
John Lawrence
(64) St. Mary at Hill
Edward Hooker
Thomas Lenthall
Francis Lenthall
Nicholas Corsellis
Edward Alston
(65) St. Mary Magdalen Milk
Street
Robert Story
Francis Waterhouse
Lawrence Brinley
Anthony Webster
John Robinson
(66) St. Mary Magdalen Old Fish
Street
Philip Owen
Andrew Neale
Thomas Lockington
Richard Gardner
(67) St. Mary Mounthaw
Nicholas Hitchcock
(68) St. Mary Somerset
Lewis Young
Richard Jones
Urian Normansell
(69) St. Mary Staining
Thomas Noell

Giles Willoughby
(70) St. Mary Woolchurch
Thomas Gower
Thomas Brace
Matthew White
Robert Thompson
John Seede
(71) St. Mary Woolnoth
Thomas Vyner
Robert Sweet
Thomas Eyres
William Hubbart
(72) St. Matthew Friday Street
John Strange
Ralph Eue
Symon Gibbon
Thomas Drinkwater
(73) St. Michael Bassishaw
Robert Alden
Robert Gardner
Clement Mosse
Edwin Browne
Miles Dixon
Walter Pell
Christopher Packe
William Flewellin
John Rutter
George Dunne
Francis Greenway
Abraham Church
William Christmas
(74) St. Michael Cornhill
Francis Mosse
John Bellamy
James Martin
William Rowell
John Bathurst
Richard Norton
Roger Rea
John Turbington
(75) St. Michael Crooked Lane
Ralph Trattle
Gabriel Binion
(76) St. Michael Queenhithe

Thomas Churchman
Edward Hurde
Henry Madox
Leonard Hammond
(77) St. Michael le Querne
Edward Honeywood
John Gillibrand
Robert Tichborne
Ralph Heygate
John Harvey
Henry Dawson
(78) St. Michael Royal
Thomas Coffin
(79) St. Michael Wood Street
John Bastwick
Thomas Underhill
Richard Payne
(80) St. Mildred Bread Street
Samuel Crispe
Thomas Brightwell
Thomas Staines
(81) St. Mildred Poultry
Philip Christian
John Sherman
Henry Dixon
Thomas Agge
(82) St. Nicholas Acons
William Ashwell
John Babington
Nicholas Skinner
James Russell
Henry Gray
(83) St. Nicholas Cole Abbey
Ralph Triplet
(84) St. Nicholas Olave
Stephen Burton
Humphrey Lynn
(85) St. Olave Hart Street
Andrew Riccard
William Harrington
Richard Ford
John Highlord
John Wolstenholm
Abraham Dawes

Thomas Dawes
(86) St. Olave Old Jewry
William Vaugham
George Almery
John Frederick
John Mascall
John Greene
Martin Noell
Moses Tryon
Edmund Wright
Richard Gurney
John Wollaston
Thomas Foote
Thomas Adams
Thomas Atkins
Ralph Harley
Thomas Bowyer
(87) St. Olave Silver Street
John Bradshaw
Abraham Chambers
Henry Pratt
(88) St. Pancras Soper Lane
Thomas Soames
Timothy Whiting
Peter Ducane
Joseph Parker
John Jurin
(89) St. Peter Westcheap
William Acton
Richard Overton
Richard Floyd
John Dod
Richard Read
Maximillian Bard
(90) St. Peter Cornhill
Thomas Lusher
George Henley
William Pease
Richard Wollaston
Philip Meade
William Bromwick
Miles Robinson
Francis Cooling
Lewis Biker

(91) St. Peter Paul's Wharf
     Isaac Finch
     James Medlicot
(92) St. Peter le Poor
     Robert Launt
(93) St. Stephen Colman Street
     Isaac Pennington
     Owen Rowe
     Caleb Cockcroft
     Samuel Avery
     Mark Hildesley
     Andrew Kendrick
     Richard Ashurst
     Thomas Barnardiston
     James Russell
     George Foxcroft
     Jeremy Sambrooke
     Joseph Silby
     Nathaniel Mickaelthwaite
     William Mountain
     John Fitzwilliams
     Thomas Fitzwilliams
(94) St. Stephen Walbrook
     John Warner
     Samuel Warner
     Arthur Juxon
     Charles Floyd
     Samual Mico
     Asabell Fairclough
     William Underwood
     William Thompson
     John Sadler
     John Jeckell
(95) St. Swithin
     Robert English
     William Bowe
     George Willingham
     William Essington
     Thomas Essington
     Henry Probie
     John Dogett
     Thomas Dawney
     William Drakeford
     Richard Lewis

(96) St. Thomas the Apostle
   Matthew Sheppard
   Andrew Cade
   John Blackwell
(97) St. Vedast Foster Lane
   Richard Glyde
   Francis Ashe
   William Daniel
   Henry Bedingfield
   John Perrin
   Nicholas Herne
(98) St. Andrew Holborn
   William Jessop
(99) St. Bartholomew the Great
   Philip Skippon
(100) St. Bartholomew the Less
   Samuel Cartwright
   Richard Lawrence
(101) St. Botolph Aldersgate
   John Johnson
   John Terry
   Miles Flesher
   Ralph Hutchinson
   Lawrence Blomley
   James Russell
   John Allen
(102) St. Botolph Aldgate
   John Hayes
   Richard Garford
   John Wildgoose
   John Lovett
   Paul Dobie
   Leonard Leonard
   Abraham Corselles
   Richard Beresford
   Alexander Bence
(103) St. Botolph Bishopsgate
   John Everett
   William Tutchin
   Edmond Denney
   John Greenhill
   William Cade
   Griffith Owen
   Martin Gardiner

Joseph Finch
(104) St. Bride
Joseph Parrott
Stephen Sedgwick
Thomas Lownes
John Banister
William Hancock
Valentine Fyge
John Alsop
Thomas King
John Baker
Robert Russell
Thomas Bakewell
Joseph Holden
Thomas Wandall
(105) Bridewell Precinct
William Knowling
(106) St. Dunstan in the West
Francis Kempe
Richard Wotton
Robert Meade
Alexander Normington
Richard Browne
William Perkins
Francis Allen
Thomas Scott
John Glover
Ralph Farmer
John Smith
Thomas Edwards
Edward East
Thomas Cooke
Matthew Hind
John King
John Hallywell
Anthony Webb
Gilbert Gynes
Praise-God Barbone
(107) St. Giles Cripplegate
Robert Manwaring
John Christmas
Henry Greene
John Great
Charles Wynn

Tobias Markham
William Rudd
Ralph Tasker
(108) St. Olave Southwark
Cornelius Cooke
Robert Houghton
George Snelling
George Thompson
(109) St. Sepulchre
Nathaniel Campfield
Edward Brooke
Thomas King
Thomas Knowles
Benjamin Potter
James Thurley
John Wilcox
Miles Petty
(110) Whitefriar Precinct

———————

Bibliography

A. THE CITY OF LONDON GUILDHALL LIBRARY MANUSCRIPTS

(V. M. = Vestry Minutes; C. A. = Churchwardens' Accounts)

GLMS 819/1	Allhallows the Great, V. M.
GLMS 818/1	Allhallows the Great, C. A.
GLMS 5062/1	Allhallows Honey Lane, C. A.
GLMS 824/1	Allhallows the Less, V. M.
GLMS 823/1	Allhallows the Less, C. A.
GLMS 4049/1	Allhallows Lombard Street, V. M.
GLMS 4051/1	Allhallows Lombard Street, C. A.
GLMS 4956/3	Allhallows Staining, C. A.
GLMS 4835/1	Holy Trinity the Less, C. A.
GLMS 7673/2	St. Alban Wood Street, C. A.
GLMS 1431/2	St. Alphage London Wall, V. M.
GLMS 1432/4	St. Alphage London Wall, C. A.
GLMS 1278/1	St. Andrew Hubbard, V. M.
GLMS 1279/3	St. Andrew Hubbard, C. A.
GLMS 2088/1	St. Andrew by the Wardrobe, C. A.
GLMS 587/1	St. Anne and St. Agnes Aldersgate, C. A.
GLMS 1045/1	St. Antholin Budge Row, V. M.
GLMS 1046/1	St. Antholin Budge Row, C. A.
GLMS 635/1	St. Augustine Watling Street, V. M.
GLMS 4384/1, 2	St. Bartholomew by the Exchange, V. M.
GLMS 4383/1	St. Bartholomew by the Exchange, C. A.
GLMS 1303/1	St. Benet Fink, C. A.
GLMS 4214/1	St. Benet Gracechurch, V. M.
GLMS 1568	St. Benet Gracechurch, C. A.
GLMS 877/1	St. Benet Paul's Wharf, V. M.
GLMS 878/1	St. Benet Paul's Wharf, C. A.
GLMS 493/1	St. Botolph Billingsgate, V. M.

GLMS 492/1	St. Botolph Billingsgate, C. A.
GLMS 4425/1	St. Christopher le Stocks, V. M.
GLMS 4423/1	St. Christopher le Stocks, C. A.
GLMS 978/1	St. Clement Eastcheap, V. M.
GLMS 977/1	St. Clement Eastcheap, C. A.
GLMS 4216/1	St. Dionis Backchurch, V. M.
GLMS 4215/1	St. Dionis Backchurch, C. A.
GLMS 4887	St. Dunstan in the East, V. M.
GLMS 7882/1	St. Dunstan in the East, C. A.
GLMS 4241/1	St. Ethelburga, C. A.
GLMS 952/1	St. George Botolph Lane, V. M.
GLMS 951/1	St. George Botolph Lane, C. A.
GLMS 1336/1	St. Gregory by St. Paul's, V. M.
GLMS 6836	St. Helen, C. A.
GLMS 6844/1	St. Helen, C. A.
GLMS 4813/1	St. James Garlickhithe, V. M.
GLMS 4810/2	St. James Garlickhithe, C. A.
GLMS 1543	St. John the Baptist, V. M.
GLMS 577/1	St. John the Baptist, C. A.
GLMS 590/1	St. John Zachary, C. A.
GLMS 1123/1	St. Katherine Coleman, V. M.
GLMS 1124/1	St. Katherine Coleman, C. A.
GLMS 1196/1	St. Katherine Cree Church, V. M.
GLMS 1198/1	St. Katherine Cree Church, C. A.
GLMS 2590/1	St. Lawrence Old Jewry, V. M.
GLMS 2593/2	St. Lawrence Old Jewry, C. A.
GLMS 3908/1	St. Lawrence Pountney, V. M.
GLMS 3907/1	St. Lawrence Pountney, C. A.
GLMS 1179/1	St. Magnus, C. A.
GLMS 4352/1	St. Margaret Lothbury, V. M.
GLMS 1175/1	St. Margaret New Fish Street, V. M.
GLMS 1176/1	St. Margaret New Fish Street, C. A.
GLMS 4571/1	St. Margaret Pattens, V. M.
GLMS 4570/2, 3	St. Margaret Pattens, C. A.
GLMS 1311/1	St. Martin Ludgate, V. M.
GLMS 1313/1	St. Martin Ludgate, C. A.
GLMS 959/1	St. Martin Orgar, C. A., V. M.
GLMS 11394/1	St. Martin Outwich, C. A.
GLMS 3891/1	St. Mary Abchurch, C. A.
GLMS 3570/2	St. Mary Aldermanbury, V. M.
GLMS 3556/2	St. Mary Aldermanbury, C. A.
GLMS 4863/1	St. Mary Aldermary, C. A.
GLMS 64/1	St. Mary Colechurch, V. M.
GLMS 66/1	St. Mary Colechurch, C. A.
GLMS 1240/1	St. Mary at Hill, V. M.
GLMS 2597/1	St. Mary Magdalen Milk Street, V. M.
GLMS 2596/2	St. Mary Magdalen Milk Street, C. A.
GLMS 2341/1	St. Mary Magdalen Old Fish Street, C. A.

GLMS 5714/1	St. Mary Somerset, C. A.
GLMS 1542/2	St. Mary Staining, C. A.
GLMS 1012/1	St. Mary Woolchurch, V. M.
GLMS 1013/1	St. Mary Woolchurch, C. A.
GLMS 1002/1B	St. Mary Woolnoth, C. A.
GLMS 3579	St. Matthew Friday Street, V. M.
GLMS 1016/1	St. Matthew Friday Street, C. A.
GLMS 2601/1	St. Michael Bassishaw, C. A.
GLMS 4072/1	St. Michael Cornhill, V. M.
GLMS 4071/2	St. Michael Cornhill, C. A.
GLMS 1188/1	St. Michael Crooked Lane, C. A.
GLMS 4825/1	St. Michael Queenhithe, C. A.
GLMS 2895/2	St. Michael le Querne, C. A.
GLMS 524/1	St. Michael Wood Street, C. A.
GLMS 3470/1A	St. Mildred Bread Street, C. A.
GLMS 62/1	St. Mildred Poultry, V. M.
GLMS 4060/1	St. Nicholas Acons, V. M.
GLMS 4415/1	St. Olave Old Jewry, V. M.
GLMS 4409/2	St. Olave Old Jewry, C. A.
GLMS 1257/1	St. Olave Silver Street, C. A.
GLMS 5019/1	St. Pancras Soper Lane, V. M.
GLMS 5018/1	St. Pancras Soper Lane, C. A.
GLMS 642/1	St. Peter Cheapside, V. M.
GLMS 645/2	St. Peter Cheapside, C. A.
GLMS 4165/1	St. Peter Cornhill, V. M.
GLMS 4458/1	St. Stephen Coleman Street, V. M.
GLMS 4457/3	St. Stephen Coleman Street, C. A.
GLMS 594/2	St. Stephen Walbrook, V. M.
GLMS 593/4	St. Stephen Walbrook, C. A.
GLMS 560/1	St. Swithin, V. M.
GLMS 559/1	St. Swithin, C. A.
GLMS 662/1	St. Thomas the Apostle, C. A.
GLMS 3989/1	St. Bartholomew the Great, C. A.
GLMS 1453/1, 2	St. Botolph Aldersgate, V. M.
GLMS 1455/1	St. Botolph Aldersgate, C. A.
GLMS 9234/8	St. Botolph Aldgate, V. M.
GLMS 9235/2	St. Botolph Aldgate, C. A.
GLMS 4526/1	St. Botolph Bishopsgate, V. M.
GLMS 4524/2	St. Botolph Bishopsgate, C. A.
GLMS 6554/1	St. Bride, V. M.
GLMS 6552/1	St. Bride, C. A.
GLMS 9163	St. Bride, poor rates
GLMS 3016/1	St. Dunstan in the West, V. M.
GLMS 2968/3	St. Dunstan in the West, C. A.
GLMS 6048/1	St. Giles Cripplegate, V. M.
GLMS 6047/1	St. Giles Cripplegate, C. A.
GLMS 3149/1	St. Sepulchre, V. M.

GLMS 3146/1	St. Sepulchre, C. A.
GLMS 1162/1A, 2, 3, 4, 5	Aldgate Ward Register of Officers
GLMS 2050/1	Aldersgate Ward Inquest Book
GLMS 4069/1	Cornhill Ward Inquest Book
GLMS 4069/2	Cornhill Ward Register of Officers
GLMS 3461/1	Bridge Ward Within Inquest Book
GLMS 3018/1	St. Dunstan in the West Register of Officers

B. THE CORPORATION OF LONDON RECORDS OFFICE MANUSCRIPTS

Journal of the Common Council, vols. 40, 41.
Letter Books, QQ

C. THE LAMBETH PALACE LIBRARY MANUSCRIPTS

LPLMS CM VIII/4
LPLMS CM VIII/16
LPLMS CM VIII/18
LPLMS CM VIII/21
LPLMS CM VIII/23
LPLMS CM VIII/25
LPLMS CM VIII/37
LPLMS CM VIII/43
LPLMS CM VIII/45
LPLMS CM IX/15
LPLMS CM IX/25
LPLMS CM IX/50
LPLMS CM IX/58
LPLMS CM IX/82

D. THE BRITISH LIBRARY MANUSCRIPTS

BL Add. MSS. 15669, 15670, 15671
BL Add. MS. 36781
BL Add. MS. 37683
BL Sloane MS 970

E. THE PUBLIC RECORD OFFICE MANUSCRIPTS

PRO SP 16/492
PRO SP 19/1
PRO SP 19/78

F. PRINTED AND TYPESCRIPT SOURCES

The following list contains only those works frequently used in this study as major sources of information. All other printed sources, whether contemporary books, pamphlets, and sermons, or modern studies, are cited in the footnotes.

Beaven, A. B. *The Aldermen of the City of London,* 2 vols. London, 1908–13.

Dale, T. C., ed. *The Inhabitants of London in 1638.* London, 1931.

Firth, C. H., and R. S. Rait, eds. *Acts and Ordinances of the Interregnum.* 3 vols. London, 1911.

Green, Mary A. E., ed. *Calendar of the Proceedings of the Committee for Advance of Money,* 3 vols. London, 1888.

Harvey, W. J., ed. *List of the Principal Inhabitants of the City of London 1640.* London, 1969.

Hill, Christopher. *Economic Problems of the Church from Archbishop Whitgift to the Long Parliament.* Oxford, 1956.

Jordan, W. K. *The Charities of London, 1480–1660.* London, 1960.

Matthews, G. A. *Calamy Revised.* Oxford, 1934.

———. *Walker Revised.* Oxford, 1948.

Newcourt, N., ed. *Repertorium Ecclesiasticum Parochiae Londinense,* 2 vols. London, 1708–10.

Nuttall, G. F. *Visible Saints: The Congregational Way, 1640–1660.* Oxford, 1957.

Pearl, Valerie. *London and the Outbreak of the Puritan Revolution.* Oxford, 1961.

Seaver, Paul S. *The Puritan Lectureships: The Politics of Religious Dissent, 1560–1662.* Stanford, 1970.

Shaw, William A. *A History of the English Church during the Civil Wars and under the Commonwealth 1640–1660,* 2 vols. London, 1900.

Surman, Charles E., ed. "The Records of the Provincial Assembly of London, 1647–1660." 2 vols. (Typescript in Dr. Willilams's Library, London.)

Tolmie, Murray. *The Triumph of the Saints: The Separate Churches of London, 1616–1649.* Cambridge, 1977.

Woodhead, J. R. *The Rulers of London 1660–1689.* London, 1965.

Index

Mead, Thomas, 226
Meade, Philip, 65, 237
Meade, Robert (St. Dunstan in the West), 175, 184, 190 n.16, 191 n.20, 240
Meade, Robert (St. Lawrence Pountney), 146 n.60, 200, 231
Medlicot, James, 238
Medlicott, William, 77
Megge, James, 133
Meggott, Richard, 142
Mellish, John, 56, 225
Meredith, Christopher, 227, 230
Meriton, John, 62, 92 n.62
Methwold, William, 76, 173, 226, 233
Michaelthwaite, Nathaniel, 238
Mico, Samuel, 60, 238
Middleton, William, 80–81, 98 n.134, 228
Mills, Peter, 71, 128, 226
Milner, Tempest, 56, 57, 192 n.59, 225
Milton, John (captain), 108, 135, 171 n.117, 184, 191 n.26, 229
Milton, John (poet), 119 n.4
Ministry, London parochial, 149–71; catechism, 163; contractual agreements, 161, 204; election of parochial ministers, 157–60, 204; examination of parishioners, 163–64; lay control, 161–62, 170 n.108, 204; maintenance of ministers, 150–51; preaching, 155–56; stipends, 151–54, 165
Monford, James, 154
Morell, Richard, 231
Morewood, Gilbert, 228
Mosse, Clement, 235
Mosse, Francis, 63, 64, 235
Mossom, Robert, 140
Mountain, William, 124 nn. 110 and 112, 194 n.89, 238
Mountney, Cornelius, 226

Nalton, James, 65, 67, 68, 159, 202
Neale, Andrew, 87, 133, 234
Nettleship, Hugh, 231
Neve, Oliver, 76, 97 n.119
Newcomen, Matthew, 73, 138, 166 n.17
Newman, Gabriel, 76, 173, 233
Newman, Joseph, 109, 121 n.46
Newman, Robert, 230
Newman, Thomas, 227
Newton, Charles, 121 n.32
Newton, George, 159
Newton, Robert, 228
Nicarius, John, 72, 227
Nicholson, Christopher, 227

Nodes, George, 227
Noell, James, 231
Noell, Martin, 237
Noell, Thomas, 231, 234
Normansell, Urian, 234
Normington, Alexander, 113, 114, 175, 184, 190 n.19, 240
Norton, Richard, 135, 139, 235
Norwood, John, 56
Nye, Philip, 106, 111, 122

Offspring, Charles, 87
Onby, Humphrey, 76, 233
Onge, John, 113, 159, 160, 162
Orlibear, John, 57, 181, 192 n.59, 227
Overton, Richard, 71, 237
Overton, Valentine, 177, 191 n.31
Owen, Griffith, 239
Owen, Nathaniel, 229
Owen, Philip, 133, 234
Owen, Richard, 128–29, 131, 145 nn. 19 and 30
Owfield, John, 85, 100 n.156, 231

Packe, Christopher, 76, 81, 98 n.141, 121 n.33, 141, 165 n.5, 235
Paget, Dr., 124 n.112
Palmer, James, 131
Palmer, Thomas, 152
Parish: democratic agitation, 174–75, 176, 177, 184; governance of, 180–82, 183–84, 204; reorganization of parish vestry, 173, 174, 175, 176, 178; restoration of old parish vestry, 177–80
Parker, Edward, 141
Parker, Joseph, 237
Parker, Philip, 231
Parrott, Joseph, 96 nn. 105 and 107, 240
Paul, John, 152
Paulson, Thomas, 190 n.16
Payne, Ephraine, 230
Payne, Richard, 236
Peake, William, 133, 192 n.62, 233
Pearson, John, 139
Pease, William, 65, 237
Peck, Francis (clergyman), 62, 159
Peck, Francis (St. Mary Aldermary), 199, 233
Pell, Walter, 81, 98 n.140, 121 n.33, 141, 235
Pennington, Isaac, 76, 83, 116, 120 n.15, 127, 129, 194 n.89, 203, 208 n.28, 238
Percival, Mr., 156
Perkins, William, 113, 114, 175, 184, 240
Perne, Andrew, 114
Perrin, John, 70, 95 n.93, 109, 239